THE CAMBRIDGE GUIDE TO

African and Caribbean Theatre

EDITED BY

Martin Banham
Errol Hill
George Woodyard

ADVISORY EDITOR FOR AFRICA
Olu Obafemi

CAMBRIDGE
UNIVERSITY PRESS

PUBLISHED BY THE PRESS SYNDICATE OF THE UNIVERSITY OF CAMBRIDGE
The Pitt Building, Trumpington Street, Cambridge, United Kingdom

CAMBRIDGE UNIVERSITY PRESS
The Edinburgh Building, Cambridge CB2 2RU, UK
40 West 20th Street, New York NY 10011–4211, USA
477 Williamstown Road, Port Melbourne, VIC 3207, Australia
Ruiz de Alarcón 13, 28014 Madrid, Spain
Dock House, The Waterfront, Cape Town 8001, South Africa

http://www.cambridge.org

First published 1994
First paperback edition 2004

A catalogue record for this book is available from the British Library

Library of Congress cataloguing-in-publication data
The Cambridge guide to African and Carribbean theatre /edited by Martin Banham, Errol Hill, George Woodyard.
250p. 24.7cm.
ISBN 0 521 41139 4 hardback
1. Theater–Africa–Dictionaries. 2. Theater–Caribbean Area–Dictionaries.
I. Banham, Martin. II. Hill, Errol. III. Woodyard, George William.
PN2969. C36 1994
792'. 096–dc20   93-36900   CIP

ISBN 0 521 41139 4 hardback
ISBN 0 521 61207 1 paperback

CONTENTS

List of Contributors   vi
Preface   vii

African Theatre   1
Introduction   3
  English-speaking Africa   6
  French-speaking Africa   7
  Portuguese-speaking Africa   10
Benin   15
Botswana, Lesotho and Swaziland   17
Burkina Faso   21
Cameroon   23
Congo, People's Republic of   25
Côte d'Ivoire   27
Ethiopia   31
Gabon and the Central African Republic   37
Ghana   38
Guinea   43
Kenya   45
Madagascar   51
Malawi   53
Mali   61
Mauritius   63
Niger   65
Nigeria   67
Senegal   93

Sierra Leone   97
South Africa   101
Tanzania   113
Togo   117
Uganda   121
Zaire   127
Zambia   129
Zimbabwe   132

Caribbean Theatre   139
Introduction   141
  The English-speaking Caribbean   142
  The French-speaking Caribbean   149
  The Hispanic Caribbean   150
Barbados   153
Cuba   159
Dominican Republic   169
Eastern Caribbean States   173
Guyana   185
Jamaica   197
Puerto Rico   219
Trinidad and Tobago   225

Index   249
Illustration Acknowledgements   261

Contributors

MARTIN BANHAM
University of Leeds
Introductions and Africa

STEPHEN CHIFUNYISE
Zambia, Zimbabwe

JOHN CONTEH-MORGAN
Fourah Bay College, University of Sierra Leone and Ohio State University, Columbus
French-speaking Africa

CHRIS DUNTON
University of Lesotho
Nigeria

MICHAEL ETHERTON
West Africa

KIMANI GECAN
Kenya

FRANCES HARDING
SOAS, University of London
Masquerades

ERROL HILL
Dartmouth College, Emeritus
English-speaking Caribbean

ANDREW HORN
University of the South Pacific
Botswana, Lesotho and Swaziland

CHRISTOPHER KAMLONGERA
University of Malawi
Malawi

ROBERT KAVANAGH (Robert McLaren)
University of Zimbabwe
Zambia, Zimbabwe

MARGARET MACPHERSON
Uganda

NGUGI WA MIRII
Kenya

PENINA MUHANDO MLAMA, JOHN MASANJA, FROWIN NYONI
University of Dar es Salaam
Tanzania

GICHORA MWANGI
Kenya

DIXON MWANSA
Zambia

OLU OBAFEMI
University of Ilorin
West Africa

DANIEL PIRES
Portuguese-speaking Africa

JANE PLASTOW
University of Leeds
Ethiopia

JULIUS SPENCER
Fourah Bay College, University of Sierra Leone
Sierra Leone

IAN STEADMAN
University of Witwatersrand
South Africa

DEV VIRAHSAWMY
Mauritius

GEORGE WOODYARD
University of Kansas at Lawrence
Hispanic Caribbean

PREFACE

The Cambridge Guide to Theatre, published in 1988, was concerned to redress the bias towards Western theatre evident in many works of reference, and to offer a truly international view of theatre – traditional and contemporary. With *The Cambridge Guide to Asian Theatre* (ed. James R. Brandon, Cambridge, 1993) we took the first step to offer a smaller volume with a specific and focused concern for one aspect of world theatre, and we now complement that with this guide to the theatre of Africa and the Caribbean.

The Cambridge Guide to African and Caribbean Theatre offers coverage of theatrical activity in all parts of sub-Saharan Africa and in the English-speaking and Hispanic Caribbean, acknowledging the Caribbean as culturally a dynamic part of the African diaspora. The concentration on these areas in a single volume has allowed us to revise and expand entries from the original *Guide*, and to direct the reader more systematically to the personalities, forms and activities of theatre within specific countries. National entries appear alphabetically and contain within them the discrete entries relating to individuals, genres or events relating to that country. Bibliographies accompany major entries.

The contributors to this volume are substantially those who wrote for the parent *Guide*, but two major contributors have been added to the writers on African theatre. John Conteh-Morgan has totally revised and rewritten the French-speaking Africa entries and Chris Dunton has revised the important entries on Nigeria. In addition Jane Plastow (Ethiopia) and Frances Harding (masquerades) have extended our coverage. Thanks are also due to Masitha Hoeane, Thula Mogobe and Sam Ukala.

All work stemming from the original *Guide* must continue to acknowledge the pioneering editorial work from Cambridge University Press of Sarah Stanton. Her work has now been taken on and developed with great commitment and skill by Caroline Bundy. Our warm thanks are due to both of them. For this volume we also wish to record our gratitude to Sue Phillpott – the most professional and helpful of copy-editors.

Martin Banham
Errol Hill
George Woodyard

Note to the reader

All the entries are cross-referenced, with a word in small capitals indicating a separate entry under that word, but where an entry is to be found within a country section other than the one you are reading, the reference goes, e.g. '...ATHOL FUGARD (see South Africa) ...'. Where an entry is cross-referenced from the Caribbean half of the book to the African one, the reference is, e.g. '...MASQUERADES IN AFRICA (see African Theatre, Introduction) ...'; but if the reference says simply, e.g. '...the UNIVERSITY OF THE WEST INDIES (see Introduction) ...' it is in the Introduction to the half of the book that you are reading that you will find the entry on UWI.

The entries in the tinted boxes which are to be found in the introductory material in both the African and the Caribbean sections apply to several countries within that section, or even the entire region.

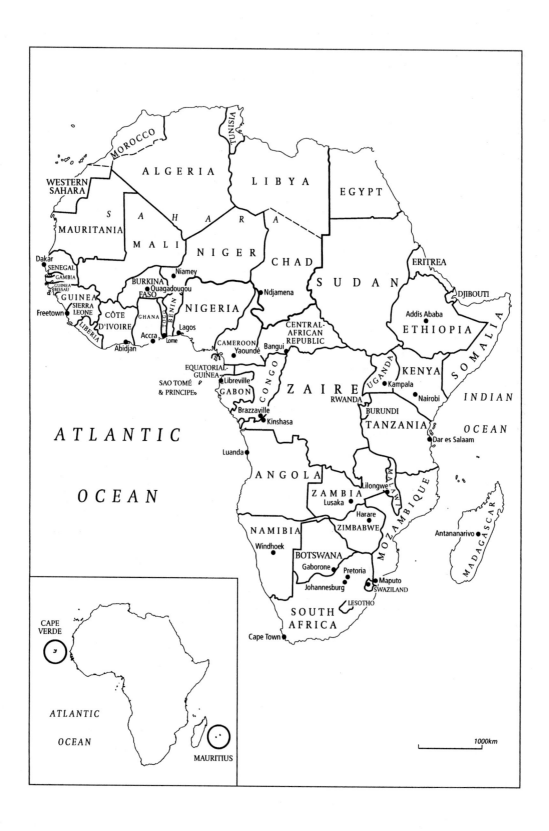

AFRICAN THEATRE

INTRODUCTION

The roots of theatre in Africa are ancient and complex and lie in areas of community festival, seasonal rhythm and religious ritual as well as in the work of court jesters, travelling professional entertainers, and storytellers. Since the late 1950s, in a movement that has paralleled the political emancipation of so much of the continent, there has grown a theatre that comments back from the colonized world to the world of the colonialists, that discusses the shared experience in the shared languages, and reasserts its own cultural and linguistic integrity. Contemporary African theatre retains a sense of function in the sense that it serves a purpose within communities and cultures that is much greater than simply that of entertainment or diversion. This functional quality gives the theatre a sense of purpose, and influences not only its material but also the nature of its performance and reception. The present-day theatre is enriched and complemented by its co-existence with traditional forms, skills and understanding.

Its vitality, diversification and variety of form and content warn us against attempting too homogeneous a view of African theatre, but centuries of European economic and political domination have inevitably influenced Africa's cultural life, and especially its theatre. During the first half of the 20th-century indigenous theatre movements often reflected Western models, whether in the Nigerian and Ghanaian 'concert party', or the vaudeville presentations of southern African theatre. The Western influences were, however, effectively subverted and eventually dominated or replaced by indigenous forms. The influence of Western-style education continues to determine elements of theatrical form and language in much contemporary drama, but here again we can see playwrights and performers working increasingly on their own terms and asserting a powerful cultural and political identity. Theatre in many parts of Africa has been at the forefront of the anti-colonial struggle, and has not relaxed its sense of purpose in the post-independence world. (Witness the banning of Hubert Ogunde's work not only by the colonial government of Nigeria in the 1940s but also by the independent government of the 1960s. Think also of the imprisonment of Soyinka during the Nigerian civil war, or Ngugi wa Thiong'o's exile from Kenya.)

In tandem with all the new activities in theatre, research predominantly by African scholars has pointed to the continuing vitality and relevance of the genuinely communal theatre manifested in festival, ritual and masquerade, with its sophisticated use of dance, mime, costuming and music, and its integral relationship between performers and observers – equal participants. It is the confidence of this resource that underlines the strength of contemporary African theatre.

FESTAC

The first 'World Festival of Negro Arts' was held in Dakar in 1966. This was followed in January 1977 by the second 'Black and African Festival of Arts and Culture' held in Lagos, for which the acronym FESTAC was coined. The festivals were planned as Pan-African celebrations; and the ingredients ranged from performance to debate, dominated primarily by dance and theatre. Further FESTACs remain an ambition; past ones evoke fond nostalgia.

MASQUERADES IN AFRICA

'Masquerade' refers both to a performance given by masked characters and to the masked performer. The term 'masquerade' will be used here to denote the performance, and 'masker' will refer to the performer. 'Mask' refers specifically to the face-covering.

The most important masquerades are those through which spirits enter the human world. In these, the human performer is not simply hidden from view, but is the embodied spirit. This supernatural and secret ability makes the mask, the masker and the masquerade sacred and powerful. The ambivalent visibility (there/not there; seen/not seen; concealed/revealed) is a visual mediation between the known world and the unknown world, legitimating temporary boundary-crossing between normally discrete categories of beings. Powerful masquerades such as the *egungun* ancestral masquerade of the Yoruba people of Nigeria, or the *dama* funeral and commemorative masquerade of the Dogon people of Mali, or the *nyau* initiation masquerade of the Chewa people of Zambia and Malawi are not performed often, and then only surrounded by considerable ritual and ceremony.

Masquerades assume many forms and can appear as spirits coming from the untamed bush into the domestic sphere, as feared and harmful spirits threatening death or destruction, or as benevolent spirits associated with abundance and the fertility of women or of crops. Whilst the majority of masquerades are specific to the people and area of their performance, some newer spirit masquerades such as *mammiwata* have a more widespread popularity. Other categories of masquerade represent humans and animals who are typically in marginal or temporary states. For example, foreigners such as traders from other areas, neighbouring people, the cattle-herding nomadic people, or Europeans are a popular category for poking fun at. Other masquerades such as the Yoruba *gelede* represent older women as 'witches' who must be appeased, but women are also represented as ideal wives, as prostitutes and as mothers. In all of these masquerades, it is male performers who represent female characters. Only rarely, as among the Sande (or Bundu) women's secret societies mainly of Sierra Leone and Liberia, do women wear masks. Other masquerades, such as those of the Idoma of Nigeria, represent diseased persons (e.g. victims of smallpox or goitre) as a gesture of support, placing them visibly at the centre of the society's concern. There are also many wild or imaginary animals, and while the sacred masquerades arouse awe and fear in the spectator, human and animal masquerades often contain a high degree of entertainment, comedy and informality and are valued for their play qualities. Masquerades can be used as a form of social control, and sometimes a masked figure will publicly reprimand an individual. Antisocial characteristics such as sexual profligacy, meanness, drunkenness or laziness are singled out and the culprit made the butt of jest and mockery. Masked figures often chase women and children to reinforce what is considered to be appropriate submissive behaviour.

The masked figure may be costumed in grasses or leaves or else in fabrics ranging from sumptuous and new to ragged and scruffy, depending on the character. The mask itself is made of wood, grasses or leaves, or of textile. Sometimes the whole body is costumed in one piece, as with the basketry masks of the Chewa. Where the primary purpose of the masquerade is to comment on social change, topical elements such as aeroplanes, motorbikes, policemen and soldiers are carved as part of the masks. Carvers, who are sometimes also the performers, develop their own style and may experiment with bold colours in gloss paint.

Almost all masquerades are performed to music, and the individual performance of any masked figure is judged and appreciated by a skilled and critical audience both for the appropriateness of the movements to a character and for the degree of skill in matching rhythm to movement. Masked figures may move in a measured and stately way, as in the sacred ancestral masquerades, or may dart about and change their shape suddenly – as, for example, in the *ekong* masquerade of the Annang people or the Tiv *kwagh-hir*, or like the *onidan* performers in the Yoruba *egungun* masquerades. To be able to change shape is not a human characteristic, so such movements emphasize the masked figure as non-human. Great skill is needed by the performer in order to effect a transformation aesthetically, and how well it is achieved is one criterion of excellence. Similarly, the masker on stilts must negotiate the crowd without falling over, for his skill reflects the ability of the community to negotiate the difficulties in the times ahead. During a performance both comic and fierce masked figures may dash up to members of the audience, startling them with their sudden attention and making the crowd laugh with excitement and admiration of their control.

Powerful masquerades whose roles arise from religious or political beliefs change little in appearance and performance over decades, but new social and economic conditions create new concerns, and so in response new masks and masquerades are created or old ones revived such as the *ode-lay* masquerades of Sierra Leone. Some, like *mammiwata* – concerning a water goddess associated with sexuality and wealth – are popular in several countries of Africa, but nevertheless develop local usage, meanings and appearance, whilst others like the Tiv *kwagh-hir* continually develop new acts and characters but remain performed only by Tiv people.

Masquerades are performed by men even when they are representing female characters. All masquerades are a demonstration of supernatural power and, with few exceptions, men monopolize the performing. Strict rules govern the appearances of all masquerades, and some sacred masks cannot even be seen by any adult who is a woman. Most masked figures cannot be touched by women, nor should women know the identity of the mask-wearer, for to do so would acknowledge the presence of the human performer in the masquerade. Theoretically, transgressions can be punished severely – previously, even by death – but in practice women frequently do know all there is to know, and yet continue to provide the supportive role of audience and chorus in the masquerade. The threat of physical and spiritual sanctions is enough to ensure that most women publicly collude in maintaining the secrecy surrounding the masquerade – a *théâtre-de-complicité*.

It seems likely that, in performance, masked performers enter a state of altered consciousness; and ritualized preparations such as fasting, sexual abstinence, prayer and sacrifice, as well as drinking alcohol, costuming and covering the face, all combine to free the performer from personal and social constraints. Sacred masquerades are performed only by ritually appropriate groups such as a specific lineage or age set, but initiation into the more secular masquerades is open to most young men.

English-speaking Africa

The universities in the anglophone nations of Africa played an important part in developing theatre activities from the late 1950s onward, both through the playwrights they produced and through the establishment or encouragement of imaginative performance venues and initiatives. The latter ranged from the travelling theatres in Nigeria and Uganda to the Chikwakwa community theatre in Zambia. With much of the new drama emerging from the universities, it is not surprising that a certain 'elitist' tone characterized much of the work – either in terms of its concern with the problems of the young educated man or woman in conflict with traditional manners and attitudes, or in the choice and use of language.

The language debate remains a crucial one: Ngugi wa Thiong'o argues that only by rejecting English can he 'decolonize the mind'. Calls have been made, by Wole Soyinka amongst others, to replace English with a Pan-African language. The Nigerian playwright Ola Rotimi proposes 'the domestication of the English language – handling it within the terms of traditional linguistic identity'. A positive move is also being made by younger dramatists towards exploring the use of pidgin as a lingua franca. It is important to remember that in notionally 'English-speaking' nations, indigenous languages are often paramount both in terms of day-to-day usage and in government and culture. Swahili, for instance, is the language of much theatre – published and unpublished – in Tanzania and elsewhere in East Africa, including the important plays of Ebrahim Hussein. Yoruba in Nigeria is the appropriate language of the immensely popular theatre of 'Baba Sala' as well as the 'operas' of Duro Ladipo, celebrating as they do the myths and history of the Yoruba people. Shona and Ndebele are the languages of much new writing for the theatre in Zimbabwe.

Growing alongside the literary theatre has been a dynamic popular theatre, often using indigenous languages and unscripted, improvised material. The nature of this theatre ranges from broad farce to serious commen-

Bibliography

See M. Banham with C. Wake, *African Theatre Today*, London, 1976; B. Butake and G. Doho (eds.), *Théâtre camerounais/Cameroonian Theatre*, Yaounde, 1988; E. Clark, *Hubert Ogunde: The Making of Nigerian Theatre*, Oxford, 1979; J.P. Clark-Bekederemo, *Collected Plays and Poems 1958-1988*, ed. and with intro. by A. Irele, Washington, DC, 1991; C. Dunton, *Make Man Talk True: Nigerian Drama in English Since 1970*, London, 1992; M. Etherton, *The Development of African Drama*, London, 1982; J. Fabian, *Power and Performance: Ethnographic Explorations through Proverbial Wisdom and Theater in Shaba, Zaire*, Madison, 1990; K. Götrick, *Apidan Theatre and Modern Drama*, Göteborg, 1984; A. Graham-White, *The Drama of Black Africa*, London and New York, 1974; T. Hauptfleisch and I. Steadman, *South African Theatre: Four Plays and an Introduction*, Pretoria, 1984; B. Jeyifo, *The Yoruba Popular Travelling Theatre of Nigeria*, Lagos, 1984; R. Kavanagh, *Theatre and Cultural Struggle in South Africa*, London, 1984; Z. Kofoworola and Y. Lateef, *Hausa Performing Arts and Music*, Lagos, 1987; Z. Mda, *When People Play People: Development Communication through Theatre*, London, 1993; O. Ogunba, *The Movement of Transition*, Ibadan, 1975; O. Ogunba and A. Irele (eds.), *Theatre in Africa*, Ibadan, 1978; Y. Ogunbiyi, *Drama and Theatre in Nigeria: A Critical Source Book*, Lagos, 1981; W. Soyinka, *Myth, Literature and the African World*, Cambridge, 1976; B. Traoré, *The Black African Theatre and its Social Function*, 1972 *Le théâtre négro-africain et ses fonctions sociales*, Paris, 1959. Journals/occasional publications with significant contributions on African theatre include *African Literature Today*, London; *Bayreuth African Studies Series*, Bayreuth; *Nigeria Magazine*, Lagos; *Research in African Literatures*, Austin, Texas; *Theatre Quarterly/New Theatre Quarterly*, Cambridge; *Theatre Research International*, Oxford.

tary and protest. Protest theatre itself is, not surprisingly, at its most effective and dynamic in South Africa, where 'township theatre' has not only produced an exceptional group of playwrights and performers, but has also determined a political agenda. One of the intriguing questions for the future of South African theatre is how a theatre geared to protest – whether through the relatively sophisticated productions of the Johannesburg Market Theatre or Cape Town's Space Theatre, or the street theatre productions of transient radical groups – will accommodate itself to the changing political scene. Having found such a challenging role in effecting change, will the theatre be able to change itself, and contribute to the new dialogue in a post-apartheid, majority-rule South Africa? South African playwrights and performers are exploring the exciting potential of interculturalism within their own nation.

Theatre-for-development, a community theatre activity designed either for propaganda (health care and hygiene, literacy, good agricultural practices and so on) or, in a more radical context, as a vehicle of conscientization, has also been experimented with and applied in many areas of the continent. The Botswana *Laedza Batanani* (*The Sun is Risen, Come Out and Work*) initiative in 1974 set in train one of the most interesting contemporary explorations of the potential of theatre, to some extent running in parallel with the experiments of practitioners outside Africa, such as Augusto Boal in Brazil, and complementing similar movements in other developing countries. The ideology and the practice of theatre-for-development has been tested and extended by the practitioners themselves in conferences and workshops, and in action through the work of companies and individuals. Typically, Oga Steve Abah in Zaria, Nigeria, through the Samaru Project, has used the resources of a university drama department to contribute to the conscientization of rural communities. Zakes Mda in Lesotho (*When People Play People*, London, 1993),

Penina Muhando Mlama in Tanzania (*Culture and Development: The Popular Theatre Approach in Africa*, Uppsala, 1991) and Hansel Ndumbe Eyoh in Cameroon (*Hammocks to Bridges*, Yaounde, 1986) have all made important contributions to the critical and methodological literature of what has become one of Africa's most buoyant theatre movements.

French-speaking Africa south of the Sahara

'Francophone' sub-Saharan Africa is the term used with increasing frequency since the 1960s, in both English and French, to describe a group of sixteen African countries where, as a result of French and Belgian colonial rule (roughly between 1885 and 1960), French is the language of government, business and administration. While these countries, from Senegal in the west through Zaire in the centre to Chad in the east, each have a unique cultural identity, they have also evolved, by virtue of their similar colonial experience (especially those under a centralizing power like France), a distinctive modern African culture.

This francophone African culture, a synthesis of local African and imported French and Belgian traditions, has found expression in many forms: in the popular music of a Franco or Tabu Ley (Zaire), in the cinema of a Sembène Ousmane (Senegal) or a Souleymane Cissé (Mali), and in the philosophical writings of a Paulin Houtondji (Benin) or Yves-Valentin Mudimbé (Zaire). But it is in literature that it has found its most powerful voice. The earliest practised genre was poetry in the 1930s, with Léopold Senghor; then came fiction in the early 50s with Camara Laye, Mongo Beti and Abdoulaye Sadji, and almost a decade later, in terms of significant published works, theatre dominated.

In spite of its relative youth, the theatre is now a vital aspect of the literature of sub-Saharan Africa in French, accounting for an important corpus of some three hundred published plays. Many of these, by playwrights like CHEIK NDAO (see Senegal), BERNARD DADIÉ (see Côte d'Ivoire), SONY LABOU TANSI and TCHICAYA U'TAMSI (see Congo, Republic of), and GUILLAUME OYONO-MBIA (see Cameroon), are of the highest standard and are regularly produced in francophone Africa. Some have been performed in France – at the Avignon Festival, and in Limoges, at the Festival International des Francophonies, launched in 1985 to promote world theatre in the French language. The Théâtre International de Langue Française, a troupe founded in 1985 by the French director Gabriel Garran, has been producing plays by U'Tamsi and Labou Tansi in theatres in Paris and its districts, while Françoise Kourilsky's Ubu Repertory Theatre has been promoting francophone African theatre in New York since 1987, by organizing staged readings and performances of plays by ZADI ZAOUROU (see Ivory Coast), SENOUVO ZINSOU (see Togo) and Maxime Ndébéka (b. 1944).

Over the years, francophone Africa has also produced actors of talent like the Paris-based Senegalese Bachir Touré and Douta Seck, Cameroonian Lydia Ewandé and, more recently, Malian Bakary Sangaré. The first three played roles in the 1960s in productions, mostly by Jean-Marie Serreau but also by Roger Blin, of plays by Jean Genet, AIMÉ CÉSAIRE (see Caribbean Theatre, Introduction) and Kateb Yacine; while over the past five years Sangaré has appeared in plays by Abdou Anta Ka, U'Tamsi and Césaire, and in a production by Peter Brook of *Woza Albert*.

That the theatre should prove an attraction to francophone Africans and become a crucial cultural nexus in their region is hardly surprising. Such a potential had always existed in this area of millennial cultures, where the performance of ancient oral narratives such as the Sunjata and Mwindo epics of old Mali and Zaire respectively by traditional bards, commonly known in francophone Africa as *griots*, as well as the enactment of rituals, takes on the quality of drama and theatre by the very circum-

stances of their performance. It is this potential, recognized in the 1930s by French educators like Charles Béart, and developed in their African students first at the Ecole Supérieure Primaire de Bingerville in the Ivory Coast and then at the École William Ponty in SENEGAL, that gave rise to the first dramatic compositions in French by sub-Saharan Africans. The best of these – Dadié's *Assémien Déhylé* (1936), for instance – were taken on tour to Paris for the Colonial Exhibition of 1937 and published in *Traits d'Union*, the cultural organ of French West African countries.

The subsequent development of francophone theatre was the result of concrete measures taken by the colonial authorities and later by the governments of some of the independent states. These include the building of theatres like the Daniel Sorano in Dakar; the founding of theatre arts institutes in Abidjan and Bamako, and other cities; the organizing of drama competitions by Radio France Internationale; and, in the immediate pre- and post-independence periods, the sponsoring of tours to Africa by French theatre directors and critics, including Raymond Hermantier, Henri Cordreaux and Jacques Schérer, to spot talent and train theatre specialists, and by theatre companies like the Greniers de Toulouse and the Théâtre des Amandiers.

Francophone African drama falls, in terms of themes, into three broad categories: historical, social and political. The first accounts for most of the plays produced so far. In exalting language, Ndao's *L'Exil d'Albouri* (*Albouri's Exile*, 1967), Jean Pliya's *Kondo le requin* (*Kondo the Shark*, first published 1966) and Séydou Badian's *La Mort de Chaka* (*The Death of Chaka*, 1962), for example, depict the careers of various 19th-century warrior-kings. In their heroic struggles to defend their territories, often against France, is conveyed a living sense of pre-colonial societies at their most glorious. This predilection for history is as much a legacy of the history-conscious oral traditions of the dramatists as it is a felt, nationalist need to present a dramatic corrective to the colonial view of the African past. With dramatists like Dadié or Charles Nokan, however, history (whether factual or legendary) is used not for glorification but for the framework and necessary safe distance (from the censor?) that it offers for a critical reflection on the present.

The dislocating effects of modern culture on traditional beliefs and customs, and the retrograde nature of some of the latter, constitute the second, social, category of mostly comic plays: such as Oyono-Mbia's *Trois prétendants ... un mari* (*Three Suitors, One Husband*, 1964), Guy Menga's *La Marmite de Koka Mbala* (*Koka Mbala's Pot*, 1969) and Protais Asseng's *Trop c'est trop* (*Enough is Enough*, 1981). The third group of plays by, among others, U'Tamsi (*Le Destin glorieux du Maréchal Nnikon Nniku*, *The Glorious Destiny of Marshal Nnikon Nniku*, 1979), Maxime Ndébéka (*Equatorium*, 1989) and Sony Labou Tansi explore the political corruption and ugly tyrannies that have sprung up in post-colonial African societies.

Over the past decade or so, francophone African theatre has moved in new directions. In the plays of dramatists like NICOLE WEREWERE-LIKING (see Cameroon) or Zaourou (*La Termitière*, *The Anthill*, 1981), ritual ceremonies – especially healing, initiation and purification rites – have provided the bases, in content and structure, for a new type of drama.

In terms of form, francophone theatre is heavily influenced by oral performance modes and the conventions of traditional genres. Elements of this influence include the episodic and undramatic nature of the action in many (especially historical) plays; the tendency to give epic grandeur to the most factual of events; the display of a vivid sense of spectacle through recourse to colourful ceremonies and to the visual and rhetorical presentation of the heroic deeds of the main characters, as in Pliya's *Kondo le requin*; the use of the cultural figure of the *griot* either as a character integrated into the action as in Eugène Dervain's *La reine scélérate* (*The Villainous Queen*, 1968) or as presenter of and commentator on the dramatized events, such as the ghost-provocateur in Ndébéka's *Equatorium* or the public entertainer in SYLVAIN BEMBA's (see Congo, Republic of) *L'Homme qui tua le crocodile* (*The Man who Killed the Crocodile*, 1972). The *griot*'s technique of acting several characters in the course of the same performance is also widely used: in Zinsou's *On joue la comédie* (*We are Acting*, 1972), for instance, in which the presenter Xuma acts the hero Chaka in a playlet within the play.

The use, as in traditional performances, of music, song and dance is also widespread. These elements signify and can contribute to dramatic action, as does the *lagyah* tune, for example, in Thiérno Ba's *Bilbassy* (1980). Sometimes they are used to entertain or to involve the audience in the action. Often, however, they degenerate into folklorism. A final legacy of oral performance to the modern theatre is to be found in the conception of scenic space as consisting of both stage and auditorium. Thus in Oyono-Mbia's *Trois prétendants ... un mari* it is the entire village community that is the stage.

Francophone theatre does not, though, merely borrow elements of form from tradition. It dramatizes actual *texts* of that tradition; that is, 'autonomous and isolated works ... highly organised as full and independent imaginative statements' irrespective of their orality, as the critic Abiola Irele has noted. An example is Dervain's *La reine scélérate*, which is a staged version of the Da Monzon epic, an oral chronicle of the 19th-century exploits of the Diarra dynasty of the Bambara people of Mali. Nor is theatrical activity in francophone Africa limited to 'art' or 'university' theatre. There also exists a dynamic modern popular theatre in the 'concert parties' and *kantatas* of Togo, and in the plays of Souleymane Koly of Côte d'Ivoire, for example, and of Zomo Bel Abel, Daniel Ndo and Jean-Michel Kankan of Cameroon.

A common thread runs through this activity: there are no scripts; the plots are improvised;

the themes treated are topical and of concern to the mass of the urban poor or unemployed who mostly constitute its audience; the language is a pot-pourri of pidgin French and local languages; and the action is conducted mostly through song and dance, though through dialogue too.

Another type of theatre in francophone Africa is the community development theatre, or theatre of social intervention. Its aim is to use the medium of the theatre to enable vari-ous target communities to better understand and participate in the development projects conceived for them. The plays are in the local languages, the actors are mostly drawn from members of the communities concerned, and the forms adopted are taken from their cultures. Mali, Niger and Burkina Faso are the great practitioners in francophone Africa of this type of theatre.

While all of this activity is, in one way or another, part of the new drama and theatre, francophone Africa is still home to a variety of traditional theatrical performances. The best-known is the *Kotéba* satirical theatre of the Bambara people of Mali, whose aesthetic is at the heart of current researches by the Groupe Dramatique of Mali to establish a new way of acting and writing.

Portuguese-speaking Africa

European theatre was introduced very early on, by missionaries, into the Portuguese colonies. The plays were religious in character, their objective being the propagation of Catholicism. The religion of the Africans was not taken into consideration: the settlers imposed on them their own religion and culture. The literary genre of drama, as seen from a Western point of view, appeared much later than poetry and prose in the Portuguese-speaking African countries. This can be explained by the fact that the colonialists provided very little in the way of facilities needed to perform a play, and that poetry could more freely express the violence experienced by the colonized peoples.

When independence was declared in 1975 in Angola, Cape Verde, Guinea-Bissau, Mozambique and São Tomé e Príncipe, illiteracy was higher than 90 per cent. This had affected both literary production and the people's interest in drama. It was very difficult to publish at all, and as writers had little incentive to do so anyway there came about a cultural stagnation. Portuguese colonialism had imposed severe

Bibliography

D. Blair, *African Literature in French*, Cambridge, 1976; J. Conteh-Morgan, 'French-language African Drama and the Oral Tradition: Trends and Issues', *African Literature Today*, 18, 1992; R. Cornevin, *Le Théâtre en Afrique noire et à Madagascar*, Paris 1970; 'Le Théâtre de langue française en Afrique Noire', *Culture Française*, 31–2, 1982/3; U. Edebiri, 'French Contributions to African Drama', *Research in African Literatures*, 6, 1975; A. Irele, 'Orality, Literacy and African Literature, in *Semper Aliquid Novi: Mélanges offerts à Albert Gérard*, ed. J. Riesz and A. Ricard, Tübingen, 1990; P. Manning, *Francophone sub-Saharan Africa 1880–1985*, Cambridge, 1988; F. Sahlien, *Panorama du théâtre africain d'expression française*, Zaire, 1983; J. Schérer, 'Le Théâtre en Afrique noire francophone', in *Le Théâtre moderne II*, ed. J. Jacquot, Paris, 1973; M. Schipper, 'Traditional Themes and Techniques in African Theatre and "Francophonie"', *Theatre Research International*, 9, 3, 1984; B. Traoré, *Le Théâtre Négro-Africain et ses fonctions sociales*, Paris 1958; C. Wake and M. Banham, *African Theatre Today*, London, 1976; C. Wake, 'French-speaking Africa South of the Sahara', in *The Cambridge Guide to World Theatre*, ed. M. Banham, Cambridge, 1988; H. Waters, *Théâtre noir: Encyclopédie des pièces écrites en français par des auteurs noirs*, Washington, DC, 1988.

censorship on newspapers and books: any expression of opinions contrary to those held by the ruling power would not be published. The principles of negritude and Pan-Africanism had formed the political and cultural background that had led to the armed struggle for liberation in 1961 in Angola, in 1963 in Guinea-Bissau and in 1964 in Mozambique. This anti-colonial war had led to their independence, after a coup in Portugal in 1974 that had overthrown the oldest dictatorship in Europe.

Negritude and Pan-Africanism influenced in part the dramatic production of these territories. Although some plays performed before independence directly challenged the ruling values, the majority were vaudeville pieces that came from metropolitan areas, their objective being mainly to amuse the white spectators. After independence Marxist regimes were formed, aiming to make good the damage done by colonialism and to build a classless society. Drama was often used as a means of politicizing people, as an instrument of the principles of socialist realism.

Angola

As elsewhere in Portuguese-speaking Africa, the subjects of the plays performed by the missionaries related to Catholicism. And as critic Carlos Vaz notes, 'the roles of the Infant Jesus, of the Angels and of Joseph and Mary could only be performed by white people, while the roles of Judas, Satan and even sometimes Herod were only performed by the blacks'. The vaudeville pieces staged mainly by theatre groups from the cities offered the only light relief.

Important 20th-century plays include Domingos Van-Dúmem's *Auto de Natal* (*Christmas Play*), performed in Luanda in 1972 and written in Quimbundo, a native language, as a reaction against the language imposed by the settlers and as a revalidation of the African culture; two plays by Orlando de Albuquerque, published in 1974, *Ovibanda* and *O filho de Zambi*

(*Zambi's Son*), on Angolan religious themes; and the children's play *Os pioneiros do futuro* (*The Pioneers of the Future*, 1974), by Júlio de Almeida and Elsa de Sousa.

A month after Angola became independent in 1975, the Union of Angolan Writers was formed. They promulgated:

At this moment when our people have just taken over full responsibility for their future as a free and sovereign nation, Angolan writers take their stand at the forefront, facing the enormous tasks of national liberation and reconstruction.

Out literary history bears witness to the generations of writers who were able in their own time to keep alive the process of our liberation by expressing the deep longings of our people, mainly those of its most exploited classes. Thus Angolan literature emerges not merely as an aesthetic need but also as a weapon for the affirmation of the Angolans.

The first step of direct armed struggle against colonialism has been made. Angolan writers in many different ways answered the call to arms, and some gave their lives on the field of honour for their fatherland.

Today, our people have entered into a new battle in this centuries-old war for our self-assertion as a free nation, in Africa and in the world. Once more, as is their duty and tradition, Angolan writers are present at the heart of this popular resistance, joining the battle on the cultural front.

This statement encapsulates the themes that dominated literature in Angola during the first years of independence. Confirming this, the then president of the republic, Agostinho Neto, himself an eminent poet, declared that 'literature in this independent country of Angola, which is marching towards a superior form of social organization – socialism – must necessarily reflect this new situation'. However, two years later, realizing that art had merely served politics, had no autonomy, and had often been reduced to political pamphleteering, Neto qualified the principles of the cultural policy thus: '... we cannot be schematic or follow stereotypes as the theoreticians of socialist realism once did'.

After the fall of the dictatorship in Portugal and during the period of transition that led to independence, a spontaneous theatre that reflected the social contradictions of a colonial society in open disintegration flourished in Angola. The plays *As duas caras do patrão* (*The Two Faces of the Boss*), *A província de Angola* (*The Province of Angola*), *Manifestação no jardim da Celeste* (*Demonstration in Celeste's Garden*), *Combate de box* (*Boxing Match*) and *Uma lição de Portugalidade* (*A Lesson in Portugueseness*) were performed by students and workers.

After independence, the aim of the Angolan theatre was to awaken the political consciousness of the people. In 1975, *Poder popular* (*Popular Power*) was performed by the Tchingange Group. In accordance with its didactic, political and doctrinal approach, it was presented in schools, factories and hospitals in Luanda and in rural areas. In 1976, the National School of Theatre was created. Once of the groups belonging to it performed *Africa liberdade* (*Africa Freedom*). In 1977, the group Xilenga-Teatro was formed, which resurrected four narratives from the rich, vast repertory of the oral tradition of the Tchokwe people. The Ngongo group were experimenting at this time in the field of the puppet theatre.

Other plays took the same political line: *A pele do diabo* (*The Devil's Skin*, 1977), by Manuel Santos Lima; *A corda* (*The Rope*, 1978) by Pepetela; *O círculo de giz de Bombó* (*Bombó's Chalk Circle*, 1979) by Henrique Guerra, adapted from Bertolt Brecht's *The Caucasian Chalk Circle*; *No velho ninguém toa* (*The Old Man is Untouchable*) by Costa Andrade; and *A revolta da casa dos ídolos* (*The Revolt in the House of the Idols*, 1980) by Pepetela. This last shows a formal and thematic depth that contrasts with the naive spontaneity that was common in the vast majority of the plays of the time.

Cape Verde

The first known play *Terra de sôdade* (*Land of Nostalgia*), was written in the 1940s by Jaime de Figueiredo. It is a sentimental four-act ballet on the theme of emigration. The only theatre group of note before independence was run by the Adriano Moreira Grammar School in the capital, Praia. After independence, theatre became a means of politicizing the people, as in the other Portuguese-speaking African countries. Using as his theme an incident in the history of Cape Verde – an uprising of slaves against colonial domination – Oswaldo Osório, heavily influenced by Brecht, wrote *Gervásio*.

Seeking to reveal the origins of the culture of Cape Verde, and combining acting with music and dance, Kwame Konde founded the theatre group Korda Kaoberdi. In 1977 he staged *Os disanimados para os infernos* (*To Hell with the Pessimists*) by Kaoberdiano Dambará. Later this group performed Augusto Boal's *A lua muito pequena e a caminhada perigosa* (*The Very Small Moon and the Dangerous Journey*), which dealt with the political activity and theory of Che Guevara. In 1979 Donaldo Pereira de Macedo's play *Descarado* (*Shameless*) was published in the USA. Its importance lies in its being the first play from Cape Verde to appear in book form, and in its being written in Creole.

The present situation is not very encouraging. there are few incentives to create or produce theatre, and previous experiments are not being followed through. Some directors, such as Leão Lopes, occasionally experiment in combining the traditional dramatic features – dance, masks, and so on – with audio-visual techniques, taking as their themes old tales, poetry and national literature.

Guinea-Bissau

Besides the traditional theatre and the vaudeville shows based on the everyday life of the settlers that flourished before independence, plays for children, based on fables, also used to be staged. Traditional dances that are still performed, such as the *dança do boi* (the dance of the ox) and the *danças dos bíjagós* (Bijagós dances), use underlying dramatic features. After independence, no dramatic activity has been reported in this country.

Mozambique

As in the other Portuguese-speaking African countries, before independence the most popular form of entertainment was the vaudeville. Notable among them were: *Crime Anica, Madalena, As aventuras de um herói* (*Adventures of a Hero*), *Sua Alteza o Criador* (*His Highness the Creator*), *Os cavaleiros do arcabuz* (*The Knights of the Arquebus*) and *Era eu* (*It was I*) by Carlos da Silva; *Polana azul* (*Blue Polana*) and *Sete de março* (*The Seventh of March*) by Fernando Baldaque and Carlos Queirós de Fonseca – all written in the first twenty years of this century; *Ponta vermelha* (*Red Point*, 1931) by Fernando Baldaque and Arnaldo Silva; *Ice-cream Today* (1932) by António Alonso Moreira, Fernando Baldaque and Arnaldo Silva; *Renúncia* (*Resignation*, 1932) by Alexandre Cabral Campos; *A palhota de Moçambique* (*The Thatched Hut of Mozambique*, 1937) and *Zona perigosa* (*Danger Zone*, 1941) by Fernando Baldaque and Arnaldo Silva; *Africa menina e moça* (*Africa Young and Lovely*) by Ruy Sant'Elmo, *Latitude sul* (*Southern Latitude*) by Luna de Oliveira, *Amor à vista* (*Love on the Way*) by José Mendonça and Fausto Ritto, *O mato* (*The Forest*) by Caetano Montez, and *Infortúnio* (*Misfortune*) by Felisberto Ferreirinha – these last performed in the 1940s.

Since censorship controlled all literary production in the years before independence, it was difficult to write plays with clear political themes. Some, however, dared to denounce the claustrophobic colonial status quo. In 1959, Afonso Ribeiro wrote *Três setas apontadas para o Futuro* (*Three Arrows Pointing to the Future*). Two characters face each other all through the play: a poet, who symbolizes an alternative future, and his boss's son, who represents colonial values. Out of the conflict between these two philosophies emerges a movement towards a new society which will be more aware of universal human values.

Lindo Lhongo's *Os noivos ou conferência dramática sobre o lobolo* (*The Engagement or the Dramatic Discourse about the Purchasing of a Bride*) follows the same theme of confrontation with colonial ideology. It was performed in 1971; an excerpt was published in the literary magazine *Caliban*, and banned soon afterwards by the political police. The play emphasized the renewal and re-evaluation of a genuinely African culture.

Not long before independence, other politically and culturally engaged plays were written: *As trinta mulheres de Muzelini* (*The Thirty Wives of Muzelini*), also by Lhongo; *Filhos da noite* (*Children of the Night*) by António Francisco, and *O feitiço e a religião* (*Sorcery and Religion*) by João Fumane.

According to the regime that emerged after 1975, the principal task was then to 'heal colonial wounds' and build a fairer society. As in the other Portuguese-speaking countries, drama was a means of propagating the ideology of the party in power. The model followed was Soviet agit-prop. These pragmatic principles were displayed in the plays of Orlando Mendes: *Um minuto de silêncio* (*One Minute of Silence*) and *Na machamb de Maria – sábado às três da tarde* (*On Maria's Small Farm – Saturday Afternoon at Three o'clock*, 1975); in the radiophonic theatrical experiment elaborated by Alvaro Belo Marques, a Portuguese voluntary worker, in 1978; in *A estrada* (*The Road*, 1979) by Leite Vasconcelos; in *O destino inimigo do povo* (*Destiny: Enemy of the People*), performed by a workers' collective; in *A Comuna* (*The Commune*, 1979), created by the students of the University Eduardo Mondlane and Mozambique railway workers; in *A Sagrada Família* (*The Holy Family*) written and performed by the Grupo Cénico das Forças Populares de Libertação de Moçambique.

Other dramatic activities include the adaptation of Luís Bernardo Honwana's tale *Rosita até morrer* (*Rosita to my Dying Day*) by a group of Brazilian voluntary workers; Sant' Anna

Afonso's *Eu não sou eu outras peças* (*I am Not I and other Plays*); *Memórias de um projecto* (*Memories of a Project*) by the Cuban voluntary workers Maité Vera; and Pedro Paulo Pereira's *Tempo de mudança* (*Time for a Change*). Theatre for children, with a basically didactic aim, is represented by *Chiquinho malandrinho* (*Naughty Chiquinho*) by Mwaparra, and *Coisas que só acontecem na flor de lótus* (*Things that Only Happen in the Lotus Flower*) by Álvaro Belo Marques.

São Tomé e Príncipe

Of first importance is *Tchiloli ou Tragédia do Marquês de Mântua e do Imperador Carloto Magno*, brought to São Tomé e Príncipe by the Portuguese settlers: it consists of a Portuguese text to which were added African features – music, masks, dances and costumes. *O Auto de Floripes*, performed in the island of Príncipe, was also brought over from Portugal. In 1965 and 1969 two plays by Fernando Reis were performed: *Os mangas de alpaca* (*The Red-Tapists*) and *D'Jambi*.

Bibliography

J. M. Abrantes. 'A procura de um Reencontro com a Realidade', *Africa*, 3, Jan./Mar. 1979; C. Andrade, *Literatura angolana* (*opiniões*), Lisbon, 1980; M. E. O. Assumípção, 'A identidade nacional na dramaturgia angolana. A revolta da casa dos ídolos e a pele do diabo', *Les Littératures Africaines de Langue Portugaise. Actes du Colloque International*, Paris, 28, 29, 30 Nov., 1 Dec. 1984, Paris, 1985; M. Ferreira, *Literaturas africanas de expressão portuguesa*, vols. 1, 2, Lisbon, 1977; R. G. Hamilton, *Literatura africa literatura necessária*, vols. 1, 2, Lisbon, 1981, 1984; F. Reis, *Povô flogá – O povo brinca*, São Tomé, 1969; B. Traoré, 'Le Théâtre négro-africain et ses fonctions sociologiques', *Présence Africaine*, 14/15, June/Sept. 1957; C. Valbert, *Le Tchiloli de São Tomé. Un Exemple de subversion culturelle. Les Littératures Africaines de Langue Portugaise. Actes du Colloque International*, Paris, 28, 29, 30 Nov. 1 Dec. 1984, Paris, 1985; C. Vaz, *Para um conhecimento do teatro africano*, Lisbon, 1978.

BENIN

A former French possession which until 1975 was known as Dahomey, Benin has, like its eastern neighbour Nigeria, a strong heritage in the traditional performing arts. Examples of these theatrical displays are the *gelede* masquerade performers (see Introduction, MASQUERADES IN AFRICA); the adjogbo dancers, who are believed to seek out evil spirits; and the watchmen, the *zangbeto*. A thriving puppet theatre also existed, up to the early 20th century, in the Ouwème region of Benin.

While these activities continue to inform the cultural life of traditional Benin, they have not provided, as in Nigeria, the framework for the emergence of a modern drama, either in the national languages or in French. In fact Benin's achievements in this area are negligible. And yet Dahomey students at the Ecole William Ponty in SENEGAL were noted in the 1930s for significant collective productions such as *La Dernière entrevue de Béhanzin et de Bayol* (*Béhanzin and Bayol, the Last Meeting*, 1933) and *L'Election d'un roi au Dahomey* (*The Election of a King in Dahomey*, 1935). But this early promise has not been borne out. Only a handful of Beninois have published plays, among them Maurice Mêlé (*Danhômé*, 1965), André Pognon (*Le trône vacant*, *The Vacant Throne*, 1975), Henri Héssou and Kossi Attiga-Tsogbe (*L'Aventurier sans scrupules*, *The Unscrupulous Adventurer*, 1982); *Droits d'auteur en Afrique*, *Copyright Laws in Africa*, 1982), and Camille Amouro (*Goli*, 1991).

Fourteen Dahomean plays are summarized by Julian Alapini in his *Les Acteurs noirs* (*Black Actors*, 1965). But of Benin's dramatists, only Jean Pliya, with his historical drama *Kondo le requin* (*Kondo the Shark*, 1981) and social satire *La secrétaire particulière* (*The Confidential Secretary*, 1973), has a reputation beyond the national frontiers. This inactivity has been partly blamed on successive governments which have failed to create the necessary infrastructure – theatre buildings, drama departments, competitions – for the growth of theatre.

However, Benin does not lack performance troupes, which are mostly concerned with presenting cultural dances and folklore. The more important are the Troupe Théâtrale et Folklorique d'Ekpe, founded in 1956; the Troupe Théâtrale Towakonou, founded in 1976 by a former footballer turned professional storyteller, Déhumon Adjagnon; and the Zamahara ('Voice of the People'), which under the Marxist-Leninist government of former president Mathieu Kérékou was little more than a propaganda machine.

Bibliography

R. Cornevin, *Le Théâtre en Afrique noire et à Madagascar*, Paris, 1970; B. Koudjo, 'La pratique théâtrale au Benin', *Notre Librairie: La Littérature beninoise*, 69, May/Jul. 1983).

Botswana, Lesotho and Swaziland

Botswana and Lesotho became independent in 1966; Swaziland, in 1968. The population of the three states totals some 3 million, including many who live and work in South Africa. Sharing the southern African subcontinent with the Republic of South Africa, the three states have had much of their modern history determined by events taking place on that troubled stage. Established as discrete nations in the early 19th century, Lesotho (formerly Basutoland) and Swaziland developed quite differently. In Basutoland, Moshoeshoe I of the Basotho welcomed immigrants of many ethnic backgrounds, and encouraged his people to engage in the emerging industrialization and urbanization of South Africa. This policy, however, had unfortunate results, as labour migrancy over the past 150 years has led to catastrophic soil erosion and the fracturing of the family unit. Religious divisions have created additional tensions within Lesotho, further worsened by the oppressive South African experience of many Basotho men. In Swaziland, a conservative ethnic exclusivity and the centralized power of the monarchy have not encouraged experimentation in the arts. Botswana (formerly Bechuanaland) – with the most varied citizenry of the three, ranging from the Khoi-Khoi and San 'bushmen' of the Kalahari to the urbanites of the modern capital Gaborone – has had the most pacific history and the greatest measure of political democracy. But scattered settlement over a large but sparsely populated territory has not, until recently, stimulated a great deal of theatrical activity beyond traditional forms.

Sharing a regional experience, playwrights of the three nations tend also to share thematic preoccupations: history (often exploring intra-communal dissonance, rather than conflicts with colonial authorities or settlers); strain between generations and between Western-Christian and customary ways, including the enduring dilemmas of bride price, polygamy and traditional magic; the changing pattern of family relations; the life of the sojourner in South African cities; the corrosive effects of apartheid; and the social and psychological consequences of labour migrancy. Interestingly, while writers working in English have tended to be identified with their nations of citizenship, writers in African languages are often seen as members of a larger transnational ethnic community. Thus, South African Joseph M. Ntsime (b.1930) is considered a Setswana-language playwright, while Sesotho-speaking B. L. Leshoai (b.1920), who writes in English, is perceived as a South African.

Of the surviving traditional performance modes in the three countries, the one with the most prominent dramatic component is the mimetic game-enactment of the hunter-gatherer Khoi-Khoi and San of Botswana's desert region. In sung and danced sketches, involving rudimentary forms of plot and characterization and the use of costuming and make-up, both animals and humans are represented. Like the cave paintings for which these cultures are noted, such plays often deal with the processes and skills of hunting.

Written drama in Setswana, the language of the Batswana people, dates only from the 1930s, with Shakespeare translations by South African Solomon T. Plaatje (1877–1932), and, later, by the Motswana Michael O. Seboni (1912–72). The first original play published in Setswana was the work of the Botswana playwright Leetile Disang Raditladi (1910–71).

Motsäsele II (1937) deals with a critical moment in the history of Botswana's Bakwena people, and was eventually followed by the tragedy, *Dinšhontšho tsa Lorato* (*The Many Deaths of Love*, 1956) and *Sekgoma I* (1967), which recounts the events of a disruptive chieftaincy dispute amongst the 19th-century Amangwato people.

Of the next generation, Ntsime's *Pelo e Ja Se Rati* (*A Loving Heart Knows No Bounds*, 1965) is a domestic comedy setting chiefly and paternal authority against decisions of the heart; his *Kobo e Ntsho* (*The Black Robe*, 1968) is a darker and partly autobiographical study of the effects of a father's pressure on his son to become a cleryman; and *Pelo e Ntsho* (*A Black Heart*, 1972) is an attack on witchcraft. But by far the most innovative theatrical initiative in Botswana in recent years had been the *Laedza Batanani* (*The Sun is Risen, Come Out and Work*) scheme, begun by Jeppe Kelepile in 1974, using theatre to encourage both discussion of and action on community problems (health, illiteracy, crime, economic issues) at village level.

The first of the three countries to have a printing operation, Lesotho has seen the greatest number of published plays, if disproportionately fewer stage productions. The first script published in the Sesotho language, Twentyman M. Mofokeng's *Sek'ona Sa Joala* (*A Calabash of Beer*, 1939), is concerned with the clash of cultures, traditional and modern. Later, numerous plays on moral and religious themes, many of them unproducible closet dramas, were circulated, often in cyclostyled form, by the Roman Catholic centre at Mazenod and the Evangelical Mission at Morija.

Lesotho's first major playwright emerged in 1947, with the publication of B. M. Khaketla's *Moshoeshoe le Baruti* (*Moshoeshoe and the Missionaries*). Khaketla (b.1913) – a teacher

A scene from *Kopana Ke Matla* (*Unity is Strength*), a play about the problems facing an agricultural cooperative, produced by the National University of Lesotho's Theatre in Community Development Project, 1984.

turned politician, and founder, in 1960, of the small Marematlon Freedom Party – is best known as a novelist, poet and polemicist. His stage pieces include the historical *Tholoana tsa Sethepu* (*The Fruits of Polygamy*, 1954), about a succession to kingship, and its sequel, *Bulane* (1958), in which the disinherited son finally becomes king. Khaketla's wife, N. M. Khaketla, is probably the most widely read Sesotho author today. Amongst her plays, which deal with both domestic and broader social problems, are *Mosali Eo U 'Neileng Eena* (*The Woman Thou Gavest Me*, 1956), in which a shell-shocked former seminarian returns from the First World War, survives difficulties in love and becomes a cleric; the two short pieces collected as *Ka U Lotha* (*I'm Posing You a Riddle*, 1976); the unpublished *Mahlopha a Senya* (*Creating and Destroying*, early 1980s), which mixes Sesotho and the local English of the streets; and *Ho Isa Lefung* (*Unto Death*).

Lesotho's best-known playwright, and one of Africa's major theatrical voices, is ZAKES MDA (see South Africa). Son of a central figure in South Africa's banned Pan-Africanist Congress, Mda emigrated to Lesotho in 1963, and began writing for the stage while at secondary school. By the mid-1980s his plays had been performed both within and outside Africa, and translated into several languages. *We Shall Sing for the Fatherland* (1978), set in an unnamed African country, examines the disparity between the promises of nationalist politicians before independence and the reality of deprivation afterwards. In *Dark Voices Ring* (1978), Mda anatomizes the system of contracted prison labour in South Africa and the psychological cost to the family of a black farm overseer of complicity with apartheid. *The Hill* (1979), his most finished piece, is a powerful tragicomedy on the social and ethical distortions created by labour migrancy. This theme is further developed in *The Road* (1982), a stark parable with resonances of Brecht, Beckett and Genet, in which a Lesotho migrant worker confronts an Afrikaner farmer in a bizarre melange of misperception, hostility and desperate territoriality.

In the mid-1980s Lesotho also saw the emergence of popular theatre, with the Theatre for Community Development Project of the National University, which combines the improvisational stage techniques of the *Laedza Batanani* scheme with radio, videotape and narrative comic-book production, and is directed at rural, urban and prison groups. From this has grown the Marotholi Travelling Theatre and the University of Lesotho Theatre Group – both working as theatre-for-development companies into the early 1990s. Playwrights and theatre workers active from the late 1980s include Masitha Hoeane, Buti Moleko and Afelile Sekhamane.

Swaziland's theatre remains the least developed in the region, with its best-known published play by a writer who is neither a Swazi nor primarily a playwright – anthropologist Hilda Kuper's statement on the position of women in Swazi society, *A Witch in My Heart* (1970). However, from the 1980s a great deal of work has been done in participatory community theatre as part of public education campaigns. Swaziland also has a rich tradition of ritual and ceremonial performance, including the six-day sacred harvest and kingship rites of the *ncwala* and the annual secular *mhlanga* (reed dance) for young girls.

Bibliography

C. M. Doke, 'Games, Plays and Dances of the Khomani Bushmen', *Bantu Studies*, 10, 1936; A Gerard, *African Language Literatures*, London, 1981; A. Horn, *The Plays of Zakes Mda*, Johannesburg, 1987; R. Kidd, M. Byram and P. Rohr-Rouendaal, *Laedza Batanani: Organizing Popular Theatre*, Gaborone, 1978; Z. Mda, *When People Play People: Development Communication through Theatre*, London, 1993; L. Nichols, *African Writers at the Microphone*, Washington, DC, 1984.

BURKINA FASO

Formerly Upper Volta, Burkina Faso gained its independence from France in August 1960. It is remembered by older French-speaking African theatre enthusiasts for the excellent performance of its Banfora Cultural Centre Troupe at the drama competitions of 1955 and 1957 organized among French West African states. But this promising beginning has not been followed up. Only two Burkina plays in French have been published to date: *Le Fou* (*The Madman*, 1986) by Jean-Pierre Guingané, playwright and Burkina theatre historian, and Pierre Dabiré's *Sansoa* (1969). The other six that exist in print were issued by the country's Ministry of Culture and are not widely available.

But theatrical activity certainly exists in Burkina Faso. The country boasts at least four notable companies that are engaged either in the creation of new plays or the staging of the many unpublished ones – estimated at five hundred by Guingané. These four are the Troupe du Théâtre Radiophonique, the Troupe de la Mutuelle Nouvelle Génération, the Atelier Théâtre Burkinabé and the Théâtre de la Fraternité, the last two being currently the most influential. The Atelier Théâtre, under the direction of Prosper Kampaoré, advocates a theatre of participation: one that breaks the barriers between actor and spectator and transforms the latter from passive consumer to creative agent. Although he is said to derive this idea from his traditional heritage, he also admits to being inspired by the forum-theatre techniques of the Brazilian playwright-director Augusto Boal. His productions are followed by debates between actors and spectators, during which the latter are encouraged to criticize the 'model' performances and propose alternative scenarios, which are then produced. Kampaoré's themes are mostly developmental. The Théâtre de la Fraternité, on the other hand, under its director Guingané, concentrates on socio-political topics. The performance style that he is trying to develop is based on that of the folk-tale, where the storyteller acts different characters, effecting costume changes in full view of the audience, and where the action is narrated, sung or dramatized.

Bibliography

B. Benon, 'Deux expériences théâtrales. Jean-Pierre Guingané et le Théâtre de la Fraternité; Prosper Kampaoré et l'Atelier Burkinabé', *Notre Librairie: La Littérature du Burkina Faso*, 101, Apr./June 1990; Thérèse-Marie Deffontaines, 'Théâtre-Forum au Burkina Faso et au Mali', *Notre Librairie: Théâtre Théâtres*, 102, Jul./Aug. 1990; J. B. Guingané, 'Du manuscrit à la scène', *Notre Librairie: La Littérature du Burkina Faso*, ibid.; J.-C. Ki, 'Dix ans de théâtre 1979-1989'. *Notre Librairie: La Littérature du Burkina Faso*, ibid.; W. Zimmer, 'Jean-Pierre Guingané, un "fou" de théâtre au Burkina Faso', *Notre Librairie: Théâtre Théâtres*, ibid.

CAMEROON

Cameroon, like Togo, was under German rule between 1814 and 1916 before passing into Franco-British control as a League of Nations mandated territory. The French section became independent in January 1961 and was joined by the British Cameroons ten months later. There is a modern Cameroonian theatre in all three languages: insignificant in German – represented by one play, Alexandre Kuma N'Dumbé's *Kafra-Biatanga* (1973), which was first written in that language – but substantial in the other two.

The modern Cameroonian theatre goes back to the 1940s, but with the exception of GUILLAUME OYONO-MBIA and NICOLE WEREWERE-LIKING it has produced no dramatists of the stature of Ferdinand Oyono in the novel, let alone of Mongo Beti. It is basically a comic theatre: refreshingly undidactic and very playable in Oyono-Mbia's works, Ndedi-Penda's *Le Fusil* (*The Gun*, 1970), Protais Asseng's feminist *Trop c'est trop* (*Enough is Enough*, 1981) and Stanislas Awona's *Le Chômeur* (*The Unemployed*, 1968), among others.

Although not comparable with the output of the Sahel countries, historical and political drama is also present, exemplified by Paul Tchakouté's *Les Dieux trancheront* (*The Gods will Decide*, 1971, written under the pseudonym Franz Cayor) and his *Samba* (1980); by Kuma N'Dumbé's *Amilcar Cabral* (1976), Ndam Njoya's *Dairou IV* (1973) and Benjamin Matip's *Laissez-nous bâtir une Afrique debout* (*Allow us to Build a Strong Africa*, 1979).

Cameroon also had in the 1940s the beginnings of a modern theatre in the local languages: its practitioners included Jean-Baptiste Obama with his *Mbarga Osono* (1943) and Adalbert Owona with *Fada Jean* (*Father Jean*, 1944); and in 1956 an erotic comedy, *Ebudundu*, was staged. But this promise of a popular theatre in the local languages did not materialize. What has emerged, however, since the 1970s is a popular, crowd-pulling theatre that uses colloquial French. It treats topics of concern to the mass of people, and depicts characters sometimes dressed in rags, singing, narrating or dancing out their many adventures. Slapstick and licentious jokes and songs figure prominently. Plays in this genre include *Le Moule cassé* (*The Broken Mould*, 1974) by Zomo Bel Abel, Daniel Ndo' *Le Mariage de Folinka* (*Folinka's Marriage*, 1976), and others, mostly unpublished, by writers such as Dieudonné Afana, Jean-Michel Kankan, Michel Ndi and Dave Moktoi.

Since the mid-1980s, under the influence of Jacqueline Leloup, the Frenchwoman who ran the University of Yaoundé theatre, there have been attempts to found a theatre based on ritual, such as Bamiléké funeral and enthronement ceremonies. Examples are Jean-Marie Tueche's *La Succession de Wabo Défo* (*The Succession of Wabo Défo*) and Leloup's *Guéido* (1984), performed at the first Limoges Festival of Francophone Theatre. Other recent plays include: D. Ndachi-Tagne's *Monsieur Handlock, ou le boulanger poétique* (*Mr Handlock, or the Poetic Baker*, 1985); R. Ekossono's *Ainsi s'achève la vie d'un homme* (*So Ends a Man's Life*, 1989); and M.-C. Mbarga's *Les Insatiables* (*The Insatiables*, 1989). The relative weakness of Cameroonian theatre, which has no national company or professional troupes, has been partly blamed on governments which prefer to sponsor activities like football rather than one that is largely devoted to criticizing their pompous and corrupt officials.

Oyono Mbia, Guillaume (1939–)

Cameroonian bilingual playwright, civil servant and university teacher. Born in Mvoutessi, Oyono-Mbia was educated at the Collège Evangélique of Libamba and Keele University, England. His plays have been widely produced in Cameroon and on British and French international radio services, where two of them – *Until Further Notice*, 1968 (*Jusqu'à nouvel avis*, 1970) and *Notre fille ne se mariera pas* (*Our Daughter will not Get Married*, 1971) – won the BBC African Service and Radio France Internationale drama competitions, respectively. But his most popular play to date is the village comedy *Trois prétendants ... un mari* (*Three Suitors ... One Husband*, 1964). In 1978 he published a fourth play, *Le Train spécial de son Excellence* (*His Excellency's Special Train*),

Oyono-Mbia's plays, mostly concerned with the disruptive effects of modern values on traditional society, are constructed principally as dramatic entertainment. Their material is not so much built on the elaborate literary effect of 'high comedy', with a properly integrated plot, as on the comic personality of stock characters that rely on mime and slapstick to perform typical numbers. Language as a source of the comic is a resource also exploited in his plays. Oyono-Mbia is also the author of three volumes of stories.

Werewere-Liking, Nicole (1950–)

Cameroonian playwright, theatre director and, with Rabiatu Njoya, also of Cameroon, and Josephine Kama Bongo of Gabon, one of the three women writing for the stage in French-speaking Africa. Werewere-Liking was born into a family of traditional musicians and had little formal education, having spent a good part of her early life being initiated into various secret societies. She taught herself to read and write French much later, skills which she subsequently used to explore for the stage those myths and rituals that were such a vital part of her early experience.

Werewere-Liking left Cameroon for the Ivory Coast in the late 1970s. As a researcher at the university there, she took part in the then ongoing debates and researches into African theatre led by playwrights like Bernard Zadi Zaourou, theatre practitioners like Niangoran Porquet, and the French ethno-sociologist and theatre critic Marie-José Hourantier. It was from her collaboration with Hourantier that her career as a playwright was born. Her published plays are *La Queue du diable* (*The Devil's Tail*, 1979), known in Cameroon as *Ngonga* after its main character and to Radio France Internationale listeners as *Les Bâtards* (*The Bastards*); *La Puissance d'Um* (*The Power of Um*, 1979); *Une Nouvelle Terre* and *Du sommeil injuste* (*A New Land* and *Of the Unjust Sleep*, 1980); *Les Mains veulent dire* and *La Rougeole arc-en-ciel* (*Hands Have Meaning* and *The Rainbow Measles*, 1987). In 1984 she founded the Ki-Yi troupe, which seeks to evolve a performance style that makes use of puppets, masks, song and dance.

Werewere-Liking's theatre constitutes a radical departure from anything yet produced in French-speaking Africa. Her plays are psychodramas, rooted in her native Bassa healing, initiation or death rituals. They invariably deal with the eruption of disorder (death, illness or crime in the life of a rural community), and their object is to purge the spectator-celebrant community of their unhealthy emotions, thereby restoring their broken equilibrium. The use of a highly esoteric language, of trance and spirit-possession techniques and of an intricate symbolism of colours, costumes and gestures, characterizes her theatre. It may also account for its obscurity and lack of wide appeal so far.

Bibliography

R. Cornevin, *Le Théâtre en Afrique noire et à Madagascar*, 1970; G. Doho, 'Théâtre et représentation au Cameroun', *Notre Librairie: La Littérature Camérounaise*, 99, Oct./Dec. 1989; C. Mbom, 'Le Théâtre camerounais en pleine mutation', *Notre Librairie*, ibid.; C. Wake, 'Cameroon', in *The Cambridge Guide to World Theatre*, ed. M. Banham, Cambridge, 1988; C. Wake and M. Banham, *African Theatre Today*, London, 1976.

CONGO, REPUBLIC OF

Formerly part of French Equatorial Africa, the Republic of Congo, renamed the People's Republic of Congo in 1969, gained its independence in 1960. Before the rapid development of the past fifteen years, modern theatre was, of all the literary genres, the poor relation. Modern theatre in the Congo started only in 1950, and even then it consisted largely of school plays put on in mission institutions and performances at the French Cultural Centre by visiting French troupes. By the end of the 1960s, the country had three troupes of its own: the Théâtre Congolais founded by Guy Menga, Patrice Lhoni and others; the Troupe Municipale; and the Kamango Players of the country's second city Pointe-Noire. Their repertory was drawn from the few existing plays: Menga's *La Marmite de Koka Mbala* (*Koka Mbala's Pot*, 1969) and *L'Oracle* (*The Oracle*, 1969); Lhoni's *L'Annonce faite à Makoko* (*The Announcement to Makoko*, 1967); and Ferdinand Mouangassa's *Nganga Mayala* (1969).

The mid-1970s saw a quickening of the tempo, which had started with the publication of SYLVAIN BEMBA's political classic *L'Enfer c'est Orfeo* (*Hell is Orfeo*, 1968), and Letembet-Ambily's prize-winning *L'Europe inculpée* (*Europe Convicted*, 1969). In addition to Bemba, who also wrote *L'Homme qui tua le crocodile* (*The Man Who Killed the Crocodile*, 1972), a comedy of manners, and *Tarentelle noir et diable blanc* (*Black Tarantula and White Devil*, 1976), the other important dramatist of the 1970s was SONY LABOU TANSI. Poets like TCHICAYA U'TAMSI with his *Le Zulu* (*The Zulu*, 1977), and Maxime Ndébéka with *Le Président* (*The President*, 1970) – both plays against dictatorship – also turned dramatists about this time. There also emerged a theatre of socialist propaganda by Jacob Owei-Okanza.

Acclaimed recent plays include: U'Tamsi's *Le bal de Ndinga* (*Ndinga's Ball*, 1987); Labou Tansi's *Moi veuve de l'empire* (*I, Widow of the Empire*, 1987); and Maxime Ndébéka's *Equatorium* (1987).

The 1980s saw the formation of troupes. Of the fifteen-odd that exploded onto the scene, only four are reported to be doing well: Labou Tansi's Rocado Zulu, Emmanuel Dongala's Théâtre de l'Eclair, both private and benefiting from financial and logistical support from the French Cultural Centre in Brazzaville; the Troupe Artistique Ngunga, and the state-run Théâtre National. What characterizes these troupes is the constant search for a new aesthetic. They all practice the technique of collective creation, and emphasize the actors' physical presence on stage and stylized body movements; they reduce the decor to the barest minimum, integrate dance, mime and song into the activity, and make use of masks and symbolism. With the Ngunga and the Rocado now earning an international reputation with their regular participation in the Limoges Festival of Francophone Theatre, Congolese theatre has come of age.

Bemba, Sylvain [Belavin, Michel; Malinda, Martial] (1934–)
Congolese dramatist and novelist. His literary career began in the late 1950s with pieces in *Liaison*, the organ of the French cultural centres of French Equatorial Africa. Before turning to playwriting he wrote sketches for radio (he was trained as a journalist in Strasbourg) under the pseudonym Belavin, and produced a short feature film and a pageant on the colonial experience of the Congo. His first play *L'Enfer c'est Orfeo* (*Hell is Orfeo*, 1966), published under the pseudonym Malinda, is about an African doctor-

intellectual, Orfeo, who finds salvation in revolutionary action from his hell of self-hatred and contempt for his pleasure-seeking social class. In its preoccupation with social and economic injustices, in its use of satire, fantasy (in the scene where the wounded Orfeo hallucinates) and popular African French speech, this play is typical of the rest of Bemba's dramatic work – which consists of four other published plays: *L'Homme qui tua le crocodile* (*The Man Who Killed the Crocodile*, 1973), *Une Eau dormante* (*Sleepy Waters*, 1975), *Tarentelle noire et diable blanc* (*Black Tarantula and White Devil*, 1976) and *Un Foutu de monde pour un blanchisseur trop honnête* (*A Rotten World for an Over-honest Laundryman*, 1979). Bemba is also the author of four novels and a collection of short stories.

Labou Tansi, Sony (1947–)

Prolific Congolese poet, novelist, dramatist and theatre director. Born in Zaire, Labou Tansi was an English teacher for several years, before founding in 1979, from the amateur theatre group Moni-Mambou, what has since become his country's leading theatre company: the Rocado Zulu Theatre. It is also beginning to gain an international reputation, with its regular participation in the annual Limoges Festival of Francophone Theatre in France, where some of its collective creations, produced by various French directors in collaboration with Labou Tansi himself, have been well received. But with seven plays and five novels to his name, it is as a writer that he is best known.

His plays highlight the dictatorships, the material and moral misery, that characterize post-colonial Africa. With their cohorts of corpses, hallucinatory shadows and Ubuesque characters, his plays create a grotesque world where events seem to conform to no logical pattern: *Conscience de tracteur* (*The Conscience of a Tractor*, 1979), *La Parenthèse de sang* and *Je soussigné* (*Blood Parenthesis* and *I, the Undersigned Cardiac Patient*, 1981), *Qui a mangé Madame D'Avoine Bergotha?* (*Who Has Eaten Madam*

D'Avoine Bergotha?, 1984), *Moi veuve de l'empire* (*I, Widow of the Empire*, 1987); *Antoine m'a vendu son destin* (*Antoine Sold Me His Destiny*, 1986). Among plays already performed but not yet published are his *La Rue des mouches* (*The Street of Flies*, 1985) and an adaptation of *Romeo and Juliet* produced by Migrations Culturelles Aquitaines in Bordeaux in 1990 under Guy Lenoir.

U'Tamsi, Felix Tchicaya (1931–88)

Congolese dramatist, poet and novelist. Born in the then French Congo, from the age of fifteen U'Tamsi lived in Paris. After his education at the Lycée Janson-de-Sailly there, he embarked on a literary career. His reputation as a writer rests principally on six volumes of dense, surrealist poetry which he produced between 1955 and 1966. In 1976 he turned to writing for the stage, establishing with *Le Zulu* (1977) – a tragedy of ambition, premiered at the Avignon Festival and published a year later – a reputation as a dramatist of talent. In addition to the short dramatic monologue *Vivène le Fondateur* (*Vivène the Founder*) published in the same volume as *Le Zulu*, U'Tamsi has also written an acutely satirical play on political dictatorship in Africa, *Le Maréchal Nnikon Nniku Prince qu'on sort* (*Marshall Nnikon Nniku, Prince Consort*, 1979). But his greatest theatrical success so far is *Le Bal de N'Dinga*. A highly poetic dance-drama on a failed exercise in decolonization, this play was first produced in October 1988 by the French director Gabriel Garran of the Théâtre International de Langue Française. It has since been performed to packed audiences in France, Africa and the French Caribbean. U'Tamsi also wrote four novels and was, until his death, an international civil servant with UNESCO in Paris.

Bibliography

R. Chemain and A. Chemain-Dégrange, *Panorama critique de la littérature congolaise contemporaine*, Paris, 1979; R. Cornevin, *Le Théâtre en Afrique noire et à Madagascar*, Paris, 1970; J.-B. Tati-Loutard, 'Itinéraire', *Notre Libraire: La Littérature Congolaise*, 92–3, Mar./May 1988; M. Turé, 'Panorama du théâtre et quelques réflexions', *Notre Libraire*, ibid..

CÔTE D'IVOIRE

Modern theatre in Côte d'Ivoire, which became independent in 1960, has enjoyed over the past seventy years a steady and richly varied development. It can be traced back to the late 1920s in Grand-Bassam, and its first signs seen in the secondary school pupils of the then Gold Coast, whose itinerant acting groups toured border regions of both countries during summer vacations, performing sketches in the common local languages. But it was in the 1930s at the École Primaire Supérieure de Bingerville that this new theatre was really to develop. The French headmaster Charles Béart, committed to nurturing his pupils' natural dramatic talent, encouraged them in their spontaneous improvisations. Beginning with extracts from French classical plays, soon the pupils were composing their own pieces and staging them to an outside audience.

This fledgeling theatrical activity was strengthened by the founding in 1938 of the Théâtre Indigène troupe by ex-Bingerville and École William Ponty Ivorians (see SENEGAL) – BERNARD DADIÉ, Koffi Gadeau and, especially, Amon d'Aby – whose period of study in the latter institution had further developed their taste for the theatre. The troupe's repertory was drawn from their historical, satirical and biblical dramas. Performances took place in the popular district of Abidjan, in a pidgin French (*francais de moussa*) that is now widely used in popular dramas. Then in 1953 the Cercle Culturel et Folklorique was formed, and its members, including the three founder-members of the by then defunct Théâtre Indigène, wrote and produced new plays that reflected their growing nationalist consciousness.

In the immediate pre-independence years, France strengthened Ivorian theatre by creating cultural centres and founding the École Nationale d'Art Dramatique for training Ivorians in the theatre arts. The newly independent state built on this programme by instituting in 1963 a scholarship programme, which sent young students to France for advanced study of the theatre, and by founding in 1967 the Institut National des Arts. Short seminars by visiting French specialists were organized, and troupes sprang up: the Kourouma Moussa, the Guézaba and the Houphouët-Boigny.

If before 1960 Ivorian theatre was dominated, in terms of sheer production, by d'Aby (with fourteen dramas by 1957) and Gadeau, the period after independence has been Dadié's. His plays, serious but also theatrical, are constantly being performed not just in his country but throughout French-speaking Africa. Other Ivorian playwrights include Charles Nokan, with his *Abraha Poku* (1971); the Martiniquan naturalized-Ivorian Eugène Dervain, with *La reine scélérate* (*The Villainous Queen*, 1968) and Amadou Koné, with *Les Canaris sont vides* (*The Pots are Empty*, 1984).

In the late 1970s, several new currents revitalized Ivorian theatre by pulling it free from its European-inspired aesthetic. Thus Niangoran Porquet with his Théâtre Griotique evolved a style of acting derived from the 'theatre-ballets' of the Guinean Fodéba Keita and the performance of the traditional *griot*, which combines the spoken word with music, song, dance and mime. Souleymane Koly, of Guinean origin, founded the Ensemble Kotéba which, like its Malian ancestor, explores social problems for a popular audience. His plays such as *Didi par-ci, Didi par-là* (*Didi Here, Didi There*, 1979) use a plurality of languages – French, pidgin

French and Dioula – and mix spoken parts with stylized dance roles.

Sidiki Bakaba is experimenting with a theatre based on collective creation – usually a collection of loosely strung episodes – where scene and costume changes are all done in full view of the audience and where the director sometimes goes on stage to act a character. But perhaps the two most notable innovators of these years are ZADI ZAOUROU with his Didiga Theatre of Symbolism, and Nicole WEREWERE-LIKING (see Cameroon), who has written plays which in content, form and function derive from ritual ceremonies.

Dadié, Bernard (Binlin) (1916–)

Ivorian novelist, poet, dramatist and politician; generally recognized as one of the founding fathers of French-language Ivorian drama. Dadié was educated in the Ivory Coast at the École Primaire Supérieure at Bingerville, and at the École William Ponty in SENEGAL, where he was involved in the school's nascent but already dynamic dramatic activities. On graduation, he worked in Dakar at the French Research Institute for African Studies (IFAN), from 1936 to 1947. Also in Dakar, under various pseudonyms he was involved in nationalist journalism, an activity he pursued on his return to Abidjan in 1948 for the Ivorian section of the Rassemblement Démocratique Africain mass political movement. Dadié has had a distinguished career in his country as a top civil servant in the Ministry of Culture and Information, then as Minister of Culture. His first play, *Les Villes* (*The Town*, 1933), now missing, was written while he was still at Bingerville. It was followed in 1934 at Ponty by a historical chronicle, *Assémien Déhylé*. Between 1955 and 1960 he wrote five sketches for the Cercle Culturel Folklorique de Côte d'Ivoire, which he had helped found: *Serment d'amour* (*Love Vow*, 1955), *Situation difficile* (*A Difficult Situation*, 1955), *Les Enfants* (*The Children*, 1956), *Min Ajao* (*My Inheritance*, 1956) and *Sidi, maître escroc* (*Sidi, Master Crook*, 1960).

But it is for the plays of his mature period that he is best known: *Béatrice du Congo* and *Iles de tempête* (*Beatrice of Congo*, 1970; *Islands of Storm*, 1973) and *Les Voix dans le Vent, Monsieur Thogo-Ghini, Mhoi-Ceul* and *Papassidi maître escroc* (*Voices in the Wind*, 1970; *Mister Thogo-Ghini*, 1970; *I Alone*, 1979; *Papassidi Master Crook*, 1975). In their preoccupation with political power and social criticism, all reflect the major concerns of the French-language African dramatist.

The success of Dadié's plays lies in the fact that they are both humanly engaging and theatrically lively. He has also written four prose narratives, volumes of poetry, folk-tales and short stories.

Zaourou, Bernard Zadi (1938–)

Ivorian dramatist, theatre director, poet and university teacher. Zaourou attended the University of Strasbourg, France; after his MA in 1970 (he has since published a doctoral dissertation on the poetry of AIMÉ CÉSAIRE (see Caribbean Theatre, Introduction)), he joined the staff of the University of Abidjan.

Zaourou is a controversial figure. While still at school, he spent a short spell in prison for extreme left-wing activities. In 1975, his agit-prop play *L'Oeil* (*The Eye*, 1974) was censored on the grounds of incitement to class hatred and violence. Since the mid-1970s, he has been at the forefront of efforts and spirited polemics aimed at renewing Ivorian theatre, in both discourse and aesthetic. After his traditional historical play *Les Sofas* (*The Sofas*, 1975), he opted, in terms of content at least, for a radical political theatre in *L'Oeil*. This play, on the growth of a revolutionary consciousness, is interesting for its use, in addition to words, of the languages of drum music, silence and mime.

The systematic exploitation of these elements is pursued in *La Termitière* (*The Anthill*, 1981), an initiation-ritual play based on the principles of the hunter narrative of his Bété people, the Didiga. These principles are the rationally illogical but mystically significant symbolism, and the language of surreal poetry. In 1980 Zaourou founded the Didiga Company, with choreographic, musical, drama and literary criticism sections, in an attempt to create a theatrical aesthetic that has roots in his community's traditional art forms. Two of his other play are *Sory Lambré* (1968) and *Les Tignasses* (*The Hair*, 1984).

Bibliography

R. Bonneau, 'Panorama du théâtre ivoirien', *Afrique Littéraire et Artistique*, 23, 1972, and 'C'est quoi même: une improvisation collective de Sidiki Bakaba', *Afrique Littéraire et Artistique*, 27, 1973; R. Cornevin, *Le Théâtre en Afrique noire et à Madagascar*, Paris, 1970; F. J. d'Aby, 'Des origines du théâtre de Bingerville', *Notre Librairie: La Côte d'Ivoire*, 86, Jan./Mar. 1987, and, *Le Théâtre en Côte d'Ivoire*, Abidjan, 1988; M.-J. Hourantier, *Du Rituel au théâtre rituel*, Paris, 1984, and 'La Parole poétique du Didiga de Zadi Zaourou', *Notre Librairie*, ibid.; A. Koné, 'La Griotique de Niangoran Porquet', *Notre Librairie*, ibid.; B. Kotchy, 'New Trends in the Theatre of the Ivory Coast 1972–1983', *Theatre Research International*, 9, 3, 1984; C. Wake, 'Ivory Coast', in *The Cambridge Guide to World Theatre*, ed. M. Banham, Cambridge, 1988.

ETHIOPIA

Ethiopia is home to one of the most prolific theatre establishments in Africa. The capital, Addis Ababa, has five state theatre companies. There are state-supported KINET (performance arts) groups in all the regions, a Theatre Arts Department at the University of Addis Ababa, and a rapidly growing number of amateur groups in many urban centres. Some three hundred original works have been staged in Ethiopian theatres this century.

Ethiopian theatre is relatively unknown outside its homeland, primarily because almost all work has been written and produced in the dominant local language, Amharic. However, the history, geography and politics of the country have also encouraged insular attitudes. Pre-20th-century Ethiopia centred on a group of highland peoples living under the feudal overlordship of emperors who traced their descent back to a liaison between the Queen of Sheba and King Solomon. These highlanders were divided geographically from their neighbours on the surrounding plains and deserts. They were also religiously different. Ethiopians strongly identified with their Orthodox Christian Church, and from the 7th century AD, as Islam swept through much of the Horn of Africa, they were increasingly culturally isolated. Traditionally, church and state reinforced each other's authority and encouraged conservative values. Control extended to censorship of the arts. As early as the 6th century AD one Bishop Grigentius published a decree stating that public singers, harp-players, actors and dancers were all to be suppressed, and that anyone found practising these arts was to be punished by whipping and a year's hard labour.

Under Emperor Menelik in the late 19th cen-
tury, Ethiopia was greatly expanded through conquest. Many new ethnic groups were brought into the Empire, so that today Ethiopia incorporates people of some seventy nationalities. The traditional performance cultures of many of these people have been little researched, although performance forms with dramatic elements such as music, dance, storytelling and ritual enactments are widespread. Within the dominant Amhara culture the church promoted certain exclusive performance arts, such as priestly dance, *shibsheba*; religious music, *aquaquam*; and oral poetry, *qene*. For the ordinary people, traditional dance accompanied by improvised songs was the most common performance outlet, although rhetorical skills were and are widely revered. Ethiopian society also developed a caste grouping of professional singers and dancers, the *azmariwoch*, or AZMARIS, who were commonly attached to noble households as praise-singers.

Modern drama was first brought to Ethiopia by a nobleman, Tekle Hawariat, who had lived for many years in Europe. His satire *The Comedy of Animals*, based on the work of La Fontaine, was performed to the Ethiopian court c.1916. The play was highly critical of the Ethiopian establishment, and as a result drama was banned at court by the then Empress, Zauditu. On his accession to the throne in 1930, Haile Selassie reversed Zauditu's ban and commissioned plays from two schoolmasters, Yoftahe Negussie and Malaku Baggosaw, who produced a succession of plays glorifying the Emperor, the Church and Ethiopian history. They had learnt the basics of modern drama by teaching in the elite European-style schools of Addis Ababa.

With the looming threat of the Italian invasion in 1935, the first national cultural group, the AGER FIKIR (Patriotic Theatre Association), was formed with a group of azmaris who were brought together to perform propaganda music, dance and theatre. The Italian occupation was a traumatic episode in Ethiopian history, and indigenous cultural production came to a temporary halt. However, after the restoration of the monarchy in 1941 there was a surge of artistic activity. The Ager Fikir was re-formed in 1942, and a second professional company was established in 1947 at the Addis Ababa City Hall. Both companies performed predominantly variety-style shows comprising short plays followed by popular music and dance. At this time, too, drama was first toured through the regions.

Populist playwrights such Mattewos Bekele and the prolific Iyoel Yohannes, who wrote some seventy plays, produced largely slapstick comedies for popular urban consumption, but during the late 1940s and 50s it became fashionable for elite intellectuals to write serious drama for aristocratic consumption. Most of these playwrights had little idea of dramatic form, and were primarily concerned with moralistic preaching. Makonnen Endalkachew was the prime exponent of the sermon play, with such works as *David and Orion*, *King David III* and *The Voice of Blood*. Patriotic and historical themes were also popular, and although some writers such as Kebede Michael with his *Hannibal* and the woman playwright Romana Worq Kasahun in her *The Light of Science* voiced mildly reformist ideals, most plays of this period reflect traditional values.

Many of the conventions for Ethiopian theatre were set during this early period. Action in serious drama is often minimal, long speeches abound, and many of the plays are written in verse form: rhetoric is the most important part of all Ethiopian plays. Characterization is generally sparse. Actors serve as symbols, and staging and lighting effects reinforce this iconographic style, which shows the strong influence of church culture. Playwrights as creators of rhetoric are honoured, and have usually come from the upper class. In contrast, actors until recently were either schoolboys or azmaris, and were regarded as mere servants of the play. Until the 1960s serious drama was still seen as an upper-class entertainment, while actors and the general populace tended to prefer traditional dance and music. A gulf has grown up between these two forms of performance art: theatre companies now have separate sections for the traditional performance arts, for modern music, and for drama. Actors now have the greatest prestige of all performers, and there is almost no interaction between the different forms of cultural representation.

Ethiopian plays may be up to four hours long and generally have no interval. Uniquely in Africa, Ethiopian theatre developed with minimal European influence. Unlike the drama of the colonized nations, Ethiopia's was always performed in the local language, dealt with matters of national concern, and was produced in ways which built on the country's cultural heritage and reflected the hierarchical, metaphysical world view of Amhara society as dominated by the Ethiopian Orthodox Church.

Haile Selassie's influence on the development of Ethiopian drama can hardly be overestimated. An autocrat who oversaw the running of Ethiopia in quite extraordinary detail, he frequently attended new productions, and no play could be published or performed without his approval. The value that the Emperor placed on drama is demonstrated perhaps most clearly in his commissioning of the 1400-seat Haile Selassie Theatre in 1955 for the Imperial Silver Jubilee. No expense was spared: the most modern technical equipment was bought from Europe, and a group of Austrians were employed to run the centre with enormous budgets for new productions.

From 1960, however, Haile Selassie's control over drama began to be challenged by a small group of young Ethiopians who had spent time abroad and who on their return started to use theatre to subtly challenge the established order. TSEGAYE GEBRE-MEDHIN, the most prominent of this group, returned home from Europe in 1960 and was given artistic control of the Haile Selassie Theatre, ousting the foreigners. In partnership with TESFAYE GESSESSE, who had studied in America and now worked primarily as a director, Tsegaye started to stage a series of plays (mostly his own), which brought new ideas of social criticism into Ethiopian drama. Works such as *Mumps*, *The Crown of Thorns* and *A Man of the Future* examined the lives of ordinary Ethiopians, looking at issues such as the oppression of the poor, the degradation of much of city life and the loss of direction suffered by urban youth. Even in plays such as *Tewodros*, which took more traditional themes, he used history to question the role of rulers and to make strongly anticlerical statements.

Tsegaye was soon joined by other new playwrights. MENGISTU LEMMA in his *Marriage of Unequals* took a comic but critical look at aristocratic arrogance, ignorance and superstition. Abe Gubegna also criticized decadent aristocracy in *The Fall of Rome*, while Tesfaye's *Yeshi* studied the massive Ethiopian problem of urban prostitution.

The new style of theatre was increasingly popular with urban audiences, who for the first time could see their own lives mirrored on stage. However, the plays continually ran into trouble with the censors. Even though criticism was generally oblique – in the tradition of Ethiopian oral literature, which is famed for its use of *doubles entendres* – the plays of the 1960s and early 70s were increasingly either cut or ordered off stage after a few performances.

The revolution of 1974, which put in power a military council, the Dergue, led to a massive expansion of drama. Although the revolutionaries quickly became committed to socialism, for some time it was not clear what sort of left-wing ideology would be espoused or how the new state would organize itself. During this time of open debate, Ethiopian dramaturgs seized the opportunity to express their views with a clarity which had previously been impossible. New plays discussing possible ways forward were now put on, and thousands flocked to this new drama of debate, so that runs lasted not for a few performances but for up to six months.

The military government quickly set up a new Ministry of Culture and Sport, and for the first time drama was used as a tool of widespread politicization. From the mass organizations that had been set up throughout the country, cultural groups were formed which started to put on short pieces of agit-prop theatre. These propaganda plays, with titles like *The Red Sickle* and *Struggle for Victory*, were crude – but popular with audiences crying out for information about the revolution. And as the Dergue tightened its hold on power and created a Marxist-Leninist state, the theatres of the capital began to put on more committed plays. Two new theatres were opened in Addis Ababa in the late 1970s, and a new generation of playwrights, writing popular agit-prop plays, came to the fore: in particular, Getachew Abdi, Tekle Desta and AYALNEH MULAT. During the early years of Dergue control the previously despised actors won considerably improved working conditions, and a Theatre Arts Department was set up at Addis Ababa University which would from now on provide the most innovative voices in Ethiopian theatre.

By 1980 the military government, now run by President Mengistu Haile Mariam, had assumed total control of Ethiopia. In the theatres this meant a crackdown on freedom of expression, which came to a head in 1983 when the Ministry of Culture assumed the right to choose all plays to be put on in the professional theatres. At the same time there was increasing disillusion with Marxist rule, and as a result many of the plays of the 1980s were non-political and chosen primarily to make money. With many of the more prominent Ethiopian playwrights having been silenced by the censors, there was a rise in the incidence of foreign translations and comic drama. However, some new voices did emerge during this time, most notably those of Astelkachew Yihun and FISSEHA BELEY. Fisseha's work is particularly significant: in plays like *Simen Sintayehu* and *Hoda Yifejew* we see for the first time Ethiopian theatre based on an understanding of rural life and traditional customs.

The greatest area of theatre expansion at this time was in the regions where an amateur arts programme was set up in 1983 to help train interested groups in music, theatre, fine art and literature skills. The programme was of limited success, as it was under-resourced and subject to strict party control. The capital's fifth theatre opened in 1990, to put on plays for children.

The overthrow of the Dergue in 1991 has already led to some liberalization of the theatres. All the old senior management have been removed and replaced by much younger graduates. The Ministry of Culture is beginning to decentralize, and control over choice of plays may be handed back to the theatres, although it is unclear at present how far this process will go. Many dramaturgs have been wary of the wish to democratize expressed by the transitional government, and in mid-1992 politics were only just starting to reappear on the Ethiopian stage. The most notable development has been the largely spontaneous emergence of many new urban theatre groups, seeking to earn an income by putting on a wide variety of improvised productions.

Ager Fikir (Patriotic Theatre Association)
The first Ethiopian professional theatre company. Established in 1935 by a prominent government official, Makonnen Hapte-Wold, the Ager Fikir was formed from a group of AZMARIS who performed music, dance and short propaganda plays in Menelik II Square to inspire the citizens of Addis Ababa to resist Italian invasion. The company was re-formed in 1942 after the restoration of the monarchy, and for many years functioned as a traditional craft centre as well as a performance arts group. Early performances comprised short plays followed by popular music and dance. The Ager Fikir acquired its present home in 1953, when Emperor Haile Selassie donated a hall originally built to display photographs of a tour to America. Nowadays the Ager Fikir presents plays three times a week in repertory, and puts on a weekly Sunday variety show. As with all theatres in Ethiopia, the building is also used as a cinema.

Ayalneh Mulat (fl. 1970s)
Ethiopian playwright. After being director of the University of Addis Ababa Cultural Centre, Ayalneh was for some years responsible for culture at the Commission for the Party of the Working People of Ethiopia. In the early days of the Marxist state he was a popular writer of pro-revolutionary, agit-prop theatre. His plays include *Isat Sined* (*When the Fire is Burning*, 1975), *Shater Beyferiu* (*Sabotage in Different Colours*), *The Peasant Woman's Beacon* (1977) and *Pumpkin and Gourd* (1979). He is now once more director of the University Cultural Centre.

azmari
The traditional performer of song and music in Ethiopian society. The *azmariwoch*, or azmaris, are a despised caste grouping, as are all craftworkers in the country. Records of azmaris go back to the 16th century, when a Portuguese traveller observed them at the court of the Emperor. Traditionally, azmaris often led armies into battle. Nobles employed them as praise-singers, although others were itinerant, travelling from celebration to celebration and improvising praises in return for gifts in cash or kind.

Azmaris may perform on a number of instruments. Most common is the *masinko*, a one-stringed violin; but also widely used are the *kraar*, a six- to ten-string lyre; the *bagana*, an eight- to ten-string harp; and the *washint*, a four-hole flute. Female azmaris seldom play instruments. Traditionally, azmaris performed alone, but when theatre companies began to form they often became part of these troupes and moved into acting as well as music and dance.

Fisseha Beley (fl. 1980s–90s)

Ethiopian playwright, the most popular of the generation to have emerged from the Theatre Arts Department of Addis Ababa University. Unusually for an Ethiopian playwright, Fisseha comes from a rural background and has drawn heavily on his understanding of rural culture and custom to create plays which have widespread appeal in both the cities and the regions. His work deals with serious social problems such as marriage rights and wife-beating, but takes the form of comedies. His plays in Amharic include *Simen Sintayehu* (1984), *Hoda Yifejew* (1985) and *Alkash Na Zefegn* (*The Mourner and the Singer*, 1988).

kinet

The term that denotes the traditional Ethiopian performance arts of music, dance and song. After the 1974 revolution the word also came to be applied to performance troupes producing these arts. *Kinet* groups became widespread, and started to produce agit-prop theatre as well dance and music. By 1988 Arsi, then the smallest region in the country, claimed to have 1300 such groups.

Mengistu Lemma (1925–88)

Ethiopian poet and playwright. The son of a senior priest, Mengistu received an Orthodox Church education, then spent seven years studying in England before his mildly socialist writings led to a summons to return to Ethiopia. He took up playwriting in order to occupy his mind, when forced to join the Ethiopian diplomatic corps in India. His two pre-revolutionary comedies in Amharic, *Telfo Bekisse* (*Marriage by Abduction*, 1962) and *Yelecha*

Gebecha (*Marriage of Unequals*, 1963), looked critically at accommodations between tradition and modernity, and were hugely successful. After the revolution Mengistu produced several more comedies, which took a critical look at changes in society. Both *Balekabara Baledaba* (*The Mighty and the Lowly*, 1974) and *Shumiya* (*Office Scramble*, 1985) examine how power corrupts. His most powerful work was probably *Kassa* (1980), a play which drew on his own childhood memories of the Italian occupation. In his later years Mengistu Lemma worked for the Theatre Arts Department of Addis Ababa University.

Tesfaye Gessesse (1937–)

Ethiopian playwright, actor and director. Tesfaye performed as an amateur actor in Ethiopia before studying drama in the USA. Returning in 1960, he worked as a director at the Haile Selassie I Theatre in Addis Ababa and at the University of Addis Ababa Cultural Centre. After the 1974 revolution he took charge of the Ager Fikir Theatre, and in 1976 assumed control of the National Theatre. His efforts to improve actors' working conditions led to his being sacked in 1983. In 1989 he was appointed chairman of the Theatre Arts Department at Addis Ababa University, but was removed and imprisoned for a short time when the Marxist government was overthrown in 1991. Tesfaye has written several plays, including *Yeshi*, which brought the question of urban prostitution to the fore; and after the 1974 revolution, *Iqaw* (1975) and *Tehaddiso* (*Renaissance*, 1979), concerned with issues of state coercion.

Tsegaye Gebre-Medhin (1936–)

Ethiopian playwright. Tsegaye started writing plays in his youth, then won a UN scholarship to study theatre in Europe, returning to Ethiopia in 1960 to become director of the Haile Selassie Theatre. Here he put on a series of his plays, which won him fame both for their poetic use of Amharic language and for their new realism and oblique criticism of society. He became the country's foremost playwright with works such as *Ye Kermasow* (*A Man of the Future*, 1965) and *Tewodros* (1966). In 1970 he left Ethiopia to study negritude theories in Senegal, but was brought back by actors' demand in 1974 to run the Haile Selassie Theatre again (renamed the National Theatre). Here he produced a series of highly popular plays in praise of the new regime. Most famous were *ABC in Six Months* and *Mother Courage*.

Tsegaye has also translated numerous Shakespeare plays into Amharic, and has written four of his own in English: a version of his *Tewodros* (1966); *Azmari* (1966); and two plays about early Ethiopian history, *Oda Oak Oracle* (1965) and *Collision of Altars* (1975). His poor treatment of actors led in 1976 to demands for Tsegaye's removal from the National Theatre, and after a brief period in prison he was appointed adviser to the Ministry of Culture where he remained until 1993 when he retired.

By the 1980s his work was increasingly critical of the Marxist government, and he was gradually forced into silence by the censors. In 1992 he produced a new play. *Ha Hu Weyim Pa Pu?* (*ABC or XYZ?*), celebrating the overthrow of the previous government but also making some criticism of the new, transitional, government of Ethiopia.

Bibliography

A. Gerard, *Four African Literatures: Xhosa, Sotho, Zulu, Amharic,* Berkeley, 1971; T. L. Kane, *Ethiopian Literature in Amharic,* Wiesbaden, 1975; D. N. Levine, *Wax and Gold: Tradition and Innovation in Ethiopian Culture,* Chicago, 1965; R. K. Molvaer, *Tradition and Change in Ethiopia: Social and Cultural Life as Reflected in Amharic Fictional Literature 1930-1974,* Leiden, 1980; E. S. Pankhurst, *Ethiopia: A Cultural History,* London, 1955; L. Ricci, *Litterature dell' Ethiopia,* Como, 1969.

GABON AND THE CENTRAL AFRICAN REPUBLIC

The modern theatre of these two Central African countries, which with Chad and Congo constituted the former French Equatorial African Federation, remains the least developed in all French-speaking Africa. Gabon, which became independent in 1960, has only one playwright of note – the former Minister of Education Paul Nyonda, with twelve plays. The two most important of these are a dramatized legend, *La Mort de Guykafi* (*Guykafi's Death*, published 1981), performed at the 1966 Dakar Festival of Negro Arts, and *Le Soûlard* (*The Drunkard*, 1981), on the problems of alcoholism. The two other Gabonese writing for the stage are Laurent Owondo with *Les Impurs* (*The Impure Ones*), and one of francophone Africa's few female playwrights, Josephine Kama Bongo, whose play *Obali* (1974) deals with problems of forced marriages.

The Central African Republic, known in colonial times as Oubangui Chari, is better known, even today, for the literature on it by the French novelist André Gide in *Voyages au Congo* (*Travels in the Congo*, 1927) and by the French West Indian René Maran in *Batouala* (1921) than for its own literary productions. It has published no dramatic works, though four plays were shortlisted in various Radio France Internationale drama competitions: *A Molengue ti independence* (*The Children of Independence*, 1960) by Abbot Benoît-Basile Siango, *La Veuve Kiringuiza* (*Widow Kiringuiza*, 1968) by A. Franck, *Le Téléphone* (*The Telephone*, 1976) by Faustin-Albert Ipeko-Etomaner, and *La Petite Leçon* (*The Small Lesson*, 1976) by Etienne Goyémidé

Bibliography

R. Cornevin, *Le Théâtre en Afrique noire et à Madagascar*, Paris, 1970, and 'Gabonese Writers and Dramatists', *The Courier: European Community–African Caribbean Pacific*, 50, Jul./Aug. 1978; E. Goyémidé, 'Le Théâtre existe!', *Notre Librairie: La Littérature Centrafricaine*, 97, Apr./May 1989.

GHANA

Ghana achieved independence under Kwame Nkrumah in 1957, the first of Britain's African colonies to do so. Nkrumah's Convention People's Party was effectively organized at the grass roots and in the first years of independence proposed radical reform at the base of society. Nkrumah himself was a committed Pan-Africanist, eager to promote the liberation of the whole continent. His speeches and actions inspired millions in many parts of Africa. However, Ghana seems to frame new discourses that are fulfilled elsewhere. Nkrumah was overthrown by the military in 1966 and died in exile in 1972.

Political and economic factors have a direct effect on modern Ghanaian drama, for in Ghana playwrights have, from time to time, played an active role in central government, rather than finding themselves consistently in opposition to it. From 1957, one of the key Ghanaians involved in the development of theatre, EFUA T. SUTHERLAND, was associated with Nkrumah. She tried to translate some of the early ideals of the state into a socially based programme for the development of drama and performance out of traditional forms combined with professionalism. She founded the Ghana Drama Studio in Accra in 1957, and was involved, with J. K. Nketia, in the establishment of the School of Music and Drama under the aegis of the Institute of African Studies at the University of Ghana in Legon. Later, playwrights AMA ATA AIDOO and Asiedu Yirenkyi, who had worked at the Ghana Drama Studio and with the university's Studio Players, held ministerial appointments in the military administration of Jerry Rawlings.

The deteriorating economy has meant that state funding for the performing arts has continually diminished. Just as new ideas have been promoted that make a virtue out of stringent economies, the funding has been further reduced. The result is that dramatic talent has been nurtured and then forced into exile – sometimes for economic reasons only, but always with a great deal of creative frustration. This has happened to Aidoo herself, as well as to another leading Ghanaian playwright and director, JOE DE GRAFT. Forced to work as expatriates in other African countries, away from the vigorous drama discourse within Ghana in which they were participating, their creative output has dwindled.

The influence of Ghanaian dramatists extends beyond their own artistic products, and to many African countries. However, the Ghanaian playwright in another African country is still classed as an expatriate and therefore caught in a contradiction: he or she is of the African culture, and yet politically separated from it. This can be particularly difficult for Ghanaian playwrights whose creative work has explored the political fusion of the traditional and the modern.

The traditional roots of drama in the oral culture are seen in Ghana as being highly significant for the forms, themes and tone of the new drama. The Ghanaian sources of theatre may be said to be dance-drama, ceremonies and storytelling. There are different traditions among ethnic groups, but research suggests that their dramatic elements all tend to emphasize the community as the basis for domestic well-being. The community can bring to light what the family may be tempted – to its cost – to hide. This can be seen in *aboakyer*, the deer-hunt festival in Winneba, which is a lord-of-misrule festival (an occasion for licensed mischief). The captured or killed deer is ceremonially sequestered while the entire community participates in an immense procession comprising bands and dancers, skits, satire and transvestism. Another feature of the oral tradition is the participation of the audience, especially in the storytelling performances. The traditions of *anansesem* (spider stories) have been extended into a modern form of performance by Efua Sutherland. She describes the conventions of *anansegoro* in the foreword to her play *The Marriage of Anansewa*. Others, like Yirenkyi, have also been involved in developing *anansegoro*. Sutherland's use of this and other interesting forms of storytelling theatre and musical performance has led her also to evolve the architecture of performance space, like the *kodzidan*, the 'story house' in the village of Atwia.

The critic Charles Angmor divides modern dramatic expression in Ghana into operatic drama and literary drama. Under the former he lists folk-opera, cantatas (of various Christian congregations) and concert parties. Folk-opera may have developed out of the staging of Gilbert and Sullivan operettas in schools, although in colonial times the Ghanaian intelligentsia also acquired a taste for European grand opera. Saka Acquaye, in particular, wanting to indigenize the operatic form, composed operas in Ghanaian languages. In a similar way, perhaps, the cantatas reflected a theatrical indigenizing of Christianity in the particular circumstances of fund-raising. However, it is in the concert parties that we find the most exciting development of theatre and dramatic form.

The concert parties of coastal Ghana and the neighbouring republic of Togo are the only professional theatre in the region, with the members of the many companies earning their livelihoods from their travelling shows. The concert parties are also called 'trios', their performers 'Comedians', and their improvised performances 'comic plays'. The content of the plays is contemporary, depicting the actuality of the lives of their rapt audiences. Concert parties are reputed to have started in 1918 with a headmaster who performed solo, one Master Yalley; but the most famous company was that of 'Bob' Johnson in the 1930s. They were first known as the 'Two Bobs and their Carolina Girl' and then as the 'Axim Trio'. Sutherland states that they did not compose *anansegoro*, but that Johnson 'took ordinary life stories and then composed plays by the method of *kasandwon* [speech and song]'. The trios flourished in the 1960s and 70s. Each company travels extensively with a large repertory of plays, which although improvised are actually maintained in a fairly stable performance 'text'. They have been researched by K. N. Bame in Ghana, and in Togo by Alain Ricard, who has published a performance on sound-tape of *Mister Tameklor* by the Happy Star Concert Band of Lomé. The great popularity of the concert parties has inspired writers like Patience Addo and Derlene Clems whose plays, *Company Pot* and *Scholarship Woman* respectively, were broadcast by the BBC (1972).

The literary form that developed in the 1960s reflected in both content and form some Western models, but also showed a strong movement away from these especially as theatre practice attempted to link the depiction of Ghanaian attitudes to the sensibilities of the audiences. This literary drama, says Angmor, 'does not operate as a rule on conflict and its resolution, but generally on consensus and consummation'. It continues to advance the discourse of traditional performance. These literary plays were prefigured by Kobina Sekyi's *The Blinkards* (1915; published 1974) which attacked European cultural influences; and, in the 1940s, by the literary and philosophical plays of J. B. Danquah and F. K. Fiawoo.

But the real flowering came only after independence. Although the corpus of published texts is small (about thirty plays, by fewer than fifteen playwrights), the drama discourse has developed with depth and consistency, despite the divergent experiences and personalities of the playwrights. The plays deal with themes and ideas which are often far-reaching in their moral and political implications. *Foriwa* (1962), by Efua Sutherland, explores the transition from the old to the new, and the social mechanism for the transformation of the community at the grass roots. *The Mightier Sword* (1973) by Martin Owusu explores history for the sake of the present, as does de Graft's *Through a Film Darkly* (1966), offering a painful analysis of black racism. *Anowa* (1970), by Ama Ata Aidoo, considered by many critics to be one of the finest modern African plays, historicizes the present by investigating the implications of slavery for people's psyche. De Graft's *Muntu* (1975) mythologizes the present. The ordinary yet important domestic problems resulting from social transformations are expressed in Aidoo's *Dilemma of a Ghost* (1964), in *Sons and Daughters* (1964) by de Graft, in *Laughter and Hubbub in the House* (1972) by Kwesi Kay and in Yirenkyi's *Blood and Tears* (1973). On the other hand, the extraordinary domestic crises that result from secret and dubious short cuts to material prosperity are variously explored in *Kivuli* (1972) by Yirenkyi, *Amari* (1975) by Jacob Hevi, Owusu's *The Sudden Return* (1973), *Edufa* (1967) by Sutherland, and in a humorous vein in Sutherland's *Anansegoro, The Marriage of Anansewa* (1975).

These plays are concerned with relationships and responsibilities within the household, which is almost always contextualized by a particularized community perspective – usually created off stage by the drama on stage. Though often not seen, the community is forever pressing in on the compound walls; and because of its absence it can also symbolize the nation-state, the well-being of which cannot be guaranteed until the family adjustments are properly made. In addition, the status of the women in the plays is often presented effectively as a problem, by both male and female playwrights. Efo Kodjo Mawugbe and other young playwrights give evidence of a new resurgence in Ghanaian theatre in the 1990s.

Aidoo, Ama Ata (1942–)

Ghanaian playwright. Born in Ghana, she graduated from the University of Legon in 1964. Her reputation as a playwright rests upon *The Dilemma of a Ghost* and *Anowa*. *The Dilemma of a Ghost* was first produced at the University of Legon in 1964, and published in London a year later. It explores the problems of a marriage between a Ghanaian who has achieved academic honours in the USA and a black American woman whom he brings home to Ghana. The play is concerned with their decision not to have children immediately, and the consequent relationship with the husband's proud Ghanaian family, who cannot reconcile the wife's slave ancestry with their prejudices. But there is eventually a reconciliation between the women of the family, and the husband is chided for his insensitivity towards mother, aunts and wife. *Anowa* (1970), too, is concerned with slavery's legacy and is written from a woman's point of view. This time the perspective is not of reconciliation and of the good sense of traditional society, but the social visionary, and the outcome is tragic. The play embodies a powerful poetic vision of social values in the context of slavery and the position of women.

Aidoo has written a collection of short stories, *No Sweetness Here* (1970), novels and poetry. She held the post of Secretary for Education in the Rawlings government. She now lives in ZIMBABWE.

de Graft, Joe [J. C.] (1924–78)

Ghanaian playwright and critic. Joe de Graft taught drama at the University of Ghana (and later in East Africa) and was active as a performer as well as a writer. In 1962 he appeared in the first performance of EFUA SUTHERLAND's *Edufa* at the Ghana Drama Studio in Accra, and in 1964 his play *Sons and Daughters* was published. This was followed in 1970 with *Through a Film Darkly*. Both plays are of their time in setting and concern, dealing with the tensions and dissensions that he suggested plagued the apparently sophisticated lives of modern educated Ghanaians. They present the 'clash of cultures' theme popular in much African theatre in the years leading up to and following independence, with young people in revolt against their parents and students abroad experiencing the humiliation of racism.

Sutherland, Efua T. (1924–)

Ghanaian playwright, director and researcher. Born in Cape Coast and educated in England and Ghana, Sutherland has dominated Ghanaian theatre since independence and over thirty years has made an incalculable contribution to the development of drama in Ghana. As a playwright she has written and devised a wide range of works in the Akan language and in English; as a director she has staged many kinds of performances, from traditional community music to modern experimental drama. She has also devoted her energies to the social production of dramatic art in Ghana. She has, for example, inspired the innovative *kodzidan* the 'story house', built by community effort in the village of Atwia as a centre for musical and dramatic performances. In the 1960s she established the Ghana Drama Studio in Accra, which she helped design and for which she raised funds, and she has explored the scope of research into traditional performance, at the Institute of African Studies, University of Ghana. Through her position of influence she found the means to set up a programme of experimental theatre (1958–61), and subsequently to explore new plays for children – e.g. her 'rhythm plays' *Vulture! Vulture!* and *Tahinta*, which she later published as a text with photographs. She later developed *anansegoro* (drama extensions of *anansesem* – storytelling performances of Ananse, the spider man). *Anansegoro* were performed by a number of groups, mainly in Akan; an English text of Sutherland's own *The Marriage of Anansewa* (1975) was published together with a brief introduction to the theory and practice of the new dramatic form. Her own earlier stage plays, *Foriwa* (1962) and *Edufa* (1967), show eclecticism and an interest in Western dramatic modes. The economic problems in Ghana constantly postpone the realization of a National Theatre for Ghana which Sutherland has consistently promoted.

Bibliography

N. Akam and A. Ricard, *Mister Tameklor, suivi de Français-le-Parisien, par le Happy Star Concert Band de Lomé (Togo)*, Paris, 1981; C. Angmor, 'Drama in Ghana' in *Theatre in Africa*, ed. O. Agunba and I. Irele, Ibadan, 1978; K. N. Bame, *Come to Laugh: A Study of African Traditional Theatre in Ghana*, Legon, n.d.; M. Etherton, *The Development of African Drama*, London, 1982; S. Lokko, 'Theatre Space: A History Overview of the Theatre Movement in Ghana', *Modern Drama*, 23, 1980; A. Yirenkyi, 'Bill Marshall and the Ghanaian Theatre of the Early Seventies', *Journal of the Performing Arts*, 1, 1, 1980.

GUINEA

Of all the French-speaking countries in Africa, Guinea had the most tumultuous relations with France. It became a French colony in 1890 and remained so until 2 October 1958, when independence was thrust upon it after it voted 'no', in a historic referendum, to a French proposal to remain part of a wider French community of African states.

Modern theatrical activity was introduced to Guinea with the advent of colonial rule, but remained modest up to independence. It consisted mostly of performances of French plays from the classical repertory and of historical pieces by former Guinean students of the École William Ponty in SENEGAL, notably *La Recontre du Capitaine Péroz et de Samory* (*The Encounter between Captain Péroz and Samory*, 1937). A typically Guinean theatrical activity of the period, which emerged in 1948 and was later to flourish, is what its founder Fodéba Keita called the 'theatre-ballet'. His play in this genre, *L'Aube africaine* (*The African Dawn*, 1965), on the shooting by French troops in Thiaroye, Senegal, of protesting, uncompensated Africans who had served in the French army during the Second World War, relates the action in the theatre-ballet tradition of mainly song and dance but also dialogue.

Since independence, theatre in Guinea has progressed. Recognizing its importance as an instrument of mass mobilization and propaganda, the socialist government of Sekou Touré (1958–84) encouraged and directed its growth. Arts festivals and competitions in which theatre played a large part were organized at district, regional and national levels. The local committees of the ruling Parti Démocratique de Guinée were charged with promoting it in their areas: the result was scores of collective productions of a fiercely anti-colonial stance on historical, political and social themes. The best of these, such as *Et la nuit s'illumine* (*And the Night is Illuminated*, 1967) or *Thiaroye* (1973) from the Labé and Dabola regions, respectively, were performed to wide acclaim, the first at the Pan-African Arts Festival in Algiers in 1969, and the second in the 1977 Lagos Arts Festival.

But Guinean theatrical activity is not limited to plays. It also includes the other performing arts, such as traditional instrumental and choral music and African ballet, which national ballet troupes like the Ballets Africains de la République de Guinée and the highly acclaimed and award-winning Ballet Djoliba were created to promote.

Although almost all Guinean drama consists of unpublished collective productions, a few plays by individual artists have been published: the historical dramas *Continent-Afrique suivi de Amazoulous* (*Continent-Africa, followed by Amazulus*, 1970) by a former Minister for Scientific Research, Condétto Nénékhaly-Camara, and Djibril Tamsir Niane's *Sikasso ou la dernière citadelle suivi de Chaka* (*Sikasso or the Last Citadel followed by Chaka*, 1976). Recent works include two by A.-T. Cissé: *Maudit soit Cham* (*May Cham be Cursed*, 1982) and *Au nom du peuple* (*In the Name of the People*, 1990).

Bibliography

R. Cornevin, *Le Théâtre en Afrique noire et à Madagascar*, Paris, 1970; J.-M. Touré, 'Mobiliser, informer, éduquer; un instrument efficace: le théâtre', *Notre Librairie: La Littérature Guinéenne*, 88–9, Jul./Sept. 1987.

KENYA

The population of Kenya is estimated at about 20 million people, inhabiting 225,000 square miles, two-thirds of which is scarcely suitable for habitation. Formerly a British colony, Kenya achieved its independence in 1963 after many years of struggle and open war waged by the Mau Mau Land Freedom Army between 1952 and 1960. Since independence Kenya has developed a form of free enterprise capitalism which has divided the society into two worlds – that of a small class of Kenyans together with their foreign business partners and the broad masses of the people – a state of affairs depicted in the 1979 play *Thi Ni Igiri* (*There are Two Worlds*).

As is to be expected in a colony with a significant settler population, theatre before independence was dominated by a tradition of 'Little Theatre', whose function was to provide its audiences with an opportunity to escape from reality and from the increasing challenge of the anti-colonial forces, who themselves were using theatre as a means of mobilizing opposition to the colonial regime. In 1952, at the height of the struggle for independence, the colonial government opened a cultural centre which also housed the National Theatre. Many of the productions performed there served to entertain and inspire the British soldiers who went to Kenya at that time, the settler community, white colonial administrators and industrial top management, as well as the educated Kenyan African petty bourgeoisie which had accepted colonial culture.

Apart from the traditional drama forms of the pre-colonial society, indigenous Kenyan drama first developed within the colonial education system and ultimately gave rise to the Kenya Schools Drama Festival, at which the set pieces, the adjudicators and the criteria were all foreign. In the late 1940s the Nairobi African Dramatic Society was formed, a group which was to initiate the idea of taking theatre to the people by performing in Machakos, Kiambu, Thika and Nakulu, all towns not far from Nairobi. In 1955 the Nairobi African Dramatic Society entered the white-dominated National Drama Festival with the play *Not Guilty* by Graham Hyslop, and won awards. Subsequently the development of indigenous theatre in Kenya was characterized either by an acceptance of the 'junior partner' tag or the struggle to find its own voice and direction. At first, most activity was very much an extension of the Little Theatre movement and the 'civilizing mission' of the mission schools. Comedians such as Athmani Suleiman (Mzee Tamaa) and Kipanga, who were trailblazers in the art of popular comedy, graced the state of the National Theatre and were much enjoyed by settler audiences for their slapstick and *kisetla* (settler) *kiswahili*. They were to continue amusing people in live shows and radio and television broadcasts after independence, setting a tradition that has found worthy successors in such modern television programmes as *Vitimbi*.

At independence, the Kenya National Theatre, like the economic and other spheres and institutions of national life, was not democratized. It continued to serve foreign interests, now widened to include the tastes of those from European countries other than Britain. Plays and musicals of no relevance to the cultural life of the majority of Kenyans were performed.

In the years that followed more and more black schools entered the National Drama Festival, at first performing European set books, but later, as African plays began to be published, their entries changed in character. At the University of Nairobi, too, African plays such as WOLE SOYINKA's (see Nigeria) *Kongi's Harvest* (1966) and Lewis Nkosi's *The Rhythm of Violence* were produced and acted by Arthur Kemoli, Ben Chahilu, David Mulwa and others. A National Drama School was set up by the National Theatre, which produced artists such as KENNETH WATENE, Titus Gathwe, Sese Njugu and Frank Kimotho. In the meantime NGUGI WA THIONG'O, who had been active at Makerere writing and publishing his early plays, had joined the then Department of English at the university (a name which he and others fought to change to 'Department of Literature'). In addition John Ruganda, FRANCIS IMBUGA and later Waigwa Wachira were developing drama there, in particular the Free Travelling Theatre, which annually toured the country performing in schools and market-places.

It was in the 1970s that the social contradictions created by neo-colonialism became clearly visible. The increasing political and social polarization expressed itself in the arts, nowhere more clearly than in the novels and plays of Ngugi, in particular his collaborative drama with MICERE MUGO, *The Trial of Dedan Kimathi* (1976), which along with Imbuga's *Betrayal in the City* – Kenya's entries for FESTAC in 1977 (see Introduction) – was performed at the National Theatre before a predominantly working-class audience. Both form and content were inspiring and created an atmosphere of communal song, dance and solidarity which served to highlight the role that a truly national theatre could play, thereby exposing the exclusiveness of the so-called National Theatre. The question of who controlled the art facilities in the country raised the more fundamental question of who controlled the economy. However, participants in this new and dynamic theatre were not ideologically united.

It is within the context of this quest for a national theatre that the performance of *I'll Marry When I Want* by Ngugi wa Thiong'o and Ngugi wa Mirii in 1977 should be seen – in its use of the Gikuyu language, the participation of workers, peasants and intellectuals of different nationalities bringing together town and rural areas – together with the move away from the National Theatre building into a more organically national context, the KAMIRIITHU Community Educational and Cultural Centre at Limuru. The potential of the Kamiriithu phenomenon to usher in a new, independent community-based theatre is best illustrated by the interest aroused by the performance of *I'll Marry When I Want* and its being able to tap and release an inexhaustible flow of creativity from ordinary people. The Kenyan government, however, moved to suppress the play. Its licence was withdrawn and subsequently Ngugi wa Thiong'o was detained without trial and Ngugi wa Mirii lost his job at the university. The Centre again, in 1982, was denied a licence to perform a play by Ngugi wa Thiong'o entitled *Mother Sing to Me*. The government publicly announced the deregistration of the Centre on 11 March 1982, thus banning all its educational and cultural activities, and sent the police to raze the open-air theatre built by peasants and workers and the unemployed youth of Kamiriithu village.

By the 1980s Kenyan theatre was characterized by three trends: the colonial theatre, the 'African theatre' patronized by Western cultural missions, and the political national theatre symbolized by Kamiriithu. There was, though, a growing tendency towards more populist activity, sometimes of a militant nature, exemplified by Tamaduni Players' collectively evolved sketches on the life of the 'parking boys' in Nairobi, and their Swahili performance of *The Trial of Dedan Kimathi* before working-class and student audiences. Independent drama groups proliferated in most townships and working-class suburbs, laying the foundations for community-based theatre movements such as Capricorn Theatre Group and Wanamtaa. And an itinerant street theatre group with preachers, jokers and charlatans came into existence, performing at the Jeevanjee Gardens in Nairobi. In 1986 these groups gathered together to organize a four-day festival at the City Hall. All this signals an increased co-option, by the working classes, of theatre as an art form that can serve their interests.

In the face of the efforts of Kenyan artists to develop an independent and relevant theatre, the Kenyan government has repeatedly acted to suppress and thwart it. In 1979 Riara Mission School outside Nairobi entered the Schools Drama Festival with the play *There are Two Worlds*. The school was raided soon afterwards by the Special Branch and the teacher in charge interrogated. In March 1982, officials tried to nullify the decision of the Schools Drama Festival judges to award a prize to the play, and it was only after a fierce struggle and because of the firm stand taken by the audience that they were forced to recognize the judges' decision. That April the government banned one school play, and in the October another. During the Teacher Training Colleges Drama Festival the Ministry of Education banned one of the entries, harassed the actors and the authors and confiscated the manuscript. The chief adjudicator at the festival commented that this intimidation was preventing young Kenyans from thinking about national issues that affected the majority, and that it suppressed not only creativity but also free democratic thinking in their everyday life.

More recently, there has been a move towards the establishment of a local repertory theatre company run along the same professional lines as the expatriate theatre companies. The first of these, Sarakasi Ltd, was established in 1990 and has recently staged two important plays, an adaptation of the Kikuyu legend *Wangu wa Makeri* and a translation in Kikuyu of the Cameroonian play *Enough is Enough* (*Ciagana ni Ciagana*). In 1992 Phoenix Players started a new professional repertory company called Miujiza Players, to put on African plays. Mbalamwezi Players and Friends' Theatre are amateur groups, but average six to eight productions a year. These companies have found it hard to survive, and the increasing need for sponsorship has sometimes meant compromising the political content of their work with the result that they have taken to reviving relatively innocuous comedies such as OLA ROTIMI's (see Nigeria) *Our Husband Has Gone Mad Again* (published 1977). The expatriate companies, Phoenix Players and Nairobi City Players, faced with a dwindling pool of European actors, find themselves recruiting more and more Africans, who are frustrated by the roles available to them in European plays.

Touring continues to be important, and Sarakasi have toured successfully with their productions, as have other companies. Interest in areas outside Nairobi has been noticeably higher when the plays have been Kenyan, such as J. Nderitu's *Wangu wa Maeri*, which in 1991 Sarakasi toured in both its English and Gikuyu versions. The idea of festivals has also caught on well and in 1990 Theatre Workshop, a group of actors drawn from both within the University of Nairobi and outside it, attempted to host one at that university which was to include Soyinka's *Kongi's Harvest*, but they were refused permission to do so. In the last three years new published writing has included adaptations of oral narrative, *Lwanda Magere* (1991) by Okoiti Omtatah and *Nyamgondho* (1990) by Alakie Mboya. These have both been performed at the French Cultural Centre, which in 1992 hosted a festival of plays performed by various local groups.

In December 1992 *Can't Pay Won't Pay* by Dario Fo was performed after the High Court granted an injunction restraining the government from banning the play for the third time. The National Theatre has also seen a revival of interest in local theatre companies, and a grand scheme to modernize the Kenyan theatre is being funded by the Japanese government. By staging the annual winners of the Schools Drama Festival in 1991 the National Theatre tried to reassert its role as a national institution, but government interference and a lack of political will have thwarted these aims and ensured the continued domination of the National Theatre by foreign and expatriate companies. Every theatre group must register with the government, and performance licences are granted only after rigorous security checks and after each script has been read and approved by the administration. Theatre in Kenya now struggles to develop in a situation of growing confrontation between two worlds, and intensifying state repression and harassment.

Imbuga, Francis (fl. 1970s)

Kenyan playwright, author of a number of works including *The Fourth Trial* and *Kisses of Faho* (1972), *The Married Bachelor* (1973), *Betrayal in the City* (1976), *Games of Silence* (1977) and *The Successor* (1979). *Betrayal in the City* was Kenya's entry to FESTAC (see Introduction) in Lagos in 1977. The play satirizes problems of independence and freedom in post-colonial African states. The same themes are seen in Imbuga's other plays, where the clashes between individuals or classes in society are used to comment on political and social tensions. The settings of the plays are usually contemporary, an exception being *The Successor*, a tale of ambition and political intrigue involved in finding a successor to a fictional emperor, set in 'semi-modern' time.

Kamiriithu

The Kamiriithu Community Educational and Cultural Centre at Limuru in Kenya was founded in 1976. An 'emergency village' during the Mau Mau War of Independence, it became after independence a labour reserve for nearby plantations and industries. Disillusioned workers and peasants in collaboration with NGUGI WA THIONG'O, Ngugi wa Mirii, an adult educator and research worker at the University of Nairobi, and other intellectuals collectively formed the Centre to embark upon a programme of 'integrated rural development',

including theatre. *Ngaahika Ndeenda* (*I'll Marry When I Want*) was its first production (1977).

Democratically devised, the play was a powerful attack on the betrayal of the Kenyan masses by local *comprador* classes and their alliance with exploitative 'foreign interests'. This is presented with great cultural richness, the peasants and workers themselves making the major contribution of language, traditional ritual, song and dance. Moreover, this production became the focus for many other collective activities in the life of the community. An open-air theatre was constructed by a 'harambee of sweat' – i.e. self-help and labour. The actual performance was 'a play of the people ... for the people by the people' (*Sunday Nation*, Nairobi). After seven weeks it was banned. Shortly afterwards Ngugi wa Thiong'o was detained. On his release a year later he returned to Kamiriithu and the community began a new play, *Maitu Njugira* (*Mother Sing to Me*), focusing on the resistance to colonial oppression of the various Kenyan nationalities. The authorities closed the Centre, refused to allow performances of the play at the National Theatre and destroyed the open-air theatre. Nevertheless thousands of Kenyans were able to see 'rehearsals' at the University of Nairobi. The Kamiriithu experience became an inspiration to artists and cultural workers in neo-colonial African countries.

Mugo, Micere Githae (1942–)

Kenyan educationalist, playwright and poet (*Daughter of My People, Sing!*, 1976) who was co-author with NGUGI WA THIONG'O of *The Trials of Dedan Kimathi* (1976). Micere Mugo's contribution to this major work of the Kenyan theatre may well be seen in its strong representation of women's role in the independence struggle and a free society. *The Long Illness of Ex-Chief Kiti* (1976) is set during the emergency in colonial Kenya, with the leading character a collaborator rejected by his children. *Disillusioned* (1976), a radio play, concerns colour prejudice in a Christian mission. She now lives in exile.

Ngugi wa Thiong'o (1938–)

Kenyan novelist, playwright and polemicist. His plays in English include *The Black Hermit* (1962), *This Time Tomorrow* (1968) and *The Trial of Dedan Kimathi* (with MICERE MUGO). With Ngugi wa Mirii he wrote the draft script of KAMIRIITHU Community Educational and Cultural Centre's Gikuyu play, *Ngaahika Ndeenda* (*I'll Marry When I Want*, 1982), and following that, also in Gikuyu, *Maitu Njugira* (*Mother Sing to Me*, 1986). Ngugi's work is characterized by a consistent development of early nationalist positions into an anti-imperialist commitment to the cause of peasants and workers in Kenya today. His work in theatre shows a parallel development – from individual authorship to collective authorship in Gikuyu and other Kenyan languages. Ngugi was detained by the Kenyan government from 1977 to 1978 and now lives in exile. Critical essays, which address issues of language and culture in theatre and literature, are contained in *Decolonising the Mind* (1986) and *Moving the Centre* (1993).

Watene, Kenneth (fl. 1970s)

Kenyan playwright. *My Son for My Freedom* (1973) is set during the Mau Mau emergency in colonial Kenya, and is concerned with the choice faced by the Kikuyu people between Christianity or the freedom fighters. Watene's play places this dilemma in a traumatic domestic context. *The Haunting Past* and *The Pot* (both 1973) are short plays dealing with the generation gap and drunkenness respectively. *Dedan Kimathi* (1974) anticipates the later play by NGUGI WA THIONG'O and MICERE MUGO on the same theme, describing the guerrilla life of the Mau Mau General, while *Sunset on the Manyatta* (1974) is a 'clash of cultures' play concerning a young Masai alienated from his people by Western education and striving to reconcile the traditional and the modern.

Bibliography

E. Gachuka and K. Akivaga (eds.), *The Teaching of Literature in Kenya Secondary Schools*, Nairobi, 1979 (includes a section on drama in Kenya); R. Kidd, 'Popular Theatre and Popular Struggle in Kenya', in *Theatrework*, 2, 6, 1982; C. D. Killam, *An Introduction to the Writing of Ngugi*, London, 1980; L. Mbughuni, 'Old and New Drama from East Africa', *African Literature Today*, 9, 1976; M. Mugo and G. Wasambu-were, *A New Approach to the Teaching of Literature in Kenyan High Schools*, Nairobi, forthcoming; Ngugi wa Thiongo, *Detained*, London, 1981; C. B. Robson, *Ngugi wa Thiongo*, New York, 1979.

MADAGASCAR

Until 1895 when it became a French possession, Madagascar was ruled by the indigenous Merina monarchy, which presided over a rigidly stratified society of nobles, freemen and slaves. The island remained a French colony until 1967, when it obtained its independence. Its theatrical activity can be divided into three categories: traditional performance, a written theatre in Malagasy, and one in French.

One traditional yet contemporary Malagasy display is the *Hira-Gasy*: a spectacle of song, dance and improvised sketches that originally took place during ceremonies. Its cast of twenty or so peasant actors known as *Mphihira-Malagasy* highlight social problems for which, on the occasion of ceremonies, the community tries to find solutions. But, reflecting the island's history, this display has undergone changes in costume, movement and dance. Originally a spectacle by villagers for villagers, it was annexed in the 18th century into the service of the monarchy. Queen Ranavalona invited *Hira-Gasy* performers to her court to entertain her European visitors. The more enthusiastic among these sometimes joined in the dancing, and to this day their steps and movements, parodied, are an integral part of *Hira-Gasy* displays, as is their outfit, which incorporates wide stripes for the soldiers and religious decorations for the missionaries, and long dresses and sometimes gold-capped teeth for the ladies. The *Hira-Gasy* remained in the service of successive governments (the French after the Malagasy monarchy, then the independent nation's) until the mid-1979s when, after a Marxist revolution, it seems to have returned to its roots as a people's theatre.

Madagascar's theatre in the Malagasy language thrived in the 19th to early 20th centuries. A few of its many representatives are Justin Rainizablolona, Tselatra Rajaonah and Arthur Rodlish, two of whose plays – *Ramoniody* (*The Rumour*, 1926) and *Sangy Mahery* (*Violent Games*, 1926), both on the theme of love thwarted because of caste differences between the lovers – were among the most popular.

With French colonial rule emerged a modest theatre in that language, practised by the poet Jean-Joseph Rabéarivelo with his dramatized legend *Imaitsoanala* (1935), and especially by JACQUES RABÉMANAJARA. In 1982 Jidy Randrianarivo published a psychological play, *Le Testament* (*The Will*). The last few years have seen the development of vigorous French-language theatre activity in Madagascar, represented by plays such as David Jaomanoro's *La Retraite* (*Retirement*, 1990), and unpublished ones such as Michèle Rakotoson's *Un jour ma mémoire* (*One Day, My Memory*) first performed in 1991, and Charlotte Rafenomanjato's *L'Oiseau de proie* (*The Bird of Prey*, 1991) and *La Pêcheresse* (*The Fisherwoman*, 1988).

Rabémanajara, Jacques (Félicien)
(1914–89)

Malagasy poet and playwright, closely associated with the negritude movement and its cultural organ *Présence Africaine*. Born in Maroantsetra, Rabémanajara was educated in Paris, where he lived from 1938 to 45. After the Second World War, he returned to Madagascar and became involved in the nationalist politics of his day. He was accused of complicity in the 1947 Malagasy rebellion against French rule, detained for more than a year, then sentenced to twenty years' hard labour; he was released from gaol in 1956. He held political office in the first government of independent Madagascar until 1972 when, after the regime's overthrow in a coup, he went to live in France.

Rabémanajara is above all a poet, but he also wrote three plays: *Les Dieux malgaches* (*The Malagasy Gods*, 1964) on the period leading to the conquest of the island; *Les Boutriers de l'aurore* (*The Boatmen of the Dawn*, 1957) on the arrival of its early South-East Asian settlers; and *Agapes des dieux, Tritriva* (*Reunion of the Gods, Tritriva*, 1962), on a tragic love story in which a father's attempt to prevent his daughter's marriage to the man of her choice ends with the death in Lake Tritriva of the lovers and of the girl's aunt. The fatal passions in these plays, presented in verse and in a context of legend and history, lend a distinct French classical tonality to Rabémanajara's theatre.

Bibliography

R. Cornevin, *Le Théâtre en Afrique noire et à Madagascar*, Paris, 1970; D. de Saivre, 'De Madagascar, un théâtre populaire: L'Hira-Gasy', *Recherche, Pédagogie, Culture*, 49, 1980; C. Wake, 'Madagascar', *The Cambridge Guide to World Theatre*, ed. M. Banham, Cambridge, 1988.

MALAWI

Theatre in Malawi has been said to 'lack the quantity and vitality of its counterpart in West Africa'. The development of drama in this region has indeed been much slower than in West Africa. Such a situation, the critic Adrian Roscoe has suggested, may have arisen out of historic, political and social causes, if not all three together. Nevertheless, there is evidence of growth, which he has attributed to 'a blend of forces: political independence, a burgeoning of new schools, colleges, and universities; the desire to repatriate the syllabus, increasing economic prosperity, the spread of radio ... and the printed word; the desire to encourage popular and effective modes of crystalising distinctly national identities, and finally the catalytic example of West Africa'.

There are two groups involved in theatre work in Malawi: expatriate amateur dramatic societies and African drama groups. This division springs from the politics of colonialism, which encouraged development, of whatever sort, along racial lines. When Africans took power after independence (1964), expatriates created their enclaves, which became their cultural reserves. Even as late as 1992 expatriate theatre groups existed in the same clubs that had housed them in the colonial days. The repertoires continue to be aimed at expatriate audiences.

'Western' African theatre has learnt nothing from expatriate amateur theatre. One needs to establish where influences on the former came from. As early as 1950 concerts and variety shows were common features in Malawi. Black South African life has played a big part in this type of recreation: Malawians have been going to work in South African mines as migrant labourers since the turn of the century. Usually such people have returned home completely changed, bringing with them not just habits, but items like record-players and bicycles, and a love for a particular type of life common amongst the city dwellers of South Africa. By the 1950s, South African blacks had already developed a popular theatre tradition which married music, dance and improvisation. The 'concert and variety show' common in Malawi in the 1950s is a by-product of this kind of theatre. Concert groups existed everywhere in the country – not just in large urban centres but also in remote mission schools and their neighbouring villages.

With the coming of independence and the consequent emphasis on promoting the indigenous cultural heritage of the people, Malawians have sought to be original in their theatre. Work is being spearheaded by particular cultural institutions, amongst which theatre groups are but one. The efforts of such institutions reveal not just the extent to which success had been achieved in theatre work, but an explanation of the way it is growing. There are now vigorous annual festivals and active travelling theatres, and good use is made of radio. The background to these operations may be found in cultural policy, education and censorship.

If an official statement regarding government involvement in the development of theatre in Malawi is sought one may refer to the Arts and Crafts Department in the Ministry of Education and Culture, whose main functions have been given as: 'to awaken, preserve and develop Malawi's culture, tradition, art, music, drama and dances; to enrich the social, cultural and material life of Malawi; to project most effectively Malawi's cultural heritage; to assist in the teaching of music, drama, and dances by holding specific demonstrations from time to time as need arises; to provide public entertainment of the highest quality'.

Of drama specifically, the department says that it is 'predominantly a secondary school and university form of entertainment'. None the less, it considers drama to be a medium through which 'the norms, values, traditions and customs of the people are easily brought to the public'. Whether this reflects the department's expectation of what drama ought to be doing, or its conception of what it is actually doing, as promoted by secondary schools and university, is not clear. Certainly, as far as effort by the department itself is concerned, the function it describes here remains to be fulfilled. If cultural activities have been promoted in the country, they have been done so largely at the people's own initiative.

Drama in Malawi schools is organized by the Association for Teachers of English in Malawi (ATEM). Formed in the 1960s to co-ordinate and encourage efforts aimed at improving the teaching of English in the country's secondary schools and teacher training colleges, its main function at first was to organize conferences for teachers of English throughout the country. From time to time it set up workshops on English-language teaching methods. Then the association started to involve students directly in its work. It organized the National Oral English Competition for secondary schools, comprising recitations of poetry and prose readings, as well as interviews conducted in English by a panel of native English speakers.

In 1969, however, this competition was dropped, and instead a drama festival was established, open to all secondary schools and post-primary educational institutions, as well as teacher training colleges and technical colleges (but not the colleges of the University of Malawi). In order to ensure that the festival still contributed to the improvement of English-language teaching, its organizers sent out rules to all schools regarding how they should pre-pare for it. But these rules were concerned only with the running of the festival itself and with ATEM's basic aim of improving the spoken English of participants; any potential audience did not feature at all. It was merely assumed that the audience would be students, either from secondary schools involved in the festival directly or from schools near the venue of the festival. As it turned out, the audience included people other than students – people from the town or city where the festival was taking place who were more than ready for entertainment of this kind. And while the organizers thought of their festival as an exercise in English-language teaching, their audience was seeing it as theatre. Since the festival was public, it was the latter who were to direct the course of events in schools drama. It was not long before people started talking of adapting plays not just for student actors, but for expected audiences. Most teacher-producers in the schools did not know the mechanics of producing a play, so they turned to ATEM to help them, either through workshops or by supplying notes on play production. Until recently English-language teaching in Malawi secondary schools and teacher training colleges has been dominated by expatriate teachers, so it is not surprising that suggestions such as the following were made: 'the producer looking for material to adapt ... should have a look at European plays from the medieval or Renaissance periods ... the periods in Europe when society most resembled society in Malawi today. The peasant population lived much the same sort of life as the Malawian villager, and you had the rapidly growing sophisticated town population that you also find here. So the situations and characters in these plays should be meaningful to our students.' The limitations of such a line of thought are obvious. The analogy holds only in so far as a large rural community is common to both. The history of the people, the experiences that they live through, and their political as well as cultural consciousness, offer no basis for comparison.

The effect of this advice has been to encourage writers to look at life in a determinist way, resigning themselves to the belief that things will happen exactly as they did in Europe hundreds of years ago, that no enhancement is called for. Thus playwrights do not write with the hope of changing the world they live in, nor are they inclined to commit themselves to particular dogmas. They are socially passive. The bulk of the plays that derive from the drama festival show a clear lack of interest in the immediate present. Instead of dealing with the lives, problems, dreams, worries and hopes of their audience, they continue to harp on themes of pre-industrial village days and ways. ATEM has claimed: 'Although the schools drama festival has been our major activity over the past few years, it is not the main aim of the association as it was established.' This perhaps indicates how popular drama has become. It also shows what pressures the demand for drama has brought to bear on the Association for Teachers of English in Malawi, whose drama work has now been taken over by the university in a more sympathetic, if academic, manner.

The Malawi government's Department of Arts and Crafts recognizes the work of the University of Malawi in the promotion of drama in the country. This work is spread over four of the five campuses making up the university – namely, Chancellor College (Zomba), Bunda College of Agriculture (Lilongwe), Zamuzu College of Nursing (Lilongwe) and the Polytechnic (Blantyre). The most active of these is Chancellor College, where there is a Department of Fine and Performing Arts under whose aegis comes the Chancellor College Travelling Theatre. Before 1981 there was no such department at the college, and all drama teaching was the responsibility of the English Department. Most of this work concerned dramatic literature rather than drama as performance. The only practical course offered was a two-hour session in 'practical drama and film' to third-year majors of English, in which stu-dents were introduced to the arts of theatre and filming. It is through this course that the Chancellor Travelling College Theatre really came into being. Although the Theatre was the responsibility of the English Department, it was an extra-curricular appendage, and thus open to staff and students from all departments of the college.

The first production to be put on there was WOLE SOYINKA's (see Nigeria) *The Trials of Brother Jero*, followed by *The Crucible* by Arthur Miller. In 1969 the British actor and teacher John Linstrum was appointed lecturer in drama, and during his two years' stay at the college he directed two plays, *The Chalk Circle* (an adaptation of Bertolt Brecht's *The Caucasian Chalk Circle*) and *Everyman* by Obotunde Ijimere. Together with a Malawian, Mupa Shumba (a veteran of the first Makerere College Travelling Theatre in Uganda), in 1970 he formed and organized the first travelling theatre in Malawi, whose first tour was confined to nearby towns. When Linstrum's term of office came to an end, James Gibbs, a British teacher with extensive experience in West Africa, took over his work (1972–8). It was during this period that the Travelling Theatre really took root, reaching almost every district in the country. The bulk of the Theatre's work remained the presentation of plays in English in schools and urban centres (never in villages). When Gibbs left, Chris Kamlongera took over, and was subsequently joined by David Kerr, from the University of Zambia. Now the company's repertoire includes vernacular plays, and tours have been extended to include drama workshops in rural areas.

The affiliation of the Travelling Theatre to the English Department at Chancellor College has had particular consequences. The department was already changing its syllabuses to include more material from Malawian oral tradition and black aesthetics – which was to have phenomenal results. Students now took to playwriting, producing plays and acting. From such activity came in 1979 the first anthology

An outdoor production of Steve Chimombo's *Wachiona Ndani*.

of Malawian plays in English, *Nine Malawian Plays*, edited by James Gibbs. Gibbs's concern with establishing theatre in Chancellor College was hampered only by a lack of space.

The Travelling Theatre constructed an open-air theatre, which became the home of all college productions until December 1982, when the Great Hall complex, with two theatres within, was opened on campus. The new open-air theatre received an unprecedented welcome from both students and staff. Now the Travelling Theatre had its own base.

Theatre life on Chancellor College campus includes visits from outside groups who perform in the open-air theatre. One such visit – which was to be memorable for the insight it offered the Travelling Theatre – was by the Zomba Community Centre Drama Group in the 1970s. They brought with them two plays: an adaptation of *The Pardoner's Tale* (in English) and Kambale: *The Famous Boy* (in Chichewa, a vernacular, and the national, language). The latter, the story of a young trickster who fools everyone around him by his antics, is the one that aroused discussion amongst theatre enthusiasts. And in spite of being merely primary school children with no formal training in drama, performers won the hearts of the audience. One critic, marvelling at the work of these children, speculated on the reasons for their success. His comments have remained at the heart of the Chancellor College Travelling Theatre's work: 'The fact that the play was in Chichewa is the most important factor: it was the language best suited to the theme, the setting, the characters, and ... the audience ... The playwright in Malawi should always decide beforehand what audience he wants to amuse and educate. If he is sensible he will first and foremost think of the man in the street most of the time; and hence use the language that best suits that man.' The Theatre's slogan is now 'Taking theatre to the people'.

It took five years to put this slogan into practice. The first time the Travelling Theatre worked with ordinary villagers was when the company went to Mbalachanda Rural Growth Centre in the Northern Region. Following the success of this tour, the Theatre has swung the weight of its work in favour of vernacular plays. Steve Chimombo's second play, *Wachiona Ndani* (1982), marks the firm establishment of Chichewa plays in the Theatre's repertoire, as well as a turning-point for Chimombo himself, who is also well known for his English verse, short stories and his first play, *The Rainmaker*.

The question of what language to use is central to any moves towards taking theatre to the people. Although Malawi is fortunate in having one national language, Chichewa, when it comes to working, for instance, in the Northern Region, it is necessary to know the local language.

Taking theatre to the people brings its own problems. First, there is the question of finance. Although the Travelling Theatre comes under the Chancellor College Department of Fine and Performing Arts, there is no money earmarked for its operations. From time to time it has thrived on support from outside bodies like the Schimmelpenninck Fund, the Morel Trust Fund, the British Council and the Christian Service Committee. Of late it has taken to charging a fee for its shows – although this in fact goes counter to its stated aims.

Because the Travelling Theatre is semi-autonomous, in that there is no financial support from the department that houses it, some organizational problems arise. Left very much to himself, the Theatre's artistic director, David Kerr, relies heavily (if not totally) on the goodwill of enthusiastic students. The extra-curricular nature of the Theatre only empha-

sizes this reliance. Kerr has identified a number of problems in running the Theatre: shortage of directors, narrow choice of plays, lack of indigenous dance groups on campus. The problem of choice, he says, is complex: 'One complexity is the Censorship Board.' The involvement of the Malawi Censorship Board is crucial to the development of theatre in Malawi. It is required by law to approve all prospective scripts before any theatre group performs them.

Moves to stop indigenous culture from disappearing in African countries usually involves proclamations by politicians, encouraging the masses to revive and take pride in their own cultural heritage on the one hand, and advocating government-controlled conservation and protection of the people's cultural heritage on the other. Governments have established departments of cultural affairs and censorship procedures in order to monitor cultural development. Theatre work is often encompassed by such censorship.

The duties of the Malawi Censorship Board include keeping a check on all theatrical activity. Before any play is performed in public, it must be passed, then previewed, by the Board. Censorship in Malawi can be political or social. Sex and nude pictures, for instance, are out. And books with a substantial political content of the 'wrong sort' will be banned outright. Describing the Censorship Board as he knew it between 1973 and 1978, the former director of the Travelling Theatre, has said: 'My impression is that the Board is ignorant and confused, but that it can tell a direct attack when it encounters one. My conclusion is that, although the Malawian writer suffers severely under the Censorship Board, the devices it forces on him are not in every way detrimental to the shaping of his work.'

When the Board was set up it determined that: 'A publication, picture, statue or record shall be deemed to be undesirable if any part thereof (1) is indecent or obscene or offensive or harmful to public morals; or (2) gives offence to the religious convictions or feelings of the public; or (3) bring any member or section of the public into contempt; or (4) harms relations between sections of the public; or (5) is contrary to the interests of public safety, or public order.' The Board has banned books, plays, newspapers and magazines. It sees part of its job as being to 'protect' Malawians from books about the anti-colonial struggle, about socialism, religious dissent and birth control, and books that deal with corruption in post-independence Africa.

In theatre, this censorship focuses on the script rather than on the performance. This is because the latter has been found difficult to censor. Although the Board insists, publicly, on a preview of all shows, distances prohibit it from visiting all theatre venues in the country. Plays submitted have been rejected on all sorts of grounds: for 'inclusion of direct and indirect sex discussion', for showing 'a woman ... deceiving her husband', for promoting political 'subversion'; for pressing the 'European way of life ... on ... African youth'; For '[making] fun of the Police and the Church by showing that the rich, the law and the Church exploit the poor'. Thus the Malawian theatre would appear to depend, for its survival, on playwrights who avoid the central problems of their society and concern themselves with the now virtually exhausted themes of traditional versus Western life, and on plays that service a conservative national ideology by offering models of chiefly wisdom, marital stability and acquiescent labour. The activities of the Board are critical in determining the way theatre will develop in Malawi.

Radio drama also offers opportunities for Malawian writers and actors. *Sewero (Kapalepale)* is a thirty-minute programme broadcast at 6.30 p.m. on Saturdays – a peak period in the Malawi broadcasting day – by the Malawi Broadcasting Corporation. Its producer-writer is Smart Likhaya Mbewe, and all the work is in Chichewa. The programme is popularly known as *Kapalepale*, which derives from the name of the leading character, who is always the centre of controversy in the drama.

Most of the episodes depict life in urban centres where the rural and the modern are in constant conflict. It would seem that Mbewe always aims at establishing, through comedy, an amicable solution to the problems that such a conflict breeds. Each presentation ends in a chief's home, where matters are sorted out to the satisfaction of all. One result of this is that the plays are heavily didactic – perhaps in keeping with the meaning of the word *kapalepale* itself, which is Chichewa for 'weeding a garden'. No scripts are written for this drama: Mbewe creates scenarios which he explains to his actors, and then, together, they improvise the dialogue.

His work has been described as: 'a weekly comedy about an urban trickster [Kapalepale himself] who lives by his wits'. 'The aim behind my plays is to teach good manners as well as to entertain people,' Mbewe has said. The initial 'trickster' idea has, over the years, given way to a more overtly didactic and moralist one. The reformed Kapalepale can no longer be seen as a man apart from his society. As Joyce Kumpukwe has pointed out: 'As playwright, Mr Mbewe can be compared to an artist in a traditional African society who functions as spokesman for the society in which he lives, sharing its prejudices and directing its dislikes against what is discountenanced.' But calling Kapalepale 'spokesman for his society' would be to romanticize. Rather, he is an artist who casts himself in the role of society's moral raider. And, working within a government-owned and controlled radio station, his morality must reflect the government's views.

Mbewe's plays are carefully calculated to produce a particular effect on Malawian audiences. The story is organized to illustrate an idea or teach a moral, and a common moral element unites the plays from week to week. The ideological element is linked to the concept of 'nation-building'. A high proportion of the Malawi Broadcasting Corporation's programmes deal with such subjects as literacy, public health, agricultural improvement, cultural traditions and social guidance.

'Theatre of the Air' is the other established MBC drama programme. Modelled on the BBC World Service's 'African Theatre', the programme is in English and broadcast at around 9.30 p.m., by which time most rural people are already in bed. It can be safely assumed that this programme is aimed at urban listeners rather than country people, who do not have the necessary electricity to continue life into the late evenings. Like most of the work emanating from the MBC, 'Theatre of the Air' carries plays aimed at projecting the culture of the country. Such plays are likely to be tragedies, handled lightly but with a serious underlying tone; material will probably be drawn from

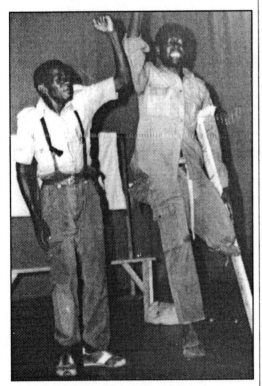

A Malawian production of Zakes Mda's
We Shall Sing for the Fatherland.

rustic society; there will be between two and six characters, and programmes will run for thirty minutes.

MBC radio drama recognizes that radio is one of the mass media that has the capacity to surmount the major obstacles to developing countries' illiteracy. This fact is used as its springboard for all drama work. The dramatization of information is gaining the upper hand and radio drama has thus, in a modest way, kindled the desire in the general public for this means of propagating information. Because of the popularity of its drama, the MBC is flooded with requests from government ministries and departments to dramatize information. The Chancellor College Travelling Theatre has been taken as an example by almost all Malawian amateur theatre groups. Once formed, a group arranges a tour of some sort; but without adequate funding to meet the logistics involved, such tours are confined to very short distances. Only three groups, apart from the Chancellor College company, have attempted nationwide tours – Lonjezo Travelling Theatre, Wakhumbata Theatre Ensemble and Kwathu Drama Group. This last, led by Charles Severe is the most successful and the oldest. The repertoires of this group and the Lonjezo ones, like those of most Malawian amateur groups, consist of Chichewa plays only, but Wakhumbata Theatre Ensemble has mostly English plays in its repertoire. The use of Chichewa, the national language by the Chancellor College Travelling Theatre and by the other amateur groups has been crucial in popularizing theatre in the country. Chichewa plays are crucial to the development of drama in Malawi, since most of the country's population does not speak English.

Theatre is certainly active in Malawi, but what is still lacking is a willingness on the part of publishers to dare to publish the many scripts that companies are producing, either through group improvisation or through individual playwrights like Du Chisiza Jr, James Mg'ombe, Enoch Timpunza Mvula, Innocent

Banda, Steve Chimombo, Vipya Harawa, Mvundula and Garton Kamchedzera. So far only a handful have been published.

Bibliography

S. Chimombo, *Wachiona Ndani*, Blantyre, 1983; J. Gibbs (ed.), *Nine Malawian Plays*, Limbe & Lilongwe, 1979, and 'Of Kamuzu and Chameleons: Experiences of Censorship in Malawi', *The Literary Half-Yearly*, 23, 2, 1982; A. Horn, 'African Theatre – Docility and Dissent', *Index on Censorship*, 9, 3, 1980; C. F. Kamlongera, 'Theatre for Development: The Case for Malawi', *Theatre Research International*, 7, 3, 1982, and 'Problems in the Growth of a Popular Art: The Relationship between Drama and Society in Malawi and Zambia', PhD thesis, Univ. of Leeds, 1984; D. Kerr, 'Travelling Theatre: Problems and Pseudo-Problems', *Muse* 60; J. Kumpukwe, 'S. M. Mbewe, Creator and Producer of Malawian Radio Plays', *BALAZA*, 1, June 1983; V. Mdovi, 'Censorship in Malawi', *Index on Censorship*, 8, 1, 1979; A. Roscoe, *Uhuru's Fire: African Literature East to South*, Cambridge, 1977.

MALI

Modern Mali, the French Sudan in colonial times but independent since 1960, is a country with an ancient history and rich theatrical traditions both old and new. Among the many oral performances of its people are the *Do* and the *Kotéba* of the Bambara. Described as sacred theatre, the *Do* takes place every seven years and marks the end of the initiation ceremony of young adolescents into the society of the same name. It takes a little over three months to perform and is open only to initiates. Its performers are masked men and their language is esoteric.

The secular version of this theatre is the *Kotéba* of central and southern Mali, which means a giant (*ba*) snail (*kote*). The shape of this animal is reproduced in the *Kotéba*'s dance formations, where a chorus of female singers in a middle circle is surrounded by five concentric circles of dancers, musicians and instrumentalists. Performed in public, unlike the *Do*, and at popular feasts, it presents satirical sketches on stereotyped subjects and characters. Its performers are young *Do* initiates and their spectacle combines mime, dialogue, song and puppetry to produce what is widely agreed to be the most total art form of the Bambara people.

Among the people of northern Mali, two interesting theatrical displays are the *Tendé* of the Tamasheq and the *Takouba* of the Bella. The first is a spectacle mounted on popular occasions, in which men and children on horse or camel back and on the ground engage in spectacular acrobatics and dances; this display is followed by dramatic sketches. The *Takouba*, or 'dance of the brave', is described as a dance of piety, with intricate steps sustained by warrior songs. The plot is sung and the action mimed.

But Mali also has a significant modern theatre in French, and several troupes such as the Nyogolon, the Kotéba National and the Troupe des Marionettes, that are engaged in building a performance style that has roots in tradition. The origins of Mali's modern theatre go back to the dramatic compositions of Malian students at the Ecole William Ponty in Senegal, such as *La Ruse de Diégué* (*The Cunning of Diégué*, 1947) on the 13th-century founder of the Mali empire, Soundjata Keita. These sketches' penchant for epic history has been continued in post-colonial Mali with, for example, Sory Konaké's *Le Grand Destin de Soundjata* (*Soundjata: A Great Destiny*, 1973), Massa Makan Diabaté's *Une si belle leçon de patience* (*So Great a Lesson in Patience*, 1972) and Séydou Badian's *La Mort de Chaka* (*The Death of Chaka*, 1962). Malian dramatists use history to kindle nationalist feelings and to justify political options (as when Badian contrives a parallel in *Chaka* between the vision of the illustrious Zulu chieftain and that of the socialist government of Modibo Keita, in which he was a minister). It is also a reflection of the strong epic traditions of their country.

Other themes dramatized are traditional practices such as ritual sacrifice or death – Alkaly Kaba's *Mourir pour vivre* (*Die to Live*, 1976), Amadou Koné's *Le Respect des morts* (*Respect for the Dead*, 1980) – and social problems, such as Moussa Konaté's *L'Or du diable* (*The Devil's Gold*, 1985). Symbolic drama also finds favour in Gaoussou Diawara's *L'Aube des béliers* (*The Dawn of the Sheep*, 1975) and Diama and Alkaly Kaba's *Les Hommes du bakschich* (*Baksheesh Men*, 1973).

Bibliography

M.-J. Arnoldi, *Bamana and Bozo Puppetry of the Ségou Region Youth Societies*, Lafayette; Ind., 1977; J. Brink, 'Bamana Koté-tlon theatre', *African Arts*, 4, Jul. 1977; G. Diawara, *Panorama critique du théâtre malien dans son évolution*, Sénégal, 1981, and 'Tende et Takouba: théâtres Tamasheq et Bella', *Notre Librairie: Théâtre Théâtres*, 102, Jul./Aug. 1990; M. Maiga, 'Le Kotéba', *Notre Librairie: Le Littérature Malienne*, 75–6, Jul./Oct. 1984; A. Sonfo and O. Kanouté, 'Le theatre historique', *Notre Libraire: La Littérature Malienne*, ibid.; C. Wake, 'Mali', in *The Cambridge Guide to World Theatre*, ed. M. Banham, Cambridge, 1988.

MAURITIUS

Mauritius, a small island in the Indian Ocean, has been independent since 1968. During French rule (1722–1810) slaves were brought to the island from Africa, and when slavery was abolished in 1834 under British rule (1810–1968) indentured labourers were brought in from India. The population (1 million) is thus multi-ethnic and multi-lingual. English is the official language, but French is more widely spoken; there are several ancestral languages of Asian origin, and Creole is the lingua franca.

Both formal and non-formal theatre have always been an integral part of the cultural scene. The slaves brought with them from Africa a type of happening known as *sega*, the Indian immigrants came with their folk-drama, and the Europeans at a very early stage of settlement showed their interest in formal theatre. According to the historian Antoine Chelin, the first theatre building was fitted up in 1754. From then onwards theatrical activities with a heavy bias towards lyrical drama, performed by French artists for a francophone

Zozef ek so palto larkansiel, a Creole adaptation of *Joseph and the Amazing Technicolour Dreamcoat*, 1982.

elite, thrived. Although Mauritius was formally ceded to Britain in 1814, the first English play was not staged until 1823. And it was only in 1932, with the founding of the Mauritius Dramatic Club, that theatre in English really started to develop.

We have to wait for the late 1930s to see the emergence of notable Mauritian performing artists like Amédée Poupard, Max Moutia and Yves Forget. During the Second World War, as a result of shortage of films from India, a new form of entertainment in Hindustani was created: *natak* (dance-drama). The post-war and pre-independence period saw the development of other new trends. First, several local writers tried their hand at playwriting in French and Hindi. Second, since the organization of the first Youth Drama Festival in 1951 the interest in theatre activities has substantially increased, to reach a much wider audience and to motivate young talents. Another boost came with the founding of the Société des Metteurs en Scène (Producers' Society, 1966).

Since independence, through stage, radio and television local writers in different languages have been able to reach an ever wider audience. The Youth Drama Festival, which originally accepted only entries in English, is now open to all the languages of Mauritius. The most spectacular development is perhaps the rise of Creole as a powerful vehicle of dramatic expression. It seems that in order to address as many people as possible and to be in a position to catch the mood and to express the major preoccupations of Mauritius, playwrights and directors have opted for Creole as the most effective language for dramatic experiment.

Asize Asgarally, who struck the imagination in the 1960s by writing and staging several plays in English, switched in the 1970s to Creole. His last play *Ritsitatane* is the first history play in a language that was until quite recently considered unfit for anything but cheap comic sketches. Henri Favory, too, has written and staged several plays in Creole, of which *Tras* is the best-known. The director Rajoo Ramana has successfully translated and adapted several plays to fit the current mood and taste. Over the last decade, the Mauritian public has been able to see and read works of Shakespeare in the new theatre language. Besides direct translation of such plays as *Othello* and *The Merchant of Venice*, Shakespeare has also inspired original creation, or re-creation. *Macbeth* has become *Zeneral Makbef*, and *The Tempest, Toufann.*

Non-formal theatrical activities still enliven important occasions such as weddings, anniversaries and end-of-the-year parties, but technological progress in the field of entertainment (particularly television and video) has considerably reduced their importance. Formal theatrical activities are dynamic, thanks to the dedication of a handful of artists (writers, actors, directors). The most original contribution of dramatic art to social and cultural growth in Mauritius is probably in the field of language. Be it original creation or re-creation through translation, dramatic literature, has greatly enhanced the process of promotion and standardization of Mauritian Creole.

Bibliography

A. Chelin, *Le Théâtre à l'Île Maurice*, Mauritius, 1954; G. A. Decotter, *Le Plaza*, Mauritius, 1983.

NIGER

An inland republic which before its independence in 1960 was part of the French West African Federation, Niger has few concrete achievements in the field of modern theatre. What existed during the colonial period was limited to a few troupes: the Amicales des Fonctionnaires de Niamey, the Elmina Renaissance and the Amis de Niamey; a couple of plays by the ex-École William Ponty graduate Mahamane Dandobi: *L'Adventure d'une chèvre* (*The Adventure of a Goat*, 1955) and *La Légende de Kabrin Kabra* (*The Legend of Kabrin Kabra*, 1957), both published in *Traits d'Union*, the cultural organ of French West Africa; and performances by William Ponty (see SENEGAL) students on tour. Although visiting French theatre troupes, under the direction of Pierre Ringel, brought Molière to supplement this scant activity, because of the language used – French – this cultural offering was accessible only to the Western-educated minority.

But theatrical activity in French has fared no better after independence, with only one full-length play in that language published to date: the historian André Salifou's *Tanimoune* (1973). Set in the 19th century, it dramatizes the successful struggle of Tanimoune, ruler of Damagaran, to overthrow the tutelage of a Bornu king and to set up an independent Hausa state.

What has flourished, however, since independence is a popular theatre in the national languages known as *teyatur* in Hausa (from the French *théâtre*) – the language most widely spoken in Niger and used in these plays. Student theatre groups, *samariyas* (mostly uneducated youth groups involved in community projects), and radio and television groups are the greatest practitioners of this genre, which also includes dance-dramas known as 'ballets'. Arts festivals at regional and national levels, and radio and school competitions, provide a forum for the various troupes and act as a stimulus to creation. This theatre has been actively encouraged by successive governments, which provide money for the troupes, construct *maisons des jeunes* (youth centres that house theatres), and programme festival plays on radio and television.

Drawing from the many play and imitative activities of traditional Hausa culture, as well as from its religious theatrical displays such as the *Kora* and the *Bori* (exorcism and spirit-possession cults, respectively), and using their resources of song, dance, mask and mime, Niger's popular theatre improves on themes that range from history through developmental issues to contemporary social ills. But because of extensive government support for it, popular theatre sometimes presents little more than the government's point of view.

Bibliography

J. Beik, *The Hausa Theatre in Niger*, New York and London, 1987; R. Cornevin, *Le Théâtre en Afrique noire et à Madagascar*, 1970.

NIGERIA

Nigeria, with over 100 million people, is the most populous country in Africa. It became independent from Britain in 1960, within boundaries created during the 19th century by European rivalry, which ignored existing African societies. The British legacy of a tripartite regional division within the country was singularly misconceived as a starting-point for Nigeria's future national political development. Relations of domination and disadvantage between ethnic groups remain a serious political problem, despite the failure of the civil war (also called the Biafran War) to split the country into independent states at the end of the 1960s. To some extent, though, inter-ethnic division has been eroded by the abandonment of the regional structure and the creation of states (thirty by 1993) under a federal system, and by the gradual creation of a governing elite and strong interest groups that cut across ethnic lines.

During the 1970s and the so-called oil boom, Nigerians were able to use massive oil revenues to create both spectacular consumption and a large-scale internal market (though the country failed to exploit these revenues to industrialize and to create a more dynamic economy). Much of this spending was channelled through the states – which proved significant for the development of drama, as each state sought to establish its own arts council and television station. In addition, there was a huge expansion in the university system, at both federal and state levels: by the early 1990s the country boasted more than forty such institutions. This has led to a significant stimulus in publishing, including that of drama texts for study as literature. A number of universities (including Ibadan, Jos, Ahmadu Bello, Ife (Obafemi Awolowo), Calabar, Ilorin, Benin, Nsukka, Port Harcourt, Abuja) have established degree courses in theatre and performing arts, and graduates from these courses initially found many new opportunities for employment in the newly founded state arts council troupes and television stations. Since the early 1980s, however, the drastic reduction in oil revenues and therefore in Nigeria's GNP has arrested the development and even the consolidation of this establishment.

There are regional variations to this general picture of substantial commitment to theatre from the Nigerian public purse. While all the states, without exception, are conscious of their heritage in the traditional performing arts, contemporary theatre is more actively encouraged by the southern states, and is most vigorous in the largely Yoruba states (Ondo, Oyo, Osun, Ogun, Lagos and Kwara). This is true both of indigenous-language drama and of drama in English, of which perhaps as much as three-quarters of Nigeria's very substantial output has been written by Yoruba playwrights. Nevertheless, theatre is neither weak or necessarily retarded in the largely Muslim Hausa and Fulani states in the north. Traditional performance there is dynamic and complex, though different from the southern masquerade traditions (see Introduction, MASQUERADES IN AFRICA); modern drama is developing in rural villages in innovative and political ways: and some young northerners, such as Sadiq Balewa, are notably channelling their dramatic talents into film-making and television. States like Benue, whose peoples are not part of the large groupings (Hausa, Yoruba, Igbo), have supplied a disproportionately large number of talented drama graduates who have become

University of Ibadan's 'Theatre on Wheels' with the touring Elizabethan theatre stage celebrating Shakespeare's quatercentenary, 1964.

actors, teachers and recorders of rich performance traditions which have received national recognition.

The states within the Nigerian federation have not entirely taken over the patronage of traditional performance. Many traditional rulers remain the ultimate authority for seasonal and religious rituals and cults. Nevertheless, the sponsorship by each state of a regional cultural identity has created the necessary conditions for contemporary drama to grow out of traditional performance, because dances, music, masquerades, festivals, storytelling, minstrelsy – all part of the oral tradition – have survived the years of colonial rule to offer now a richer historical view than that drawn from written colonial records. This forms the basis of both discourse and aesthetic in the emerging Nigerian theatre.

For example, J. A. Adedeji's pioneering study of *Alarinjo* theatre in the Oyo Yoruba empire shows how that theatrical art evolved in the 14th century out of the *egungun* masquerade, becoming eventually both court masque and professional popular travelling theatre. This research is complemented by other studies of *egungun*, exploring, for example, the mimetic satire of the *gelede* masquerade which imposes

Theatre in the Round at Ahmadu Bello University, Zaria, 1984.

animated wooden puppetry upon the mask. *Egungun* is given a complex metaphysical significance by the playwright WOLE SOYINKA, both in his writing and in his aesthetic theory. In fact, many Yoruba playwrights, writing either in Yoruba or in English, find both content and style in *egungun*, the popularity of which is, if anything, on the increase. A later outcome of the professional popular travelling theatre *Alarinjo*, itself an outgrowth of the *egungun* masquerade, was the YORUBA TRAVELLING THEATRE, and this in turn has developed into a prolific and commercially successful Yoruba television and film drama.

The *Ozidi* saga of the Ijo people is an example of a full-scale dramatic performance, still put on today, within the tradition. It takes a number of years to rehearse, and three nights and days to perform. It engulfs the whole village in which it takes place (see J. P. CLARK BEKEDEREMO). Similar in dramatic scope is the drama *Ekong* (Ibibio), which takes six years to rehearse and involves in the enactment of its narrative every aspect of performance. Scholars like D. Adelugba, J. Amankulor, M. Echeruo, O. Enekwe, M. Nzewi, O. Ogunba and N. Ugonna have variously and extensively researched and analysed the relationship between theatre and drama on the one hand, and trance, festivals, masquerades and rituals on the other – for example, in the Igbo Ekpe dance-drama which occurs in December at the close of the Ekpe cycle within the religious-ritual year.

These ancient traditional performances can still extend their scope and are able to represent modern Nigeria; one vividly contemporary yet traditional theatrical display is the *kwagh-hir* of the Tiv people in Benue state, which consists of highly complex animated puppets, either in tableaux on mobile platforms depicting modern Tivland, or as giant bestiary and shamanesque masks. They are non-affective and are presented in a night of competition between villages. Each village's puppet team is backed up by a chorus of women singers and a large orchestra of traditional instruments. The playlets performed by these teams frequently use satire in a biting depiction of contemporary social custom. The assessment, by a team of judges, is an aesthetic one and seeks to relate the depiction of modern Tivland to established traditional aesthetics, especially in song and music.

In the north, there are nascent theatrical elements in the grand spectacle of the Fulani emirs' *Sallah* processions on the high feast days of Islam. Hundreds, sometimes thousands, of people take part in each *Sallah*, either on caparisoned horses and camels or on foot, costumed and in armour. In the midst of this pomp, and often ridiculing it, are the *'yankama*, whose entertainment, *'yankamanchi*, is made up of satirical skits, songs and scurrilous surrealism. The *'yankama* are travelling minstrels who entertain both at the emir's court and in the market-place. They belong to guilds, and are sometimes protected and patronized by an emir; they are an accepted part of the cultural life of the emirates. Not so *Bori* (researched variously by D. Adelugba, A. Horn, M. Onwuejeogwu), which is an ancient Hausa ritual possession cult, pre-Islamic, practised by women who live sequestered within their own compound. *Bori* has an affective healing context with access to the spirit world; it also has a pure entertainment mode, the enjoyment of which derives from a complex aesthetic. *Bori* is not acceptable to Islam, or to the traditional rulers. Yet another sort of traditional performance among some Hausa villages is the lord-of-misrule festival, an example of which is

Kalankuwa in Zaria, Kaduna state, organized by the young male farmers. There is a strong contemporary satire in the mimetic role-play, with people in naturalistic costume acting the parts of national and local rulers and bureaucrats, in the context of twenty-four hours of total licence within the village.

The years of the struggle for independence were accompanied by a flowering of dramatic talent at all levels in society, which has not abated in the thirty-five years since independence was achieved. Inspiration comes from many directions, though the traditional arts are dominant. The main legacy of performance traditions to new Nigerian drama is the concept of 'total theatre'. This applies whether the play is performed in English or, say, Yoruba, or in pidgin, or even in a mixture of languages and language registers. The linguistic dimension is itself a part of total theatre which also includes significant non-naturalistic idioms: masks, masquerades, music, dance, rhythm and movement, incantation and word-play. Many of these elements are fused to create surrealist physical imagery. Plays which vividly demonstrate total theatre are the Yoruba operas developed in the 1950s by people like HUBERT OGUNDE and at the Mbari Clubs at Oshogbo and Ibadan, where DURO LADIPO's great success *Oba Ko So* (1964) was created. Other important examples of total theatre are Soyinka's *A Dance of the Forests* (1960) and WALE OGUNYEMI's *Langbodo* (1980).

Some playwrights deal with the supernatural as content, but avoid its direct meaning through symbolism in the style of the play. Sonny Oti's *The Old Masters* (1977) deals naturalistically with the clash between Church and cult; and the brilliant actor E. K. Ogunmola, in his adaptation of Amos Tutuola's *The Palmwine Drinkard*, retreats from Tutuola's surrealism. Since the mid-70s, a new generation of dramatists has emerged whose work inclines towards a radical appreciation of the problems of society. Here again the principle of total theatre is still highly valued, and plays such as FEMI

Osofisan's *Morountodun* (1982), Ola Rotimi's *If* (1983) and Bode Sowande's *Ajantala-Pinocchio* (1992) stimulate audience consciousness through a rich and constantly modulating range of theatre resources.

Many dramatists promote a serious debate on Nigeria's social formation, though re-creating traditional performance modes. Folklore, myth, magic and ritual become the framework for engaging in rigorous analysis of the class structure and polarities inherent in the neo-colonial state. Notable works of this mode are Osofisan's *The Chattering and the Song* (1976), Kole Omotoso's *The Curse* (1976) and *Shadows in the Horizon* (1975), Olu Obafemi's *Suicide Syndrome* (1987) and Akanji Nasiru's *Our Survival* (1982). Ben Tolomoju, Stella Oyedepo, Tess Onwueme (*The Desert Encroaches*, 1985; *Legacies*, 1988, among others), Bode Osanyin and Fred Agbeyegbe (e.g. *The King Must Dance Naked*, 1990) also belong to this emergent radical theatrical tradition.

The synthesizing, multi-referential nature of much of the most challenging Nigerian drama is seen also in the way playwrights draw on quite diverse models from world theatre: Ladipo's *Eda* from von Hofmannsthal's *Jedermann* (*Everyman*); the Zaria Performing Arts

Ogunmola's production of Amos Tutuola's *The Palmwine Drinkard*.

Company's *Lawal Kung Fu Kaduna* from Udall's *Ralph Roister Doister*; Rotimi's *The Gods Are Not to Blame* from Sophocles' *Oedipus the King*; Osofisan's *Who's Afraid of Solarin?* from Gogol's *The Government Inspector*. All these have become distinctly Nigerian plays. Their audiences neither know nor care about the originals; they receive the plays as yet further contribution to the rich texture of Nigerian theatre today.

Other plays of social criticism are far more exclusively reliant on (often didactic) dialogue. Writers and performers are influenced by naturalism, on television and in the cinema as well as in the theatre. A direct representation of contemporary life on stage appeals to actors as well as to audiences, who take pleasure in the acute observation of human behaviour at a time of extensive social change. Naturalistic drama is exemplified in the plays of James Ene-Henshaw, such as his *Dinner for Promotion* (1967). Plays concerned with personal morality in sexual and social relationships among upwardly mobile Nigerians tend also to be crafted and performed naturalistically: Meki Nzewi's *Two Fists in One Mouth* (1976), 'Laolu Ogunniyi's television plays such as *Candle in the Wind* (1977), ZULU SOFOLA's *The Sweet Trap* (1977), and Rashead Gbadomosi's *Echoes from the Lagoon* (1972) all exemplify this. Naturalism, though still present, is less obvious in a number of theatrically effective historical dramas, like *Ovonramwen Nogbaisi* by Rotimi, as well as in some pidgin plays such as 'Segun Oyekunle's *Katakata for Sofahead* (1978) – about a group of petty criminals who, in gaol, act out the poverty and petty thieving of the latest convict to join them. Tunde Lakoju's *Moonshine Solidarity* (1980), a political satire on the 1979 civilian government elections in Nigeria which uses the newspaper cartoon-strip character Pappy Joe, is read naturalistically by Nigerian audiences – as are pidgin adaptations of Brecht.

If there is an underlying aesthetic in contemporary Nigerian theatre, it is the way in which quite disparate styles are effortlessly combined in performance. Life is presented on the stage, directly; but it is mediated by symbolic representations of a further, or 'other', reality. This may result from performing to eager audiences with eclectic tastes.

A significant extension of Nigerian theatre is seen in the work of Nigerian playwrights living in the USA or Britain. Tess Onwueme has been based in the USA since 1990; Biyi Bandele-Thomas, living in London, continues to address that central concern of Nigerian drama, the state of the state (*Marching for Fausa*, 1993). Nigerian myth may still provide core thematic material for an Anglo-Irish–Nigerian playwright such as Gabriel Gbadamosi (*Eshu's Faust*, 1992).

Practitioners in Yoruba-language theatre (Ladipo, Ogunde, MOSES OLAIYA ADEJUMA) were able to form professional, commercial theatre companies from the outset. From the 1960s onwards there were also many attempts by university-based practitioners to form performance companies: Soyinka and the Orishun Theatre, Rotimi and the Ori Olokun theatre (Ife), Onuora Enekwe, Kalu Ika and Meki Nzewi with the Oak Theatre in Nsukka.

With the end of the oil boom and the ever deepening economic crisis of the 1980s and 90s – exacerbated, as throughout Africa, by government's adherence to World Bank/IMF-imposed economic programmes – theatre might have been expected to decline through lack of audience support. Yet Nigerian theatre continues to attract a substantial audience, a tribute to its entertainment value as well as to its ability to speak to popular perception of current realities. Further more, even though the audience for Nigerian theatre is still often centred on universities and/or is made up of members of the elite (productions sponsored by banks and other organizations are now a familiar feature of Lagos social life, for example), there are signs of an interaction between popular and literary theatres and of the existence of a broad-based audience for companies prepared to perform outside prestige venues. The last fifteen years have seen a growth in the establishment of

Bibliography

D. Adelugba (ed.), LACE Interview series, Univ. of Ibadan; *Nigerian Magazine* (Lagos); *Nigerian Stage* (Univ. of Ilorin); M. Banham and C. Wake, *African Theatre Today*, London, 1976; E. Clark, *Hubert Ogunde: The Making of Nigerian Theatre*, London, 1979; J. P. Clark, *The Ozidi Saga*, Ibadan, 1977; B. Crow, *Studying Drama*, London, 1983; H. J. and M. T. Drewal, *Gelede: Art and Female Power among the Yoruba*, Bloomington, Ind., 1983; C. Dunton, *Make Man Talk True: Nigerian Drama since 1970*, London, 1992; M. Etherton, *The Development of African Drama*, London, 1982; B. Jeyifo, *The Yoruba Popular Travelling Theatre of Nigeria*, Lagos, 1984, and *The Truthful Lie: Essays on a Sociology of African Drama*, London, 1985; Z. Kofoworola and Y. Lateef, *Hausa Performing Arts and Music*, Lagos, 1987; O. Ogunbiyi (ed.), *Drama and Theatre in Nigeria: A Critical Source Book*, Lagos, 1981; W. Soyinka, *Myth, Literature and the African World*, Cambridge, 1976.

fully professional and commercial theatre companies, often formed by formerly university-based dramatists: J. P. Clark-Bekederemo's PEC Repertory Theatre (Lagos) has been joined in the 1990s by Bode Sowande's Odu Themes Meridian (Ibadan) and Ola Rotimi's African Cradle Theatre (Ife). Other significant companies include the Dasuku Living Theatre (Port Harcourt) and the Ayota Community Theatre, based in a low-income area of Lagos.

Adejumo, Moses Olaiya [Baba Sala] (1936–) Nigerian actor-manager and founder-owner of the Alawada theatre ('theatre of the one who entertains'). Olaiya, whose stage name is Baba Sala, is one of the most popular comedians in Nigeria today and his company (both acting and trading) is the most commercially successful, despite performances being almost entirely in Yoruba. The fact that the company is licensed to produce plays, run musical groups and hotels, and produce records and magazines is a clear indicator of Olaiya's vigorous business sense.

He started his first theatre group in 1963, and developed what is now his unique comic format in 1965, when he won first prize (a tour of West Germany) in a Nigerian television drama competition. He was denied the prize as his company was considered too coarse to represent Nigeria – its membership, being non-literate in English, might blemish the image of Nigeria abroad! He was, however, compensated with a permanent slot on local television. Ironically, this made his name and ensured the future success of his travelling theatre. Since 1965 he has performed continuously all over Nigeria and coastal West Africa.

Olaiya is a religious syncretist who, though Christian, has many wives and children. The strength of his hard-working company resides in its use of an aspect of Yoruba traditional theatrical heritage, the *yeye* (fun-making, also called *efe*), to treat diverse areas of human experience. Unlike his predecessors, in the genre, Hubert Ogunde and Duro Ladipo, Baba Sala does not take any noble roles in his plays, which always centre on the comic escapades and misadventures of one Lamidi Sani (Baba Sala himself). His comedies are improvised, witty and extremely funny, ensuring the popularity and the huge commercial returns that sustain his travelling theatre. The critic B. Jeyifo contends that, despite the plays' debunking of all social pretensions, Olaiya's potential for social protest is neutralized by the 'amoral, cynical social posture of this great satirist and parodist'.

Like Ogunde and Ade Afolayan, Baba Sala has branched into film-making, in which since the late 1970s he has been increasingly involved. In common with many practitioners in the Yoruba Travelling Theatre, by 1990 he had virtually abandoned live performance. He began using film by projecting shorts – often film material culled from other sources – as inserts in plays such as *Kunkusi, De Director* and *Tokunbo*, then turned to producing full-length films such as *Orun Mooru* (*Heaven is Heated*). Subsequently he has turned to video as a medium. His videos are designed for projection before an audience, not for distribution as cassettes for sale to the public. Recent video productions include *Ore Adisa* (*Friend of Adisa*) and *Ashale Gege* (*Pamperer of Prostitutes*). He continues also to film for television.

Clark-Bekederemo, J(ohn) P(epper)
[J. P. Clark] (1936–)

Nigerian playwright, poet, critic and academic. J. P. Clark-Bekederemo was born in Kaigbodo in Ijo country in the Niger Delta. In 1958, as an undergraduate at Ibadan University, he edited the poetry magazine *The Horn*, which created both context and outlet for a new literacy discourse in Nigeria amongst the young Nigerian

Cameroonian actor and playwright, Hansel Ndumbe Exoh, in *The Raft* by Clark-Bekederemo at the Workshop Theatre, University of Leeds.

'Euromodernists' (as they were later called). After a spell in journalism, Clark-Bekederemo held research fellowships at Princeton and Ibadan. Three early plays in English were widely acclaimed, despite some reservations about their use of a stylized, metrically organized variety of English. The first, *Song of a Goat*, is a tragedy of two brothers, one of whom becomes impotent. His younger brother sleeps with his wife, which results in both men committing suicide. *Masquerade* is the tragedy of the child of that wife's coupling with the husband's brother. *The Raft*, the third play, is a quasi-existentialist work about four men adrift on the Niger on a lumber raft; like *Song of a Goat*, it has been widely produced (all published 1964).

Clark-Bekederemo has continued to publish poetry, with a collection on the Nigerian civil war arousing fierce controversy (*Casualties*, 1970). His reputation for outspoken social criticism was confirmed by his account of his visit to the USA in *America, their America* (1964). His years as an academic were marked by his creative and scholarly work on the monumental Ijo saga of *Ozidi*, a substantial piece of sustained research into the traditional antecedents for Nigerian theatre. This resulted in his own English-language play, *Ozidi* (1966), and a transcribed version of the full saga (1977). In 1980 he resigned his Chair of English at Lagos University, and in 1982 he founded with Ebun Odutola Clark the Pec Repertory Theatre in Lagos. This is a commercial venture committed to the professional presentation of outstanding African plays in English before a subscription audience and, through this initiative, to the creation of a theatre industry in Nigeria. Since the early 1990s the repertory theatre has been leased to other performing companies, such as that run by Chuck Mike.

Amongst Clark-Bekederemo's more recent plays are *The Wives' Revolt* (1985) and *The Bikoroa Plays* (1981; published 1985). The action of the *Bikoroa* trilogy extends from the beginning to the close of the colonial period. Essentially a domestic chronicle, set in the Niger Delta, it offers oblique insights into Nigeria's social and political history.

Fatunde, Tunde (1951–)

Nigerian playwright, critic and journalist. Fatunde was born at Makurdi, Benue state. He studied at the Universities of Ibadan and Bordeaux, and later taught at the University of Benin. Among Nigerian playwrights he is the most notable exponent of agit-prop theatre. His plays challenge economic exploitation in an authoritarian state that he sees as divided along class lines. Critical opinion is sharply split as to whether he has achieved an effective revolutionary theatre, raising his audience's consciousness, or whether his drama is 'ultimately reductionist ... [ignoring] the complexities with which [his] audience is daily contending', as the critic David Richards has said. His earliest plays, *Blood and Sweat* and *No More Oil Boom* (both 1985), deal, respectively, with the exploitation of labour in apartheid South Africa and with corruption and exploitation in the Nigeria of the oil-boom years. *No Food, No Country* (1985) dramatizes the massacre of peasants at Bakolori, northern Nigeria, as the government attempted to sequester land for a large-scale irrigation project. This play is significant as the first Fatunde wrote in pidgin, in an attempt to widen his potential audience and to bring his theatre's contents closer to the experience of working people. His later plays, *Oga Na Thief Man* (*The Big Man is a Thief*, 1986) and *Water No Enemy Get* (1989), also written in pidgin, deal again with the themes of economic deprivation and attempts by workers to organize opposition to exploitation. Fatunde lectures at the Lagos State University. Since the early 1990s he has been an activist in Nigeria's Civil Liberties Organization.

Ladipo, Duro (1931–78)

Nigerian musician, dramatist and performer; a notable composer of Yoruba folk opera, and founder of the Duro Ladipo Theatre. Born in Oshogbo in what was then the Western Region of Nigeria, Ladipo discovered his theatrical inspiration in the oral tradition of Yoruba history, and in the Oshogbo masquerades and festivals (see Introduction, MASQUERADES IN AFRICA), which rubbed against the grain of his stern Christian upbringing. He established the Mbari-Mbayo Centre (1962) in Oshogbo, with a performance of his first opera *Oba Moro* (*The Ghost Catcher*, published 1964). Aided by Chief Ulli Beier and Suzanne Wenger, Mbari-Mbayo became a hothouse for young Yorubas talented in the arts, some of whom went on to achieve international fame as painters, sculptors or performers. Ladipo's most famous opera, *Oba Ko So* (*The King Did Not Hang*, 1964), concerns the religio-mythic figure of Sango, god of lightning in the Yoruba pantheon. The opera, with Ladipo as Sango, remained in the repertory of his company for more than twelve years and was performed in many parts of the world, always with great success. Other operas which appealed to Yoruba audiences and achieved critical acclaim were *Oba Waja* (*The King is Dead*), based on an incident in Nigeria's colonial period when a British district officer tried to stop a sacred ritual suicide; *Moremi*, based on the legend of a Yoruba woman who allowed herself to be captured so that she might learn the secret of the success of her people's enemy; and *Eda*, his adaptation of von Hofmannsthal's *Jedermann* (*Everyman*). Ladipo also composed sketches for television, and made a series, *Bode Wasinmi*. He was a gifted musician; and this talent was enhanced by the further gift of a strong visual sensibility. His work derived from Yoruba history, and indeed his art was more concerned with a specifically Yoruba aesthetic, as part of a wider Nigerian theatre aesthetic. His early death was a tragedy for Nigerian theatre.

Obafemi, Olu (1951–)

Playwright, director, actor, poet, critic and journalist. Obafemi was born in Akutupa-Benu, Kwara state, and studied at Ahmadu Bello University in Zaria, then took a doctorate at

Leeds, England, in 1981. He founded the Ajon Players, a theatre group based in Ilorin, which performs in both town and village venues such as schools, adapting his English-language plays with inserts of Yoruba, pidgin and Hausa. All of Obafemi's plays address exploitation, both political and economic, in the Nigerian state. He is especially concerned with the way state authorities, government officials, employers and other members of the elite impose their preferred interpretation of the world on the people they exploit, and with the ways in which people can develop a clear understanding of this indoctrination. *Nights of a Mystical Beast* (1986) draws on myth and history to establish a continuity of exploitation. *The New Dawn* (1986), like most of his plays, focuses on a radical group and their possibilities for contesting authority. In *Suicide Syndrome* (1987) he uses alternating scenes to demonstrate the gulf between the lifestyles of rich and poor. This play also uses an on-stage orchestra, whose punctuation of the action has a caustic satirical effect. His latest play, *Naira Has No Gender* (1993), develops his previous themes through reference to the social institution of wedding ceremonies. Obafemi is professor of English at the University of Ilorin.

Ogunde, Chief **Hubert** (1916–90)
Nigerian playwright and musician, founder of the Ogunde Theatre, and of the Association of Theatre Practitioners of Nigeria (with a membership of over one hundred professional travelling theatre companies). Ogunde is sometimes described as the father of Nigerian theatre, or the father of contemporary Yoruba theatre. His work was mainly in Yoruba, and reveals some largely Yoruba influences: the traditional *Alarinjo* theatre which derived from the *egungun* masqueraders, the Lagos concert parties, and the (Lagosian) Church of the Lord. Yet for nearly forty years he travelled the length and breadth of Nigeria, developing a national view in the years before indepen-

dence. He began his theatre career in 1944, when he was a poorly paid policeman, with his first folk-opera *The Garden of Eden and the Throne of God*, to raise money for his Church. The following year he resigned from the police to start his own professional travelling theatre company. During the next thirty-five years he composed over fifty operas, plays and melodramas. During a full life he took titles, reputedly became a millionaire, and was in his later years a film-maker and arts entrepreneur. His productions over the years are a record in performance of a popular perception of all the major events in Nigeria's recent history.

Between 1946 and independence in 1960 he identified closely with the political struggle, and his plays were banned by the colonial authorities: *Tiger's Empire* (1946), *Strike and Hunger* (1946), *Bread and Bullet* (1950). He was commissioned to write a play for the independence celebrations, *Song of Unity* (1960). His almost agit-prop operas were interspersed with other folk-operas based on myths and love stories. After independence he became embroiled in the political turbulence in the Western Region, as the country began to slide towards civil war, and his most famous political play, *Yoruba Ronu!* (*Yoruba Awake!*, 1964), resulted in his being banned from performing in the Western Region. He produced *Otito Koro* (*Truth is Bitter*), records his biographer Ebun Clark, 'as a biting answer to this ban'. He composed and produced the opera *Muritala Mohammed* in 1976, after the traumatic assassination of that Nigerian head of state.

He always worked hard to remain in touch with popular sentiment; and he subjected himself as well as his company to gruelling touring schedules, even when it was no longer financially necessary for either himself or his company to reach so many distant audiences. In turn, Ogunde always sought to increase a national awareness among his largely Yoruba audiences. He was a superb entertainer: able to catch the mood of an audience and then suddenly heighten it – thus transforming rather

Okan mi ko ja gara
si ohun ti awǫn enia
wǫnyi wi, bẹni nko fẹ
ki wǫn ni ikunsinu
loni ǫdun ....

Hubert Ogunde's plays also appear as photocomic books.

bland tales of love, heroism and evil politicians into exciting theatrical performances that are observant, witty, and full of meaning for their enraptured audiences.

Ogunde was the first of the YORUBA TRAVELLING THEATRE practitioners to see the commercial possibilities of full-length film-making. In films like *Aiye* (1980) and *Jaiyesimi* (1981) he was able to use the resources of cinema especially to emphasize the supernatural aspects of his plots. Shortly before his death he worked with Bruce Beresford as casting director for the film of Joyce Cary's *Mister Johnson* (1990), and also played the role of Johnson's father-in-law.

Ogunyemi, Chief Wale (1939–)

Ogunyemi was born in Igbajo, Osun state. He worked with WOLE SOYINKA as a member of Orisun Theatre. Particularly in the late 1960s and 70s, the University of Ibadan provided a focal point for productions of his work by, amongst others, Soyinka and Dapo Adelugba. These productions, of plays dealing with Yoruba history and myth, made considerable impact on younger Nigerian dramatists, especially because of their vigorous pursuit of 'total theatre', employing music, dance, song and dialogue.

A versatile actor and director, Ogunyemi is

one of the most prolific dramatists in Nigeria, freely admitting that he can no longer list all the plays he has written and that he no longer has copies of some! His plays can be broadly divided into three categories. The first deal with traditional and mythical themes, with the intervention of gods in human affairs and with disputes amongst the gods themselves. These plays, which offer vivid insight into Yoruba conceptualization of the religious pantheon, include *The Scheme* (1967), *Obaluaye* (1968) and *Eshu Elegbara* (1970). Closely associated with these are two adaptations: a fiercely effective condensation of *Macbeth* entitled *Aare Akogun* (1969), and *Langbodo* (1980), a dramatization of D. O. Fagunwa's novel *Ogboju Ode* (first translated by Soyinka as *The Forest of a Thousand Daemons*). The latter, in Adelugba's production, was Nigeria's FESTAC (see Introduction) entry for the London Commonwealth Arts Festival, 1976. It exemplifies both the spectacular brilliance of Ogunyemi's stagecraft and his radical conservatism. The second category embraces such historical plays as *Ijaiye War* (1970) and *Kiriji* (1976), both of which explore the fratricidal conflicts among the Yorubas in the 18th and 19th centuries. Here Ogunyemi brings a fresh, raw vigour to a subject treated by other Nigerian playwrights, including OLA ROTIMI and Adebayo Faleti. The third category comprises satirical comedies such as *Business Headache*, a pidgin work from the early 1960s, and *The Divorce* (1977), one of the most frequently performed of all English-language plays in Nigeria.

Based at the Institute of African Studies, University of Ibadan, since 1967, Ogunyemi is now Senior Executive Officer there.

Omotoso, Kole (1943–)

Playwright, novelist, essayist, actor, critic and journalist. Omotoso was born in Akure, studied French and Arabic at Ibadan University, and took his doctoral degree in Edinburgh in 1968. Committed to a specific socialist ideology, his plays include the part-absurdist and part-political *The Curse* (1976) and *Shadows in the Horizon* (1975), in which he explores the vulgarity of bourgeois wealth and the essence of revolutionary action by the oppressed. In the former work a servant revolts against his greedy master, kills him and his erstwhile colleague and takes over the estate. Professional praise-singers who praised their first master return to laud their new one, and the cycle continues. The play states explicitly that a revolution that aims at achieving the values of those removed will bring no change but perpetuate evil in greater proportion. Between 1981 and 1982 Omotoso produced for the Nigerian Television Authority thirty serial episodes entitled *Life Off the Course*.

Onwueme, Tess (1955–)

Nigerian playwright, director and critic. Onwueme was born in Ogwashi-Uku, Bendel state. She studied at the Universities of Ife and Benin, completing a doctoral thesis on the work of FEMI OSOFISAN. As a lecturer at the Federal University of Technology, Owerri, she founded an innovative theatre group whose members comprised junior (non-academic) staff and science students, and which was responsible for the first performances of many of her early plays. Onwueme's work is notable for its constant experimentation with form, language and theatrical technique. *A Hen Too Soon* (1983) and *The Broken Calabash* (1984) are essentially realistic domestic dramas on familiar themes in Nigerian theatre, such as parental opposition to love partnerships. *The Desert Encroaches* (1985) and *Ban Empty Barn* (1989) are extremely ambitious animal allegories, audacious in their use of language, exploring political and economic oppression both within the authoritarian African nation-state and at an international level. These early plays achieved high prominence, with productions at the National Theatre and on Nigerian television. *Cattle Egret Versus Nama* (1989) is a short play of ferocious impact set in a Nigerian prison cell. Two much longer works, *The Reign of Wazobia* and *Legacies* (both 1988), scrutinize traditional value systems and structures of government: the two plays focus, respectively, on women's organization and on the relationship between African and African-American communities. Since 1990 Onwueme has been teaching in the USA.

Osofisan, Femi (1946–)

Nigerian playwright, poet, novelist and critic. Osofisan was born in Iloto, Ijebu-Ode, Ogun state. He studied French at Ibadan University, then pursued postgraduate studies at the Universities of Dakar and Paris. He took his doctorate at Ibadan, and after lecturing there in French and theatre arts was appointed professor of theatre arts at the University of Benin in 1983. After a period in journalism, helping to found the most reputable daily in Nigeria today, the *Guardian*, he returned to Ibadan where he is now professor of theatre arts.

Osofisan's critical writing reflects his exposure to some of the Marxist criticism and structuralist philosophy in French intellectual circles in the 1960s and 70s. With fellow Nigerian playwrights like KOLE OMOTOSO and left-wing critics like Biodun Jeyifo, Osofisan has helped shape a new discourse which places contemporary political class analysis at the centre of the literary and theatrical enterprise. This has involved a critique of the work of established writers such as WOLE SOYINKA and J. P. CLARK-BEKEDEREMO. Two of his plays *No More the Wasted Breed* (1981) and *Another Raft* (1989), are direct replies to Soyinka's *The Strong Breed* and Clark-Bekederemo's *The Raft*, respectively. Osofisan rejects the older playwrights' metaphysics and what is regarded as their unreconstructed view of myth and African history. Yet he does not simply ignore or discard myth: rather, as the critic David Richards has noted, 'he subjects tradition to scrutiny and reinterpretation'. He admits the persuasive-

ness of Soyinka's drama, a legacy it is impossible for him not to engage with, however critical that engagement may be.

Osofisan's own vigorous analysis of materialism and culture in Africa appeals to many Nigerian students and young writers in the post-oil-boom, SAP (Structural Adjustment Programme)-ridden 1990s. In the later 1970s the discourse was publicly extended in the periodicals *Afriscope* and *Positive Review*. Taking up where Soyinka's *Ch'Indaba* (formerly *Transition*) left off, it attempted to situate art, history and literature in a class-based analysis of Nigeria's social formation. At the same time, Osofisan's writings on culture are profoundly concerned to analyse the aesthetic. This binary emphasis obtains in his plays also: as Jeyifo has said, 'a consummate *artistry* [exists] side by side with a passionate advocacy of social justice'.

Performances of Femi Osofisan's plays on Nigerian university campuses have reinforced his popularity among radical students and intellectuals. *Red is the Freedom Road* (1969) is a play on the Yoruba wars of the 19th century, a subject also tackled by OLA ROTIMI and WALE OGUNYEMI. This was followed by the publication of a satirical novel, *Kolera Kolej* (1975; later dramatized and produced at Ibadan by DEXTER LYNDERSAY (see Trinidad and Tobago)); and then by a widely performed version of Gogol's *The Government Inspector* entitled *Who's Afraid of Solarin?* (1978). This brilliantly transforms Gogol's satirical model to dissect the behaviour of Nigeria's governing elites.

In 1976 appeared the first of three plays that established Osofisan's reputation as one of Nigeria's foremost dramatists, *The Chattering and the Song*. This complex and subtle play explores the relationship of a number of intellectuals towards a revolutionary movement – and towards each other as their real affiliations emerge. This was followed in 1978 by the first production of *Once upon Four Robbers*, an attack on the Nigeria military government. Niyi Osundare has commented: 'The play revolves around a magnificent irony: the real armed robbers [the soldiers] are those set to catch the four robbers.' In 1979 his most ambitious work to date, *Morountodun*, was premiered: the first version had a running time of four to five hours. The play combines the myth of the heroine Moremi with the 1969 uprising of farmers in western Nigeria. The synthesis is made in the context of an enactment of the latter by a 'Theatre Director' and 'Actor', in order to show 'the urgent necessity to deploy the energies of the past to struggle against and defeat the forces of oppression and injustice that ensnare our people in the purgatory of poverty and insecurity' (*Positive Review*).

Osofisan's satirical flair was shown again in *Midnight Hotel* (1982), his adaptation of Feydeau's farce, *Paradise Hotel*. In his later plays he addresses his major themes – the gaining of self-knowledge, the contestation of oppression, the ability to achieve an undistorted reading of history – through a remarkable range of different storytelling techniques, always thoughtful and yet never ponderous or too wordy. Music and the imaginative use of role-play episodes are primary resources for his theatre, as is comedy, though the latter arguably sometimes clouds his work's critical pungency. Most of his plays are published and some are amongst the most frequently performed in Nigeria (especially *Once upon Four Robbers* and the short play *The Oriki of a Grasshopper*).

Among the most important of Osofisan's later plays are three that occupied him through the 1980s: *Farewell to a Cannibal Rage* (published 1986), *Esu and the Vagabond Minstrels* and *Aringindin and the Nightwatchmen* (both 1991). *Esu*, a highly entertaining piece that has gained a popular audience, uses Yoruba myth to explore individual conscientiousness; *Aringindin* is a grim investigation of the nurturing of violence as a method of, and pretext for, totalitarian government. *Yungba Yungba and the Dance Contest* (1993), which has an all-female cast, is a display piece for Osofisan's stagecraft; it also exemplifies, as Chris Dunton has said, his 'firm, sober confidence in the value of debate and reflection'. After this play, Osofisan's theatre seems likely to head in new directions: during the early 1990s he has begun work on an ambitious project, a trilogy on Nkrumah, Sekou Touré and Cabral. The first part, a massive play on Nkrumah in exile, was completed in 1993.

Performing Arts Company of the Centre for Nigerian Cultural Studies

Nigerian professional performing arts company, based in Zaria in northern Nigeria and subsidized by the Cultural Institute of Ahmadu Bello University (ABU). The company is loosely connected through its personnel with the ABU Studio Theatre – the 'Mud Theatre' – purpose-built by traditional Hausa craftsmen in the style of a Hausa compound, with decorated mud and thatch, as a facility for African theatre research.

The Performing Arts Company of the Centre for Nigerian Cultural Studies (CNCS) travels within Nigeria and abroad. It has its own training school which exports talent and expertise around Nigeria and which has acted as a catalyst in establishing the performing arts all over northern Nigeria. DEXTER LYNDERSAY (see Trinidad and Tobago) established the company in Kano; he was succeeded by Andrew Horn who with Peter Badejo, the dancer and choreographer, created the dance-mime *Fadakarwa* in 1976, which achieved notable success. The CNCS Performing Arts Company also included the brilliant actor and playwright Kasimu Yero, whose weekly television plays in Hausa, which he devised through improvisation with a group of actors, had huge ratings in the 70s. Other CNCS actors were absorbed into film-acting, such as the late Umaru Ladan who starred in the film of his own play *Shehu Umar*. In the 1980s Badejo's choreography combined with the Nigerian-music experiments of jazz musician Yusuf Lateef to create balletic pieces which greatly extend a Hausa-Fulani and partly Islamic performance aesthetic.

The 'Mud Theatre' has enabled drama students from all over Nigeria to develop a pidgin drama for the Nigerian cities. The plays of 'Segun Oyekunle (who has now branched into film-making) and of Tunde Lakoju were premiered in the theatre in the late 1970s.

Rotimi, Ola (1936–)

Nigerian playwright and theatre director. Born in Sapele in the Niger delta, in what is now Bendel state, Rotimi went to Boston and Yale Universities in the USA. He returned to Nigeria to a research fellowship at Ife University, where he founded the Ori Olokun Acting Company (later the Ori Olokun Players). The popularity of this theatre in the late 1960s and early 70s was the result not only of the talents of Rotimi as writer and director, but also of the considerable musical talents of the composer Akin Euba. Rotimi began writing plays in America. *Our Husband Has Gone Mad Again* was premiered at Yale, directed by Jack Landau, in 1966 (although it was published only in 1977, after Rotimi had made his theatrical reputation in Nigeria). A comedy, set in a Nigeria in the throes of a general election, it concerns a retired Nigerian army major who has made money in cocoa farming and is now determined to get himself and his party elected to power – so that he can make more money.

The comedy arises mainly out of the major's marital condition: he has two Nigerian wives about whom he has failed to tell his 'abroad' wife. She unexpectedly flies into Lagos as the election is in progress. The play has an earthy wit, often appropriately communicated through pidgin phrases. This work is especially interesting in the light of Rotimi's play *If*, which was first performed in Port Harcourt, Nigeria, in 1979 (published in 1983). In *If* the action takes place in the middle of a general election but, unlike *Our Husband* of thirteen years before, *If* has a serious political intent and is wholly concerned with a group of ordinary working-class Nigerians. The electoral candidate, who is also their oppressive land-lord, is depicted as an evil figure (seen only at the beginning and end of the play) against whom good people struggle and fail. The racy dialogue, as in *Our Husband*, reflects the linguistic texture of Nigeria.

However, the difference in tone between the two plays could not be more striking. The transition is perhaps an indication of Rotimi's disillusionment with the political processes in Nigeria and the increasing politicization of his dramatic art. The play also contains a number of elements characteristic of his craft as a playwright: a strong theatricality combined with touches of melodrama (such as the death of the little boy from asthma, and the use of music to heighten emotion), which builds to a tragic and moving climax.

One of Rotimi's best-known plays is *The Gods are Not to Blame*, a Nigerian version of Sophocles' *Oedipus the King*. It was the first production of the Ori Olokun Acting Company in 1968, and published in 1971. Rotimi has hinted that the play is an allegory of the Nigerian civil war: the ethnic pride of Nigerians, and not fate or 'the gods', was responsible for the slide into war in 1966. Its first performance during the civil war might well have been read in this way; its later success comes from its appealing theatricality.

Rotimi then turned to creating Nigerian history on stage, and from a Nigerian perspective. *Kurunmi* (premiered by Ori Olokun in 1969; published in 1971) depicts an aspect of the internecine wars amongst the Yorubas in the mid-19th century, and creates an Aristotelian tragic hero out of the Yoruba commander Kurunmi. This was followed in 1971 by *Ovonramwen Nogbaisi*, enacting the sack of Benin by the British in 1897 and the exile of the eponymous Oba. Again, the playwright's vision is tragic, though historically the central figure, the Oba, is less susceptible to this heroic treatment.

Rotimi moved from Ife to Port Harcourt, to become head of drama at the university there;

A libation scene in *Kurunmi* by Ola Rotimi.

and he formed a new company of players to stage his work. Here *If* was premiered, preceded by *Holding Talks: An Absurdist Drama* (published in 1979), which was popularly received. *Hopes of the Living Dead*, produced in Ibadan in 1985, is based on the life of Ikoli Harcourt-Whyte, who was a leper from the age of nineteen: 'Leprosy ... is a grand metaphor for a social, political and psychological disease which, though daunting and stigmatising, can be tackled,' the critic Osundare has noted. One of the most striking features of Rotimi's drama has been his development of a 'trans-Nigerian idiom' through the use of indigenous theatre means such as music, specific musical instruments, gesture, dance, chant. In *Hopes of the Living Dead* this takes on a new dimension, as he saturates the play with dialogue in a dozen Nigerian languages. As the lepers strive to communicate with each other, to achieve effective solidarity, Rotimi creates a powerful image for group commitment.

In 1991 he left the University of Port Harcourt to found, the following year, a professional theatre company, African Theatre Cradle, based in Ife. The group gave performances of a number of his plays in prestige venues in Lagos. ACT folded in 1993 through lack of funds.

Sofola, Zulu (1935–)

Nigerian playwright and director. Sofola was born at Isele-Uku in Bendel state, and studied at the Catholic University, Virginia, USA, and at the University of Ibadan, researching into traditional Nigerian religious and political systems. Her plays employ elements of magic, myth and ritual to examine conflicts between traditionalism and modernism in which male supremacy persists. Her most frequently performed plays are *Wedlock of the Gods* (1972) and *The Sweet Trap* (1977). In the former, the heroine experiences a sense of liberation after the death of a husband she has never loved. She and her new lover are hunted down after breaking their society's marital taboos. *The Sweet Trap* has a contemporary setting, but again examines a conflict of authority in marital relations. Sofola's treatment of women's rights and of class difference here have sharply divided critical opinion: does her work offer a blueprint for liberation, or is it inherently conservative? *King Emene* (1974), *Old Wines are Tasty* (1981), *Memories in the Moonlight* (1986) and *Song of a Maiden* (1991) all examine traditional values and conflicting notions of authority. Other plays range outside her primary interest in traditional value systems. *The Wizard of Law* (1975) is a highly skilful adaptation of the medieval French play, *Maistre Pierre Pathelin*. *The Operators* (unpublished) deals with a familiar theme in Nigerian theatre – armed robbery. Sofola is professor of performing arts, University of Ilorin, Nigeria.

Sowande, Bode (1948–)

Nigerian playwright, director and novelist. Sowande was born in Abeokuta, and studied at the Universities of Ife, Nigeria and Sheffield. He is a founding member of the Ori Olokun Players and a scriptwriter in WOLE SOYINKA's Orisun Theatre. The first work of Sowande's to gain widespread attention was the trilogy comprising *The Night Before, Farewell to Babylon* and *Flamingoes* (produced 1972–82). These plays deal with the totalitarian state and with problems of leadership and loyalty amongst a radical group, first seen as students, who contest oppressive authority. Increasingly through the 1980s Sowande's plays embraced Brechtian techniques of dislocation, which readily graft on to the Nigerian theatre's convention of mixing song, music, dance and role-play episodes. These techniques are seen in *Afamako – the Workhorse* (1978), a play dealing with the exploitation of labour, and even more in the satirical *Monkey's Gold* (1993). *Tornadoes Full of Dreams* (1990) is a powerful, large-scale treatment of the Haitian revolution, commissioned by the French Cultural Centre in Lagos to commemorate the bicentenary of the French Revolution. The same organization commissioned *Arede Owo* (1990), a free adaptation of Molière's *The Miser*. Sowande's increasingly bold stagecraft and growing use of song and dance are seen in *Mammy-Water's Wedding* and *Ajantala-Pinocchio* (both 1992, unpublished). He taught at the University of Ibadan until 1990, when he resigned to devote more time to Odu Themes Meridian, which was transformed in 1993 into a fully professional and commercial theatre company.

Soyinka, Wole (1934–)

Nigerian playwright, poet and novelist; generally recognized as Africa's greatest living playwright, and considered by some critics to be one of the foremost writers of his generation. Soyinka was born in Aké, in what was then the

Wole Soyinka.

Western Region of Nigeria, the son of a canon in the Anglican Church. He has recreated his childhood in a reminiscence, *Aké: The Years of Childhood* (1981). The tensions between the Christian home and the Yoruba *egungun* masqueraders (see Introduction, MASQUERADES IN AFRICA) among the people have helped create the dynamic of his poetic vision. He treated the conflict early in his career in a radio play about an adolescent emerging into a tense world of confused adults, *Camwood on the Leaves*, broadcast on Nigerian radio in 1960 and on the BBC World Service in 1965. *Aké* is more the sustained recollection, in maturity, of the writer's youth.

Soyinka went to University College, Ibadan, and then to Leeds University, England, in 1956. He became involved in the new drama at the Royal Court Theatre, London, where he became a playreader in 1959–60. With a company of actors whom he had brought together, he developed three experimental pieces there. While he was still in England, two of his plays were produced in Nigeria: *The Swamp-Dwellers*, about the moral realignment necessary to make the land productive and the community whole in rural Nigeria; and *The Lion and the Jewel*, a comedy in which a village chief and the schoolteacher vie with each other for the hand of the village belle. Soyinka returned to Nigeria in 1960 and founded the 1960 Masks, which presented his first major play, *A Dance of the Forests*, for the independence celebrations. The play was not what was expected. It offered a critique of pre-colonial history while diminishing the cultural significance of the colonial period. Many of the themes of Soyinka's later plays are present in this complex work: the notion of the three parallel and interlocking worlds of the past, the present and the future (the dead, the living and the unborn); Nature, conceived metaphysically in a romantic vision of the moral imperative laid upon the questing hero;

the need for sacrifice; the role of the artist in society; the presence of the god Ogun.

The theatre company the 1960 Masks acted as an umbrella, administratively, for the younger, fully professional Orisun Theatre Company, whose actors Soyinka trained between 1962 and 1965. The company premiered two series of sketches containing some pungent political satire: *The New Republican* and *Before the Blackout*. During these years some of his major plays appeared in print, following performances in Nigeria: Their publication acted as a spur to young dramatists in other countries in anglophone East and West Africa: *The Trials of Brother Jero*, a satirical comedy recounting the adventures, sexual and otherwise, of a mendicant Christian preacher on Lagos's Bar Beach; *The Strong Breed*, an ironical exposition of the context for human sacrifice today; and *The Road*, also concerned, metaphysically, with sacrifice, but in the context of wanton death on Nigeria's roads and the rubbishing by society of a lumpen working

A scene from Soyinka's *The Road*, Talawa Theatre Company, London, 1992.

class. *The Road* suggests that in modern Nigeria the *egungun* masquerade can offer a Nigerian audience a more contemporary discourse than can a naturalistically presented materialism. The mask can discover a meaning for those at the base of society for their wasted lives and random deaths – even though the class-based nature of their oppression remains 'hidden' in the play.

In 1965 Soyinka published his first novel, *The Interpreters*, about, again, meaning in the lives and deaths of a group of young Nigerian artists and intellectuals. He also had two plays broadcast by the BBC, London. Then, in the October, he was arrested for allegedly seizing the Western Region radio studios and making a political broadcast disputing the published results of the recent elections. He was acquitted in December. His next play, *Kongi's Harvest*, about the abuse of power and the tyrant's ability to corrupt a whole people, was performed at the Dakar Festival of Negro Arts in 1966. It was published in 1967, as was his collection of poems *Idanre and Other Poems*.

Nigeria slid into civil war. In August 1967 Soyinka was detained without trial, and released only in October 1969. He made notes during this period of incarceration, secretly and was able to publish them on his release under the title *The Man Died* (1972) – 'The man dies,' he wrote, 'in all who keep silent in the face of tyranny.' This work forms a quartet: with his next major play, *Madmen and Specialists* (premiered in Connecticut, USA, 1970); with another collection of poems, *A Shuttle in the Crypt* (1971); and with the novel, *Season of Anomy* (1973). *Madmen and Specialists* is set in the civil war – also known as the Biafran War – and is an intensely moral play about man's responsibility to his fellow men, in his control both of his own nature and of an external Nature. The quartet shows how Soyinka's intense vision of people corrupted and debased by power-play transcends any single genre, moving vividly through them all.

After his release in 1969, Soyinka went into exile. He became editor of the cultural and political magazine *Ch'Indaba* (formerly *Transition*), which he intermittently edited from Ghana between 1970 and 1975. He was appointed professor of comparative literature at the University of Ife, but was not able to take up the position. He wrote for the National Theatre in London a version of *The Bacchae of Euripides* (the title of his play), which was performed in London in 1973. He had a visiting professorship at Sheffield University and a fellowship at Churchill College, Cambridge. Out of his reaction to this last experience came a collection of essays, *Myth, Literature and the African World* (1976), a theorizing of African aesthetics. This important text develops, among other things, the relationship of myth to performance today. Soyinka has a vision of the transformation of the physicalities of space and time in the act of performance. In particular, he explores the significance of Ogun – the god of iron, war and creative fire – in the Yoruba pantheon. He is seen by Soyinka as the embodiment of contradiction; he is the original sacrifice, the one who dares chaos and the abyss. In connection with the concept of the co-existence of the three worlds of the dead, the living and the unborn, Soyinka emphasizes the importance of the masquerade for a new moral consciousness: through the rites of passage there is 'movement of transition' between these worlds, which open upon each other. The mask – and, by extension, the modern actor – can actualize this metaphysic.

While at Cambridge Soyinka also wrote *Death and the King's Horseman* (1975). This play reworks a moment in Nigeria's colonial past from inside the Yoruba metaphysic: it is about the halting of the ritual suicide of the equerry of the Alafin of Oyo by the local British district officer, in 1946. The incident had already been handled in an opera by DURO LADIPO. The play in performance is the praxis of Soyinka's theory. Together, theory and drama are a summation of his work up to his return to Nigeria. Many of the plays of this period require the dia-

George Harris in Soyinka's *Death and the King's Horseman*, Royal Exchange Theatre, Manchester, 1990.

logue to carry the burden of the playwright's philosophical preoccupations. The writing is dense and Soyinka has been criticized for overloading the language – through his play on words, control of rhythm and assonance, and with metaphor piled on brilliant metaphor. His own sensibility often seems to outstrip his audience's.

He returned to Nigeria, to Ife, in 1976. After directing a production of *Death and the King's Horseman* there in the same year, he set about generating a new drama. The Guerilla Theatre Unit, based at the University of Ife, presented plays and sketches attacking corruption and political oppression; eschewing formal stage presentation, the Unit operated on a 'hit-and-run' basis, mounting its satirical playlets in car parks and markets and at street corners. Soyinka has always seen this type of theatre as a necessary activity, parallel to the metaphysical explorations of plays such as *The Road* and *Death and the King's Horseman*. A related production is his recording 'Unlimited Liability Company' (1983), which satirizes the corruption and hypocrisy of the Shehu Shagari regime. One song in particular, the caustic 'Etiko Revo Wetin?', became a popular hit.

In December 1977 Soyinka produced *Opera Wonyosi*, a Nigerian amalgam of Gay's *The Beggar's Opera* and Brecht's *Threepenny Opera*. The play is a full-frontal satirical attack on Bokassa, the self-crowned emperor of the short-lived Central African Empire, and, at the same time, an attack on the values of the Nigerian petty bourgeoisie who benefit materially from such tyrants. The onslaught was continued in his next work, *A Play of Giants* (1985). Using Genet's *The Balcony* as a model, Soyinka parodies some of Africa's worst modern tyrants – in particular, Idi Amin of Uganda. The play also attacks the Superpowers and the United Nations, which he sees as sanctioning the megalomania and butchery of these dictators. *Requiem for a Futurologist* (1985) is a Swiftian satire on the cult of bogus fortune tellers and astrologers, with a witty exposure of false prophets – who make Jero (of *The Trials of Brother Jero* and *Jero's Metamorphosis* (1973)) seem positively benign – manipulating a gullible public. These plays, and the work of the Guerilla Theatre Unit, are complemented by Soyinka's film *Blues for a Prodigal* (1985), in which he attacks the power-play and corruption of the civilian government of Shagari. Banned in Nigeria, the film was screened privately in London in 1985 on the occasion of his Herbert Read Memorial Lecture, in which he reaffirmed his commitment to a political praxis in his dramatic art.

Soyinka was awarded the Nobel Prize for

Literature in 1986. The occasion provided a fresh opportunity for those critics who see his art as elitist to condemn him for 'writing for the West', but it also occasioned considerable and widespread national pride that Nigeria had 'bagged' Africa's first Nobel. Soyinka has retained a high profile in Nigerian public consciousness ever since, with his work (until 1993) as chairman of the Road Safety Corps and with his frequent public comments on human rights abuses on the part of Babangida's military regime. Since the mid-1980s, Soyinka has written little new work for the theatre. His major publications have been the poetry collection *Mandela's Earth* (1990) and a fictional extension of *Aké*, a study of his father's circle of friends entitled *Isara: A Voyage Around Essay* (1989). *Art, Dialogue and Outrage* (1988) is a major collection of his essays on drama, literature and criticism, which offers many insights into the world-view that underlies his theatre. A new play for radio, *A Scourge of Hyacinths*, was broadcast by the BBC in 1991; *From Zia with Love*, first performed in Siena, Italy, in 1992, is an expansion from this play. Here Soyinka focuses once more on corruption and on civil rights abuses under Nigeria's military regime: in common with many other Nigerian plays – notably

Segun Oyekunle's masterly *Katakata for Sofahead* – the action takes place in a prison cell.

Soyinka is a political playwright; but, rather than being didactic, his work demonstrates the dialectic within the term 'political art'. He thinks politically, and can see no other way of thinking as an artist in Africa today. Thus, the greater Soyinka's commitment to his art, the more political it becomes; and the greater his commitment to praxis, the more artistically compelling are the plays which come out of his experience.

Unibadan Masques [University of Ibadan's School of Drama Acting Company]
Nigerian professional theatre company, subsidized by the University of Ibadan. It has encouraged the development of Nigerian theatre by giving professional performances of new Nigerian plays, and by linking these to detailed research of traditional performance, epitomized in WALE OGUNYEMI's 'total theatre' plays. The company was founded in 1967 as part of the School of Drama in the university. Its first director, Geoffrey Axworthy, was succeeded by WOLE SOYINKA, who could not take up his appointment because he had been detained without trial during the civil war. On Soyinka's instructions, DEXTER LYNDERSAY (see Trinidad and Tobago), with the help of tutors in the School of Drama, set up the six-month crash programme of training which brought a company of twelve actors into being, six of whom had had training already in Soyinka's own Orisun Theatre.

Even while training was in progress, the Company performed weekly on television in the Orisun Television Series, directed by Dapo Adelugba, in order to meet some of its financial commitments. When Soyinka was released in 1969 he took over the directing and, together with Adelugba, took the troupe to Waterford, Connecticut, where they premiered Soyinka's new play *Madmen and Specialists* (August 1970).

Bibliography

Dapo Adelugba *Before Our Very Eyes: Tribute to Wole Soyinka*, Ibadan, 1987; Martin Banham, *A Critical View on Wole Soyinka's 'The Lion and the Jewel'*, London, 1981; James Gibbs, (ed.), *Critical Perspectives on Wole Soyinka*, Washington DC, 1980, London, 1981; *Wole Soyinka*, London, 1986; Eldred Jones, *The Writing of Wole Soyinka*, London, 1988; Ketu Katrak, *Wole Soyinka and Modern Tragedy: A Study of Dramatic Theory and Practice*, Westport CT, 1986; Obi Maduakor, *Wole Soyinka: An Introduction to his Writing*, New York, 1986; Gerald Moore, *Wole Soyinka*, London, 1978; Oyin Ogunba, *The Movement of Transition: A Study of the Plays of Wole Soyinka*, Ibadan, 1975; Derek Wright, *Wole Soyinka Revisited*, New York, 1993.

The Company was disbanded in 1971, then formally reconstituted in October 1974 as Unibadan Masques, with Lyndersay as its director. In its first season it presented a musical review by Ogunyemi, *Day of Deities*, and FEMI OSOFISAN's *Kolera Kolej*. Adelugba succeeded as director, directing Ogunyemi's *Langbodo* for FESTAC in 1977 (see Introduction), and taking it on tour in Europe in 1985. The group has also staged plays by ZULU SOFOLA and Tunde Aiyegbusi, and has introduced, as well as Osofisan, new writers like BODE SOWANDE and Bode Osanyin. It was with the help of the *mise-en-scène* talents of Demas Nwoko (stage and scenic design) that they were able to develop as playwrights. Nwoko subsequently set up his own fully professional New Culture Studios, which designed theatres and furniture and offered in-house training in the plastic and performance arts. These three theatre practitioners – Soyinka, Lyndersay and Nwoko – have made a considerable contribution to the present direction and status of theatre within Nigeria.

Yoruba Travelling Theatre

For some three decades, from the mid-1950s, the most widespread theatrical enterprise in Nigeria. The Yoruba Travelling Theatre attained the status of a movement with a sense of group identity within, as B. Jeyifo has noted, a 'divergent and distinct stock of conventions, staging techniques and modes of organisation'. This corporateness was recognized by the founding and nurturing, by the late HUBERT OGUNDE (d.1990), of an umbrella structure called the Association of Theatre Practitioners of Nigeria (ATPN), to which most of the troupes belonged. After three decades spent taking theatre to the people, from the early 1980s onwards the Yoruba Travelling Theatre turned increasingly from live performance to film, television and video production. By the early 1990s live performance has become a rarity; though companies continue to thrive, they now work almost exclusively through electronic media. The term 'Yoruba Travelling Theatre' is now, therefore, something of a misnomer. It has been retained here, however, because there is substantial continuity between the aesthetic and theatrical methodology of the component companies' earlier live performances and those of their current video and television productions.

In its modern form, the Yoruba Travelling Theatre movement's professional existence is just fifty years old, having taken off with Ogunde's 'concert party' in 1945. But its genesis must be seen in the centuries-old religious and secular oral performing arts of the Yoruba, blending with the performances and entertainments which evolved out of the contacts with Western European culture.

Historically, the Yoruba have a long theatre tradition. As Bruce King and other critics of African theatre have established, the 'preference for drama among Yoruba ... has a tribal basis. Yorubas often speak of their various forms of masquerade [see Introduction, MASQUERADES IN AFRICA] and ritual as dramatic art.' The ritualist origin of the Yoruba theatre has even been traced to the 'theatrogenic' nature of a number of the deities in the Yoruba pantheon, such as Obatala the god of creation, Ogun the god of creativeness and Sango the god of lightning, whose 'cults of worship', as Jeyifo has commented, are vitally connected 'with drama and theatre and their symbolic and psychological uses'. WOLE SOYINKA tells us that both Obatala and Ogun are prototype 'personalities' in the emergence of Yoruba drama. But the rituo-secular protoform of the modern Yoruba Theatre is the Alarinjo tradition, the most advanced form of the traditional theatre among the Yoruba people. The *Alarinjo* is an itinerant professional troupe of masked dancer-mummers. They present satirical skits assembled from a range of stereotypical characters, employing music, mime, drama, acrobatics and spectacle. *Alarinjo* is the predominant influence on the modern Yoruba

Travelling Theatre, to which it bequeaths its structural and thematic characteristics. European-derived influences include operetta, variety shows and, especially, the biblical dramas that were performed by Lagosian social and church societies from the turn of the century and well into the period when Ogunde was developing his stagecraft.

Initially, the term 'operatic' applied to the Travelling Theatre's performance mode especially during the first decade of Ogunde's concert-party enterprise between 1945 and the mid-50s, when the limited dialogue linked singing in the tradition of opera. But the predominant mode of the Travelling Theatre later changed, with the performance being delivered through elaborate and eloquent acted dialogue and robust action. The essential Yoruba Travelling Theatre is dramatic rather than musical or operatic. The other common, and more appropriate, appellation of 'folk-theatre' derives from the Theatre's cross-class character as opposed to the elitist 'high-culture' literary theatre. The Yoruba Travelling Theatre is primarily a popular cultural expression and secondarily, though no less importantly, theatrical and dramatic expression. (Jeyifo, 1984)

Notable scholars of this theatre movement have ascribed to it an almost inviolable conventional format, viewing the Yoruba Travelling Theatre as a structural derivative of the performance idioms of traditional Yoruba art forms (specifically the *Alarinjo* theatre, the *Ewi* poetic chants and the performances of the *egungun* society), with an 'opening glee', the 'play proper' and 'closing glee'. This format was imposed on the modern Travelling Theatre, and to deviate from it was seen as an aberration – in critic Ebun Clark's words, 'a dissociation of content with form'. At best, this model may be proposed as a means of delineating a certain aesthetic specific to the Yoruba Travelling Theatre movement, which distinguishes it in all its divergent forms. This aesthetic comprises (1) the language of the performance, (2) the uti-lization and exploitation of the indigenous traditional artistic resources, and (3) the basic underscoring *oeuvre* which informs the practitioners' presentation. But apart from most of Ogunde's productions, the other stalwarts of the Yoruba Travelling Theatre have hardly adhered to the traditional format; MOSES OLAIYA ADEJUMA, still arguably the greatest commercial success story of this tradition, is radical to the point of having introduced into the start of his performances film projections of foreign documentary and other cinematic productions. Indeed, this novelty was the genesis of the eventual abandonment by Yoruba Travelling Theatre of live performance in favour of film and video.

Yoruba is the primary language of communication and performance of the Yoruba Travelling Theatre troupes, performing in the Yoruba sub-region of over 20 million Nigerians as well as in neighbouring states. (A few troupes, including Hubert Ogunde's, used to perform in pidgin in eastern and western states to non-Yoruba audiences.) Aesthetically, the competence in discourse characteristic of Yoruba oral literature – one of the most highly articulate in Africa – also informs the theatre. The success of the performance is determined by the dexterity of the artists, and their fidelity to the Yoruba verbal arts. Hence, the less illusionistic their theatrical display – which they achieve through the simultaneous use of drumming, singing, costuming, acrobatics and movement, blended with the Yoruba verbal arts of oratorical chant, vocal music, word-play and poetry, mime and costume – the more authentic the performance and the more the audiences value it. As Jeyifo has observed, the Yoruba Travelling Theatre is a 'highly liberating, actor-oriented theatre where the outcome of any performance is a factor of the mode of rapport between the actors on stage and the popular audience'.

Essential to the Yoruba Travelling Theatre is the moralist stance of most of its practitioners (beginning with Ogunde himself, and especially Kola Ogunmola). This moralism is a reflection of the living experiences of the popular masses at whom the performances are aimed. Indeed, the artistic success of the troupes' performances is determined, mainly, by the degree to which the plays impress the popular audiences and deal with their reality. Issues that carry concrete and direct economic, political and social implications for the lives of their audiences attract the troupes' attention. Hunger, squalor, social deviance, corruption, and all the other issues of the daily working lives of the people, provide the Theatre with its main themes. At the same time the social norms projected by this theatre can be seen, in certain respects, to be highly conservative and have been questioned by radical English-language dramatists such as FEMI OSOFISAN. The Yoruba Travelling Theatre's tendency to stereotype has ideological implications: in the case, for instance, of its frequently dismissive treatment of independently minded or non-submissive female characters.

Only a few of the troupes and the artists of the Yoruba Travelling Theatre are well known –

A concert-party troupe entering Bida, northern Nigeria, in 1970.

Ogunde, Olaiya, Jimoh Aliyu and a few others. However, by 1988 there existed nearly 150 troupes in the movement, with the body of plays in the various repertoires numbering several thousands. The companies constitute themselves into their professional guild, founded by its doyen and patron Hubert Ogunde, the Association of Theatre Practitioners of Nigeria (ATPN). They are not all necessarily made up of full-time employees: many of the practitioners who give their name to a company hire artists on an *ad hoc* basis.

During the period when the Yoruba Travelling Theatre was mainly devoted to live performance, companies would go out from their home base (usually Lagos) to reach all corners of Nigeria, as well as West African countries such as GHANA, TOGO and BENIN, to become the most mobile theatre movement in African history. Each live performance was generally preceded by heavy publicity via radio and television advertising, newspaper items and notices, printed handbills and direct contact with troupe patrons. All these prepared the eager popular audiences, on whom the commercial success of the troupes depended. On the evening of the performance a rousing campaign would be staged on company buses, from which music and songs were broadcast. The performance was tailored to the environment and to the tastes of the specific audience, while the comedy and song, the dance and the skits, all reflected the trademarks of the particular troupe. The orchestras of most travelling theatre troupes blended European instruments with indigenous traditional ones, though some relied solely on Yoruba instruments. Some troupes opened their performance with comic dialogues and monologues alternating with ribald songs and dances.

Besides undertaking road tours, from 1959, when the first television studio in Africa, Western Nigerian Television (WNTV), was established, the Yoruba Travelling Theatre battled successfully to supplant foreign programmes on Nigerian television screens. The main electronic medium for spreading theatre, the radio, had been slow in taking off. Ogunde, and later Baba Sala (alias Moses Olaiya Adejumo), had significant exposure through the radio. But it was television that really gave prominence to the travelling theatre – from the broadcasting of live performances to the adaptation of Yoruba novels and historical documentaries into television dramas (for example, Oyin Adejobi's group appeared in *Ekuro Oloja*, while *Efunsetan Aniwura* featured Oshola Ogunshola's troupe, both on WNTV Ibadan).

From the late 70s practitioners of Yoruba Travelling Theatre began to experience constraints in live performance, and to seek other outlets. The most attractive was film. The reasons are not far to seek. Ade Afolayan had blazed the trail into the glamorous arena of movies with his *Ija Ominira*, and now, after over three decades on stage, Ogunde looked in that direction. The cinema provided a more satisfying medium, offering flexibility and limitless expansion in the content and range of their work. Awareness of the transitory nature of their productions – largely non-scripted and improvisational – drove the Yoruba Travelling Theatre to seek more permanent modes. Unlike stage productions, which may vanish after a few performances, films enjoy a high degree of permanence. All the major protagonists of the Yoruba theatre entered the film industry as a complementary enterprise to their main stagecraft.

A number of outstanding films result from this: after Afolayan's *Ija Ominira* came Moses Olaiya Adejumo's *Orun Mooru* and *Aare Agbaye*, and the remarkable and large-scale cinematic creations of Ogunde. Ogunde was the most accomplished professionally, recording his films on a permanent location, a film village that he built in Ososa, his home town. Having started in 1979 with a metaphysical Yoruba epic, *Aiye*, he followed rapidly with *Jaiyesimi*

(1980), *Aropin N'tenia* (1983) and *Ayanmo* (1988). The films of most of these practitioners tend to offer mystery and mysticism, with a large dose of magic and exoticism. They are full of macabre and grotesque images rooted in Yoruba mythology. The films revolve around the central theme of morality: the perennial conflict between good and evil, with good constantly triumphing. The films' titles reveal both their reliance on these themes and the need to attract the attention of potential customers with the lure of the sensational or scandalous: *Iya m l'aje* (*My Mother is a Witch*) and *Ashewo to re Mecca* (*A Prostitute Goes to Mecca*), for example.

In the early 1990s a further technological development has taken place, as the companies have moved away from reel film and turned to video. Some, such as Olaiya's, record on video for screening in cinema auditoriums, jealously guarding against piracy; others screen their videos over a year or two and then duplicate them for market retail. The more successful companies continue to work on television too.

Bibliography

J. Adedeji, 'The Church and the Emergence of the Nigerian Theatre', *Journal of the Historical Society of Nigeria*, 6, 1 and 4, 1971, and 'Alarinjo: the Traditional Yoruba Travelling Theatre', in *Theatre in Africa*, ed. O. Ogunba and A. Irele, Ibadan, 1978; K. Barber, 'Radical Conservatism in Yoruba Popular Plays', in *Drama and Theatre in Africa*, Bayreuth, 1986; E. Clark, *Hubert Ogunde: The Making of Nigerian Theatre*, Lagos, 1979; B. Jeyifo, *The Yoruba Popular Travelling Theatre of Nigeria*, Lagos, 1984; Y. Ogunbiyi, *Drama and Theatre in Nigeria*, Lagos, 1981; O. Rotimi, 'Drama', in *The Living Culture of Nigeria*, ed. S. O. Biobaku, Lagos, 1976; W. Soyinka, *Myth, Literature and the African World*, Cambridge, 1976.

SENEGAL

Senegal, formerly the capital of the French West African Federation and independent since 1960, has the longest tradition of modern theatre in French West Africa. And until the late 1970s, when the centre of dramatic production and theatre research moved to countries such as the Ivory Coast, the Congo and Mali, it was also the strongest.

Theatrical activity in Senegal goes back to before the First World War, when visiting troupes, on their way to South America, staged performances in Dakar to a mostly French expatriate audience. The subsequent founding in that country of the École William Ponty, and the large part that it devoted to theatrical activity, made of that school and, by extension, Senegal – as the drama historian Robert Cornevin has noted – the 'great laboratory of African drama'. Through the school's annual *fête d'art indigène* (festival of indigenous art), in particular, which presented dramatic works by student groups based on the history or folklore of their countries, Senegal became the centre of theatre activity in the Federation.

This role was reinforced in 1954 with the construction of the modest Théâtre du Palais, replaced in 1965 with the grand Théâtre Daniel Sorano, complete with a Conservatory of Dramatic Arts, an African ballet troupe, a theatre company proper and a traditional ensemble of *griots*. Under the direction of Sonar Senghor and with the collaboration of the French theatre producer and former pupil of Jacques Copeau, Raymond Hermantier, and of the Haitian playwright Gérard Chenet, the Daniel Sorano mounted performances as varied as the Senegalese CHEIK NDAO's *L'Exil d'Albouri* (*Albouri's Exile*, 1967), Shakespeare's *Macbeth* and Gogol's *The Government Inspector*

(1836), adapted by Senghor as *Monsieur Pots-de-vin et consorts* (*Mister Bribery and Company*). The 1966 first World Festival of Negro Arts in Dakar consecrated that city's reputation as a leading sub-Saharan capital of the modern arts and, with its cohorts of visiting troupes and their productions, acted as a stimulus to the creative activity of its theatre practitioners.

Senegal has given some notable works to French-language African dramatic literature, among them Amadou Cissé Dia's *Les Derniers Jours de Lat Dior suivi de la mort du Damel* (*The Last Days of Lat Dior Followed by the Death of The Damel*, 1966); Abdou Anta Ka's *Amazoulou* (1972); Cheik Ndao's *L'Exil d'Albouri* and *Le Fils de l'Almamy* (*The Son of the Almamy*, 1973); Thiérno Ba's *Bilbassy* (1980); Seyni Mbengue's *Le Procès de Lat Dior* (*The Trial of Lat Dior*, 1971); Ibrahim Sall's *Le Choix du Madior* (*The Choice of the Madior*, 1981), and not least Léopold Senghor's dramatic poem for two voices and a chorus, *Chaka* (1956). What these plays have in common is a preoccupation with the African past. But their treatment of it is not uniform; not only are there differences in technique, but there is also a sharp difference in the vision of the past presented in plays like Cissé Dia's and Anta Ka's written before independence, on the one hand, and the rest written after. Where the former's folklorish vision is consistent with that of official colonial history, the latter's is robustly nationalistic, idealizing ancient kings like Lat Dior (whom Cissé treats rather negatively), Albouri Ndiaye, Chaka and Samory Touré.

Some of Senegal's plays are technically distinguished. Ndao's *L'Exil d'Albouri*, for example, stands out in its epic quality created by the movement of crowds and the use of vast open spaces and battle scenes. It also conveys a high

Scene from the dramatization of a tale by Birago Diop, *L'Os de Mor Lam*, staged in Senegal in 1967 and subsequently adapted for Peter Brook's repertory of the Bouffes du Nord Théâtre, Paris.

sense of drama in its handling of situation and character. Ba's *Bilbassy* is striking in its music, which functions as an integral part of the action and not just as an exotic extra, while Abdou Anta Ka excels in the poetry of his works and in the theatricality of their language.

If Senegal's long cultural contacts with France enabled it to produce a leading modern theatre in the immediate pre-independence years and for almost a decade and a half later, it is those contacts that are also responsible for a certain sterility currently presented in that theatre. While elsewhere in French-speaking Africa creative energy is being channelled into ways of evolving a truly African theatre aesthetic derived from the traditional performing arts, Senegal, the home of negritude, continues paradoxically to produce historical dramas that merely nod politely at the African arts.

Ndao, Cheik (Sidi Ahmed) (1933–)
Senegalese dramatist and English teacher, educated in Senegal and at the University of

Swansea, Wales. The author of a volume of poetry, short stories and a novel, Ndao has also written five plays in French including one of the earliest francophone history plays and winner of the first prize in the 1969 Algiers Art Festival: *L'Exil d'Albouri* (*Albouri's Exile*, 1967). This play has the distinction among French-language history plays of being more than just a picturesque spectacle of song, dance and movement. It presents a unified plot with a solid core of moral dilemmas and individualized characters. His other plays include *Le Fils de l'Almany and La Case de l'homme* (*The Almamy's Son, The Hut of Manhood* (on the practice of circumcision), 1973); *L'île de Bahila* (*The Island of Bahila*, 1975); *Du Sang pour un trône* (*Blood for a Throne*, 1983) and *La Décision*, on the problems of race in the USA. Ndao's plays mostly deal with the resistance of African princes to French imperial conquest in the 19th century. He has also published two in English: *Tears for Tears* (1977) and *Love but Educate* (1978).

Bibliography

R. Cornevin, *Le Théâtre en Afrique noire et à Madagascar*, Paris, 1970; M. Diouf, 'Un baobab au milieu de la brousse: le théâtre de langue française', *Notre Librairie: La Littérature Sénégalaise*, 81, Oct./Dec. 1985; C. Wake, 'Senegal', in *The Cambridge Guide To World Theatre*, ed. M. Banham, Cambridge, 1988; C. Wake and M. Banham, *African Theatre Today*, London, 1976.

SIERRA LEONE

Sierra Leone, in West Africa, has been independent since 1961. The land on which its capital, Freetown, now stands was first settled in 1787 by a group of freed slaves from Britain. In 1792, about 1100 freed slaves, mostly from Nova Scotia, landed on the peninsula and founded Freetown. Christian with European acculturation, in the 19th century they later intermixed with much larger numbers of men and women whom British anti-slavery patrols had freed from illegal slave ships. Together, this group of settlers came to be known as the Creoles (now called Krios). They acquired formal education and were very British in outlook, but developed a language which has become the lingua franca of Sierra Leone: Krio.

The published drama of Sierra Leone largely reflects the urban black settler culture of the Freetown Krios. There is, first of all, a less secure base in the traditional roots of drama than obtains in NIGERIA or GHANA. However, a vibrant traditional performance culture persists among the indigenous ethnic groups. The Mende, for instance, have a vigorous story-telling tradition. But the character of the independence struggle precluded the emergence of the traditional culture as the means of expressing black aspirations. A Europeanized Krio culture was already in place.

Modern theatre in Sierra Leone has its origins in the 19th-century Church, which used drama as a means of elucidating Bible passages. This activity developed into a kind of variety-concert performance that came to be known as the 'pleasant Sunday afternoon gathering', with a drama sketch as its centrepiece. Up to the 1950s, it was the most popular form of entertainment in Freetown.

Apart from this, pre-independence Sierra Leone theatre was dominated by performances of published European and American plays. Notable exceptions were the works of Sierra Leonean writers including Gladys Caseley-Hayford and Professor N. J. G. Ballanta-Taylor in the 1930s, and John Akar in the 1950s. Caseley-Hayford dramatized folk-tales, while Ballanta-Taylor wrote 'African' operas. Akar wrote and produced plays which had distinctive African themes, enhanced by his use of song and dance. The production of his play *Valley without Echo* by the Hans Crescent Society in London in 1954 was described by one critic in *West African Review* as 'the first significant play about African village life'. Akar was also instrumental in setting up the Sierra Leone National Dance Troupe in 1963.

A moralizing critique of post-independence Sierra Leonean society is presented by the plays of the Freetown medical practitioner, R. Sarif Easmon: the prize-winning *Dear Parent and Ogre*, and *The New Patriots* (both 1965). The plays explore the private lives of the new Sierra Leonean political elite. Love affairs, corruption and matters of state are combined in tight plots with obvious moral lessons. A high-art reaction against what might be seen as a limiting naturalism is reflected in Gaston Bart-Williams's *The Drug*, an experimental drama which owes something to the influence of Peter Weiss's contemporary experimentation in German theatre, and was first broadcast on West German radio in 1972.

Perhaps the most important development in post-independence theatre in Sierra Leone is the emergence of KRIO THEATRE. This is the product of the pioneering work of Thomas Decker, whose translation of Shakespeare's *Julius Caesar* into Krio in 1964 marked the watershed in Sierra Leone theatre. Although Decker pioneered the introduction of Krio drama, it was Juliana John, Dele Charley (d.1993) and YULISA AMADU MADDY who spearheaded its development as an alternative class-based theatre. John wrote the first original full-length plays in Krio – *Na Mami born Am* and *I Day I nor Du* in 1966. Both had unusually long runs for the time, playing to packed houses in Freetown. Charley founded the Tabule Experimental Theatre in 1968, the group responsible for the popular Krio play *Titi Shine Shine* (1970) and the even more successful *The Blood of a Stranger*, performed more than twenty times between 1975 and 77 and entered for FESTAC in 1977 (see Introduction). Maddy founded the group Gbakanda Afrikan Tiata in Freetown in 1969, but because he then went to Zambia to train the new Zambian National Dance Troupe, it did not really take off until he returned to Freetown in 1974. He was head of radio drama before going to Zambia, and became acting Director of Culture on his return. But he has had a stormy relationship with the Sierra Leonean government, and has been imprisoned for his outspoken criticism of it, both on and off the stage.

The 1980s witnessed the flowering of theatre in Sierra Leone. With the building of the city hall in 1978, which could seat over a thousand people, groups found that they could make money out of theatre. The theatre now became popular in both outlook and structure; plays assumed an episodic plot structure, and contemporary and commonplace themes and situations could be used. The popularity of the theatre eventually caused it to fall foul of government, and, spurred by Kolosa John Kargbo's production of his socio-political satire, *Poyo Tong Wahala*, in 1979 it introduced censorship.

Although the city hall was closed to theatre in 1986, the popularity of the theatre did not wane. Theatre groups proved very resilient, and took their art on to the streets, hotel courtyards, bars, nightclubs and community halls. This period saw the rise to prominence of the Freetong Players, a group led by Charlie Haffner, which has been largely responsible for popularizing street theatre and giving it respectability, and of Spence Productions, directed by Julius Spencer.

Krio theatre

A highly popular theatre tradition in Sierra Leone. Krio, which is the lingua franca in Sierra Leone – a country in West Africa of approximately 4 million people – is an English-based Creole language which developed out of interchange between freed slaves settled in the capital Freetown, their European colonial masters, and the indigenous people of the region. Krio, though largely an urban language, is the language of the home and of commerce, and is spoken by approximately 60 per cent of the population.

Krio theatre was pioneered by Thomas Decker, who mounted a campaign spanning several decades for the use of Krio in literary endeavours. The breakthrough came in 1964 when his translation of Shakespeare's *Julius Caesar* was performed in the grounds of State House by the National Theatre League, an umbrella organization for theatre in the 1960s and early 70s. Decker later wrote an adaptation of Shakespeare's *As You Like It*, which he called *Udat Di Kiap Fit*. These plays, combined with his writings in newspapers and radio plays, provided the impetus for the flowering of Krio drama. Juliana John took Decker's experiment a stage further by writing original plays in Krio, using a theme song and dance sequences. Her work started the process of popularizing Krio theatre. Dele Charley, YULISA AMADU MADDY and a host of other playwrights carried this process of popularization to fruition. Today, Krio theatre operates side by side with theatre in English.

Perhaps because Krio is the language of the urban masses, Krio drama is peopled by characters drawn from this social sector, and deals with issues common to them in a down-to-earth way. Krio theatre is therefore popular theatre which, although appreciated and patronized by a wide cross-section of society, draws the bulk of its audience from the working classes.

The unique feature of Krio theatre is the dance-drama, which came into existence in 1977 with Dele Charley's creation of *Fatmata*. Krio dance-drama usually takes the form of storytelling theatre in which theme and action are welded together through dance, music, mime, choral speaking and narration. Not a dance-drama in the true sense of the term, it relies on a narrator and a chorus to present the story verbally but the individual characters, except for occasional songs, perform in a non-verbal mode through dance and mime. All verbal presentations (apart from the songs) are structured with a distinctive beat, thus facilitating their rendition to the steady rhythm of drums.

Maddy, Yulisa Amadu (1936–)

Sierra Leonean playwright, theatre director and novelist; founder of the Gbakanda Afrikan Tiata theatre group. Maddy was educated in Freetown and at the Rose Bruford College of Speech and Drama in Kent, England. He has made a powerful impact on theatre in Sierra Leone, as well as in other African countries. He had also promoted black theatre and African performing arts during lengthy sojourns in Denmark, Britain and the USA. Although he is an imaginative and experimental director – his production of Alem Mezgebe's *Pulse* at the Edinburgh Festival in 1979 won a Fringe award – his greatest contribution to African theatre is probably as a playwright.

Maddy comes out of the urban Creolized context of Freetown. Increasingly, he writes in Krio, an urban language suitable for a theatre depicting the West African urban milieu, and bases his dramas within a class analysis. He has always written about the oppressed and their sense of a collectivity within communities

which have lost hope. The humanist overview within the plays is always a complex one. The characters rarely find easy solutions to their oppression, as they struggle towards a fairer society within the scope of their limited resources. *Yon Kon* (published 1968) is about a criminal in gaol who is top dog amongst the other prisoners. Inside and outside the prison an amoral world is created through the language of conventional morality. The drama is developed, through a series of short scenes, to its ironic conclusion. Another early play – one with Sartrean overtones – is *Life Everlasting*, in which recognizable Sierra Leonean types arrive dead in Hell, and are organized by 'Big Boy'. An anthology of his plays (1971) includes *Obasai* and *Gbana Bendu*. *Obasai*, about community renewal being spearheaded by the least likely people in that community, is a quasi-naturalistic play with emotive songs and some vivid theatrical imagery. *Gbana Bendu*, a wholly integrated piece of 'total theatre', breaks new ground. It enters into the penumbra of the masquerade (see Introduction, MASQUERADES IN AFRICA) and the secret cult, in order to explore alternative paths to social justice.

Big Berin, which Maddy produced in the early 1970s in Sierra Leone, is set in a compound of multiple occupancy among the urban poor. It explores the secret desires of its occupants; relates these desires, surrealistically, to the hegemony of the state; and shows the immoral implications of individualistic materialism. Since his production of this play, Maddy's work seems to have stagnated. Perhaps his imprisonment by the Sierra Leone government, as a result of his outspoken criticism of the corruption prevalent in the society of the 70s, has embittered him. Since the early 1980s, his productivity both as playwright and as director has diminished.

Forced to live in exile after his release from detention in the late 1970s, Maddy returned home periodically in the late 80s and early 90s, and has attempted to re-establish himself in the local theatre.

Bibliography

M. Banham and C. Wake, *African Theatre Today*, London, 1976; D. Cosentino, *Defiant Maids and Stubborn Farmers: Tradition and Invention in Mende Story Performance*, Cambridge, 1982.

SOUTH AFRICA

Political relations in a racially heterogeneous population of nearly 40 million people have produced fundamental cultural tensions in South Africa in the latter half of the twentieth century. In the early 1990s, as it strives for identity as a non-racial democracy, the country is in a condition of low-level civil war.

These tensions have found expression for decades in a multiplicity of theatrical forms and traditions, mainly dealing with race and politics. As a result of colonization and the subsequent control of the means of production and distribution of resources, nearly 5 million 'white' people of European descent wielded political power over the rest of the population, of whom nearly 30 million were disfranchised blacks of African descent.

This latter group comprises descendants of the Bantu-speaking aboriginal peoples who had settled in the subcontinent before the arrival of European settlers in the 17th century. These Africans of the pre-colonial period practised various forms of dramatic enactment – in, for example, songs and storytelling narratives. Some of these, like the Xhosa *intsomi* and the Zulu *inganekwane*, would be invoked by later dramatists and theatre practitioners as important models for 'authentic' African theatrical dialogue and action. In addition, the Zulu *izibongo* tradition of 'praise poetry' employed mimetic narrative and dance in a form which incorporated oral communication as well as broadly gestural enactment. Religious rituals and military and political ceremonies also called for dramatic enactment through movement, speech and singing. The occasion of such performance was a major determinant of form and theme: the pieces were functional in relation to the tribal social structure or to religious custom.

These indigenous performance traditions are by no means based upon merely archaic forms: they are still constantly practised and re-created, changing in theme and style in relation to historical developments. They have continued into the present in two ways. First, many of them have been commodified. The most obvious arena for their contemporary performance is the gold-mining compound, where tribal groupings are often maintained. In some cases traditional forms have undergone metamorphosis in accordance with the changed circumstances of the migrant labourer. One such contemporary form of oral poetry is *sefela*, which enacts the life and experience of the migrant labourer temporarily uprooted from his rural home. Second, some of the aspects of visual and oral communication derived from narratives and praise poetry have been incorporated into contemporary theatrical forms. Many plays, especially in the 1980s, relied heavily in performance on the traditions of narration and solo enactment that have their roots in the early indigenous forms: in the 1980s, for example, MBONGENI NGEMA's *Asinamali!* and the workshop-produced *Woza Albert!*.

Apart from these modes of performance among the Bantu-speaking peoples, there is evidence of other modes in the cultural traditions of other ethnic groups: e.g. in the games and ceremonies of the nomadic Bushman communities which roam over vast areas of semi-desert terrain in the Cape Province are found the *Khoi-San* traditions of dance, mime and narrative enactments whose history goes back more than six thousand years. Thus, many roots of African performance were already

Market Theatre production of *Asinamali!*

firmly established when the European settlers arrived.

As part of the strategy to maintain white hegemony, authoritative accounts of South African cultural history for decades largely ignored these indigenous African traditions and focused instead on the European influence. Thus a performance of Beaumarchais's *The Barber of Seville* given in 1783 by French troops at the military barracks in Cape Town (at that time an important refreshment station on the sea route to the East) was commonly considered to be the earliest recorded instance of theatrical performance in South Africa. From this event one can trace the growth and development of European tradition in South African theatre – although alongside this tradition there were always alternative indigenous and syncretic forms – one of the earliest of which was the Anglicized Dutch dramatic poem *Kaatje Kekkelbek*, in the first decade of the 19th century.

The dominant cultural influence from the beginning of the 19th century coincided with British rule over the Cape Colony. After the founding in 1801 of the first theatre – the African Theatre in Cape Town – visiting professionals and entrepreneurs imported European plays and players. Actor-managers and impresarios arriving from England and elsewhere in

Europe developed theatre under the influence of European theatrical models. Then the discovery of diamonds in 1867 and of gold in 1886 brought an influx of immigrants, which in turn determined the growth of amateur theatre in the different European languages to cater for the needs of a new cosmopolitan audience. By the end of the century, Afrikaans drama had appeared. The first Afrikaans play, S. J. du Toit's *Magrita Prinslo*, was produced in 1897. After the Anglo-Boer War in 1902 Afrikaans nationalism found expression in a wave of patriotic writings such as C. J. Langenhoven's drama *Die Hoop van Suid-Afrika* (*The Hope of South Africa*) in 1912, and in numerous other Afrikaans plays which were toured by companies to the rural areas – at that time dominated by Afrikaans farming communities.

By the beginning of the 20th century the large cities boasted numerous well equipped theatre buildings modelled on London's West End theatres, and during the first quarter of the century both Afrikaans and English companies established an infrastructure for professional theatre. In addition, again in both languages, there was a thriving amateur theatre industry. Perhaps less influential in the development of South African theatre, but nonetheless an important strand in the spectrum of performance styles and forms, were equestrian spectacles, pantomime and melodrama, vaudeville and music hall, the circus and popular entertainments from France, Germany, England and the USA. Anglo-European political dominance was reinforced by cultural activities in which the theatre played an important role.

While the second quarter of the century witnessed the consolidation of this process, important developments were taking place in theatre among black communities. In 1927 the first published Xhosa drama was G. B. Sinxo's *Debeza's Baboons*; and in 1935 HERBERT DHLOMO became the first black person to publish a play in English, with his drama about Xhosa legend, *The Girl Who Killed to Save: Nongqause the Liberator*.

The black middle class began to assert a taste for theatre based on European models of dramatic literature, and elitist clubs were formed, such as the Johannesburg Bantu Dramatic Society in 1932. Meanwhile, a popular form of theatre among working-class blacks began to make an impact. Mthethwa's Lucky Stars was founded in Natal in 1927 as the first professional black troupe, and toured the country with plays based on Zulu legends and customs, performing in the vernacular to popular acclaim.

During the 1930s and 40s the urbanization of Africans, gathered in slum yards and communities in and near the big cities, produced syncretic forms of music and theatre. The synthesis of tribal and traditional with Western models of performance, especially from the USA, would lead eventually to the important point when, in 1959, the black musical *King Kong*, about the rise and fall of a heavyweight boxer, brought African musicals and actors to the attention of theatre-goers in Johannesburg, London and New York.

Meanwhile, English and Afrikaans theatre profited from a number of developments. The growth of professional and amateur theatre until the end of the Second World War was rapid but eclectic, and some cohesion was necessary. In 1938 a nationwide co-ordination of amateur theatre groups had been achieved when P. P. B. Breytenbach founded the Federation of Amateur Theatrical Societies of South Africa. Then in 1947 emerged the National Theatre Organization, and Breytenbach soon became chairman of this first state-funded body for professional theatre. During the 1950s the NTO provided important training and experience for a new generation of actors and directors, and in 1963 the process of consolidation was crystallized with the formation of provincial performing arts councils. This coincided with the entrenchment of rigid racial segregation in theatres, and a consequent international playwrights' boycott. As it came of age, the state-funded theatre found itself symbolizing the political system that had brought South Africa international disrepute.

In opposition to this theatre, alternative forms emerged among practitioners determined to defy government policies on racial segregation. One important group was Union Artists, which co-ordinated activities on behalf of black musicians and actors. This was the group which produced *King Kong*. It also gave encouragement to an important generation of theatre practitioners, among them ATHOL FUGARD and GIBSON KENTE. Both were to forge independent careers in the 1960s, 70s and 80s – Fugard as a white liberal exploring on stage the relationships of South Africans frustrated by social and political pressures, and Kente as a black entrepreneur creating popular musicals about life in the black townships. While, for two decades after 1963, Afrikaans theatre was confined almost totally within the performing arts councils, a number of English writers emerged to present their work in fringe theatres, though none achieved the sustained success of Fugard's work. Far more important for English-language theatre after 1963 was the training and experience gained in the performing arts councils by a number of theatre practitioners who would make an important contribution to the 1970s. The experimental theatre that emanated from the Arena Company, under the auspices of the performing arts council of the Transvaal in Johannesburg, and from the Space Company, in Cape Town, provided arguably the most innovative theatre amongst English-speaking whites in the 1970s.

At the same time, an important development occurred with the growth of black nationalism. The Black Consciousness movement began in the universities and quickly spread to other sectors of the black populace. Black Consciousness led to radical changes in black politics, and black cultural expression became one way of asserting an alternative South African cultural identity. Militant political theatre emerged from groups like the People's Experimental Theatre and the Theatre

Council of Natal. Both were cited in the charge sheet at a trial under the Terrorism Act for their involvement in the dissemination of 'subversive' plays and literature. Significantly, the groups involved in what was defined as 'black' theatre in the 1970s comprised, in addition to Africans, the other population groups categorized by the state as 'Indian' and 'coloured'. Throughout the country, among all three population groups, theatre became a means to assert black nationalism. Even Gibson Kente introduced a more pronounced political theme into his musicals, and the title of his play *How Long?* attained a symbolic importance in the revolutionary action which developed among schoolchildren in the townships in 1976. Meanwhile, one of the most radically innovative groups, Workshop '71, began its work. Creating plays in 'workshop', this non-racial group challenged the conventions of South African theatre, making plays out of the experiences of its participants, and produced an impressive range of forms and themes, in plays such as *uNosilimela*, *Survival* and *Crossroads*.

These workshop techniques, as well as the wave of black political militancy, did not fail to influence white theatre practitioners, and in the 1970s fringe groups emerged, producing plays about South African politics and race relations. The Market Theatre in Johannesburg and the People's Space Theatre in Cape Town were two of the most innovative, providing venues for many of Fugard's works as well as for works by a number of other young writers and directors. The extraordinary international success of John Kani and Winston Ntshona, the actors who created *Sizwe Bansi is Dead* (1972) with Fugard, inspired many groups to adopt improvisatory methods in the creation of theatre, and by the end of the 1970s South African theatre had rejected many of its European and American models and discovered its own voice.

After 1976 the home for most of this new work was the Market Theatre, which focused on developing theatre about the cultural contradictions of South African life. In the 1980s

Winston Ntshona in *Sizwe Bansi is Dead* by
Fugard, John Kani and Ntshona.

one of the most successful plays to emerge was
Woza Albert!, created in workshop by director
Barney Simon with actors Percy Mtwa and
Mbongeni Ngema. Four other factors were

related to the developing political crisis in the
1980s. First, as various black trade unions produced plays about working conditions and
union solidarity as one way of educating workers about these important issues, trade union
workers' theatre emerged. Second, the township musical, which remained the dominant
form of theatre in the townships in the hands
of people like Kente, began to be supplemented
by political plays. Major exponents of black
political drama included Dukuza ka Macu,
Matsemela Manaka, Maishe Maponya,
Mzwandile Maqina, Percy Mtwa and Ngema.
Third, a new wave of white Afrikaans playwrights appeared. These included Deon
Opperman and Reza de Wet, whose work was
innovative with regard to forms and techniques, and frequently involved experimental
pieces dealing with sexual and psychological
taboos related to political anxiety. Fourth,
English-speaking playwrights began to recognize the importance of multi-lingualism in
South African theatre, and a new generation of
playwrights like Paul Slabolepszy, Sue Pam
and Opperman exemplified these discoveries
by creating plays which provided insights into
the fears and anxieties, the hopes and aspirations, of the younger generation of South
Africans facing a post-apartheid society.

Apart from politically committed theatre
there also existed a popularly supported commercial theatre. In the 1970s African musicals,
backed by white capital and marketing expertise, enjoyed lengthy seasons both in South
Africa and abroad. Though popular with audiences, these were often criticized as inauthen-
tic 'tribal musicals' exploiting indigenous
culture for commercial gain – the visiting card
of black Africa in Europe. Most prominent of
the genre was the musical *Ipi-Tombi*, while
Umabatha, a Zulu adaptation of *Macbeth*,
achieved critical acclaim at the 1972 World
Theatre Season in London. White commercial
theatre also flourished in South Africa's major
cities, despite (and perhaps partly because of)
the introduction of television in 1976. From

The Ukukhanya Players in a Community Theatre presentation of *Moments*, a play on voter education by Peter Ngwenya.

the 1950s to the 80s these commercial theatre enterprises relied almost exclusively on British and American farces and whodunnits. By the 1990s, however, the partial breakdown in racial exclusivity began to influence even these bastions of Anglo-American culture in South Africa, and some cross-over work began to find its way into the commercial theatres.

In 1992, as the country's major political players negotiated a non-racial future government, the performing arts councils and the civic and commercial theatres began to reflect these developments by employing black artists in key positions. Not all of these appointments were cosmetic: many of the appointees were able to exert pronounced influence in some of the old bastions of apartheid theatre. At the same time, a new union, the Performing Artists 'Workers' Equity, an organization dedicated to eradicating all vestiges of race and gender discrimination in theatre in South Africa, began to effect major changes in policy within the theatre industry.

By the mid-1990s South African theatre had built up an impressive infrastructure. Political theatre and theatre based on the country's unique social problems has given birth to a new identity, after decades during which Eurocentric models predominated. Commercial success associated with the new forms of theatre has given rise to independent professional companies. Training facilities proliferate as universities and colleges offer courses in all aspects of the performing arts. The fledgeling television and film industries are providing new expanding outlets for graduates, and each of the major cities can boast impressively equipped theatre buildings. As the apartheid system has been steadily dismantled, the theatre appears to have arrived at full maturity.

Akerman, Anthony (1949–)
South African playwright and director. His plays are written in English but incorporate South African slang and idiomatic expressions from Afrikaans and Zulu. His first, *Somewhere on the Border* (1983), was written while he was living in exile in Amsterdam. An indictment of the South African military and its participation in the Angolan War, the play was banned in South Africa before its first performance by exiled actors in Holland. Then followed *A Man out of the Country* (1985), an exploration of the existential problems faced by exiles, and *A World Elsewhere* (1987), a mini-epic about growing up in South Africa during the apartheid era. All these plays deal with individuals trying to come to terms with their South African identity, and examine the ethical choices they feel compelled to make – themes further explored in *Dark Outsider* (1991), set in the 1920s and 30s and dealing with a period in the life of the South African poet Roy Campbell. After nineteen years in exile, Akerman returned permanently to South Africa in 1992. His most recent play, *First Loves* (1993), deals with memory and a returned exile's confrontation with his past.

Dhlomo, Herbert (1903–56)
South African playwright, poet and essayist. Known in South Africa as 'the father of black drama', H. I. E. Dhlomo was the first black man to have a play published there in English. He wrote heroic historical dramas such as *Dingane* (1937), *Cetshwayo* (1936) and *Moshoeshoe* (1937),

as well as plays that explored the social and political relations of his time such as *The Girl who Killed to Save: Nongqause the Liberator* (1936) and *The Workers* (1940). Frequently misrepresented as a middle-class intellectual appropriated by European liberal discourse, Dhlomo was in fact one of the most important progressive thinkers of his time. He grappled with the crucial themes for black South Africans of modernization and urbanization, rejecting tribalism at a time when political figures in South Africa were embarking on retrogressive 'native' policies which sought to entrench tribal identities in order to retard black development. He exerted an important influence on the development of black writing in English which matured in the 1950s before it was effectively truncated by political repression in the 60s. An essayist of considerable stature, he wrote about art and politics in South Africa. His *Collected Works*, edited by N. Visser and T. Couzens (1985), reveal him as the most prolific black writer of the mid-century in South Africa.

Fugard, Athol (1932–)
South African playwright; educated at the University of Cape Town, where he studied philosophy. Fugard's plays are written in English but incorporate many regional dialects and slang derived from vernaculars. His first plays and a novel (*Tsotsi*) were written from 1958 while he associated with black writers and intellectuals in the freehold suburb of Sophiatown outside Johannesburg. In the 1960s he wrote what are often referred to as 'the family plays' – including *The Blood Knot* (1961), *Hello and Goodbye* (1965) and *Boesman and Lena* (1969) – about the loneliness and isolation of working-class people of different races. In the early 1960s he worked through improvisation with actors to create what are referred to as 'the workshop plays', like *Sizwe Bansi is Dead* (1972) and *Statements after an arrest under the Immorality Act* (1972), plays which dealt more directly with the oppression brought about by

apartheid. In the second half of the decade he began writing alone again, and this period produced plays like *Master Harold ... and the Boys* (1982) and *The Road to Mecca* (1984), focusing on relationships and with a backdrop of politics. Indeed his plays are permeated by South African politics, but Fugard maintains that he is simply a 'regional' writer, and that his concern is with individual loneliness and pain in specific situations: politics, he suggests, provides only the context.

With the radical changes occurring in South Africa during the first half of the 1990s, however, his work has become more actively engaged with the political situation. His play *My*

Children, My Africa! (1989) depicts characters actively confronting the violence of the streets which characterizes South Africa in the 90s: a society caught in civil war brought about by apartheid. And *Playland* (1992) depicts characters trying to find some way of communicating with each other and with themselves in the light of a history that has bruised every South African. Castigated by some for being a white liberal out of touch with the realities of black suffering and resistance, Fugard nevertheless succeeds in articulating an image of South Africa's peoples trying to live out their lives in a society deformed by race prejudice and all the insecurities spawned by such prejudice.

Athol Fugard directing John Kani and Sean Taylor in *Playland*, Market Theatre, 1992.

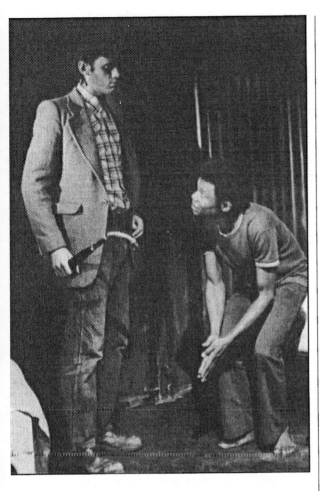

University of Leeds Workshop Theatre production of Fugard's *The Bloodknot*.

Junction Avenue Theatre Company

An experimental theatre company based in Johannesburg. It has created a number of plays which have challenged ideas of content and form in the development of South African theatre. Since its foundation in 1976 with the production of their play *The Fantastical History of a Useless Man*, the company's policy has been to workshop plays which 'critically reflect South African society, reclaim hidden history and restore a voice to the voiceless'. Committed to non-racialism in a society where racial defini-

tions have been the norm for most of the century, the company works collectively, sometimes spending up to six months researching, workshopping and improvising a text, then editing and rehearsing it for production. Using principles of music hall and popular theatre, African music and dance, and ideas derived from Workshop 71, Brecht and Grotowski, plus later elements of social realism, Junction Avenue has consistently engaged creatively with the relationship between theatre and political action.

Many of its plays, influenced by revisionist historiography emanating from, for example, the University of the Witwatersrand, attempt to reveal the history of repression in South Africa. Under the direction of Malcolm Purkey, plays such as *Randlords and Rotgut* (1978), *Marabi* (1982) and *Sophiatown* (1986) reveal aspects of the history of apartheid and its brutal influence over people's lives. In the late 1970s, inspired by the emergent trade union movement, members of the company, determined to push out in new directions, began working on short plays and sketches to take to union meetings and workers' halls. In 1980 *Security* and *Dikitsheneng* (*The Kitchen*), examples of this work, were presented in a double bill under the title *People's Plays*. Company members were subsequently invited by activists in the trade union movement to help devise plays with trade union members. The result was *Ilanga Lizophumela Abasenbenzi* (*The Sun Will Rise for the Workers*, 1979), a seminal trade union theatre production.

The company has produced popular children's theatre and experimental works such as *Will of a Rebel* (1979), based on the life of poet Breyten Breytenbach, and an African version of *The Bacchae* (1983). It has also written and produced an award-winning television film, *Howl at the Moon* (1981). *Tooth and Nail* (1989) represents a departure in style: constructed as a series of flashes of South African life, the play suggests some issues to be confronted in a post-apartheid society.

Kente, Gibson (1932–)

South African playwright and director. In 1967 Kente became South Africa's first black independent producer of theatre, and for the next quarter of a century remained virtually unrivalled as a theatrical entrepreneur, producing and directing on average more than one new play a year, all of them box-office hits. Even in by the 1980s Kente's name remained virtually unknown in the established white theatres of the cities, but amongst black audiences he was the leading exponent of the 'township musical' and the unrivalled leader of the entertainment world. As writer, choreographer, composer and director of all his productions, Kente is a strict disciplinarian, and each of his productions has been likened to a course of study in a theatre school, in which new generations of performers have obtained their first rigorous training in the craft of theatre. Ranging from plays with a political message, such as *How Long?* (1971), *I Believe* (1972) and *Too Late* (1973), to simple township musical melodramas like *Hard Road* (1978), *Lobola* (1980) and *Mama and the Load* (1981), all of Kente's work draws upon popular cultural expression, refined and performed with extraordinary energy and professionalism, and his brand of musical melodrama has opened a window on the lives of black people in the townships. Many of his actors have gone on to establish careers as playwrights, directors and actors with an international reputation, but Kente has chosen to address his plays to the people of the townships.

Manaka, Matsemela (1955–)

South African poet, playwright, musician and graphic artist. Born in the township of Alexandra, Manaka now lives in Diepkloof, Soweto. He first achieved prominence in 1980 when his play *Egoli* (*The Golden One*, literally: 'Johannesburg') was performed at the Erlangen Festival in Germany – the first time a black playwright had presented work there. A founder member of the Allahpoets, a group of 'performance poets', and founder of the Soyikwa Africa Theatre group, he is a prominent figure in the black theatre movement on the Witwatersrand. He has also published some poetry and a number of critical articles on the theatre, and exhibited his graphics both locally and internationally.

For a time employed by Ravan Press in Johannesburg, Manaka was the editor of the literary magazine *Staffrider*. Influenced in his early work by GIBSON KENTE, the first attempt he made at writing a play resulted in a musical called *The Horn* (1977), inspired by Kente's *How Long?* The play was based on a theme to which Manaka would return: the dispossession of the migrant worker. In 1979 he produced *Egoli* in Cape Town; later it transferred to the Market Theatre in Johannesburg, and was invited to West Germany. After its staging at the Erlangen Festival the play toured to Frankfurt, Augsburg, West Berlin and other cities. Also in 1979 Manaka created, out of improvisation, the play *Imbumba* (*Unity*) – the first production of his newly formed Soyikwa Africa Theatre. Later plays were *Pula* (1982), *Vuka* (1982) and *Children of Asazi* (1984). As the organizer of the Drama Committee of the Funda Centre in Soweto in 1984, Manaka coordinated a vigorous theatre programme for aspirant young black theatre practitioners.

Maponya, Maishe (1951–)

South African playwright, actor and director, born in the township of Alexandra. When Maponya was eleven, his family was forcibly removed under apartheid legislation and resettled in Diepkloof, Soweto, where in 1975, when he was an insurance clerk in one of South Africa's giant corporations, he began writing plays. His writing career took off when he joined Medupi Writers' Association, which, along with many other organizations including newspapers, was banned in October 1977. That year he founded the Bahumutsi Drama

Group, and in 1978 he co-founded the Allahpoets, a group of 'performance poets'.

His first play, in 1976, was *The Cry*, written before the political uprising of 16 June; this was followed by *Peace and Forgive* in 1977, first performed in various townships and later at the Market Theatre in Johannesburg. In 1981 his play *The Hungry Earth* left South Africa for a lengthy tour of Britain, Switzerland and West Germany. As an example of a Sowetan drama created by Maponya independently of white managements, it was invited to perform in community centres, universities and fringe theatres and also at the Edinburgh Festival, which it did to critical acclaim. The play toured to Germany again in May 1983, along with Maponya's new play *Umongikazi* (*The Nurse*, about health and working conditions in hospitals); both plays were enthusiastically received. Harassment from police and political organizations did not prevent him from creating two further plays in 1984: *Gangsters* and *Dirty Work* interrogated the methods and tactics of the South African security police. In 1986, in *Jika* (written when he was taking a postgraduate degree in theatre studies at Leeds University) he explored the potential for political change in his country, and in 1987 he co-authored with Amani Blackwood a play about the Incas in South America, *The Valley of the Blind*. Maponya is a lecturer in drama at the University of the Witwatersrand in Johannesburg.

Mda, Zakes (1948–)

South African playwright, writer on theatre, poet and painter. Mda was born in the Eastern Cape Province of South Africa, and educated in Lesotho, Switzerland, the USA and South Africa. His first prominent play was *Dead End*, produced in 1979. In the previous year he had won an Amstel Merit award for his play *We Shall Sing for the Fatherland*, and in 1979 he won the Amstel Playwright of the Year award for *The Hill*. These three plays dealt, respectively, with the relationship between prostitution and apartheid, the betrayal of liberation fighters by post-independence politicians, and the effects of South African race policies on labour migrants in the subcontinent. *Dark Voices Ring* (1979) and *The Road* (1982) similarly deal with labour and politics. Mda differs from the major South African theatre exports of his time in that he never foregrounds political debate, but rather focuses his action upon the interplay of characters who happen to be formed by their political context. More recently, he has concentrated on the uses of theatre-for-development, and in 1993 published a major scholarly treatise on the subject, *When People Play People*. He also works as a UNICEF consultant on rural development.

Ngema, Mbongeni (1955–)

South African playwright, actor and director. Ngema first attracted international attention with his performance in the play *Woza Albert!* in the early 1980s. Spending much of his youth in Zululand, he drew upon traditions of Zulu music and dance which, using his experience as an actor in the township musicals of GIBSON KENTE, he incorporated into his later work. His play *Asinamali!* (1985), influenced by the work of the Chicano American group El Teatro Campesino, exemplifies his approach to performance. Depicting the experiences of black prisoners in apartheid South Africa, it utilizes mime, dance, song and rhythmic movement and gesture to create powerful theatrical images of political oppression and resistance. Later plays have focused on music and singing, *Sarafina* (1987) and *Township Fever!* (1990) being praised in New York as musical representations of the black struggle against apartheid; and *Magic at 4.00 am* (1993), a spectacular musical mounted in Johannesburg's Civic Theatre, heralding Ngema's now central role in professional theatre in South Africa. He has established a company called Committed Artists, which is both a training school and a production company, focusing on the presentation of what he calls 'theatre of liberation'.

Slabolepszy, Paul (1948–)

South Africa's most prolific new playwright. Slaboleszy has a performer's diploma from the University of Cape Town. His carefully textured plays seldom refer directly to the political context which determines the action, but inscribed in every one is dialogue which reveals the damage wrought by apartheid politics. His work is characterized by accurate representation of the idiosyncrasies of poor whites, primarily with respect to language. All of his plays employ a rich multi-lingual dialogue, and his comic characterizations of apartheid's children have made his works extremely popular. Major plays are: *The Defloration of Miles Koekemoer* (1980), *Saturday Night at the Palace* (1981), *Karoo Grand* (1983), *Under the Oaks* (1984), *Over the Hill* (1985), *Boo to the Moon* (1986), *Making like America* (1986), *Travelling Shots* (1988), *Smallholding* (1989), *The Eyes of their Whites* (with David Kramer, 1990), *One for the High Jump* (1990), *Braait Laaities* (1991), *The Return of Elvis du Pisanie* (1992), *Mooi Street Moves* (1992), *Pale Natives* (1993), and *Victoria Almost Falls* (1993). His plays have been translated into German, Swedish and Hebrew.

Smit, Bartho (1924–86)

Arguably the most prominent Afrikaans playwright; also a theatre critic. Smit was a controversial figure, his plays frequently censored in South Africa. He was active in professional theatre for many years, directing for the National Theatre Organization and the performing arts councils. His work spans three decades, from *Moeder Hanna* (*Mother Hanna*, 1959), a drama about the futility of war, through *Don Juan Onder die Boere* (*Don Juan among the Boers*, 1960), *Die Verminktes* (*The Maimed*, 1960) and *Putsonderwater* (*Well Without Water*, 1962), an absurdist study of religious bankruptcy in modern life, to *Bacchus in die Boland* (*Bacchus in the Highveld*, 1974), in which Bacchus visits a wine estate and makes the white farmer switch roles with his black staff. *Die Keiser* (*The Emperor*, 1977) adapts the Hans Christian Andersen story *The Emperor's New Clothes* to present a satirical look at the absurdities of social mores. His best-known play is *Christine*, commissioned for the opening of the Nico Malan Theatre in Cape Town in 1971, but then cancelled and produced two years later in the Transvaal. It is a richly allusive play focusing on Nazi Germany and developing themes of Calvinist guilt and racial prejudice. A young and an old Christine appear simultaneously on stage, as the play moves through past and present exploring its central character's existential anxieties and guilt. His plays have frequently been censored, yet he has also been recognized through the *Encyclopedia Britannica* Award (for *The Maimed*) and a number of local prizes.

Bibliography

D. Coplan, *In Township Tonight: South Africa's Black City Music and Theatre*, Johannesburg, 1985; A. Fuchs, *Playing the Market: The Market Theatre, Johannesburg, 1976–1986*, Chur, 1990; T. Hauptfleisch and I. Steadman, *South African Theatre: Four Plays and an Introduction*, Pretoria, 1984, and (eds.), *South African Theatre Journal*, Univ. of Stellenbosch; International Defence and Aid Fund for Southern Africa, *Black Theatre in South Africa*, London, 1976; R. Kavanagh (ed.), *South African People's Plays*, London, 1981, and *Theatre and Cultural Struggle in South Africa*, London, 1985; A. von Kotze, *Organise and Act: The Natal Workers' Theatre Movement 1983–87*, Univ. of Natal, Durban, 1988; M. Orkin, *Drama and the South African State*, Univ. of Witwatersrand, 1992; I. Steadman, 'Theatre beyond Apartheid', *Research in African Literatures*, 22, 3, 1991, and 'Performance and Politics in Process', *Theatre Survey*, 33, 1992.

TANZANIA

Over 90 per cent of the 20 million inhabitants of Tanzania subsist on agriculture. The 123 ethnic groups are linguistically united by Kiswahili, the national language, which has greatly influenced the growing nationalist theatre movement, especially after the adoption of *Ujamaa* (socialism) in 1967.

The theatre of pre-colonial times was a conglomeration of many forms derived from a variety of pre-capitalist production modes and their resultant cultures. These can be broadly categorized into four types: ritual theatre, especially relating to initiation; celebration dances related to some social event such as weddings and harvest festival with the basic aim of reinforcing social values, e.g. *nindo*, which is found among the Wagogo; *mkwajungoma* (the Wazaramo), *maseve* (the Wangoni), *selo* (the Wazigua) and *hiari ya moyo* (the Wanyamwezi); storytelling, called *Simo* (a Wagogo tradition) and *Hadithi* (found among coastal groups); and heroic recitations.

Colonization by the Germans and later by the British brought about significant changes. Though the British – by means of missionaries, colonial educators and administrators – discouraged or prohibited traditional theatre performances, regarding them as 'barbaric' and 'uncivilized', most forms stubbornly survived. In 1948, however, colonial policy changed, and traditional theatre performances were encouraged at agricultural exhibitions and trade fairs as well as at colonial festivals such as Empire Day, to ensure wider publicity and to distract the people from their discontent with the colonial situation. This resulted in the formation of over fifty-eight 'dance associations' in the urban areas by 1954. The colonialists also encouraged certain new dances that were considered 'appropriate' for 'enlightened natives', e.g. *beni*, whose movement, costuming and music borrowed from colonial military bands, and *mpendoo*, which was devised especially to distract the Christian and 'educated' Wagogo people from their traditional *nindo* and *msunyunho* dances. Later, however, the colonial government again discouraged these traditional dance groups because of their subversive potential.

Western theatre was introduced in the early 1920s, and by 1952 almost all schools were staging the works of, among others, Shakespeare, Shaw, and Gilbert and Sullivan. In 1957 the British Council launched a school drama competition to foster British culture and to emphasize 'correct and proper' English speech. Because of their exposure to exclusively British bourgeois theatre, the Tanzanian colonial elite came to look upon this kind of theatre as the one and only. *Vichekesho*, an offshoot of Western theatre, was very popular in colonial times in the schools alongside the imported Western drama. Based on improvised sketches, directed and performed by students, *vichekesho* sought to 'cause laughter' among the audience by making fun of the 'uncivilized' and 'uneducated' masses for not being able to use such items of 'civilized' life as a fork, a sprung bed or a mirror.

Expatriate theatre was established in the form of two 'little theatres' – the Dar es Salaam Players (1947) and the Arusha Little Theatre (1953). These remain to this day oblivious of any theatre tradition inside or outside Tanzania other than that of Broadway and the West End. As a result, they have exerted no influence on the development of Tanzanian theatre.

The attainment of political independence in Tanzania in 1964 brought little change to the theatrical scene. The formation of the Youth Drama Association in 1966 under the patronage of expatriates and of the Tanzanian elite resulted in the emergence of original Swahili plays by Tanzanian playwrights, such as *Mukwava wa Uhehe* (*Mukwava of the Hehe People*) by M. Mulokozi. *Vichekesho* lived on, but the emphasis changed from laughing at the 'uncivilized' to rebuking the educated for looking down on their own people, as in *Zabibi* (*The Raisin*), a radio play, and *Martin Kayamba*, both by G. Uhinga.

More significant changes came with the Arusha Declaration, the blueprint for *Ujamaa*, in 1967. Plays for foreign dramatists were discouraged and theatre in Kiswahili gained the upper hand. More than twenty published Tanzanian playwrights emerged during this period. The plays written during 1967–77 portray a general enthusiasm and support for socialism, while pointing out hurdles in its implementation. Such works include *Kijiji Chetu* (*Our Village*) by N'GALIMECHA NGAHYOMA, *Haitia* (*Guilt*) by P. Muhando (see PENINA MLAMA), *Mwanzo wa Tufani* (*Beginning of the Storm*) by K. Kahigi and A. Ngemera, and *Giza Limeingia* (*The Dawn of Darkness*) by EMMANUEL MBOGO. Plays produced after 1978 present a more critical analysis of the socialist construction process, portraying the disillusion and helplessness of the masses in the face of mounting corruption and exploitation by members of the ruling class: e.g. *Kaptula la Marx* (*Marx's Capital*, c.1985) by E. Kezilahabi; *Nguzo Mama* (*Mother the Main Pillar*) and *Lina Ubani* (*There is an Antidote for Rot*), both by P. Muhando, *Harakati za Ukombozi* (*Liberation Struggles*, 1982) by A. Lihamba and others, and *Ayubu*, c.1985, by the Paukwa Theatre Association. *Vichekesho* continued, to become the core of workers' theatre.

Another theatre form that developed during this period was *ngonjera*, based on traditional poetic forms and constituting a recital accompanied by dramatic movement and gesture,

costumes and props. Commonly performed at Party functions, national festivals and other official occasions, *ngonjera* answered President Nyerere's call for poets to 'go out and publicize *Ujamaa*'. *Ngonjera* troupes now exist in all schools, and it is one of the most popular theatre forms. Traditional dance, too, has transformed itself into an appropriate bearer of the new messages of the *Ujamaa* era. Over thirty dance troupes, some professional, are active in Dar es Salaam alone. These groups also engage in slapstick improvised drama.

The search for a Tanzania-based theatre has been the preoccupation of the University of Dar es Salaam's Department of Art, Music and Theatre, the Bagamoyo College of Art and the Butimba Arts College of Education. Drawing on traditional and contemporary local resources as well as on foreign theatre traditions, they have produced performances and writings both based in Tanzanian cultural reality and of contemporary relevance, such as *Shing'weng'we* (*Monster*), *Harakati za Ukombozi* (*Liberation Struggles*) and *Nyani na Mkia Wake* (*The Monkey and its Tail*) (by the university), *Tunda, The Challenge and the Gap* and *Chakatu* (by Bagamoyo) and *Azota na Azenga* (*Azota and Azenga*) (by Butimba). The same trend is apparent in the writings of those who are the products of these institutions – MLAMA, Lihamba, EBRAHIM HUSSEIN – and in the work of the amateur theatre groups such as Paukwa and Sayari, as exemplified in the former's *Ayubu* and *Chuano*.

In the 1980s the theatre-for-development movement emerged in Tanzania, spearheaded by the university's Department of Art, Music and Theatre. Long-term projects and short-term workshops have been conducted in Malya (Manxwa Region), Mosoga and Bagamoyo villages in Coast Region, and Mkambalani in Morogoro Region. Other theatre-for-development workshops have been based at Namiyonga (Mtwara Region, 1989), and Misalai, Mbuyuni and Kisiwani villages in Tanga Region in 1990, 91 and 92 respectively. In 1993 the

Scene from a programme of youth and community work created by the University of Dar es Salaam.

university embarked on a major theatre-for-development initiative in eight villages in Rukwa Region. Work of this nature has also been undertaken by a range of government and non-government development agencies, including the National Arts Council, UNICEF and the National Aids Control Programme. In addition, local communities have adopted theatre-for-development processes as a vehicle for local political and economic debate.

Theatre for children and youth is another important activity, promoted by the university's Art, Music and Theatre Department since 1978. A five-year programme (1991–6) of training for primary school teachers aims to provide the methodology and stimulus for theatre in schools. Arising from this programme is an annual festival of theatre for young people, presented by schools participating in the training programme and by children's theatre groups from Dar-Es-Salaam, Bagamoyo College of Arts and Morogoro Region.

Hussein, Ebrahim (1943–)
Tanzanian playwright. Published plays include *Kinjeketile* (1970) originally in Swahili and translated into English, *Wakati Ukata* (*Time is a Wall*, 1970), *Alikaona* (*The One Who Got What She Deserved*, 1970), *Mashetani* (*Devils*, 1971), *Arusi* (*Wedding*, 1980), *Jogoo Kijijini* (*The Dock in the Village*, 1976), *Ngao ya Jadi* (*The Traditional Shield*, 1976). Hussein's themes are closely related to the struggle for a just society in Tanzania, from

the depiction of the Maji Maji uprising against the Germans in *Kinjeketile* to his portrayal of the unfulfilled dream for a better society in *Arusi*. Not only are his themes relevant to the Tanzanian situation but in many cases so are his forms, particularly his use of the traditional storytelling structure. Hussein was formerly Associate Professor in Theatre Arts at the University of Dar es Salaam.

Kaduma, Godwin (1938–)

Tanzanian playwright. He has written two plays, both in Swahili, one published, the other not: *Dhamana* (*Pledge*, 1980), on the proper use of education, and *Mabatini* on the frustrations of the poor peasantry. Kaduma is Director of Culture in the Ministry of Culture, Youth and Sports.

Mbogo, Emmanuel (1947–)

Tanzanian playwright. He has published two plays in Swahili, *Giza Limeingia* (*The Dawn of Darkness*, c.1980) on the advantages of *Ujamaa* villages, and *Tone la mwisho* (*The Last Drop*, 1985), on the liberation struggle in Zimbabwe. Mbogo is a Research Fellow at the Institute of Kiswahili Research at the University of Dar es Salaam, but presently is working at Moi University, Kenya, where his playwriting activities continue.

Mlama [Muhando], Penina (1948–)

Tanzanian playwright and director. All her published plays are in Swahili and include *Haitia* (*Guilt*, 1972); *Tambueni Haki Zetu* (*Recognize Our Rights*, 1973); *Heshima Yangu* (*My Respect*, 1974); *Pambo* (*Decoration*, 1975); *Talaka si Mke Wangu* (*I Divorce You*, 1976); *Nguzo Mama* (*Mother the Main Pillar*, 1982); *Harakati za Ukombozi* (*Liberation Struggles*, 1982), with A. Lihamba and others, and *Lina Ubani* (*There is an Antidote for Rot*, 1984). Like other Tanzanian playwrights, Mlama deals with the problems of the struggle for liberation and a just society, as in *Tambueni Haki Zetu, Harakati za Ukombozi* and *Lina Ubani*. She also explores more personal problems, as in her treatment of the effects of divorce on children in *Talaka* and hypocrisy in *Heshima Yangu*. She is concerned with women's rights, and her *Nguzo Mama* shows the conflicts and contractions in the Tanzanian struggle for the liberation of women. She also takes an active part in the theatre-for-development movement. Her book *Culture and Development: The Popular Theatre Approach in Africa* (1991) discusses theatre-for-development programmes and strategies. Mlama heads the Department of Art, Music and Theatre at the University of Dar es Salaam.

Ngahyoma, Ngalimecha (fl. 1970s)

Tanzanian playwright, working with the Audio-Visual Institute in Dar es Salaam. He has published two Swahili plays: *Huka* (1973), which portrays the problems of a young school-girl trapped and destroyed by the evils of city life, and *Kijiji Chetu* (*Our Village*, 1975), which deals with some of the social problems arising from the creation of *Ujamaa* villages.

Bibliography

E. Hussein, 'On the Development of Theatre in East Africa', PhD thesis, Humbolt Univ., 1975; A. Lihamba, 'Politics and theatre in Tanzania after the Arusha Declaration, 1967–1984', PhD thesis, Leeds Univ., 1985; L. Mbughuni, 'Old and New Drama from East Africa', *African Literature Today*, 8, 1976; P. Muhando [Mlama], 'Traditional African Theatre as a Pedagogical Institution', PhD thesis, Univ. of Dar es Salaam, 1984. 'African Theatre – the Case of Tanzania', UDSM, unpublished paper, and *Culture and Development: The Popular Theatre Approach in Africa*, Scandinavian Institute of African Studies, Uppsala, 1991; M. Rugyendo, 'Towards a Truly African Theatre', *Umma*, 1, 2, 1974).

TOGO

Togo was a German territory from 1884 to 1914. In 1919 it came under Franco-British control as a League of Nations mandated territory, with the British western third joining independent Ghana in 1957 and the French section becoming the independent Republic of Togo in 1960. The division of Togo's largest and most influential ethnic group, the Ewe, into Ghanaian and Togolese, and the irredentist feelings this has fostered, are at the heart of the distrust and disputes between the two affected countries.

Togo's triple colonial heritage has had a direct influence on its modern culture, especially the theatre. For it was the mid-19th-century work of early German missionaries (followed by the British) in standardizing the Ewe language for evangelical purposes that laid the foundations for the emergence of a modest Ewe literary theatre. This theatre is basically didactic and proselytizing, and its chief representatives are F. Kawasi Fiawoo (graduated 1929, last play performed 1944), author of *Toko Atolia* (*The Fifth Lagoon*, 1937) and winner of the International African Institute prize, and his contemporary B. H. Setsoafia, playwright and translator of Shakespeare into Ewe.

Ewe literary theatre went into decline partly as the result of an aggressive French policy which promoted literacy in French at the expense of Ewe, and was replaced in the 1940s by a church-based Ewe religious theatre, the *kantata*. Of missionary origins, the *kantata*, which spread from Ghana, dramatizes Bible stories and moralities as in, for example, *La Vie de Daniel* (*The Life of Daniel*) and *Le Mariage d'Isaac et de Rebecca* (*The Marriage of Isaac and Rebecca*). Danced and sung to Christian music on the piano – notably in the hands of its first Togolese practitioner Morehouse Apedo-Amah – it later evolved to include dialogue. But some *kantatas* were lay, improvising on Togolese or oriental lore: examples are *Mille et une nuits* (*One Thousand and One Nights*) and the hugely popular *Ali Baba et les quarante voleurs* (*Ali Baba and the Forty Thieves*) which ran from 1947 to 1954. The lay *kantata*, unlike its religious counterpart, is sung and danced to traditional Togolese music and instruments. It also has a greater element of fantasy which, according to the theatre historian Alain Ricard, derives from its original

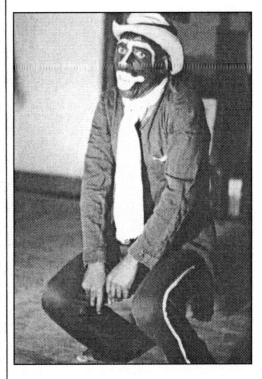

Ben Amegee in a Happy Star Concert, Lomé.

subject-matter as well as from the influence of popular Indian films, aspects of whose scenography and choreography it reproduces.

It is this theatre which from the late 1960s gave rise to the only truly popular Ewe theatrical form to date, the 'concert party'. Resolutely oral, without (unlike the *kantata*) even a written outline and aimed at a mass audience (it is despised by the literate elite), the concert party, whose origins are also Ghanaian and Nigerian, is an evening of musical and theatrical entertainment. It comprises a warming-up session of 'highlife' music, a prologue of skits and storytelling, and an improvised play on topical and moral issues. It uses a mixture of Ewe and pidgin French and combines the comic, the burlesque and the satirical. The performers, untrained and mostly recruited from among the urban unemployed and petty employee class, invent the action as they go along, relying on their imagination and, in the

tradition of the Pantaloons that they are, on their talents as mimics, dancers and singers. They depict stock characters like the prostitute, the houseboy and the trader, who are easily recognizable by their costumes.

Side by side with this popular activity goes a theatre in French. But in spite of the efforts of the French and the Togolese authorities to promote it, it has not produced any writers of note. The exception is SENOUVO ZINSOU. But even he integrates many concert-party and traditional performing arts techniques in his plays in French, such that he can be considered as continuing in the language the modern Togolese popular theatre tradition.

Zinsou, Senouvo (Agbota) (1946–)
Togolese playwright and former civil servant. Born in Togo, Zinsou showed an early interest in the theatre, writing his first play *L'Amour*

Hotel Tonyeviadji in downtown Lomé where Happy Star performed weekly in the 1970s.

d'un sauvage (*The Love of a Savage*) in 1968. He played an important role, while still at school, in the formation of an inter-secondary school dramatic society, L'Entente Scolaire pour le Théâtre et le Folklore. He attended the University of Togo and the Institut d'Etudes Théâtrales of the University of Paris, where he studied under the noted French drama critic Jean Schérer. On his return to Togo, Zinsou was appointed to the Ministry of Culture, where he founded the National Company for the Performing Arts, which he headed until 1992.

His first published play, *On joue la comédie* (*We are Acting*, 1975), won first prize in the Inter-African Radio competition organized by Radio-France Internationale, and was performed in Lagos during the second Pan-African Cultural Festival. His other published plays are *Le Club* (1983) and *La Tortue qui chante, La Femme du blanchisseur* and *Yévi au pays des monstres* (*The Singing Tortoise, The Laundryman's Wife* and *Yévi in the Country of Monsters*, 1987). His originality as a dramatist lies in his skilful exploitation of Togolese popular theatre traditions, both ancient in his 1987 plays and modern (concert party and *kantata*) in *On joue la comédie*. His work reflects a self-consciousness that is absent from most French-language African plays and is, among other things, a reflection on the art of playwriting.

Bibliography

S. Amégbléame, 'Le Théâtre dans la littérature ewe', *Afrique Littéraire et Artistique*, 51, 1979, and 'L'Influence biblique dans la littérature Ewe', in *Mélanges offerts à Albert Gérard*, ed. J. Riesz and A. Ricard, Tübingen, 1990; A. Ricard, 'Concours et concert: théâtre scolaire et théâtre populaire du Togo', *Revue d'histoire du théâtre*, 1, 1975, and *L'Invention du théâtre*, Lausanne, 1986.

UGANDA

Uganda became a unit in 1900 when the agreement which made it a protectorate was signed, uniting four separate kingdoms and several other separate societies. Although it is a multi-lingual society with two major ethnic groups, the country's pre-theatre traditions have common features from which a recognizably Ugandan theatre is developing. In the past, both religious and social occasions have employed dance and music in close conjunction, and in a dialogue which could be seen as dramatic. Whether within the northern and eastern Nilotic culture, or the western and southern Bantu tradition, the lead singer sets both chorus and musicians in motion with verbal commands, and the musicians then inspire the singers and dancers. All participate, and improvisation within a set rhythm is valued. Whether the occasion is an attempt to exorcize an evil spirit or the celebration of a marriage, the performance is a mass emotional experience. There is no audience – all are part of the happening. Basic steps are taught and sometimes rehearsed (as in the Masaba circumcision dances), and there is a set form of words for some traditional stories. Royal courts used to maintain a professional team of musicians and dancers (including a jester in the kingdom of Bunyoro), and there are still itinerant performers who can be invited to weddings and other celebrations, following the traditional pattern. Individual improvisation is still seen as a mark of excellence. Unlike in West Africa, story-telling was a family entertainment that took place around the evening fire rather than in the market-place, and while the narrator, often a senior woman, would grip the audience by her versatile role-playing, the form did not develop into theatre as we know it, although it

provided a wealth of material for theatre treatment. These forms are still current in rural areas.

After 1877 Christian missionaries established schools, and British administrators concerned themselves with social welfare. Schools and colleges, while discouraging traditional forms of entertainment, began to present performances, before an invited audience, which were rehearsed and in which the spoken word was the major means of communication. Plays in English helped with learning set books, but the students also enjoyed improvised vernacular farces, usually of a topical nature. Later, in community centres, social welfare assistants and Mothers' Union officers developed for didactic purposes the traditional form of cantor/response into a sung dialogue, with coordinated dance-mime and gesture. With hindsight, this can be seen as the beginnings of real Ugandan dramatic communication. In the 1950s, the emergence of songs that were a reaction to current situations showed one way in which this mode could develop: for instance, the strike of Mulago nurses – who were objecting to being made to wear badges with identity numbers – produced the dramatic song 'Namba, Namba'. The early missionaries had tried to suppress the indigenous entertainments, but by 1946 Mukono Theological College, like the medieval European Church, had seen the value of drama and was teaching its students to employ acting as a means of understanding. The major Bible stories were used to create plays drawn from the imaginations of the students and expressed in the mother tongue. The most notable was *Were You There?* (1949). A further development of this form later produced scripted plays from traditional stories – another step in the development of theatre (*The Cows of Karo* and *Kitami the Queen*, for instance).

Since 1946, all forms of theatre have been encouraged by organized competitions within and between youth groups, schools, colleges and adult groups, and at national level. At first drama was separated from other forms of theatre, but increasingly they have come together again. All the earliest-known writers first reached the public in festivals. The majority are graduates of Makerere University, which served all East Africa until the break-up of the East African Community. Its Department of Literature not only produced plays and encouraged writing but began a drama diploma course which has generated a full Department of Music, Dance and Drama, offering degree and postgraduate courses. A creative writing fellowship, financed for several years, was held largely by playwrights, including ROBERT SERUMAGA, BYRON KAWADWA, ELVANIA ZIRIMU and John Ruganda. Despite several attempts to establish professional groups, Ugandan theatre is still largely amateur, although the recent development of full-scale dramatic presentations by such professional musical groups as that of JIMMY KATUMBA may be a significant new feature. A national dance group has been formed from time to time, and schools and colleges are now often able to teach traditional dance and music from all parts of Uganda.

The National Theatre in Kampala was built in 1959, before independence, and in its first five years was used largely by expatriate groups. Stimulated by radio serials and, after 1962, by television, a local audience began to emerge and by 1966 more local than expatriate groups were performing: two landmarks were the premières of *The Black Hermit* (1962) by NGUGI WA THIONG'O (see Kenya), the first full-length play in English by an East African, and *Gwosussa Emwani* (*The One You Despise*) (1963) by WYCLIFFE KIYINGI-KAGWE, the first full-length Luganda-language play produced and acted entirely by Ugandans in the theatre. A further notable development came with the collaboration of BYRON KAWADWA and Wassanyi Serukenya in *Makula ga Kulabako* (*Kulabako's Wonderful Gift*, 1970), where original music in the Ugandan idiom was combined with a romantic story told in the form of a light opera. The number of original plays presented in the National Theatre grew impressive, but Luganda is so much the dominant language that critics suggest it is a regional rather than a national theatre.

There is a taste for theatre entertainment throughout the country. In Kampala the National Theatre is only one of many venues. This tiny theatre cannot satisfy demand; some groups have taken over cinemas and halls, and there are frequent outdoor performances in the capital. Elsewhere a similar increase can be observed. Every village provides an audience for travelling concert parties. Nearly all schools and colleges offer an appropriate venue, and presentation in community centres, market squares and churches is showing more versatility. Uganda is blessed with an equable climate, and in many parts a natural hill can provide an amphitheatre with minimum effort, although the increasing dependence of musical groups on electrical amplification for their instruments can be a complication. Transport is extremely expensive, but travelling groups now perform to full houses wherever they go. The first of the social welfare groups to attempt to tour villages were the Uganda Pilgrim Players, who from 1958 to 1960 took adaptations of medieval plays to parts of Buganda. The Makerere Travelling Theatre extended its itinerary to the whole of Uganda in the summer of 1965, and in its heyday travelled to Tanzania and Kenya as well. This kind of intracultural exchange is all too limited now.

The standard of performance of the current touring groups varies, and upcountry groups are seen too infrequently in Kampala, although the annual appearance of Namasagali Secondary School is a highlight in the theatre year. Dance-drama is increasingly popular. It both solves the language problem to some extent and builds on the traditional forms. There is a large audience for farce, which has been encouraged by the TV serials about office immorality, nagging wives, drunken husbands, corruption and trickery. Audiences like to escape from the problems of raging inflation, disease and inefficient administration into laughter. Performing groups can claim to have a didactic purpose – although how much effect their efforts have on attitudes is debatable. Some plays, scrappily scripted and naive in story line, are so heavily didactic that it is only the music, plus the ability and charisma of individual actors, that attract the audience. Many such performances, running for as long as four hours and sometimes changing direction in the middle, would seem interminable to a more sophisticated public. Rivalry and fear of plagiarism, and cost and difficulty of publication as well as the continued emphasis on improvisation, discourage literary development. Serious writers, producers and actors in the 1970s made their protests under cover of satire, mostly in English, the language of the educated audience, and now are trying to educate by the same means.

There is no closet drama. All playwrights – including Elvania Zirimu, Nuwa Sentongo and Robert Serumaga – write for performance, usually by a specific group, and often working through to a final script via group improvisation. The most popular plays are in local languages, usually Luganda – used, for instance, by Byron Kawadwa and Kiyingi-Kagwe, for many years the best-known dramatists. Serumaga, whose aim was to build on traditional forms and appeal across language divisions, attracted limited 'intellectual' audiences in Uganda, although he was for some time the best-known Ugandan theatre practitioner overseas. For a few years he ran a professional group, developing a theatre form dependent on movement, sound, music and dance which looks as though it will become the dominant form – although not in the shape he envisaged.

Serumaga has been followed in recent years by ALEX MUKULU, whose plays – such as *Twenty Years of the Banana* (1993) – are well shaped and presented; John Ruganda's influence in Uganda has been limited since he left the country, but his plays are published and studied in schools there and he is still attacking the evils of Uganda, if from a distance. Elvania Zirimu, a gifted actress and producer as well as lecturer in theatre arts, in the 1970s formed and led a group of graduate players and was a wider influence than her limited number of published plays suggests. CLIFF LUBWA P'CHONG, who was her husband, has been writing continuously as well as teaching and producing plays. He encourages the dramatization of traditional material as well as using comedy as a means of outspoken social criticism. He contributes to the raising of standards by his productions and his acting as well as by his writing. Eli Kyeyune, Zirimu's brother, writes didactic satire. Kiyingi-Kagwe has turned increasingly to writing series for television, where his work has always been most popular. But his plays have been published and are now on the Luganda school syllabus. His *Muduuma Kwe Kwaffe* (*Muduuma Our Home*, 1977) was originally an excellent stage play that has become a popular series. It was during the years of oppression (1971–86) that the majority of these writers learned the art of protest, instantly recognized as such by the target audience, but not by anyone else. Since 1986 it has been possible for criticism to be more explicit.

An interesting recent development has been the creation of the satirical story as a framework for the music of an increasing number of popular music groups, of which the best known and most dynamic has been Jimmy Katumba and the Ebonies. Making full use of recording studios, highly sophisticated equipment and technical knowledge, they led the way in the commercial theatre. But Katumba is now in the USA, and the raising of standards of composition and general performance is still hindered by the proliferation of largely amateur groups, exploiting the immense but unselective demand for theatre entertainment. The didacticism, reminiscent of medieval European morality plays, is often heavy-handed and unsubtle, but much current work is vigorous, there is an increasing sensitivity to the need for wit in both dialogue and music, and the combination of music, dance and drama would appear to point the way in which Ugandan theatre is going.

The present government and many international agencies have recognized the educative value of theatre and commission plays to be taken on tour to encourage awareness of AIDS and of the need to halt the spread of malaria. Under the guidance of Professor ROSE MBOWA a community-based drama (theatre for development) is tackling similar problems from the grass roots. A leader goes to a village, gathers potential performers, discusses local problems and identifies the one considered most urgent. Then, under his guidance, together they improvise a play, lasting usually some thirty minutes, highlighting the problem and often suggesting a possible solution. The play is rehearsed until fixed, then performed in school, in church after a service, or in the market-place, with the audience summoned by drums. At the close the audience is asked to discuss the problem – role-playing moving easily into reality – and suggest solutions. The play is occasionally so successful that the players perform it in neighbouring villages.

At all levels of performance, interaction between actors and audience is of great importance. Most forms of theatre in Uganda, while sometimes using very sophisticated means of communication (video interpolation drawing on TV narrative forms, for instance), concentrate almost entirely on local subjects. A wider knowledge and experience of drama from elsewhere would give Ugandan theatre a greater resonance.

Katumba, Jimmy (fl. 1970s–80s)

Ugandan musician and entrepreneur. In the late 1970s Katumba formed a musical ensemble which became very popular – the Ebonies. The group developed a large business enterprise, owning sound studios which produce Jimmy Katumba records. In 1988, extending their activities to drama, they formed the Ebonies, a group of actors who perform at the Theatre Excelsior, a converted school hall in Kampala. John W. Katunde's *The Dollar* (1988) and *The Inspector* (1990) are detective plays which are developed in performance by improvisation. *The Dollar* attacks materialism and corruption through a search for a murdered woman. In *The Inspector*, the main object of attack is hospital mismanagement and the medical profession. Both plays use the music for which this group is well known. Katumba now lives in the USA, and the group has become less active.

Kawadwa, Byron (c.1940–77)

Ugandan playwright, producer and director. Kawadwa was educated at Aggrey Memorial School, Kampala, and founded the Uganda Schools Drama Festival while still a student. On leaving school he worked at Radio Uganda but was arrested and imprisoned after the 1964 disturbances. On his release he worked with KIYINGI-KAGWE and his group. By 1965 the Kampala City Players had been formed with Kawadwa as writer and director and members drawn largely from young men and women in the Kampala business, commercial and government world. He was admitted to the Makerere University drama course in 1968. He was appointed artistic director of the Uganda National Theatre in 1973 and held a concurrent Creative Writing Fellowship at Makerere for one year. A staunch royalist, he used palace themes in his two most important works, written in collaboration with musician Wassanyi Serukenya. *Makula ga Kulabako* (1970) tells the love story of Kulabako, a princess, and a commoner. It was immediately popular and has been made into a film. *Oluimba lwa Wankoko*

(*The Song of Mr Cock*, 1971) tells of the attempt to oust the rightful heir to the throne by an ambitious politician. A covert satire on the political situation in Buganda after the ousting of the Kabaka in 1966, it was later Uganda's entry to FESTAC (see Introduction) in Lagos and is said to have been the cause of Kawadwa's murder. In both plays the music matches the words and the theme is both original and Ugandan.

Kiyingi-Kagwe, Wycliffe (1934–)

Ugandan playwright and producer, regarded as the doyen of Ugandan theatre. Educated at Kings College, Budo, and Makerere University, he founded the African Artists' Association, the first all-Ugandan dramatic society, in 1954. He writes well constructed topical satire and farce, and was first successful with his radio series *Wokulira*, which began in 1961 and was then suppressed under Amin, but a new series is running in the 1990s. With the introduction of television in 1962, he began a very popular series, *Buli Enkya, Buli Ekiro* (*Day In, Day Out*) and, with radio and TV reputation already made he produced *Gwosussa Emwanyi* (*The One You Despise*, 1963), the first full-length play performed in Luganda language in the Uganda National Theatre. (It was published in 1967 and is a school set book.) In 1965 he spent a year studying theatre in Bristol. Another of his satirical farces, *Lozio ba Cecilia* (*Lozio, Cecila's Husband*, published in 1972, is also a set book. Kiyingi-Kagwe acknowledges his debt to G. B. Shaw and Sean O'Casey, and is still writing and producing plays for stage, TV and radio. *Muduuma kwe Kwaffe* (1977) contrasts the exploiting Asian shopkeeper with the equally exploiting but less obliging Ugandan businessman in a witty three-act satire that gave rise to a TV series, which is a vehicle for much social comment.

Lubwa, Cliff p'Chong (1946–)

Ugandan playwright, actor and producer. Lubwa was educated at Sam Baker School,

Gulu, the National Teachers' College, Kyambogo, and at Makerere, Durham and Exeter Universities. He was Creative Writing Fellow at the University of Iowa in 1987, and lectures in drama-in-education at the Institute of Teacher Education, Kyambogo. His plays (published in English) are *Generosity Kills* and *The Last Safari* (1975), *The Minister's Wife* (1983) and *Kinsmen and Kinswomen* (1986). He has also published poems and other writings.

Mbowa, Rose (fl. 1970–)

Ugandan playwright and academic. Educated at the Universities of Makerere and Leeds, where she gained a BA and MA and a diploma in drama, Mbowa now heads the Department of Dance and Drama at Makerere. She has collaborated with JIMMY KATUMBA in overseas tours. Her play *Mother Uganda* (1987) links music and dance from all parts of Uganda with a simple story in which 'Mother Uganda' attempts to bring all her warring children into harmony. The play has toured in Europe as well as Uganda. Mbowa and her students are deeply engaged in community-based theatre projects. Her plays are usually written in response to a particular need, involve all the theatrical arts and, while written in English, translate easily.

Mukulu, Alex (fl. 1980s–90s)

Ugandan actor and performer, playwright and director. Mukulu first drew attention in the early 1980s with a group which paid more attention to competent presentation than most companies, performing plays that incorporated plenty of dance and music, in the pattern of BYRON KAWADWA and ROBERT SERUMAGA: most recently *Wounds of Africa* (1990) and *Thirty Years of the Banana* (1991). As well as writing the plays and directing, Mukulu usually takes the leading role and is reported to maintain rigid discipline within the company. His songs are dramatically topical and often satirical, and, while there is a bias towards the Luganda language, his plays appeal over the language barrier, through mime, dance and music.

Serumaga, Robert (1940–81)

Ugandan playwright and producer. Educated at Trinity College, Dublin, Serumaga trained at the BBC and in theatre in Europe before returning to Uganda in 1966. He founded Theatre Ltd, later known as the Abafumi Players, gathering together outstanding actors and backstage personnel from existing dramatic societies (largely expatriate in the beginning) to form a semi-professional group. After producing several plays by other writers he concentrated on producing his own. Subsequently he gathered together a group of school-leavers whom he trained as professional performers and with whom he travelled widely, creating two notable dance dramas: *Renga Moi* (1972) and *Amerykitti* (1974). He held the senior Creative Writing Fellowship at Makerere University for one year. In the last two years of the Amin regime (1977–9) he found it easier to operate his company from Nairobi. He was briefly (1979) Minister of Commerce in the Lule government. He returned to the Abufumi Players in Nairobi, where he died. His published works are *A Play* (1967), *The Elephants* (1970) and *Majangwa* (1971).

Zirimu, Elvania (Namukwaya) (fl. 1960s–70s, d. 1979)

Ugandan playwright, producer, actress and academic. Already a talented actress at Kings College, Budo, she attended Makerere University from 1961 to 63, where her play *Keeping up with the Mukasas* won the English competition and the Original Play award in the Ugandan Drama Festival. In 1963 she went to Leeds University, where she took a degree in 1966. On her return she became tutor at the National Teachers' College, Kyambogo, and later also at Makerere University. She formed the Ngoma Players, with the declared policy of writing and producing plays in a Ugandan mode, and was actively concerned with the National Theatre. She had been appointed to the embassy in Ghana when she was killed in a car crash. Her published plays are *Keeping up with the Mukasas* (1965), as well as *When the Hunchback made Rain and Snoring Strangers* (1975), and *Family Spear* (1973).

Bibliography

M. Banham and C. Wake, *African Theatre Today*, London, 1976; E. Breitinger, 'Popular Urban Culture in Uganda', *New Theatre Quarterly*, 8, 31, 1992; D Cook, *In Black and White*, Nairobi, 1976; D. Duerden and C. Pieterse, *African Writers Talking*, London, 1972; R. Grandquist (ed.), *Signs and Signals: Popular Culture in Africa*, Umea, 1990; E. Jones, *African Literature Today*, No.8, London, 1976; A. Roscoe, *Uhuru's Fire*, Cambridge, 1977.

ZAIRE

After seventy-five years of colonial rule, the former Belgian Congo, now Zaire, was hurriedly granted independence in 1960. The new state had very little experience in self-government and it was soon engulfed in a civil war during which its first prime minister, Patrice Lumumba, was assassinated. The events of this period have been dramatized in various plays, the most important of which are AIMÉ CÉSAIRE's (see Caribbean Theatre, Introduction) *Une Saison au Congo* (*A Season in the Congo*, 1966), and *Murderous Angels* (1968) by the Irish diplomat and academic then with the United Nations, Conor Cruise O'Brien.

Modern Zairian theatre has not produced a work of the significance of *Une Saison*. Because of a Belgian colonial policy which encouraged education in the national languages, the theatre in French did not start until the 1950s. Its pioneers were Albert Mongita, a former teacher and post office employee who wrote *Soko Stanley* (1954) to commemorate the fortieth anniversary of the death of the explorer Stanley, *Mongenge* (1956) and *Ngomba* (1957), on traditional customs and folklore; L. S. Bondekwe, whose *Athanase et les professeurs de lumière* (*Athanasius and the Enlightened Teachers*, 1957) satirizes the so-called *évolués*; and Hippolyte Kabamba with a play on the Luba dynasty, *Nkongola* (1957).

After the civil war in 1966 there was a flowering of theatrical activity, with the founding of troupes such as the Lovanium University-based Théâtre de la Colline, Théâtre de Zaire and the Union Générale des Amis de la Musique et de la Culture of Lumumbashi, one of whose founders, Valérien Mutombo-Diba, wrote several plays including a comedy, *Beau Michel* (*Handsome Michel*, 1966), and a historical play, *Tamouré et les seigneurs de Garengazé* (*Tamouré and The Lords of Garengazé*, 1966).

Contemporary Zairian theatre has also produced many plays, whose themes range from ritual: Yoka Mudaba's *Tshiré* (1984) and Mwamb'a Mangol's *Muzang* (1977); through political struggles and corruption: Lisembé Elébé's *Simon Kimbangui ou le Messie noire* and *Le Sang des noirs pour un sou* (*Simon Kimbangui or the Black Messiah* and *The Blood of Blacks for a Penny*, 1972) and Nkashama Ngandu's *Bonjour Monsieur le Ministre* (*Good Morning Mr Minister*, 1983); to traditional customs and practices: Charles Ngenzhi's *La Fille du forgeron* (*The Blacksmith's Daughter*, 1960) and Saturnin Ngombo's *Coutumes et usages du roi Ntinu Wene* (*Customs and Practices of King Ntinu Wene*, 1979).

Bibliography

R. Cornevin, *Le Théâtre en Afrique noire et à Madagascar*, Paris, 1970; U. Edebiri, 'Le Théâtre Zairois à la recherche de son authenticité', *Afrique Littéraire et Artistique*, 40, 1976; C. Wake, 'Zaire', in *The Cambridge Guide to World Theatre*, ed. M. Banham, Cambridge, 1988.

ZAMBIA

Until independence on 24 October 1964, Zambia was the British colony Northern Rhodesia. The population of over 8 million falls into six major language groups – Bemba, Nyanja, Lozi, Tonga, Lunda and Kaonde.

Before the advent of colonialism, traditional dances, dance-dramas and ritual plays were performed at seasonal and religious festivals and rites of passage, such as the *makishi* masquerade (see Introduction, MASQUERADES IN AFRICA) of North Western Province and the *nyau kasinja* funeral dance of the Eastern Province. Other ceremonies include the *nachisungu*, a puberty rite of the Northern Provinces; the *mutomboko*, which celebrates the accession to the throne of Mwata Kazembe, king of the Lundas; the *kuomboka*, which marks the movement of the Lozi king from his winter to his summer capital; and the *ncwala*, which commemorates the victories of the Nguni people during their migration from South Africa. In addition to these forms, there is a rich tradition of narrative, the most famous of which are the stories of Kalulu the hare.

With colonization and the subsequent urbanization, some of these forms were modified and some new ones developed from the old. As with much cult drama in early societies – the rites of Dionysus in Greece and the Yoruba masquerades of Nigeria, for instance – the *nyau* masquerades developed in line with social changes from a clan cult performance into a secret society, then into family guilds, and ultimately into professional performing groups. In the process new masks were added, comic and satiric plots elaborated, and the original cult taboos were set aside in favour of inventive entertainments which were performed for money, before multi-ethnic audiences. Ultimately, content was stripped of original meanings and functions.

Other syncretic modern performance forms based on the traditional culture are *kayowe* (a courtship dance based on a cock and hen choreography), *kalela* (satirical of white dress and manners), *fwembu* (an acrobatic dance developed by soldiers returning from the Second World War) and *kachala* (based on spirit possession (*mashawe*) and puberty rites (*nachisungu*), and incorporating mimed satire of contemporary mores). During the period of agitation for independence, the nationalist youth groups made effective use of these performing modes for political mobilization. They were later incorporated into the repertoire of the National Dance Troupe, established in 1965, which under the directorship of Edwin Manda adopted a dynamic approach to the traditional forms, producing full-length dance-dramas such as *Nsombo Malimba* (the names of musical instruments). These in turn influenced other dramatists, including MASAUTSO PHIRI and S. J. CHIFUNYISE (see Zimbabwe).

The European settlers introduced Western theatre into Zambia, forming in 1952 the all-white Northern Rhodesia Drama Association, which with independence became the Theatre Association of Zambia (TAZ). Between 1954 and 1958 a number of theatres were built for the exclusive use of expatriate and settler communities. In 1958 a multi-racial group founded the Waddington Theatre Club and challenged the colonial colour bar by, after heated debate, gaining membership of TAZ. Though the white settlers claimed that 'very little interest was shown by Africans in theatre', from 1958 to 1962 the Northern Rhodesian Youth Council held an annual drama and choir festival, which came to an end only when the clubs became involved in the political campaigns of the nationalist organizations. In 1958 a fifteen-minute radio programme was introduced, broadcasting plays in a number of Zambian languages by, among others, Edward Kateka, Asaf Mvula, Y. L. Zulu, Wilfred Banda and Patterson Mukanda. Andreya Misiye was the first Zambian to write a full-length play, *The Many Lands of Kazembe*. A weekly series in Tonga, *Malikopo*, and another in Nyanja, *Tambwali*, became extremely popular.

Formed in the year before independence, the Zambia Arts Trust, a national association of indigenous theatre enthusiasts, toured the country on a grant from the new Zambian government with plays in English and Zambian languages including Gideon Lumpa's *Iyi Eyali Imikalile* (*The Way We Lived*), John Simbotwe's *Ifyabukaya* (*Our Customs*), KABWE KASOMA's *The Long Arm of the Law* and others by Shaw, WOLE SOYINKA and OLA ROTIMI (see Nigeria), and Obutunde Ijimere. They organized theatre festivals and were virtually the only organization at the time performing plays in Zambian languages. In 1969 a local publisher, Titus Mukopo, recruited Yulisa Amadu Maddy (see Sierra Leone) to found the Zambia Dance Company, but a venture to establish a professional theatre company was not a success.

Possibly the most significant new development after independence was the emergence of drama at the new University of Zambia. A student dramatic society (UNZADRAMS) became active on the campus; its policy favoured locally written plays, and its earliest productions included Kasoma's *The Long Arm of the Law*, Michael Etherton's adaptation of G. Oyono-Mbia's novel *Houseboy*, *Che Guevara* and *Kazembe and the Portuguese*. In 1969 drama courses were established by Michael Etherton and Andrew Horn, and in 1971 with the construction of an open-air theatre the CHIKWAKWA THEATRE was born. Chikwakwa took theatre in English and Zambian languages to the people by touring plays, developing plays with local

schoolchildren and holding workshops and festivals. It also produced a journal, *The Chikwakwa Review*. The Chikwakwa example inspired many new developments, and the concept of travelling theatre has been continued by the Centre for the Arts, founded at the university in 1983.

Bazamai Theatre (1970–2) was a Chikwakwa outside university walls. Founded by Masautso Phiri and Stephen Moyo, it produced the dance-drama *Kuta*, Moyo's *The Last Prerogative* and an adaptation of Chinua Achebe's *Things Fall Apart*. Another development of Chikwakwa was Tikwiza, founded in 1975, which became a *de facto* national company, dominating Zambian theatre for nine years and representing Zambian theatre at the 1972 FESTAC (see Introduction) and in CUBA, Botswana (see Botswana, Lesotho and Swaziland), and KENYA. Its actors included some of the best Zambia has produced, such as Matildah Malamamfumu, Mumba Kapumpa and Haggai Chisulo. Its work was characterized by the political emphasis of plays such as Masautso Phiri's *Soweto* and Dickson Mwansa's *The Cell*.

The extent to which the Chikwakwa tradition had become the basis for an alternative indigenous Zambian theatre movement is demonstrated by the formation of the Zambian National Theatre Arts Association (ZANTAA). With a large membership in schools, colleges and community theatre groups, ZANTAA organized annual festivals. Nearly ninety plays were produced, mostly unpublished. In 1983 a national debate culminated in the merger of the two existing theatre organizations, TAZ and ZANTAA.

Starting as an opponent of Chikwakwa, David Wallace became a leading advocate and practitioner, via his Theatre Circle, of theatre based on traditional orature, especially the Kalulu (hare) tales. Bakanda Theatre's production in 1980 of Dickson Mwansa's *The Cell*, Tithandize Theatre's performances of plays by Craig Lungu and ZANASE Theatre, a full-time company attached to the Zambian National Service, have all been influential.

In the 1980s there was spectacular growth in community-based theatre in working-class residential areas. One group, Kanyama Theatre, became Zambia's first full-time professional theatre group, touring Zambia and Zimbabwe widely.

Television drama, too, has been influenced by the indigenous Zambian theatre movement. In response to government directives to scrap foreign material in favour of local work, Zambian television introduced the 'Play for Today' series, which has produced many popular Zambian works such as Chifunyise's *I Resign* and *A Thorn in Our Flesh*, Mulenga N'gandu's *Jobless Existence* and Kwalela Ikafa's *Dambwa*, as well as a number of dance-dramas. The National Dance Troupe had an influential weekly one-hour slot in which it performed dance, dance-drama and sketches, in Zambian languages – constituting a breakthrough, as only English had hitherto been used on television.

Chikwakwa Theatre

An open-air theatre established at the University of Zambia in 1971 as a venue for practical drama work by students, and in order to promote the democratic development of popular performing arts in Zambia as a whole. Plays produced there were original and indigenous in content and form, and, with its tours to all parts of the country, Chikwakwa pioneered the concept of taking theatre to the people. Many of Zambia's playwrights and actors received their decisive training experience there. The spirit of Chikwakwa is perhaps best expressed by Michael Etherton, one of its founders: 'Chikwakwa theatre is more than an open-air theatre building in the bush near Lusaka. It is a commitment to the development of theatre in Zambia from existing cultural roots as they are manifested in the performing arts and in ritual.' One of Chikwakwa's most influential productions was *Che Guevara* at the third summit meeting of the Non-Aligned Movement in 1970. Chikwakwa also produced a theatre review.

Kasoma, Kabwe (fl. 1970s)

Zambian playwright, whose published work includes *The Black Mamba* trilogy of plays on Kenneth Kaunda and the struggle for independence (1975). Kasoma is director of the University of Zambia dance troupe and of the Centre for the Arts.

Phiri, Masautso (fl. 1970s)

Zambian playwright, director, novelist and poet. Active in theatre since 1963, he co-founded with Stephen Moyo the Bazamai Theatre Group in 1970 while a student, and Tikwiza Theatre in 1975. He has written and directed a number of plays including a trilogy on Soweto, plus novels and poetry.

Bibliography

Chikwakwa Review, Univ. of Zambia, Lusaka. M. Etherton, *The Development of African Drama*, London, 1982, and 'The Dilemma of the Popular Playwright: The Work of Kabwe Kasoma and V. E. Musinga', *African Literature Today*, 8, 1976.

ZIMBABWE

After years of bitter armed struggle against the white settler regime of Ian Smith, the new state of Zimbabwe (formerly Rhodesia) came into existence on 18 April 1980. The majority of its 10 million inhabitants speak Shona, while Ndebele is a significant minority language and Tonga, Kalanga, Venda and English are also spoken.

When a soldier called William King put on a variety concert soon after the Pioneer Column first occupied the country in 1890, he was said to have staged the 'first major theatrical entertainment in the country'. However, indigenous theatre forms existed many years before the coming of the settlers, as illustrated by the wide practice amongst the Shona people of the *mahumbwe*, a young people's harvest performance, and the comic 'funeral drama' in which the deceased's major achievements are dramatized. In addition, there were many other ritual ceremonies, dances, games and narratives that contained significant dramatic elements.

By the 1950s the white settlers had established segregated theatre clubs in most major towns, and in 1958 these formed the Association of Rhodesian Theatrical Societies, later to become the National Theatre Organization, holding an annual theatre festival adjudicated by 'experts' from Britain or South Africa. With few exceptions, this organization confined itself to segregated colonial drama, a situation which changed only slowly after independence.

The organization of theatre amongst the black majority was left to a variety of bodies: to the colonial government, which organized festivals of prescribed plays; to the Salisbury city council, which employed Basil Chidyamathamba to foster traditional dancing and establish the Neshamwari Festival of Music, Dance and Drama in 1965; to various church organizations from whose activities emerged active personalities such as BEN SIBENKE, Walter Muparutsa and Dominic Kanaventi; and to a number of amateur clubs often associated with the mining companies – namely the Torwood African Theatre Society, the Wankie Dramatic and Choral Society and the Kamativi African Players. Then, in the 1970s, the escalating war of liberation began to restore to the people a theatre practice based on the indigenous traditions of Zimbabwe. Political cadres of the nationalist movements organized dramas in the guerrilla camps and all-night *pungwes*, night-time political meetings conducted by freedom fighters in the countryside where songs, folk-tales, dance and drama articulated the motivations behind the struggle. The theatre of the pungwe featured prominently the heroes of the first anti-colonial resistance of the 1970s, colonial repression, and the new Zimbabwe that would emerge from the struggle.

Theatre in the post-independence period is characterized by a mixture of trends established in the colonial regime and of new ones generated by the changed circumstances of independence. Artists who had been active in the colonial period found more room to expand. Whereas before independence N. Chipunza's *Svikiro* (1978), mangled by the white director into *My Spirit Sings*, was the only play written and acted by black Zimbabweans to be performed in a white theatre, now both the People's Company – with locally written plays by Sibenke and Karl Dorn – and the Sundown Players, specializing in the plays of ATHOL FUGARD (see South Africa), began competing in the previously all-white National Theatre Festival. In 1982 Basil Chidyamathamba's traditional-based musical, *Sounds of Zimbabwe*, was produced. In 1985 Kanaventi, Muparutsa and Sibenke came together to form the Zimbabwe Arts Productions, with impressive performances of Fugard's 'workshop play' *Sizwe Banzi is Dead* and *The Island*. They went on to join up with Andrew Whaley, performing his play *Platform Five*, about tramps on Harare's streets. Subsequently Whaley and the actor Simon Shumba formed Meridien Players, staging Whaley's *Nyoka Tree* (1988) and *The Rise and Shine of Comrade Fiasco* (1990), a controversial treatment of the liberation struggle and post-independence society.

It was the post-independence government of Robert Mugabe, however, which made innovations that were to influence the development of theatre in Zimbabwe – namely the foundation of the National Dance Company and the community-based theatre movement organized by the Zimbabwe Foundation for Education with Production (ZIMFEP); and the work of the new Ministry of Youth, Sport and Culture. The National Dance Company was formed in 1981 and its first production, *Mbuya Nehanda – the Spirit of Liberation*, choreographed by Peggy Harper, Karium Welsh-Asante and Emmanual Ribeiro, continued the spirit of the revolutionary *pungwe*. Subsequently, though, the company confined itself to the performance of indigenous dance, until its demise in 1991.

In 1982 the then Ministry of Education and Culture employed the Kenyans Ngugi wa Mirii and Kimani Gecau to develop a community-based theatre movement under the auspices of ZIMFEP. With the Chindunduma School community they produced *The Trials of Dedan Kimathi* by NGUGI WA THIONG'O and MICERE MUGO (see Kenya) in Shona and English, and toured nationally, demonstrating widely the concept of community-based theatre. The ministry followed this up with a UNESCO-sponsored African Workshop on Theatre for Development in Murewa in 1983, involving local participants and theatre artists from twenty-two African countries.

Ngugi wa Mirii, with ZIMFEP, and S. J. CHIFUNYISE as Director of Arts and Crafts in the new Ministry of Youth, Sport and Culture, continued the tradition by holding various theatre-for-development and drama-skills workshops and forming community-based theatre groups. The Vashandi Workers' Theatre Group, the Avondale Domestic Workers' Theatre Group, the Chindunduma School Drama Group and Habbakuk Musengezi's community theatre group in Centenary in northern Zimbabwe were early examples of this movement's growing importance. Groups were established all over the country, performing both scripted and original plays in schools, mines, community halls and factories. Amakhosi Productions of Bulawayo, directed by Cont Mhlanga and a representative example, includes among its productions *Workshop Negative* (1987), *Citizen Mind* (1989) and *Stitsha* (1990).

In 1987 many of these groups came together to form the Zimbabwe Association of Community Theatre. ZACT and the National Theatre Organization are the two main theatre organizations in Zimbabwe. The NTO holds an annual festival, formerly called the National Theatre Festival but now renamed Winterfest. It also organizes a national school festival and a Play of the Year competition. The NTO is no longer exclusively white and colonial, but a clear difference in orientation and ideology has distinguished the two organizations. With the change in the international balance of forces and the introduction of the economic structural adjustment programme in Zimbabwe, this distinction has in recent years become less marked. But the struggle to survive on the part of the community-based theatre groups has become intense. This has led to a change in content and to an increased professionalism, with greater attention being paid to issues that are likely to be supported by sponsors and donors, and to other commercial considerations. A play on AIDS, *Manyanya* (1989), by the theatre group Batsiranai (meaning 'help each other') is a case in point.

A particularly influential development has been the growth of indigenous television drama, including the regular Shona comedy series *Mhuri ya Mukadota* (*The Mukadota Family*) featuring Safirio Madzikatire and Susan Chenjerai, both veterans of Shona radio drama since the early 1960s; plays by Chifunyise and by THOMPSON TSODZO, Charles Mungoshi, Agnes Gwatiringa and Aaron Moyo, as well as by Ndema Ngwenya with his MAWA (Mthwakazi Artists and Writers Association) Theatre Group; and MAWA Theatre Group's *Tshaka Zulu* (in Ndebele). Madzikatire also plays in a popular stage show which includes sketches and is in the popular theatre format reminiscent of GIBSON KENTE (see South Africa) or HUBERT OGUNDE (see Nigeria).

In 1984 the University of Zimbabwe introduced undergraduate courses in drama and began to participate actively in the community. In addition to productions staged as a part of coursework, a major production was introduced as an annual feature and a political theatre group, Zambuko/Izibuko, formed. The university worked closely with the Ministry of Youth, Sport and Culture and with ZIMFEP in the development of the community-based movement, establishing courses in theatre-for-development and theatre-in-education. A major feature of the university's work was the involvement of actors from the community. Since its first production, in 1984–5, of *Mavambo, First Steps*, based on Wilson Katiyo's novel *A Son of the Soil*, the university and Zambuko/Izibuko have produced a number of influential original and scripted plays, including *I Will Marry When I Want* by Ngugi wa Thiong'o and Ngugi wa Mirii translated into Shona, N. Pogodin's *Kremlin Chimes*, and Zambuko/Izibuko's *Katshaa!* (1986), *Samora Continua* (1988) and *Mandela, the Spirit of No Surrender* (1990). All these productions were staged both at the university and throughout Zimbabwe.

Since independence, Zimbabwean publishers have devoted more attention to publishing plays in English, Ndebele and Shona, including those of Chifunyise, Bertha Msora and Habbakuk Musengezi; G. Mujajati, Andrew Whaley, Cont Mhlanga, Aaron Moyo, William Chigidi and T. Dangarembga. The university's Faculty of Arts began publication of a 'University Playscript' series of cheap acting editions of Zimbabwean and African plays in 1986. In addition to the growth of theatre amongst adults, the development of children's theatre has been greatly facilitated by the establishment of the Children's Performing Arts Workshop, which has staged its own original plays and plans to publish material specially for children.

A considerable upsurge in interest in indigenous theatre and in theatrical activity transformed the depressed situation of the pre-independence years, but the present harsh economic climate threatens to undermine the progress made.

Chifunyise, S. J. (1948–)

Zimbabwean playwright, educated in Zambia and the United States. A CHIKWAKWA THEATRE (see Zambia) product, he taught at the University of Zambia and was national director of Culture. He is now Director of Arts and Crafts at the Ministry of Youth, Sport and Culture in Zimbabwe. His short plays and dance-dramas are extremely popular in both Zambia and Zimbabwe. Some of these have been published in his collection, *Medicine for Love* (1984). Chifunyise is now Deputy Secretary, Culture, in the Ministry of Education and Culture, and active in many cultural and arts organizations.

Sibenke, Ben (1945–)

Zimbabwean playwright and actor, founder

member of the People's Company, and author of, among other plays in both English and Shona, *My Uncle Grey Bhonzo*, a comedy on the need for cultural roots, and *Chidembo Chanhuwa* (*The Polecat Stank*), a play set in the rural areas after independence.

Tsodzo, Thompson (1947–)

Zimbabwean playwright, novelist and writer on education. Formerly a teacher, he joined the government at independence. Many of his plays in Shona have been televised. He also produced his *The Storm* in 1982 with S. Chikwendere, commemorating Zimbabwe's struggle for independence. His published plays include *The Talking Calabash* (1976), *Tsano* (*The Brother-in-law*, 1982) and *Shanduko* (*Changes*, 1983). His focus is generally moralistic, though *The Storm* and *Shanduko* show an interest in modern political developments in Zimbabwe.

Bibliography

G. P. Kahari, *The Imaginative Writings of Paul Chidyausiku*, Gweru, 1975; *Journal of Southern African Studies*, 16, 2, 1990; *Tulane Drama Review*, 36, 1, 1992; *Zimbabwe Theatre Report*, Univ. of Zimbabwe 1989; R. M. Zinyemba, *Zimbabwean Drama: A Study of Shona and English Plays*, Gweru, 1986.

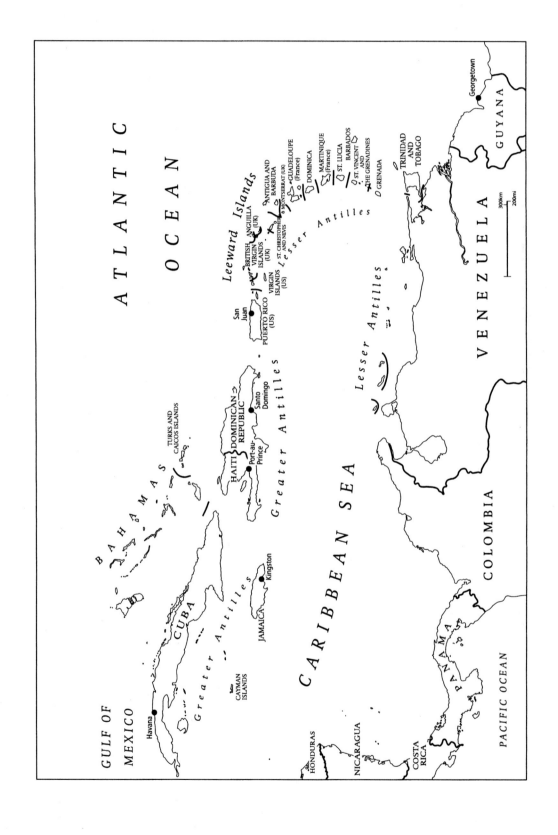

CARIBBEAN THEATRE

INTRODUCTION

Until the first third of the present century theatre in the Caribbean was representative of a stratified and hierarchical multicultural society. Having eliminated the indigenous Amerindians who inhabited the Caribbean islands, the European colonizers began their settlement of the region with the creation of large plantations on which the production of sugar proved most profitable. Chief among the Europeans vying with each other for a share of the spoils of conquest were the Spanish, French, English and Dutch nations, each of whom left the residue of its rule in the language used by present-day Caribbeans.

Cheap labour required for work on the estates was supplied by slaves brought over from West Africa and, after the slaves were emancipated in the 19th century, by indentured workers from India who replaced them in colonies such as Guyana, Trinidad and Jamaica. In addition there were Portuguese from Madeira, Chinese from mainland China, Syrians and other waves of immigrants who came seeking their fortune in the fabled isles of the west.

Theatre in such a polyglot society will have many strands. Its most formal manifestation occurred when companies of travelling professionals from Europe and later America visited the Caribbean, more or less regularly, beginning in the 17th century.

They brought plays contemporary with their times and played in a variety of public halls when no proper playhouse was available. Along with these career actors were military thespians of officer rank who whiled away the hours of inactivity by staging plays for their fellow officers, government officials and friends among the local society.

The next level of theatre occurred when local amateur groups, in imitation of the professionals, staged plays by young men and women for the general public. Often intense rivalry erupted among these groups with partisan reviewers favouring one group of players over another. Recruitment into these amateur companies usually came from graduates of high schools where there existed a tradition of speech training and elocution with student performances as end of the school year exercises. Some of these youthful players would eventually find themselves on professional stages abroad.

Yet another type of performance activity came from the non-European, numerically dominant segment of the population; slave, indentured, and free workers who sought to retain traditions of their distant homelands by re-enacting them in their new environment. The Africans told stories of their folk hero, the spider Anansi who, among the frailest of creatures, could survive only by using his wits. They composed and sang songs of praise and derision using homemade instruments for accompaniment. They danced and masqueraded when allowed to join in festive holidays and they worshipped their orishas (African gods) in private ceremonies.

When slavery was abolished in 1834 indentured workers from India brought in to replace slave labour also carried with them various traditional festivals. Chief among these was the celebration of Muharram, the first month of the Muslim year, during which tribute was paid to Hasain, grandson of the prophet Mohammed and a victim in the battle of Karbala to reinstate his family's rule. At this public parade highly decorated, sacred moon objects or *tadjahs* were borne through the streets to the beating of Indian drums and were later thrown into the river or sea. In a few decades the parade was joined by Hindu and Afro-Caribbeans that suggested a growing solidarity among the labouring classes. The Chinese also for many years displayed their dragon dance on city streets to herald the birth of a new year but this festival is no longer continued. Such were the types of public performance that continued through the 19th and into the first decades of the 20th century.

Although isolated plays had been written by Caribbean authors prior to the 1930s, it was only in that decade that the first serious attempts were made to write and present plays relevant to Caribbean life that would appeal to a broad cross-section of the population. In Jamaica in 1930 Marcus Garvey produced three dramatic pageants at his open-air stage in Kingston stressing the need for an end to colonialism. In London the Trinidad-born writer C.L.R. James presented his drama *Toussaint l'Ouverture* on the Haitian revolution in 1936. And in Puerto Rico a national theatre was established in 1938 with the staging of three plays by native authors dealing with national themes.

Three further developments helped bring the live theatre home to Caribbean people. The first was the establishment in 1947 of the University (College) of the West Indies whose extramural tutors helped to encourage the writing and publication of local plays throughout the English-speaking Caribbean and to spread the notion of a popular theatre using the vernacular where appropriate rather than a grammatically correct but artificial language.

Next came the movement towards political independence and the granting of self-government to most territories beginning with Jamaica and Trinidad in 1962. This led to a deeper sense of belonging to a nation and a search for forms of presentation in speech, drama, movement, dance, music and rhythm, in verbal and visual imagery that would free theatre creators from inherited customs and inhibitions of the past.

Finally, there has been a movement, largely promoted in Cuba but adopted by several sister territories, to use theatre as a means to raise the social, political and aesthetic consciousness of the people through what has been called the theatre of collective creation. Community based, this movement adopts the method of research into problems of a given geographic area in which the theatre is located with attempts to solve these problems in a dramatic presentation with community involvement. Performances are followed by serious discussions with scholars, writers and workers. The first national festival in this movement known as Teatre Nuevo was held in Cuba in 1969.

English-speaking Caribbean

The Caribbean or, more correctly, the Commonwealth Caribbean (hitherto and incorrectly called the West Indies) consists of some fifteen island governments and the two coastal states, Belize and GUYANA, that border the Caribbean Sea. They were British colonies until 1958, when most of them united in the West Indies Federation. When the Federation was dissolved in 1962, individual countries took different constitutions. Some, like TRINIDAD AND TOBAGO and Guyana, eventually became republics; JAMAICA and BARBADOS claimed full nationhood; others formed a loose association of self-ruled EASTERN CARIBBEAN STATES; others, like Anguilla and the Cayman Islands, retained colonial status. All, however, joined Britain in the new Commonwealth of Nations, although they continue to seek a closer cultural unity and identity with neighbouring nations in the Caribbean basin. Separate articles will be found on the theatre in Barbados, Guyana, Jamaica, Trinidad and Tobago, and on three of the Eastern Caribbean States: Antigua, Dominica, and St Lucia.

The anglophone Caribbean has had formal

Carifesta

The Caribbean festival of creative arts is a periodic two- or three-week gathering of creative writers and artists in one of the major territories of the region. It is government-sponsored and reaches beyond the anglophone Caribbean to embrace all islands and coastal nations around the Caribbean basin. (The first Caribbean regional festival – the precursor of Carifesta – in which fourteen territories participated, had taken place in 1952 in PUERTO RICO, and second has been held in Trinidad to mark the opening of the short-lived West Indian Federation in 1958.) The idea was promoted by the government of GUYANA, which hosted the first Carifesta in 1972. Since then there have been festivals in JAMAICA in 1976, Cuba in 1979, BARBADOS in 1981 and TRINIDAD AND TOBAGO in 1992. Apart from exhibitions and presentations of various kinds, publications such as *A Time and a Season: 8 Caribbean Plays* (1976), edited by ERROL HILL (see Trinidad and Tobago), were issued for the Jamaican festival.

Césaire, Aimé (1913–)

Martiniquan poet, politician, essayist and playwright. Césaire has enjoyed a successful career as a politician and author, being one of the founders (with Léopold Senghor) of the negritude movement in the 1930s. He is better known as a poet than as a playwright, but his plays were among the most important new French-language work of the 1960s. They administered a shock to the French theatre world very similar to that produced by WOLE SOYINKA's (see Nigeria) work in England. An early play, *Et les chiens se taisaient (And the Dogs were Silent)*, celebrates the themes of revolt to be found in his major plays, but remains essentially a poetic work.

His three plays for the theatre were written in the 1960s, partly under the influence of Jean-Marie Serreau, who directed them. In *La Tragédie du Roi Christophe (The Tragedy of King Christopher*, 1964) the historical figure of Christophe (King Henry of Haiti, 1811–20) is used to present the conflicting views of black African liberation current in the 1950s and 60s. The play has a vigorous, Brechtian epic structure, combined with a rich and powerful French poetic idiom, drawing on the language of Africa and the Caribbean as well as that of France. Through the very different dramatic style of the African hero play, with its flattering depiction of its subject, *Une Saison au Congo (A Season in the Congo*, 1967) centres on Patrice Lumumba's attempts to establish an independent Congolese Republic. European critics misunderstood its intentions, but it is as powerful in its own way as *Christophe*, and very much more critical of the effects of white decolonization. This theme is taken up in *Une Tempête* (1969), a brilliant reworking of Shakespeare's *Tempest*, in which Prospero represents a white settler and Caliban a black slave, follower of Shango. The play ends differently from Shakespeare's, with Prospero unable to leave the island, remaining locked in a power struggle with Caliban which he is doomed, in the end, to lose.

Césaire turned to the theatre to reach a broader audience than the readers of his poetry and to deal directly with African politics. His plays are revered more than they are performed in France, but his work has become a staple for young racially aware theatre companies in the USA.

Eastern Caribbean Popular Theatre Organization (ECPTO)

A group whose aims are to help communities identify problems of daily living and to find solutions through the performance process, as well as to promote the development of artistic and cultural activities in the region. ECPTO was launched at Layou, St Vincent, in April 1983, when four theatre groups decided to collaborate under one umbrella. These were the New Artists Movement of St Vincent and the Grenadines, the Movement for Cultural Awareness in Dominica and the Folk Research Centre of St Lucia (see Eastern Caribbean States), and the Ministry of Education and Culture in Grenada. Harambee Open-Air Theatre of Antigua (see Eastern Caribbean States) and the Popular Theatre Organization of BARBADOS joined the organization in December 1983 and June 1986 respectively. ECPTO has been represented at international popular theatre festivals held in Canada and at important meetings, conferences, workshops and seminars on popular theatre methods.

Harquail Theatre

Built in 1986 at a cost of US$4 million with funds provided by Mrs Helen Harquail in memory of her husband, the 330-seat playhouse on Grand Cayman is managed by the National Cultural Foundation of the Cayman Islands. The Foundation is funded primarily by an annual government grant and from voluntary contributions; it conducts an annual playwriting competition and produces the prize-winning plays at the theatre. Other locally produced plays and productions from elsewhere in the Caribbean are accommodated at the Harquail. The current programme director is Guyanese HENRY MUTTOO.

Reichhold Center for the Arts

Constructed in 1978 as a gift from Henry H. Reichhold of Reichhold Chemicals to the island of St Thomas in the US Virgin Islands, the Center is an 1196-seat amphitheatre with a covered stage on two levels. The upper level consists of an ample proscenium stage, orchestra pit, greenroom and star dressing-rooms, while the lower level houses chorus dressing-rooms, rehearsal space, scene storage and staff offices.

From 1978 to 89 the Center was run by an independent board as a roadhouse for largely American shows and artists. Occasionally it hosted Caribbean-generated events. In 1992, after a hiatus of three years caused by hurricane damage, the Center reopened as an integral part of the University of the Virgin Islands. While it seeks to enrich the cultural and social life of the university and its community with programmes from across the globe, it now has a particular interest in presenting items from the Caribbean and Central American region, and there are plans to install a core professional acting company. The Center's new director is DAVID EDGECOMBE (see Eastern Caribbean States).

Theatre Information Exchange (TIE)

A regional organization formed to provide information on theatre to the scattered territories of the anglophone Caribbean. Funded by the Inter-American Foundation (IAF), TIE was inaugurated at the first conference of Caribbean dramatists held in St Lucia (see Eastern Caribbean States) in 1976. The first coordinator was Pat Charles, then resident extramural tutor at the UNIVERSITY OF THE WEST INDIES. In 1978–9 the IAF funded a one-man secretariat run by KEN CORSBIE (see Guyana) in BARBADOS, where the second conference was held in 1978. A third took place in St Thomas, US Virgin Islands, in 1981. During his tenure Corsbie travelled to seventeen territories and conducted sixty interviews with theatre people. The organization disbanded in 1984 for lack of sustaining funds. Its membership had reached seventy-one individuals and eight theatre organizations.

University [College] *of the West Indies* (UWI)

Founded in 1947 as a university college in special relationship with the University of London, UWI achieved full university status in 1963. It has played a special role in the development of theatre in the anglophone Caribbean, first through the University Dramatic Society, next through the work of the Extramural Department, and third through the establishment of Creative Arts Centres on the campuses in JAMAICA and Trinidad (see Trinidad and Tobago).

The University Dramatic Society was started in Jamaica in 1948. Students from all parts of the Caribbean participated in its activities. It won many awards in the annual adult drama festival in Jamaica, fostered the writing and production of Caribbean plays, and in 1961 began to tour the other territories, thus stimulating local dramatic effort. Graduates who had been members of the UWI Dramatic Society would continue their theatre activity on returning to their home countries.

Since 1963 the Extramural Department (now the School of Continuing Studies), particularly through its roving drama tutors, has offered training courses in theatre arts to all territories affiliated to the university, from Belize to GUYANA. The tutors have regularly conducted playwriting seminars and organized vacation schools in the creative arts. In Trinidad and Tobago a vacation school has been offered annually since 1964. The Department collected and printed a wide range of Caribbean plays in the 1950s and 60s when such plays were unobtainable beyond their place of first production.

The Creative Arts Centres, established in Jamaica in 1967 and in Trinidad in 1986, have formalized the teaching of drama and theatre techniques for the university curriculum. The Jamaican centre has provided an auditorium and stage for campus productions as well as for productions from elsewhere. Since 1968 residential halls on the Jamaican campus have organized an annual theatre festival with help from the drama tutor and the use of the Centre's facilities.

dramatic theatre for centuries. Jamaica, conquered by Britain in 1655, had a public theatre by 1682. Barbados had organized dramatics in 1728, and in 1751 gave a performance of George Lillo's *The London Merchant* before George Washington, who would become the first president of the USA. Antigua opened its first theatre in 1788, with Thomas Otway's *Venice Preserv'd*; Guyana converted rooms in the Union Coffee House into its first Theatre Royal in 1810 and opened with a performance of *The London Merchant*, using its subtitle *The History of George Barnwell*; coloured amateurs in Grenada staged a Shakespearian tragedy in 1828, and in 1832 St Lucia launched a theatre for English- and French-speaking players. Trinidad, taken from Spain in 1797, boasted three theatres in the 1820s, for English, French and Creole amateur performers.

Up to the abolition of slavery in 1834, and beyond, Caribbean theatre was merely a reflection of English and European. British, and occasionally French and American players, travelled to the then colonies with an established repertoire including Shakespeare, Molière and a quantity of farces and melodramas. Less frequently, Spanish and Italian troupers brought musical plays and opera. The Hallam Company, for instance, which arrived in America from London in 1752, made two extensive tours of Jamaica between 1754 and 58 and 1775 and 85, returning to the mainland only at the end of the War of Independence. Between the visits by professionals, local players known as 'gentlemen amateurs' occupied the theatres and performed similar works. British forces stationed in the territories also gave plays, at times combining their talents with amateurs to present spectacular dramas and pantomimes. The audiences for these shows consisted primarily of the 'upper crust': the planters, well-to-do merchants, military and naval officers, government officials and civic leaders.

From time to time plays romanticizing Caribbean life, by foreign authors, would be produced, such as Richard Cumberland's *The West Indian* (1771) set in London, Isaac Bickerstaffe's comic operetta *The Padlock* (1768), and the romantic *Inkle and Yarico* (1787) by Colman the Younger, set on a plantation in Barbados. Some members of Hallam's company wrote comic sketches of Jamaica which they played as afterpieces; but the first attempts to produce an indigenous Caribbean drama came later. In the 1820s Jamaican newspapers carried in serialized form some anonymous plays on the slavery issue, meant to be read rather than performed. In Trinidad E. L. Joseph, a Scottish resident, wrote and produced a group of plays on Trinidadian subjects, including the musical farce *Martial Law in Trinidad* (1832), which pokes fun at the annual muster of troops that took place during the Christmas holidays to safeguard against slave rebellion. The play draws characters from the different racial strains on the island and uses native dialects. In Jamaica the newspaper reporter Charles Shanahan wrote a historical tragedy, *The Spanish Warrior* (1853), that traced the career and death of the New World Spanish explorer Balboa. The play was produced at Kingston's Theatre Royal along with an afterpiece, also written by Shanahan, called *The Mysteries of Vegetarianism*, ridiculing a dietary trend then current in the city.

Throughout the 19th century attempts were made to establish permanent playhouses in Caribbean towns. Theatre buildings that were erected or converted from existing halls after much debate and fund-raising were often destroyed by fire, storm or creeping decay, then painfully rebuilt. Native plays continued to appear sporadically for local consumption. In the 1860s and 70s Jamaica produced three monologuists in HENRY G. MURRAY and his two sons Andrew and William, who between them delighted town and country audiences for some thirty years with recitals of 'The Customs and Characters of Jamaican Society a Generation Ago'. Topics such as the annual troop muster, the Christmas-time masquerades of the Set Girls and John Canoe, and the Festival of the New Yam, as well as contemporary events, written in sparkling dialect and skilfully presented with appropriate songs, were enormously popular.

Trinidad observed the centenary of British rule in 1897 with a drama festival that included two original (and sentimental) plays. *Carmelita, the Belle of San José* by L. O. Inniss was a love story set against the conquest of the island by British forces, aided by native Indians. The other, *The Violet of Icacos*, author unknown, was about domestic intrigue on a rural plantation. The next year Inniss returned to his theme of the noble savage despoiled by Spanish invaders with *Mura, the Cacique's Daughter*. Remarkably, his two works honouring a hundred years of British control ignored the presence of black Africans who, at the time in which his plays were set, constituted some 80 per cent of the population.

The turn of the century saw a resurgence of touring professionals such as the Frank Benson Shakespeare Company and, some years later, the Florence Glossop-Harris Dramatic Company. In 1911 George Bernard Shaw visited Jamaica and advised the country, if it wished to create a truly indigenous theatre, to 'do your own acting and write your own plays ... with all the ordinary travelling companies from England and America kept out'. In fact, serious interest in the native culture was already developing. J. A. Van Sertima of Guyana had brought out his *Scenes and Sketches of Demerara Life* (1899), the anthropologist Walter Jekyll had published *Jamaican Song and Story* (1907) and six years later would appear the Jamaican Astley Clerk's lectures on *The Music and Musical Instruments of Jamaica* (1913). In Trinidad the carnival and calypso had begun on their long path towards respectability and national acceptance (see TRINIDAD CARNIVAL).

The focus on indigenous culture brought to the fore native comedians, notably ERNEST CUPIDON of Jamaica and SAM CHASE of Guyana, both of whom wrote and performed comic sketches before admiring popular audiences. Cupidon would later be the first to dramatize a favourite Caribbean novel, H. G. DeLisser's *Susan Proudleigh* (1930), which played at Kingston's Ward Theatre and enjoyed numerous revivals with Cupidon himself performing the female lead. Other stage versions of prose works followed. At another level Tom Redcam (pen name of T. H. McDermot, a respected Jamaican journalist and poet) hoped to create a literary drama with his historical play *San Gloria* (c.1920s), written in prose and verse, which dealt with episodes in the third voyage of Columbus when his ships were driven aground on Jamaica's north coast. Many years would pass before other Caribbean poets like Roger Mais and the Nobel laureate DEREK WALCOTT (see Eastern Caribbean States) would write for the stage.

In the late 1920s, forces in the Caribbean were beginning to challenge colonial overlordship. Strong leaders of grassroots political parties and labour unions emerged. Left-wing literary magazines began to appear, and in the theatre a new self-awareness asserted itself as participation became more widespread. The Jamaican MARCUS GARVEY, leader of a global African uplift movement, opened a theatre for the masses in 1929 and presented a series of farces written by the Jamaican comedian RANNY WILLIAMS, as well as three of his own epic pageants on black nationhood. UNA MARSON's (see Jamaica) play *Pocomania* (1938) dealt with the pervasiveness of a banned religious cult, and Frank Hill's *Upheaval* (1939) spoke boldly of labour unrest leading to social revolution. The Guyanese writer Esme Cendrecourt produced her first play, *Romance of Kaiteur*, and her compatriot NORMAN CAMERON began his series of quasi-religious–historical dramas with *Balthazar*, both in 1931.

In Trinidad in the 1920s, Cecil Cobham formed the Paragon Players in Port of Spain, and presented a number of original pathetic dramas under such titles as *False Honeymoon*, *Retribution* and *Sold But Not Lost*. F. E. M. Hosein, mayor of Arima, wrote and staged *Hyarima and the Saints* (1931), a martyr play on the killing of Spanish priests by Amerindians at their mission near the town. Arthur Roberts, a schoolmaster, produced a decade of delightful if circumspect plays on topical issues such as divorce, slander, personal hygiene and child-rearing, which were performed by his boy pupils before vociferous audiences. Another schoolteacher, DeWilton Rogers, dealt more astutely with questions of colour prejudice and political chicanery in *Blue Blood and Black* (1936) and *Trikidad* (1937). New ground was broken when the historian and political activist C. L. R. James had his drama on the Haitian revolution, *Toussaint L'Ouverture* (1936), produced in London for a special showing by the Stage Society. In the cast were the American actor Paul Robeson as Toussaint, the Guyanese Robert Adams as Dessalines, John Ahuma as Christophe, and the Nigerian Orlando Martins as Boukman. In 1934 Trinidad calypsonians began annual visits to New York to cut recordings and appear on metropolitan boards.

In many respects the 1930s represented a breakthrough for Caribbean theatre. The need to show more local life and history on the stage was recognized; the theatre's ability not merely to entertain but to address issues of common concern was accepted. That plays of this nature could gain attention abroad had been demonstrated. Local drama groups in schools and communities were encouraged in their efforts. But colour and class barriers, though steadily being dismantled, still existed in the theatre. In particular, working-class characters in plays frequently lacked dignity, and dialect speech was allowed mainly for comic relief. However, as the outbreak of the Second World War brought an influx of American and British servicemen to the region, native entertainers catering to this new clientele with exhibitions of folk culture began to enjoy considerable approbation.

The next two decades witnessed steady progress towards the establishment of a Caribbean theatre. Several important theatre groups came into being many of which are still extant. THE LITTLE THEATRE MOVEMENT OF JAMAICA (LTM) was inaugurated in 1941 and the Caribbean Thespians in 1946. The LTM by 1961 had built its own theatre, laid the foundations for a national drama school, and given the country its most unique theatre form, the JAMAICA PANTOMIME, that still performs annually to tens of thousands of playgoers. The Whitehall Players (later renamed the COMPANY OF PLAYERS) started in Trinidad in 1946, the ARTS GUILD OF ST LUCIA in 1950 (see Eastern Caribbean States), and the THEATRE GUILD OF GUYANA in 1957.

In Barbados Joyce Stuart's *Revuedeville*, a variety show of Caribbean customs, culture and folklore, although popular, saw only five productions between 1938 and 1950. Meanwhile, Caribbean drama was gaining a foothold overseas. In New York William Archibald's *Carib Song* (1945) starring the dancer Katherine Dunham had a fair reception on Broadway, and Moss Hart's *Climate of Eden* (1952) dramatizing a novel by the Guyanese writer Edgar Mittelholzer was a gallant if unsuccessful attempt. In London that year Derek Walcott's verse play *Henri Christophe* showed well in production at the Hans Crescent International House with ERROL JOHN (see Trinidad and Tobago), formerly of the Whitehall Players, in the leading role. John would later win the London *Observer* prize for the best Commonwealth drama, with his sensitive 'yard play' *Moon on a Rainbow Shawl* (1957).

The new movement was distinguished by as serious a commitment to the craft of theatre as to the development of a Caribbean dramatic form. Local companies sponsored training classes conducted by resident professionals – efforts that were reinforced by the timely appointment at the UNIVERSITY OF THE WEST INDIES (see Introduction) of extramural drama tutors who travelled around the region organizing workshops, summer schools and drama festivals, and collected, published and distributed locally written plays. The result of this activity was a cadre of skilled theatre artists and young dramatists who indicated high promise for the future. Among playwrights to emerge at this period were BARRY RECKORD, SAMUEL HILLARY and CICELY WAITE-SMITH of Jamaica, DOUGLAS ARCHIBALD, ERROL HILL and Errol John of Trinidad, Derek Walcott and his twin brother RODDY WALCOTT of St Lucia (see Eastern Caribbean States), and FRANK PILGRIM and SHEIK SADEEK of Guyana. At a 1957 drama festival held at the Ward Theatre in Kingston, the adjudicator could boast that 'side by side with plays from England, America and France, have been plays from Trinidad, Grenada, St Lucia and Jamaica – and we have not suffered by the comparison'. The work of this period peaked in 1958 with the staging in Trinidad of a commissioned epic drama, *Drums and Colours*, written by Derek Walcott and performed by the finest acting talent assembled from the region, at the inaugural ceremonies of the short-lived West Indies Federation.

Succeeding decades have witnessed the spread of Caribbean theatre to countries overseas. The TRINIDAD THEATRE WORKSHOP, established in 1959, has regularly toured its productions to neighbouring islands and to North America. Playwrights resident abroad such as MUSTAPHA MATURA (see Trinidad and Tobago) and Michael Abbensetts in England, LENNOX BROWN (see Trinidad and Tobago), Lorris Elliott and Roddy Walcott in Canada, and EDGAR WHITE (see Eastern Caribbean States) and Derek Walcott in the United States, as well as those who remain at home like TREVOR RHONE of Jamaica, now have their plays produced on metropolitan boards. Meanwhile, the search continues for a narrative theatrical form that captures the expressive qualities of Caribbean life. Elements of indigenous culture culled especially from the carnival and from folk religions and speech patterns are incorporated into plays. The Jamaica School of Drama (see Jamaica, CULTURAL TRAINING CENTRE) has focused part of its programme on developing

Bibliography

I. Baxter, *The Arts of an Island*, Metuchen, NJ, 1970; W. Bennett, 'The Jamaican Theatre: A Preliminary Overview', *Jamaica Journal*, 8, 2 and 3, 1974; E. K. Brathwaite, *Folk Culture of the Slaves in Jamaica*, London, 1971; K. Corsbie, *Theatre in the Caribbean*, London, 1984; E. Hill, 'The Emergence of a National Drama in the West Indies', *Caribbean Quarterly*, 18, 4, 1972, and *The Jamaican Stage, 1655–1900: Profile of a Colonial Theatre*, Amherst, Mass., 1992; J. W. Nunley and J. Bettelheim, *Caribbean Festival Arts: Each and Every Bit of Difference*, Seattle, Wash., 1988; K. Omotoso, *The Theatrical into Theatre: A Study of Drama and Theatre in the English-speaking Caribbean*, London, 1982; R. Wright, *Revels in Jamaica*, rev. edn, Jamaica, 1986.

an idiomatic Caribbean theatre. In the tradition of the Anansi storyteller, solo dialect performers like the veteran LOUISE BENNETT of Jamaica, Shake Keane of St Vincent and PAUL KEENS-DOUGLAS of Trinidad continue to enjoy wide popularity. Paralleling the work of dramatists and actors is the contribution made by the choreographers in establishing theatrical dance forms based on Caribbean material. Chief among these are BERYL MCBURNIE of the Little Carib Theatre in Trinidad, and IVY BAXTER and REX NETTLEFORD of Jamaica.

The French-speaking Caribbean

Haiti

Few events in modern history have engendered the writing of as many plays as the Haitian war of independence (1791–1804). The idea of a successful slave revolt against the imperial forces of France and Britain accompanied by the tragic deaths of the revolutionary leaders seized the imagination of playwrights in the western world. Vèvè Clark has estimated that from 1796 to 1975 no less than 63 dramas were published or performed about the event. Whilst most of these plays originated in Haiti, about one-third came from writers in England, France, Germany, Ivory Coast, Martinique, St Lucia, Sweden and the United States.

During the period of the American marine occupation of Haiti (1915–34) several patriotic plays were written, some of which were censored by the authorities, such as Dominique Hippolyte's *Le Forçat (The Prisoner*, 1929). In 1953 playwright Felix Morriseau-Leroy produced his *Antigone in Creole* in response to Haitian intellectuals who felt that serious drama could not be written in Creole, the language of the ordinary Haitian. The play was successful in performances both on Haiti as well as in Paris, New York and Montreal. Morriseau-Leroy also wrote a Haitian version of *King Creon* in which Creon was clearly meant to represent the Haitian dictator François Duvalier.

More recent playwrights have experimented in other ways. Franck Fouché, who died in 1978, not only had five of his plays performed in Creole but, according to Clark, he employed Epic Theatre techniques combined with Catholic and Vodoun ritual in his major work *Général Baron-la-Croix ou le silence masqué (General Baron of the Cross or Masked Silence*, 1971) yet another play in Creole, Kaselezo (*Womb Waters Breaking*, 1985) represents the collective creation of playwright, director and three actresses who play a blind Vodoun priestess and her two daughters.

Hispanic Caribbean

The Caribbean Sea washes the shores of several nations including Central and northern South America, but the Caribbean theatre included in this volume focuses on the three principal islands: Cuba, the Dominican Republic and Puerto Rico. All three locations possess a long and sustained tradition of theatrical activity, dating back to the time of the conquest, and some evidence of pre-Columbian theatrical activity has been preserved. While each of these island-nations has followed its own course at its own pace, the Spanish cultural patterns imposed during the colonial period have produced many common characteristics. The extermination of indigenous populations, the importation of an African workforce, the development of an insular mentality and the slow movement towards independence all provided cultural anthropologists and sociologists with evidence of heterogeneity and consistency that distinguish these political entities not only from Haiti, with which the Dominican Republic shares a border, but also from neighbouring nations across the Caribbean water.

For Cuba and Puerto Rico independence from Spain did not come until the Spanish–American War of 1898, and during the 20th century repeated American intervention in the political and economic structures of all three islands has left its mark on the culture, including the theatre. Cuba's identity has been largely prescribed by its proximity to the USA, first by an intimate and corrupt relationship during the first half of the century, then by a nearly complete separation as a result of the political and economic blockade since the Castro Revolution in 1959. Puerto Rico continues to struggle with the question of its identity either as an independent nation or as the 51st state of the USA, as an alternative to continuation of the commonwealth status that has been in

Bibliography

Vèvè A. Clark, 'Haiti's Tragic Overture: (Mis) Representation of the Haitian Revolution in World Drama (1796-1975)' in *Representing the French Revolution* ed. James A. W. Heffernan, Hanover, NH 1992, pp. 237–60); Vèvè A. Clark, 'When Womb Waters Break: The Emergence of Haitian New Theatre (1953–1987)' in *Callaloo* 15, 3, (1992), 778–86.

place since 1952. Even though the Dominican Republic has nominally enjoyed autonomous status since the 19th century, American marines have occupied the country many times this century to protect American vested interests.

All of these interventions have left their mark on the cultural and theatrical development of each island. The widespread staging of the plays of Eugene O'Neill, Tennessee Williams and Arthur Miller in their prime, for example, reflected great admiration for the stagecraft of the American masters. These island-nations may be geographically remote, but they are by no means isolated: theatre artists and practitioners have regularly visited or studied in New York and other world theatre centres. But these contacts do not preclude productions that clearly reflect strong resentment towards the USA for its involvement in internal affairs and for the attempted imposition of American values on the Hispanic system.

During the colonial period – which extended from the time of Columbus's arrival until the 19th century – theatre activity normally took the form of visiting theatre troupes from mother Spain, although some vestigial music and dramatic forms survived the early invasions. For the most part, colonial theatre reflected continental patterns with an occasional effort to incorporate local themes and characteristics. The flowering of theatre in Spain during the so-called Golden Century did little to stimulate the Caribbean theatre.

The stimulus for local development came in the 19th century, when playwrights and theatre artists showed interest in capturing the island flavour and characteristics in their plays. The romantic models imported from Spain and France often brought a similar predilection for remote times and places (e.g. SALVADOR BRAU's play on 13th-century Sicily),

but a parallel current stressed the importance of local colour and customs, known in Spanish as *costumbrismo* (from *costumbre*, custom). When realism as an aesthetic mode swept Europe in the 19th century, its impact was little noticed in the Americas, which developed a second wave of romanticism.

The 20th-century theatre is complex because multiple sources of influence from Europe, the USA and especially from other Latin American nations have brought an increasing stridency to questions of political, social, racial, religious and cultural identity. Latin American theatre in general, after a period of experimentation with its independence in the 1930s and 40s, began to flower in the 1950s; the theatre of these three islands participated fully in this movement by developing styles and standards that sought to define issues of political, social and psychological importance within the aesthetic and artistic parameters of each location. Attention is paid here to the characteristic features of each island-nation, including popular and commercial theatre as well as major plays, playwrights and groups, and African influences.

Bibliography

S. J. Albuquerque, *Violent Acts: A Study of Contemporary Latin American Theatre*, Detroit, 1991; J. J. Arrom, *Historia del teatro hispanoamericano, epoca colonial*, Mexico, 1966; F. N. Dauster, *Historia del teatro hispanoamericano, siglos 19 y 20*, rev. edn, Mexico, 1973; R. Perales, *Teatro americano contemporaneo*, Colección Escenología, vols. 1 and 2, Mexico, 1989, 1993; D. Taylor, *Theatre of Crisis: Drama and Politics in Latin America*, Lexington, Kentucky, 1991; A. Versényi, *Theatre in Latin America: Religion, Politics and Culture from Cortés to the 1980s*, Cambridge, 1993.

BARBADOS

Most easterly of the Caribbean island chain, Barbados had been deserted by indigenous Carib Indians by the time it was settled by the English in 1625. The first African slaves were brought to the island in 1627, and by 1668 its population consisted of 40,000 blacks and 20,000 whites. Today the population is virtually homogeneous, with more than 90 per cent of African descent and the rest of European or non-African mixed ancestry.

Because, at 66 square miles, the island is relatively small and its open terrain allows access to all parts of the country, it has been assumed that the slaves, engulfed by the dominant European culture, lost all traces of their African past. While this conjecture may be partly true of the coloured middle class, there is little doubt that Barbadian working-class blacks, like those in other Caribbean islands, retained aspects of an African-Caribbean performance culture that was despised or, at best, tolerated during the colonial period. Since the achievement of political independence in 1966, these performance modes have been openly encouraged in events such as the annual Crop Over festival, the Kadooment carnival, the Talk Tent and the calypso contest; and in the Landship marching band and the Tuk music band.

As far as formal theatre is concerned, the 18th century witnessed spurts of dramatic activity: in 1729 by local 'gentlemen players', and in 1752–3 and again in 1783–4 most probably by travelling players from England or America. The plays shown were standard works for the period – for instance, George Lillo's *The London Merchant, or, The History of George Barnwell* and George Farquhar's *The Beaux' Stratagem*. Although press advertisements referred to the theatre venues as 'playhouses', they were most likely large rooms fitted up for the purpose, such as Marshall's Great Room in the city of Bridgetown used in 1752.

During the 19th century several theatres were opened, the most important being the Theatre Royal, built in Bridgetown in 1810 at a cost of £10,000. It was destroyed by a hurricane in 1831 and was succeeded two years later by a second Theatre Royal built of wood, which was demolished in 1844. The British garrison in 1818 set up its own theatre space at St Ann's for the entertainment of troops, their families and friends. Known as the Garrison Theatre and set up in one hall after another, it survived into the mid-20th century. Speightstown, the second town of importance, also boasted at least two theatres in the 19th century. Professional players, mainly from North America, visited the island quite regularly in the latter half of the century. These included the J. W. Lanergan Company, Brooks and Fyffe's Dramatic Combination, an Italian opera company, and the E. A. McDowell Vaudeville Company that came in 1881, 1882 and 1886 and performed Gilbert and Sullivan's *HMS Pinafore* for the first time in Barbados. Although these touring companies played for no more than two weeks at a time, their appearance usually stirred the local thespians into renewed activity, so that over a four-year period performances were given by no less than six different amateur groups.

The final decade of the 19th century brought Bridgetown yet another theatre – Wilhelmina Hall. Erected in 1894 by J. H. Inniss, with seating for 900, it became the principal venue for visiting companies such as the Russ-Whytal Dramatic Company from New York in 1900, and the Frank Benson Shakespeare Company (in 1905) and the Florence Glossop-Harris Dramatic Company (in 1920) from England. The hall was eventually converted into a cinema and renamed the Olympic Theatre. The urge to build a proper civic theatre had existed since the 1880s, when a group of Barbadian businessmen jointly offered shares to the public in order to raise capital of £8,000. This and other similar schemes proved abortive, until 1918 when construction was begun on the Empire Theatre on Probyn Street. At a cost of £15,000 this handsome, spacious, limestone-brick playhouse opened its doors to the public in 1922, by which time it had been decided that the city could not support a theatre of stage productions only. The opening bill consisted of vaudeville items and screen snapshots, and it was inevitable that film shows would eventually overwhelm theatre productions.

Up to the 1930s, live theatre in Barbados was primarily a white concern, both participants and audiences comprising resident Europeans and the military, native-born whites or near-whites. Exceptions to this pattern were rare. As far back as 1805, when members of the free coloured population of Bridgetown staged John Home's tragedy, *Douglas*, one critic, while favourably impressed with the performance, felt constrained to point out that non-whites should not have been permitted to engage in this sort of cultural activity. His remarks had the effect of increasing the attendance of whites at subsequent performances. Then in 1830 the Lyceum Amateur Theatre on Reed Street was organized by Samuel Jackman Prescod and other leading coloured figures of the community, but the group was apparently active for only a few months.

At no time before the 1930s do the records disclose the production in Barbados of a locally written play or a play of local relevance. *The West Indian*, a sentimental comedy chosen for the opening of the newly built Theatre Royal in 1810, had been written by the English dramatist Richard Cumberland, and though it was about a rich, hot-blooded, young Jamaican planter who becomes entangled in a love affair, it was set in London. This situation would change in the years ahead.

The first real departure came when the Guyana-born Joyce Stuart, a coloured woman who had studied dance in New York and London, staged her first *Revuedeville* at the Drill Hall in 1938, featuring students from her dancing academy. A second presentation took place the next year, and in 1950 the show was revived at the Empire Theatre as a musical comedy under the title *Passport to Heaven*. It introduced to the stage the inimitable comedian JOE TUDOR. According to one critic, the show had 'broken virgin ground, filled with possibilities and promise for the future'. Stuart took her show to Trinidad, making it one of the first Caribbean productions to travel to a neighbouring country – an event that had become commonplace two decades later.

In the 1930s other popular revues were staged at the Empire Theatre, displaying the talents of local writers and performers, among them FRANK COLLYMORE who became one of the island's leading actors. Amateur groups such as the Bridgetown Players and the Barbados Dramatic Club (which merged into the Green Room Theatre Club in 1953) continued to function. As these observed a finely drawn colour line, it was left to the British Council, which set up regional offices in the Caribbean in the 1940s, to provide a pocket theatre at its own premises where fledgeling drama groups that could not afford the cost of hiring the Empire Theatre or other commercial halls could stage their plays. The Council also undertook to sponsor theatre arts workshops, conducted by drama officers of the Extramural Department of the UNIVERSITY OF THE WEST INDIES (see Introduction) and others; the contribution of DAPHNE JOSEPH-HACKETT, as organizer and producer of these sessions, was substantial. With the growth of indigenous theatre groups, the 250-seat theatre in Queen's Park House (now the Daphne Joseph-Hackett Theatre) was put into service, and it has proved an ideal home for intimate productions.

As racial barriers in the theatre began to come down, two major concerns were voiced. First was the issue of interracial casting, and second was the need for more Caribbean plays. These issues, raised in articles published in the *Advocate*, were soon overtaken by events. In 1955 the university's extramural drama office began publishing a series of Caribbean plays which were quickly disseminated throughout the area, encouraging new writers who wished to take advantage of a wider field. Meanwhile, graduates who had been members of the University Dramatic Society in JAMAICA returned home and mounted plays with mixed casting, as they were accustomed to do in their campus productions.

Strides in dramatic production were paralleled in music and dance. Beginning in 1966 and continuing for over a decade, the Barbados Festival Choir produced a series of original musicals called *Bimshire*, loosely patterned on the annual JAMAICA PANTOMIME. The originators of this experiment were NOEL VAZ of Jamaica and Joseph-Hackett. The Barbados Dance Theatre Company, founded in 1968, has gone from strength to strength in its annual season of dance, much of it theatrical in form, which has attracted increasingly enthusiastic audiences. The company has presented original dances based on folklore or historical anecdote, such as the ritual dance *Shango* and *Yarico*, a legend about an Arawak girl (1973); the ingenious *Licks for Six*, based on Barbados cricket (1974); and *Dreams and Visions*, inspired by Caribbean poetry (1983).

With the attainment of independence in 1966, competitive festivals for schools and adult groups were introduced under the aegis first of the Barbados Arts Council and later of the NATIONAL CULTURAL FOUNDATION. These festivals spurred the writing and production of more Barbadian and other Caribbean plays. The leading playwright in Barbados is ANTHONY HINKSON, and others of note include Winston Farrell and the New York-based dancer-drama-

tist Glenville Lovell, whose play *When the Eagle Screams* deals with the 1983 American invasion of Grenada. Popular theatrical experiments include *Laff It Off*, an earthy, vernacular romp set in a bar in a Barbadian village and directed by Thom Cross; the satiric *Pampalam*, a series of staged encounters in rhyme written by journalist Jeannette Layne-Clark; and the Talk Tent – initiated by director EARL WARNER and based on the 19th-century fund-raiser known as a tea meeting with its emphasis on speechifying and song. The popularity of these forms of theatre has pushed the homegrown effort towards professionalism.

Another type of production is epitomized by the Popular Theatre Movement, a group that encourages rural communities to participate in solving communal problems through research and play enactment, using a variety of expressive forms. The programme is part of the EASTERN CARIBBEAN POPULAR THEATRE ORGANIZATION (see Introduction), based in Dominica. Perhaps the most notable recent development in Barbadian theatre has been the establishment of professional organizations that aim to put the theatre on a sound financial footing while ensuring that the best talent is able to travel throughout the islands and abroad. Stage One, organized in 1978, has over twenty-five productions to its credit, and W.W.B. Productions (1987) has recruited Caribbean-wide performers and toured its productions to other territories and to London.

Collymore, Frank (1893–1980)

Barbadian teacher, poet, essayist, actor and graphic artist. As editor of *BIM* literary magazine for over thirty years, Collymore inspired many new writers, including novelists George Lamming and Austin Clarke of Barbados, and DEREK WALCOTT of St Lucia (see Eastern Caribbean States). In *Notes for a Glossary of Words and Phrases of Barbadian Dialect* he pioneered the study of folk idioms and expressions. His acting career was principally with the Bridgetown

Players and the Green Room Theatre Club during the 1940s and 50s. He favoured character parts and gave memorable performances in roles such as Sheridan Whiteside in Kaufman and Hart's *The Man Who Came to Dinner*. Named in his honour are the Frank Collymore Hall, a performing space in Bridgetown seating 483, and the Frank Collymore award for the best entry in the National Independence Festival of Creative Arts.

Hinkson, Anthony (1942–)

Foremost playwright in Barbados, and drama teacher at the Garrison Secondary School in Bridgetown. Hinkson began writing in 1972 as a member of the Writers' Workshop, and has written over thirty plays, several of them winning awards in the local arts festivals, including *God's Daughter* (1979), *Children of the Moonlight* (1980) and *Jackpot* (1982). *The Candidate* (1986), on political campaigning, was cancelled on opening night on account of charges of bias, but was allowed to continue its run after viewing by members of the National Cultural Foundation. Theatre groups that have staged his plays include the Pinelands Theatre Workshop, for which he wrote *Nigger Yard* (1978) and *High Rise. Unchanged* (1972) and *Village Life* (1988) incorporate writings of other Caribbean authors, and have musical settings. His works have been performed in GUYANA and JAMAICA as well as in Barbados.

Joseph-Hackett, Daphne (1915–88)

A Latin teacher at Queen's College, Barbados, native-born Joseph-Hackett was also for over thirty years a dynamo in the Barbadian theatre – as tutor, producer, adjudicator, scriptwriter, actress and director. She worked with drama schools and theatre workshops conducted by the extramural tutors of the UNIVERSITY OF THE WEST INDIES (see Introduction), helped to write and stage the annual pantomime presented by the Barbados Festival Choir, and facilitated the productions of little theatre groups through her energy and skill. As an actress she is remembered for her role in the popular local radio serial, *The Brathwaites of Black Rock*. She received the Barbados Silver Star award, and named after her is the prize for the most outstanding drama performance at the National Independence Festival of Creative Arts. In October 1991 the Little Theatre in Queen's Park, Bridgetown, was renamed the Daphne Joseph-Hackett Theatre.

National Cultural Foundation (NCF)

A statutory corporation established by the government of Barbados in 1983 to promote cultural development on the island. Cultural officers are employed in the literary and theatre arts, and in the fields of dance, music, fine arts and folklore. The NCF conducts training sessions in these art forms and organizes the annual (July–August) Crop Over festival and the National Independence Festival of Creative Arts (NIFCA), which coincides with the anniversary of independence each November.

Tudor, Joe (1922–70)

Barbadian comedian, actor and entertainer. Tudor made his stage debut in 1950 at the Empire Theatre, Bridgetown, in Joyce Stuart's musical comedy *Passport to Heaven* in which he played several comic parts and was hailed as the best actor on stage; he reappeared as the lead in the 1952 production. He hosted a radio talent show called *Flying High*, and presented other radio programmes in which he welcomed the participation of children. He promoted and hosted live shows at the Globe Cinema, Bridgetown, featuring prominent black entertainers from America, and helped to improve the image of the local entertainer by taking his shows into first-class hotels.

Warner, Earl (1952–)

Barbadian director whose skills are sought after throughout the Caribbean and by Caribbean communities in England and America. Warner trained in drama at the University of Manchester and at the Jamaica

School of Drama (see Jamaica, CULTURAL TRAINING CENTRE), where he studied under Jamaican DENNIS SCOTT, late director of the Yale School of Drama. He was a co-founder of the Barbados Writers' Workshop. Warner believes in theatre as a teaching vehicle and as an agent for change in society, and is interested in the effects of the Caribbean element on stage design, acting, speech, spatial qualities and performance styles. His directing credits include three plays by DEREK WALCOTT (see Eastern Caribbean States): *Remembrance* (1982), *Beef, No Chicken* (1985) and *A Branch of the Blue Nile* (1985); EARL LOVELACE's (see Trinidad and Tobago) dramatization of his novels *The Dragon Can't Dance* at the Eugene O'Neill Center in Waterford, Connecticut (1985), and *The Wine of Astonishment* in Trinidad (1988); the experimental *Lights* (1985), a play about women woven through improvisation from works by various authors; TREVOR RHONE's (see Jamaica) *Smile Orange* (1986); the premiere of EDGAR WHITE's (see Eastern Caribbean States) *I, Marcus Garvey* (1987); and Glenville Lovell's *A Silver Web* (1989).

Wilson, Cynthia (1934–)

Barbadian actress, dancer, choreographer, songwriter and producer. She played her first leading role at the age of six and continued her interest in theatre through school and at the University of the West Indies. She has performed in several Caribbean countries, in Britain and the USA. She is a founding member of Stage One Theatre Company and an active member of the Barbados Dance Theatre Company. She played Titania in a Caribbean version of *A Midsummer Night's Dream* (1985) directed by MICHAEL GILKES (see Guyana), and participated in the experimental play *Lights*, from its conception in 1985 and through its revivals in JAMAICA, England, Trinidad; and Dominica and Antigua (see Eastern Caribbean States). Wilson is a co-founder, administrative director and resident producer of W.W.B. Productions in Barbados.

Bibliography

W. Alleyne, 'A Tradition of Theatre', *The Bajan and South Caribbean*, 333–6, 1981; K. Corsbie, *Theatre in the Caribbean*, London, 1984.

CUBA

Early manifestations of theatrical activity in Cuba parallel those of the other Caribbean islands. The *areytos* of the indigenous peoples were complex theatre-dance forms that incorporated music with full-dress costume to recount the historical, religious and cultural repertoire of the society. When the Spanish colonizers banned the *areytos* in 1512 on grounds of primitive hereticism, they extinguished an important part of the indigenous culture and took another step towards obliterating the native population itself. Later, when black slaves were imported to work the developing sugar plantations, other cultural traditions and art forms came to exert an influence.

Cuba's strategic location in the Caribbean has generated a long struggle for military and economic control of the island. The British occupied Havana in 1762-3; French refugees from Haiti arrived in the late 18th century For centuries, sugar has been the single most important product, and its fluctuating price has determined the local prosperity. Between 1500 and 1700, there was only sporadic theatrical activity. The first Cuban play is considered to be *El príncipe jardinero y fingido Cloridano* (*The Presumed Gardener Prince Cloridano*) by Santiago Pita. Published in Spain c.1730, this play treats chivalry in a mythical Grecian setting far removed from Cuba's reality. Beginning late in the 18th century, a round of theatre construction facilitated local productions: the Coliseo (1775), later restored as the Teatro El Principal (1803); the Diorama (1820), the Tacón (1838) and others. The acknowledged father of the Cuban national theatre is Francisco Covarrubias (1775-1850). Impresario, actor and author of more than twenty plays, he was famous for his representations of the 'negrito' (the white actor in black face), probably before the famous roles created by Thomas Rice and Daniel Decatur Emmett in the USA. Covarrubias integrated popular Cuban figures into forms of the Spanish *sainete* (see Dominican Republic, GÉNERO CHICO), but without the political implications or character development of that genre; no play has survived.

During the 19th century Cuba continued to chafe under colonial domination, as the Spanish-American struggle for independence during the period 1810-25 bypassed the island. In other countries the new freedom ushered in the unrestrained liberties of romanticism; Cuba was not unaffected by this trend – as early as 1836 *Don Pedro de Castilla* by Francisco Javier Foxá (1816-65) was staged. This Dominican exile's play drew a storm of protest – and censorship – because of its unconventional techniques. The island was not yet ready to accept romanticism as a new aesthetic mode. José María Heredia (1803-39), Cuban poet and patriot who spent years of exile in the USA and Mexico, wrote romantic poetry, but his plays, translations and adaptations retained neoclassical styles and techniques. José Jacinto Milanés (1814-63) took the figure of *el conde* Alarcos (in *Count Alarcos*, 1838) as a dramatic symbol of tyranny and oppression; in his later plays he turned towards picturesque popular figures presented in natural language, as in *El mirón cubano* (*The Cuban Busybody*, 1840), which consists of several scenes of a costumbristic nature in which Milanés censures habits and customs of the age. The outstanding figure of the period was GERTRUDIS GÓMEZ DE AVELLANEDA, an extraordinary poet, novelist and playwright. With an output of twenty plays, she was a major literary figure of the Americas who dominated both tragic and comic form, and knew how to create solid characters while avoiding the excesses of romanticism.

At mid-century the theatre was replete with writers whose humour and use of comic intrigue reflected the foibles of a developing society, and the problems created by politics, social status and racial mixtures. José Agustín Millán wrote his *Una aventura, o El camino más corto* (*An Adventure, or the Shortest Route*) in 1842, a play considered to signal the beginning of Cuba's national comedy, a form characterized by its humble, popular language and comic intrigue. Joaquín Lorenzo Luaces (1826–67) was the best Cuban playwright of the 19th century. His *El becerro de oro* (*The Golden Calf*), *La escuela de los parientes* (*School for Relatives*), *Dos amigas* (*Two Friends*) and *El fantasmón de Aravaca* (*The Ghost of Aravaca*), like the rest of his plays, capture the same comic style as, and anticipate, the BUFO theatre that took Havana by storm in 1868. The US minstrel shows that had visited Havana in 1865 had left an influence on this musical-dance theatre that specialized in parody, caricature and satire. The linguistic salad of the *bufo* drew on a French, English and black cuisine, and though its popular format excited the Cuban public, the colonial regime was not pleased. The havoc of the Ten Years' War (1868–78) suspended the activities of the *bufos habaneros* (Havana *bufos*), but they were to return for a second cycle from 1879 to 1900.

Late in the century the great Cuban poet and patriot José Martí (1853–95), who also wrote nationalistic and moralistic plays, was killed while spearheading an invasion of the island by the government in exile. Spain was ready to concede defeat, but the sinking of the battleship *Maine* in Havana harbour provoked American intervention, and in 1898 Spain relinquished Cuba as well as Puerto Rico and the Philippines to US control. The USA ruled Cuba militarily for four years, then withdrew as planned, leaving the island to self-rule under the Platt Amendment (1901), although the USA reserved the right to intervene 'as nec-

essary'. A series of inept and corrupt presidents led to the tyrannies first of Gerardo Machado (1925–33) and later of Fulgencio Batista (1934–59).

The 20th century ushered in the Alhambra Theatre, which was the centre of popular theatre in Havana. The music and dance revues programmed by Regino López as principal actor and Federico Villoch as impresario championed the popular Cuban character types in lavish and colourful productions that entertained Cubans for some thirty-five years. Efforts to organize a serious theatre movement came in 1910, with the formation of the Sociedad de Fomento del Teatro (Society for the Promotion of Theatre), later redesignated the Sociedad del Teatro Cubano (Society of Cuban Theatre). In spite of the enthusiasm of such distinguished participants as José Antonio Ramos (1885–1946) and Max Henríquez Ureña (1885–1968), these efforts failed. Ramos did write serious plays, and his *Tembladera* (*Tremor*, 1917) was a precursor of the theatre of protest against exploitative bourgeois policies.

Another impetus came in 1928 when Luis A. Baralt (1892–1969) launched the Teatro La Cueva (Cave Theatre), which represented an early attempt to bring vanguard European techniques to the Cuban theatre. The Academia de Artes Dramáticas (Dramatic Arts Academy) was established in 1941, the Patronata del Teatro (Patrons of Theatre) in 1942, and the Teatro Experimental (Experimental Theatre) of the University of Havana in 1949 – all fundamental to the development of an internationalized theatre capable of stimulating national playwrights and directors. Nevertheless, authors such as Francisco 'Paco' Alfonso (b.1906), Carlos Felipe (1911–75) and Rolando Ferrer (1925–76), the most established playwrights during the 1950s, wrote without benefit of an atmosphere conducive to serious theatre. Alfonso's *Cañaveral* (*Cane Field*, 1950) is typical of his propagandistic and bombastic style. Felipe's work also spans many years and political periods, ranging from the Pirandellian *El chino* (*The Chinaman*, 1947) to *Réquiem por Yarini* (*Requiem for Yarini*, 1966). The decadence of Havana during the later Batista years yielded to prostitution and commercialized, semi-pornographic shows catering primarily to the tourist trade. In the years immediately preceding the Castro Revolution, few theatre companies existed and few serious plays were presented. Only forty new Cuban plays were premiered in the last decade of the Batista regime. Nevertheless, some dedicated artists, having studied or worked in New York or in Europe, made heroic efforts to bring new techniques, such as Stanislavski method-acting, to the Cuban stage.

When Batista was ousted by Fidel Castro and his followers on 1 January, 1959, the singular importance of this political event for theatre in Cuba could hardly have been anticipated. Along with a period of Marxist domination, Castro brought with the Revolution a new perspective on theatre and the arts. Under the new regime, government support was available and theatre became, in fact, an arm of the revolutionary process. Salaries were provided for writers, directors, actors and technical crew. Buildings, some of them old movie houses, were adapted for use as theatre space, but the theatre also took to the streets and parks. The Escuela de Instructores de Arte (School of Art Instructors) was established in 1961 and the Escuela Nacional de Arte (National School of Art) in 1962. By the mid-70s a wide network of sites offered instruction in theatre, music, plastic arts, ballet and dance to nearly 5000 students. An active publication programme accompanied the literacy campaign; plays were published in great numbers and the theatre journal *Conjunto* (established by Manuel Galich in 1964) began publishing criticism, plays and information about theatre from countries throughout the Americas.

The theatre of the period belongs not only to the playwrights who were writing new theatre but also to the many groups that were spawned and to their valiant and creative directors. Of those playwrights whose careers coincide with the recent period, ABELARDO ESTORINO is foremost. He joined the Teatro Estudio (Studio Theatre) group in 1960, and became a professional writer the following year. His *El robo del cochino* (*The Theft of the Pig*, 1961) signalled his ability to create true-to-life characters in the tense political situation that anticipated the Revolution. His subsequent plays, such as *La casa vieja* (*The Old House*, 1964) and *Morir del cuento* (*To Die from the Story*, 1983), lived up to the original promise: he was the only writer who continued to write in Cuba over an extended period. Less realistic in technique is ANTÓN ARRUFAT, who wrote an absurdist play, *El caso se investiga* (*The Case is Being Investigated*), as early as 1957, followed by several others during the early revolutionary years. After his *Los siete contra Tebas* (*Seven against Thebes*) won the UNEAC (Unión Nacional de Escritores y Artistas Cubanos; National Union of Cuban Writers and Artists) Prize in 1968, the play was censured for its alleged counter-revolutionary spirit, along with Heberto Padilla's poetry. Arrufat has continued writing for the theatre, but his later plays have not been staged.

JOSÉ TRIANA became Cuba's best-known writer internationally for *La noche de los asesinos* (*Night of the Assassins*, 1965), a brilliant and intriguing metatheatrical play and winner of the Casa de las Américas prize for 1965, about three adolescents playing various roles as they enact the ritual murder of their parents. Although his earlier plays pointed towards a successful career, the political fall-out of *The Assassins* thwarted further activity. In 1980 Triana settled in Paris; his recent plays provide revisionist perspectives of Cuban society in previous periods, mostly 19th-century, and normally as metaphorical comment on current conditions.

An interesting transitional figure is VIRGILIO PIÑERA, often cited as having been an absurdist writer before the French wave of Beckett and Ionesco. His *Electra Garrigó* (1948) plays with the Greek myth within a milieu of colourful and satirical Cuban characters trying to survive the absurdity of the Cuban sociopolitical system. *Aire frío* (*Cold Air*, 1962) is an autobiographical work that chronicles the disintegration of family structure during the Batista years. *Dos viejos pánicos* (*Two Old Panics*, 1968), which captures the chilling effects of fear on a society, also has absurdist tones.

Other writers of the early years of the Revolution include José Brene (b.1927), whose *Santa Camila de la Habana vieja* (*St Camille of Old Havana*, 1962) dramatizes the conversion of a low-life parasite to a revolutionary ideology. At the age of fourteen the precocious Nicolás Dorr (b.1946) presented a remarkably mature picture of human relationships captured in a farcical and even absurdist style. In this vein are his *Las pericas* (*The Parrots*, 1961), *El palacio de los cartones* (*The Cardboard Palace*, 1961), and *La esquina de los concejales* (*The Councillors' Corner*, 1962); later works, though, are more realistic, such as *La chacota* (*The Racket*, 1974) and *Confesión en el barrio chino* (*Confession in the Chinese Quarter*, 1981). In his controversial *Confrontación* (*Confrontation*, 1989) he examines the personal needs *vis-à-vis* the professional obligations of a woman soldier. As director of Teatro Popular Latinoamericano (Popular Latin-American Theatre), in the 1970s Dorr launched an ambitious programme for Cuban theatre and continued writing ideologically oriented plays about the new society. In 1964 Héctor Quintero wrote, and the imaginative Sergio Corrieri staged, *Contigo pan y cebolla* (*With You Bread and Onions*), one of Cuba's most popular though structurally defective comedies about basic human needs and aspirations.

As early as 1960 the government established the Teatro Nacional de Cuba (National Cuban Theatre), the enabling agency that created other groups. The first revolutionary group, the Studio Theatre, was consolidated in 1959 after the Revolution and dedicated to Marxist-Leninist principles. In short order there appeared the Grupo Rita Montaner (1961) and the Conjunto Dramático Nacional (1962), with many others to follow. The effort reached out from Havana to stimulate theatre throughout the island, with parallel activity for children sponsored through the Departamento de Teatro Infantil. The repertoire consisted of both old and new Cuban plays, as well as many foreign classics. Additional activities included theatre seminars and festivals, all intended to raise the level of theatre-consciousness within the Cuban public while communicating basic principles of the Revolution.

By 1968 the theatre in Cuba had entered a second phase. The Grupo Teatro Escambray (Escambray Theatre Group), established that year by Corrieri in the province of Las Villas, was representative of the search for the methods and contacts that would lead to the so-called 'new theatre'. The term refers to the anti-bourgeois theatre that grew out of close interaction between theatre groups and the public it served. The Escambray group, for example, developed a model of interviewing regional people about their concerns, attitudes and values in order to develop meaningful dramatic experiences for them. The plays relied on local language and colour, and almost always used music (although the Cuban penchant for music is so strong that most productions automatically incorporate some musical background). The history of Escambray, in its search for a style that suited its objectives, in some respects illustrates the history of the collective theatre movement in Cuba. Over several years, the group staged Onelio Jorge Cardoso's *Los cuentos* (*The Stories*, 1971), Albio Paz's *La vitrina* (*The Showcase*, 1971), Gilda Hernández's *El juicio* (*The Trial*, 1973) and Roberto Orihuela's *La emboscada* (*The Ambush*, 1978). The quality and spirit of these performances served as an inspiration across the island.

Other groups with a similar orientation soon followed, including La Yaya (1973–6), directed by Flora Lauten; Teatro de Participación Popular (1973), directed by Herminia Sánchez and Manuel Terraza; Teatrova (1974), a group from Santiago that depended greatly on music;

The Cubana de Acero in Albio Paz's *Huelga* (*Strike*), Havana, 1981.

Teatro Juvenil Pinos Nuevos (Pinos Nuevos Children's Theatre, 1974) and Cubana de Acero (Cuban Steel) (1977). Cuban Steel operated directly out of the steel factory, and performances took place between shifts. Juglars y su Peña Literaria (the Minstrels and their Literary Group) performed in Lenin Park in Havana. The Cabildo Teatral [Town Hall Theatre] de Santiago (1973), reconstituted out of its original Conjunto Dramático de Oriente (1961), has enjoyed unusual success with Raúl Pomares' *De cómo Santiago Apóstol puso los pies en la tierra*

(*About How the Apostle James Set Foot on Earth*, 1974), a performance combining pantomime and dance with African and Cuban rhythms and movement, often performed in public parks and squares.

In 1976 the Cuban theatrical world was moved by the production of *María Antonia*, a tragedy by Eugenio Hernández Espinosa (b.1936) rooted in the mythical Afro-Cuban universe that reflects the marginal society preceding the 1959 Revolution. Hernández is the Cuban playwright who reflects with greatest authenticity the world of the blacks, in such works as *Oba y Shangó* (*The King and Shangó*, 1980) and *Odebí el cazador* (*Odebí the Hunter*, 1980).

Even though the Cuban theatre has operated in a collective style, individual authors have played a prominent role. Others of note are Lázaro Rodríguez, Rafael González, Freddy Artiles and Abraham Rodríguez. Herminia Sánchez and Flora Lauten, in addition to their work as directors, are both accomplished playwrights. Francisco Garzón Céspedes has devot-

ed his talents in recent years to reviving the art of storytelling through a process known as *narración oral escénica* (staged oral narration). Of the most recent performances, two deserve special mention: Víctor Varela's *La cuarta pared* (*The Fourth Wall*, 1987) and the Ballet Cubano's presentation of 1988.

Cubans in exile have maintained a high level of theatrical activity completely disconnected from that of the island. José Triana has resumed writing and staging in Paris. The multi-talented Matías Montes Huidobro, professor of literature at the University of Hawaii, writes plays and scholarly studies while running an active theatre publication programme (he has his own press). The centre of Cuban theatre in exile can be found in Florida, where numerous groups appeal to the large Hispanic population, primarily Cuban. Teatro Avante, under the direction of Mario Ernesto Sánchez, has completed eight cycles of an annual theatre festival that attracts groups from the USA and Latin America.

The immediacy of the revolutionary process

Cabildo Teatral de Santiago in Raúl Pomores's *De cómo Santiago Apóstal puso los pies en le tierra* (*About How the Apostle James Set Foot on Earth*), Santiago, 1975.

in Cuba called special attention to education, to male/female roles and relationships, to work ethics, and to an individual commitment to revolutionary goals – all in a rapidly changing economy and society. The theatre did not merely reflect the process, but because of its popular nature it became instrumental in helping to shape attitudes and opinions. Especially since the 1970s, Cuban playwriting frequently signals a recognition of current themes by means of a critical investigation of reality. The Cuban government has continued to invest heavily in theatre and art programmes. The theatre festivals sponsored on the island have helped to create a sense of solidarity among theatre practitioners. Over the years the government has invited many distinguished artists to Cuba, including the Argentine Osvaldo Dragún, who directed the Seminar of Latin-American Dramaturgy as early as 1962 and since 1989 has lived in Cuba, where he directs the Institute for Latin American Theatre. The Cubans have regularly participated in international theatre festivals and seminars sponsored throughout Latin America and Europe. In 1982 a new theatre journal, *Tablas* (*Boards*), edited by Rosa Ileana Boudet, complemented the longstanding publication programme of the Casa de las Américas (the Cuban cultural centre responsible for promoting ideology and art), the most prolific on theatre in all the Americas.

Ideological theatre still dominates in Cuba, while the search for new forms continues. The basis of that search derives from the desire for a new language and new images that convey the essence of Cuban reality. In part, it relates to the effort to avoid the monotony of productions bound by the forces of the Revolution. Many theatre groups and organizations throughout Latin America have maintained solidarity with Cuba, but with many external sources of inspiration closed off by political and economic restrictions, it has become increasingly difficult to infuse creativity into the system. Paradoxically, in the midst of copious activity and strong state support, the Cuban theatre remains one of the most impoverished in all of Latin America. No plays of transcendental value have emerged from Cuba since the production of *The Night of the Assassins* in 1965. In the 1990s the collapse of the Soviet system has obliged the Cuban theatre to become even more resourceful – when there are no lights for productions and no paper for printing.

Arrufat, Antón (1935–)

Cuban playwright and poet, who abandoned his university studies to be a writer. His first efforts were two one-act absurdist plays *El caso se investiga* (*The Case is Being Investigated*) and *El último tren* (*The Last Train*), both written in 1957 and both unsuccessful. *El vivo al pollo* (*Chicken for the Living*, 1959) uses traditional BUFO theatre to parody a natural fear of death in the case of a woman who embalms her husband. With *La zona cero* (*Zero Zone*, 1959), the illogical patterns and comedy routines that he developed earlier reach a climax in a Beckett-style absurdism. After *La repetición* (*The Repetition*, 1963), a repetitive process that shows the influence of the Revolution, and *Todos los domingos* (*Every Sunday*, 1965), he wrote *Los siete contra Tebas* (*Seven against Thebes*), which won the UNEAC (National Union of Cuban Writers and Artists) Prize for 1968, but he was censured along with Heberto Padilla for a work considered antithetical to revolutionary goals. He remains in Cuba and works as a journalist/writer. His later plays are unpublished and unstaged: *La tierra permanente* (*The Solid Earth*), *Retrato de Juan Criollo* (*Portrait of John Creole*) and *La divina Fanny* (*Divine Fanny*). His search for language adequate to express new concepts is a strong characteristic of his work.

bufo

The Caribbean, especially Cuban, equivalent of the *sainete* (see Dominican Republic, GÉNERO CHICO), a popular theatre form that incorporates the types, characters and language typical of the lower social classes. *Bufo* also implies a criticism of some aspect of life and is normally presented with the intention of destroying false illusions. After a period of relative disuse, the form has been reincorporated into Cuba's new social theatre.

Corrieri, Sergio (1938–)

Cuban actor and director. He was a charter member of the Teatro Estudio (Studio Theatre) in 1958, a pre-revolutionary group that became instrumental in indicating new directions, and in 1968 he founded the Grupo Teatro Escambray in the provinces of Las Villas. As artistic director he sought to bring revolutionary ideology to the people through theatre. The plays they developed often depended on interviews the group itself conducted into local problems, and regularly involved direct interaction with the public, both during and after the performances. Many of Cuba's new generation of writers, such as Albio Paz, Gilda Hernández and Roberto Orihuela, were launched by the Grupo Teatro Escambray, which by 1975 had earned for Corrieri the plaudits of Cuba's president and a post as delegate to the First Congress of the Cuban Communist Party.

Estorino, Abelardo (1925–)

Cuban playwright and director. He was born in Matanzas and studied at the University of Havana, then practised dental surgery for three years. In 1960 he joined the Studio Theatre, Cuba's first revolutionary theatre group, and in 1961 was contracted by the government as a professional writer. He often directs and occasionally acts and designs sets. Estorino interprets contemporary situations and immediate problems of Cuban reality into transcendent theatrical pieces. The constants in his work are the focus on family units and marital issues, along with the need for openness, fairness and equality in human relationships. Essentially a

realistic writer, he has remained loyal to the revolutionary ideals while in later plays experimenting with metatheatrical techniques. His best-known works are *El robo del cochino* (*The Theft of the Pig*, 1961), *La casa vieja* (*The Old House*, 1964), *Los mangos de Caín* (*Cain's Mangoes*, 1967), *La dolorosa historia del amor secreto de don José Jacinto Milanés* (*The Tragic Story of the Secret Love of don José Jacinto Milanés*, 1974), *Ni un sí ni un no* (*Neither a Yes nor a No*, 1981), and *Morir del cuento* (*To Die from the Story*, 1983).

Gómez de Avellaneda, Gertrudis (1814–73)

An extraordinary poet, novelist and playwright whose work reflects little of the Cuban reality of the time. Twice widowed, beset with major personal problems and mostly unappreciated in her native Cuba, she spent most of her life in Spain where she aspired to courtly grandeur. Her theatre belongs primarily to Spain, although she is considered one of the major women playwrights of the Americas, dominating both tragic and comic forms. Of her twenty plays, her principal tragic works are *Munio Alfonso* (1844) and *Baltasar* (1858), the latter relating the Spanish crown to its biblical antecedents. On the lighter side, *La hija de las flores* (*Daughter of the Flowers*, 1852) and *El millonario y la maleta* (*The Millionaire and his Suitcase*, 1870) are entertaining comedies with good humour. For the most part, Tula, as she was called, managed to avoid the excesses of romanticism and to create developed characters with a sound psychological basis.

Piñera, Virgilio (1912–79)

Cuban playwright, poet and fiction writer. Piñera studied philosophy and letters at the University of Havana and lived in Argentina from 1946 to 58. His first play, *Electra Garrigó* (1948), set off a heated scandal for its bold Cuban treatment of a classical myth. His theatre is characterized by absurd black humour and by a depiction of reality in intellectual and, on occasion, abstract terms. In contrast his *Aire frío* (*Cold Air*, 1962), considered a classic Cuban play, is a totally realistic vision of a middle-class family before the Revolution. Among his most significant works are *El flaco y el gordo* (*The Thin Man and the Fat Man*, 1949), *Jesús* (1950), *El filántropo* (*The Philantropist*, 1960) and *Dos viejos pánicos* (*Two Old Panics*), the latter a recipient of the Casa de las Américas prize in 1968.

Triana, José (1931–)

Cuban playwright. He studied literature at Santiago de Cuba, wrote poetry in Spain, then returned to Cuba to espouse revolutionary programmes. His first plays, *Medea en el espejo* (*Medea in the Mirror*, 1960) and *La muerte del ñeque* (*Death of the Strong Man*, 1963), both contain elements of classical Greek tragic figures integrated into a lower-class Cuban environment, where violence and criminality prefigure the game symbolism – representing the machinations within society at large – in his later theatre. His masterpiece, and Cuba's best-known play internationally, is *La noche de los asesinos* (*The Night of the Assassins*, 1965), a brutal work with metatheatrical techniques that involves three adolescents in the myth, ritual and exorcism of killing their parents. No other plays appeared until, on a trip to Paris in 1980, Triana defected. *Ceremonial de guerra* (*War Ceremony*), written during 1968–73, and *Diálogo de mujeres* (*Women's Dialogue*, 1979–80), are both set in Cuba at the turn of the century. In 1986 the Royal Shakespeare Company staged the latter play (retitled *Palabras comunes* in Spanish) as *Worlds Apart*, a study of Cuba from 1894 to 1914.

Bibliography

N. González Freire, *Teatro cubano* (1927–61), Havana, 1961; R. Leal, *Breve historia del teatro cubano*, Havana, 1980; M. Montes Huidobro, *Persona, vida y máscara en el teatro cubano*, Miami, 1973; J. R. Pereira, 'The Black Presence in Cuban Theatre', Afro-Hispanic Review, 2:1 (Jan. 1983).

DOMINICAN REPUBLIC

On this Caribbean island, one of Columbus's first settlements, the native *taínos* practised both the *areyto*, a historical music-dance drama that transmitted the cultural heritage orally, and the *cohaba*, a priestly ceremonial dance induced by hallucinogenic drugs. The early extinction of the indigenous population through the imposition of a Spanish hierarchical system and the importation of European diseases reduced the demand for catechetical theatre. In the colonial years, theatre tended to reflect religious concerns in the form of *loas, entremeses* and *comedias* (see GÉNERO CHICO), although a secular theatre, realistic and comic, sometimes in open opposition to Catholic dogma, was performed and naturally censured by the Church.

Cristóbal de Llerena, born on the island, is the first playwright of record native to the New World. He wrote several works, but only his *entremés* performed in 1588 survives. The work reflects social conflicts and corruption within Dominican society during a period of external and internal piracy. Sir Francis Drake had recently sacked Santo Domingo, and Llerena's brief, two-scene play resulted in his immediate but temporary deportation. From 1616–18 Tirso de Molina, the famous Spanish playwright of the Golden Age, lived on the island, but there is no record that his plays were performed there or that his idealistic conception of the world left any lasting impact on Dominican theatre.

New governors, slave rebellions and political instability – produced by invasions and by the wars between Spain, France and England – characterized life on the island during the 17th and 18th centuries. Theatrical events took place in the churches, squares and viceregal houses and palaces, but no plays are preserved. The 19th-century occupation first by the Haitians (1822–44) and then by the Spanish (1861–5) perpetuated the turbulence, but such theatre groups as the Trinitarians, the Philanthropics and the Dramatic Society attempted to maintain a semblance of activity, generally with foreign plays by such authors as Alfieri and Francisco Martínez de la Rosa.

Don Félix María del Monte is considered the first national playwright, with a work that criticizes the first president of the nation for the assassination of the patriot Antonio Duvergé – *Antonio Duvergé, o Las víctimas del 11 de abril* (*Antonio Duvergé, or The Victims of 11 April*, 1856). Indigenous and heroic tendencies, embedded in a romantic framework, were typical of the other major authors of the period, such as Javier Foxá (1816–65) and Javier Angulo Guridi (1816–84), who wrote *Iguaniona* (1867). Groups such as La Juventud (Youth, 1868) and Amigos del País (Friends of the Nation, 1871) contributed to the theatre movement.

After 1911 cultural societies began to produce comedy sketches, and the North American occupation of the island (1916–24) inspired some political plays. However, Rafael Damirón's (1882–1946) *Alma criolla* (*Creole Soul*, 1916) continued the romantic tradition, with elements of the *zarzuela* (see GÉNERO CHICO). The early years of the century generally saw little new development.

Roughly one-third of the century belongs to Rafael Trujillo, who held power from 1930 to 1961. The material progress he brought to the country, as well as the great profits for himself, were achieved at the cost of personal freedoms. Criticism of the dictator was not permitted, and the theatre of the period is generally impoverished. In the 1940s the arrival of Spanish immigrants, refugees of the Civil War, gave some new impulse to the theatre, but in general the Trujillo years are characterized by foreign plays and by local playwrights little engaged with Dominican reality – largely because of the stringent conditions of the police state. From 1930 to 61 only 9.5 per cent of all productions were plays written by Dominicans. In 1946 Generalissimo Trujillo's wife urged the creation of the Fine Arts Theatre. The theatre occupies a handsome building; currently the government provides regular, though minimal, salaries.

A new sense of experimentation in the Dominican theatre began to emerge in the mid- to late 1950s, through the efforts of three playwrights in particular: MANUEL RUEDA, MÁXIMO AVILÉS BLONDA and FRANKLIN DOMÍNGUEZ, all using newer techniques in their work. Rueda's *La trinitaria blanca* (*The White Pansy*, 1957) relies on a Dominican setting to explore a case of psychological anguish produced by a religious experience; Avilés Blonda in *Las manos vacías* (*Empty Hands*, 1959) also explores religious conflicts vis-à-vis human values. All three are major authors with a commitment to serious theatre. Domínguez – most recognized of the island's playwrights in international circles – produced *Un amigo desconocido nos aguarda* (*An Unknown Friend Awaits Us*) in 1958, but achieved greater success with *El último instante* (*The Last Moment*), a monologue that penetrates both existential and social conditions.

The years following the Trujillo assassination have been marked by political instability and regrouping, along with the gradual rebuilding of the artistic infrastructure of this island nation. But the new freedom of political expression brought no quick response in improved drama quality. An early wave of Greek-based plays, such as Marcio Veloz Maggiolos' *Creonte* (1963) and HÉCTOR INCHÁUSTEGUI CABRAL's *Miedo en un puñado de polvo* (*Fear in a Handful of Dust*, 1964), eased the transition into a period of greater social awareness and commitment. A revival of Tennessee Williams's realistic plays set a new standard, as the Dominican theatre sought not only to create a new dramaturgy but also to develop a public appreciative of plays of commitment in contrast with the customary plays of simple entertainment. The later generation includes such writers as Carlos Esteban Deive (b.1935), IVÁN GARCÍA GUERRA, Carlos Acevedo, Rafael Añez Bergés, Juan Carlos Mieses (b.1947) and Efraím Castillo. This last has published two plays: *Viaje de regreso* (*Return Trip*) and *La cosecha* (*The Crop*). Of special importance is García Guerra, whose *Más allá de la búsqueda* (*Beyond the Search*) incorporates elements of the Afro-Antilles milieu. He is committed to the social issues of Dominican reality, condemning hypocrisy and injustice in political, religious and military spheres.

Playwright and director Rubén Echavarría (or Echevarría) was responsible for two major successes in the mid-1970s. Before the brilliant production of Domínguez's *El último instante* (*The Last Moment*) in 1975, he had staged the previous year his own play, *La obra que no tiene nombre* (*An Unnamed Play*), an exposé of the nation's system of justice (or injustice), from its earliest times to the present, combining Brechtian techniques with 'total theatre'. The innovative staging of Peter Weiss's *Marat-Sade* in 1981 is widely considered another milestone in Dominican production history.

The experimental movement spawned such groups as the Jockey Club Group (1975), the Popular Experimental Theatre (1976), Intec Projection (1978) and Chispa (Spark). Domínguez created his own independent group; and the Gratey Theatre, directed by Danilo Ginebra and others, has been involved in a wide range of publications and activities, including the first national popular theatre festival in 1983. Delta Sota and María Castillo have done important work with the Nuevo Teatro (New Theatre). In 1985 Reynaldo Disla won the coveted Casa de las Américas prize in

Cuba for the best new play, *Bolo Francisco*, which makes a strong statement about oppression and the struggle for liberation. A 1987 theatre competition resulted in five new published plays; first prize went to Juan Carlos Campos for *Hágase la mujer* (*Let Woman Be Created*), an entertaining piece in which God loses control and man's request for a companion brings an unexpected response.

Theatre activity in the Dominican Republic continues to be sporadic, centred mostly in the capital city, Santo Domingo, and embracing non-professional, independent and university theatre work – which includes that of the Autonomous University of Santo Domingo, Pedro Henríquez Ureña National University and the Technical Institute of Santo Domingo. Isolated activity in the provinces includes the work of RAFAEL VILLALONA with the Teatro Popular del Centro de la Cultura, and that of Lincoln López with the theatre programme of the Catholic University Madre y Maestra, both located in Santiago de los Caballeros. The Dominican theatre still suffers from a lack of infrastructure, and the many extant groups create false expectations about the availability of staged performances.

Avilés Blonda, Máximo (1931–)

Dominican playwright and poet with degrees in philosophy and law, and founder-director of the University Theatre. *Las manos vacías* (*Empty Hands*, 1959) is a study of spiritual emptiness following the Second World War; *La otra estrella en el cielo* (*The Other Star in the Sky*, 1963) deals metaphorically with a 15th-century Italian struggle for power. *Yo, Bertolt Brecht* (*I, Bertolt Brecht*, 1960) is a vanguardist collage of epic scenes from a dozen of Brecht's plays set in Avilés's framework, and *Pirámide 179* (*Pyramid 179*, 1969) applies Brechtian techniques to national hatred over the Haitian boundary issue.

Domínguez, Franklin (1931–)

Dominican playwright, director and actor. A graduate of the National School of Dramatic Art in 1949, he was instrumental in creating the experimental theatre movement in the Dominican Republic. With degrees in philosophy (1953) and law (1955), he has occupied important positions in national theatre and culture. He has served as director of the Fine Arts Theatre and has his own theatre group, Franklin Domínguez Presents. An eclectic writer, his works have been translated and staged in French, German, English, Portuguese, Flemish and Chinese. Among his thirty-odd plays are: *El último instante* (*The Last Moment*, 1957), the anguished monologue of a suicidal prostitute; *Se busca un hombre honesto* (*The Search for an Honest Man*, 1963); and *Lisístrata odia la política* (*Lysistrata Hates Politics*, 1965), a socially committed play based on Aristophanes. His plays have won prizes in many countries.

García Guerra, Iván (1938–)

Dominican professor and playwright, author of, among other plays, *Más allá de la búsqueda* (*Beyond the Search*, 1963), a combination of classical themes and Caribbean techniques and motifs; *Don Quijote de todo el mundo* (*Everyman's Don Quijote*, 1964), about injustice and corruption; *Un héroe más para la mitología* (*Another Hero for Mythology*, 1965), denouncing military supremacy; and *Fábula de los cinco caminantes* (*The Fable of the Five Travellers*, 1965), about the irrationality of mankind within the grotesque and absurd framework of the modern world. García Guerra employs techniques ranging from the absurd to the epic in order to denounce the social and political problems of his country.

género chico

Spanish generic term for the short one-act play, having its origin in the medieval church, but by the 16th century entirely secular. The essence of the works that constitute the genre, including the *paso*, the *loa*, the *entremés* and the *sainete*, is that they provided comic relief and variety between the acts of a full-scale play. The *loa* was a short theatre piece of sacred origin, normally with music, and common in Spain and Latin America during the years of conquest and colonization. The principal object was to praise high-level officials on special occasions. The *entremés* was usually performed after the first act of the *comedia*. Music was an important element, especially in the *zarzuela*, which inspired the popular theatre forms that began to develop in the 19th century.

Incháustegui Cabral, Héctor (1912–79)

Dominican poet, critic, fiction writer and playwright. Born in Baní, he practised journalism in his youth. He belonged to the group of 'independent poets' who produced important social poetry during the 1930s–50s. His *Miedo en un puñado de polvo* (*Fear in a Handful of Dust*, 1968) is a collection of three plays based on Greek classics that express universal constants of the human spirit; but his theatre is more theatre of ideas than of action.

Rueda, Manuel (1921–)

Dominican poet, musician, playwright, fiction writer and critic; born in Monte Cristi. Rueda is considered one of his country's most important writers. His play *La trinitaria blanca* (*The White Pansy*) won the National Prize for Theatre in 1957, and was anthologized in 1968 along with *Vacaciones en el cielo* (*Vacations in Heaven*), *La tía Beatriz hace un milagro* (*Aunt Beatriz Works a Miracle*) and *Entre alambradas* (*Inside Fences*), the latter dealing with the US occupation of the Dominican Republic in 1965. Rueda's theatre is characterized by balance of form, his poetic language and humour, and dramatic action. *El rey Clinejas* (*King Clinejas*) won the National Prize for Theatre in 1979 and, as popular theatre, has been well received for its poetry and fantasy.

Villalona, Rafael (1942–)

Dominican director. A graduate of the Lunacharsky Institute in Moscow, Villalona has promoted good theatre in his country by establishing theatre groups (Compañía Nuevo Teatro, 1969; Teatro Popular del Centro de la Cultura de Santiago, 1970; Casa de Teatro, 1974), by staging innovative productions of both domestic and foreign plays (including García Lorca, Ibsen, Ionesco and Tennessee Williams), and by representing national theatre interests at home and abroad.

Bibliography

D. Ginebra (ed.), *Teatro dominicano*, vol. 1, Santo Domingo, 1984; P. Henríquez Ureña, *Obras completas: El teatro de la América española*, vol. 7, Santo Domingo, 1978; J. Lockward, *Teatro dominicano: Pasado y presente*, Santo Domingo, 1959; José Molinaza, *Historia crítica del teatro dominicano*, vol. 1 (1492–1844), vol. 2 (1844–1930), Santo Domingo, 1984, and '1863–1987: Del indigenismo a la dramaturgia de los ochenta', in *Escenarios de dos mundos: Inventario teatral de Iberoamérica*, vol. 4, Madrid, 1989.

EASTERN CARIBBEAN STATES

When the West Indies Federation collapsed in 1962 with the withdrawal of JAMAICA and TRINIDAD AND TOBAGO, the smaller English-speaking islands of the eastern Caribbean sought to establish a loose association from which they might benefit economically as trading partners. At present they use the same currency, although politically they range from crown colony to fully independent states. With a total population of about 600,000, these islands – referred to as the Windward and Leeward Islands, according to whether they are in the path of the trade winds and thus subject to rain, or on the lee side and therefore drier – form the eastern rim of the Caribbean basin. The Windwards comprise Grenada, Martinique, St Vincent and the Grenadines, St Lucia and Dominica. The Leewards are Montserrat, Antigua and Barbuda, St Kitts and Nevis, and Anguilla. Entries are given only on the three states where theatrical activity is of particular interest, but there are entries on individuals from states that are not entered.

The islands were first inhabited by Arawak Indians who were driven out by the fiercer Carib Indians from South America. These in turn were crushed by the Spanish adventurers who followed Columbus to the area. In the 1500s and 1600s Great Britain and France fought over these Eastern Caribbean States, which had become British colonies by the early 1800s. Little is known of early theatrical activity in the islands, but English companies no doubt put on performances in the area from the late 18th century. A Leeward Islands company of comedians is reported to have performed *King Lear, Richard II* and other popular plays of the day at Christiansted, Danish West Indies, in 1771.

Antigua

A party of amateurs opened Antigua's first theatre in 1788 with Otway's *Venice Preserv'd*, after which visiting companies came for a few weeks' run, their performances reinforced by local actors. The West India Sketch Book (1835) mentions a theatre in Antigua with amateurs performing Goldsmith's *She Stoops to Conquer* along with a pantomime called *Harlequin Planter, or The Land of Promise*. This latter – containing 'aboriginal savages', their evil spirit Maboya, white settlers, black slaves, Astraea the goddess of justice, members of the Anti-Slavery Society, Harlequin and Columbine – might count as one of the earliest pieces of native Caribbean theatre, dealing as it does with the local scene. The audience of white, coloured and black, freemen and slaves, were said to be delighted by the performance.

Antiguans recall, from the 1930s, the operettas and musicals presented by one Nellie Robinson of the TOR Memorial High School. In 1952 the Community Players were formed, causing a stir in local circles when, led by the drama tutor of the UNIVERSITY OF THE WEST INDIES, (UWI, see Introduction), they created the village play *Priscilla's Wedding* using local dialect, thought at the time to undermine the teaching of 'proper' English. The Players have since performed their folksongs and operettas internationally. In 1956 the UWI extramural tutor based in St Kitts organized the first Leeward Islands drama festival, and in 1967 the Antigua University Centre was established, with a 400-seat open-air theatre. Several short-lived theatre groups sprang up at this time. The Little Theatre, led by Bobby Margetson, presented Caribbean plays including two from Antigua by Oliver Flax: *The Legend of Prince Klaas*, entered in the CARIFESTA (see Introduction) in Guyana in 1972, and *A Better Way* (1976), directed by Edgar Davis. The Grammarians took their *Obeah Slave* (1969), by Lester Simon, to Montserrat and BARBADOS, and the Open-Air Theatre travelled to St Kitts and Barbados in 1971 with Lonne Elder's *Ceremonies in Dark Old Men*.

These last two groups merged in 1972, under DORBRENE O'MARDE, to become the Harambee Open-Air Theatre, considered the most important group of recent times. The Third World Theatre led by Leon Symester, also known as Chaka Wacca, presented two protest plays, *Voices of Protest* (1976) and *Time Bomb* (1977), dealing with the political situation in Antigua. *Time Bomb* was considered libellous and not allowed to be entered in the local festival, but drew crowds when it played at the University Centre. Chaka Wacca left Antigua in 1980 for New Jersey, where he practises law. Eliston Adams, known also as Nambulumba, in 1979 started the Rio Revealers Theatre for staging what have been described as his 'slapstick plays', which the company took to Montserrat, St Martin (Dutch) and St Thomas (American). In 1988 the Popular Theatre Movement was started in village communities, where role-playing, discussion and creative play-making help to identify issues and suggest solutions. The group toured their self-made play, *Rising from the Ashes*, to Dominica. In 1990 Rick James began his fully professional Theatre Ensemble, playing short plays with small casts at beach hotels.

As in Antigua, groups in other island states have taken productions to neighbouring islands in order to extend their run, improve working skills and advance careers. But this constant movement has posed survival difficulties, because such groups tend to be disparate and short-lived instead of becoming consolidated under strong, lasting leadership.

Dominica

The only Eastern Caribbean island with a history of significant Carib and free African populations, Dominica was captured from the French by the British navy in 1761. Its mountainous terrain was not suitable for large plantations, and thus peasant farming controlled by French mulattos from neighbouring Guadeloupe and Martinique remained the dominant mode in coastal villages. From this mélange of Carib, African, and French mulatto, plus a small English administrative community, emerged a rich heritage of folk-songs, dances, music-making, storytelling and masquerades, cultural manifestations in which the Creole language predominates.

According to the historian Lennox Honychurch 'there is no tradition of theatre or creative interpretative dance in Dominica'. Only in this century have productions of Gilbert and Sullivan's operettas been organized, and in 1945 an adaptation of Jane Austen's novel *Pride and Prejudice* was memorably staged. In 1964 a Shakespeare festival brought to the fore Amah Harris and ALWIN BULLY. Harris formed the Little Theatre, which she led during 1965–70 before leaving for Toronto. Bully took a BA at the Cave Hill, Barbados, campus of the UNIVERSITY OF THE WEST INDIES (see Introduction) during 1967–71. On his return to Dominica he directed Daniel Caudeiron's *Speak, Brother, Speak*, a social commentary with music and dance which was produced for the Little Theatre in 1972. He then formed his own group, the People's Action Theatre (PAT), whose intention was to be socially active, taking productions to village audiences. In 1975 Bully's play *Streak* confirmed this approach.

The work of the PAT inspired the formation of other groups such as, in 1976, the Aquarian Xpression group; in 1977, the Karifouna Cultural Group, dedicated to the preservation and promotion of Carib culture; in 1982, the Movement for Cultural Awareness which, as part of the EASTERN CARIBBEAN POPULAR THEATRE ORGANIZATION (see Introduction), focused on popular theatre in the villages; and in 1984, the New Dimensions Theatre led by playwright-director Steve Hyacinth, principal of the Mahaut Government School. This group has produced six of Hyacinth's plays, all taken on tour to village audiences. In 1990, combining the talents of the People's Action and New Dimensions Theatres, the Popular Theatre Movement produced *The Swine and the Pearl*, written by Hyacinth, Philbert Aaron and Delmance Moses and directed by Nigel Francis. Dealing with issues pertinent to the Year of Environment and Shelter, to which it was a contribution, the play was presented in the capital, Roseau, and to ten communities around the island. Creole translations of plays such as DEREK WALCOTT's *Ti-Jean and His Brothers* and ERROL JOHN's (see Trinidad and Tobago) *Moon on a Rainbow Shawl* have proved popular in a country where the first, and sometimes only, language of the people is Kweyol (Creole). Demonstrating the theatre's consciousness of the needs of its public, both plays have been staged in Dominica, the latter having also been taken to the Martinique Theatre Festival in 1989.

The most serious and successful dance-drama group is the Waitukubuli Dance Theatre Company led by Raymond Lawrence. ('Waitukubuli' is the Carib name for Dominica, to be interpreted as 'tall is her body' or 'land or many battles'.) Founded in 1971, the company has produced four dance-dramas: *Kabouki* (1977), *Papa Toussaint* (1978); and two biblical pieces, *The Resurrection* (1986) and *The Power and the Glory* (1987). It has also presented works set to the poetry of Dominican writers.

The major problem facing theatre and dance companies in Dominica is the lack of a proper performing space. For years theatre groups have endured inadequate school halls, and even today, troupes in Roseau are obliged to perform in an old, hurricane-damaged cinema.

St Lucia

A Theatre Royal was first established in the capital, Castries, in 1832. The theatre was used by English and French amateurs, aided by a company of artists from Martinique under the direction of one M. Charvet. They performed two or three times a week for six months. The historian Henry Breen has commented: 'it was a spectacle at once novel and pleasing to behold the same audience successively applauding the representations, on the same stage and in different languages, of *Othello* and the *Médicin malgré lui*'. Charvet brought his company for a second visit in 1834, when they were joined by amateurs from the Royal Regiment stationed on St Lucia. The phenomenon of French and English performers sharing the same stage reflects the duality of the colonial powers that, for over 160 years, contended for the island. Eventually, in 1804, the English prevailed, but, as with Dominica, the French left their mark on the language and customs of the island, with its population of basically African or part-African, as well as bequeathing them what is still their principal religion – Roman Catholicism.

Any theatre performed up to the mid-20th century might be expected still to be European in content, if not always in personnel. In 1950, however, a new era was ushered in with the founding of the ARTS GUILD OF ST LUCIA by Maurice Mason and DEREK WALCOTT. Within months Walcott left St Lucia to take up a scholarship at the UNIVERSITY OF THE WEST INDIES (see Introduction), and the leadership of the Guild was taken over by his twin brother RODDY WALCOTT. With members recruited primarily from pupils and ex-pupils of Castries's secondary schools, the Guild started with an ambitious programme to promote the arts in general, but soon found itself drawn primarily to the theatre. For over twenty years it was the principal play-producing organization in the country, with a growing emphasis on Caribbean drama. In 1966 the Creative and Performing Arts Society – primarily a training operation supported by the university extra-mural tutor, Patricia Charles – came into being. Tutors were drawn from among the

British residents on the island who were trained in theatre, and from Jamaica and Trinidad in the case of workshops in dance. As well as indigenous works, the society produced plays such as Shaw's *Dark Lady of the Sonnets*, Henri Ghéon's *Christmas in the Market-Place*, ERROL HILL's (see Trinidad and Tobago) *Square Peg*, and Eric Roach's *Letter from Leonora*.

The Society ceased to exist in 1974, but it was in that year that the Folk Research Centre was established. George Alphonse, one of its foundation members, was sent for two years (1983–5) by the St Lucia government to the CULTURAL TRAINING CENTRE in Jamaica, and on his return he organized popular theatre groups in villages around the country, as well as conducting an annual festival for them. His work is closely associated with the EASTERN CARIBBEAN POPULAR THEATRE ORGANIZATION (see Introduction). Allan Weeks, a former Arts Guild member now teaching at the Community College, formed the St Lucia Creole Theatre Workshop, for which he has translated into Creole several St Lucian and other Caribbean plays and performed them in Castries, in Vieux Fort and on tour to Martinque.

In 1989 the government of St Lucia opened a cultural centre with funds provided by the French government, but since the fees charged for both rehearsal and performance are reportedly too high to encourage its frequent use by individual theatre groups, Kendal Hippolyte, another past member of the Arts Guild, has opened the Lighthouse Theatre in Castries, seating up to 120. Plays recently performed there include his own *The Drum Maker*, LENNOX BROWN's (see Trinidad and Tobago) *The Trinity of Four*, Derek Walcott's *Pantomime*, and Fernando Arrabal's *Picnic on the Battlefield*. Apart from the Walcott brothers and Hippolyte, the most important St Lucian playwright is Stanley French, a University of London graduate in civil engineering who now lives in Barbados. His plays include *The Rape of Fair Helen* (1962), *Ballad of a Man and Dog* (1967), *No Rain No Play* (1967),

Bibliography

H. Breen, *St Lucia: Historical, Statistical and Descriptive*, London, 1834, repr. 1970; D. J. Crowley, 'Festivals of the Calendar in St Lucia', *Caribbean Quarterly*, 4, 2, 1955; E. Hill, 'The Emergence of a National Drama in the West Indies', *Caribbean Quarterly*, 18, 4, 1972; K. Omotoso, *The Theatrical into Theatre: A Study of the Drama and Theatre of the English-speaking Caribbean*, London, 1982.

The Light and the Dark (1968), and *Under a Sky of Incense* (1977).

Arts Guild of St Lucia

Founded in 1950 by Maurice Mason and DEREK WALCOTT, and composed of ex-pupils of the two secondary schools in the capital Castries, the Arts Guild set out to raise the level of the fine and performing arts in the island. To bring originality to its art, it sought to use the folk forms as expressed in the flower festivals, in carnival and in the poetic quality of the spoken dialects. They opened with an exhibition of paintings by Walcott and Dunstan St Omer, followed by a performance of Walcott's play on the Haitian revolution, *Henri Christophe*. In several ways this production forecast the Guild's future. It introduced themes such as leadership and identity in an ex-slave society – issues that would recur in Walcott's work. Written mostly in Elizabethan verse, the play gave the Guild a stature it was eager to claim. But staging the play at a convent hall required approval by the Roman Catholic authorities, who sanitized the script, removing altogether the scene showing the murder of Dessalines. When several key members left to seek higher education abroad, the Guild decided to devote its activities primarily to drama.

When Derek Walcott left for the UNIVERSITY [College] OF THE WEST INDIES, (UWI, see Introduction) in Jamaica on a scholarship, his twin brother RODDY WALCOTT assumed leadership of the Guild, which he headed for the next eighteen years. For the first four years Guild productions consisted of some early one-act plays by Derek Walcott and others by Marlowe, Chekhov, Christopher Fry and Saroyan, as well as scenes from Shakespeare. Roddy became the Guild's leading director, designing as well as acting in some of the plays. In 1954, after a visit to St Lucia by the UWI extramural drama tutor ERROL HILL (see Trinidad and Tobago), the Guild began to concentrate on producing Caribbean plays. In that year it staged Derek Walcott's *The Sea at Dauphin*, then in 1956 three plays by his brother Roddy: *The Harrowing of Benjy*, *Shrove Tuesday March* and *The One-Eye King*. In 1957 came Derek's *Ti-Jean and His Brothers*, directed and costumed by Roddy. Guild member Allan Weeks wrote and produced *Talk of the Devil*, and other Guild productions included works by DOUGLAS ARCHIBALD and Errol Hill of Trinidad, SAMUEL HILLARY of Jamaica, and Wilfred Redhead of Grenada. Overseas ties were strengthened when four members attended an extramural drama workshop under NOEL VAZ (see Jamaica) held in Grenada in 1956, Roddy Walcott attended a summer school in Jamaica in 1957, and the Guild made its first overseas tour, to Dominica, in 1958.

A setback occurred when the plays chosen for St Lucia's contribution to the 1958 federal arts festival in Trinidad – Derek Walcott's *The Sea at Dauphin* and Roddy Walcott's *The Banjo Man* – were banned by the Catholic Church as immoral. The first featured an angry fisherman who reviles the sea and God for his hard life; and the second, a roving troubadour who seduces young women with his music and songs. Disappointed, the Guild decided to withdraw altogether from the festival, but the next year it took six one-acters, four by Roddy Walcott and two by Derek, to three venues in Trinidad.

In 1960 the Guild initiated a week-long annual festival of arts in St Lucia, which it conducted for seven successive years. This consisted of choral and instrumental recitals, and creative dances plus the occasional art exhibition, as well as drama by the Guild. When the festival folded, the Guild had produced thirty-four plays – nineteen foreign ones and fifteen Caribbean, including six from St Lucia. Its most successful production was Lorca's *The House of Bernardo Alba* directed by Allan Weeks, with which it toured St Vincent.

In 1968 Roddy Walcott left for Canada to pursue advanced studies in theatre arts. In this year that St Lucia achieved statehood, the Guild was involved in a national open-air production entitled *L'Histoire Hélène*, along with revivals of *The Sea at Dauphin* and Roddy Walcott's *A Flight of Sparrows*. Curiously, the start of a national effort in drama witnessed the decline of the Guild. For a series of national cultural presentations – including *Soirée St Lucien* for Grenada Expo in 1969, for St Lucia's Development Day in 1971, for CARIFESTA (see Introduction) in GUYANA in 1972 and for the Heads of Government Conference in 1974 – it became necessary to recruit talent more broadly than hitherto. Presentations were now usually billed as produced by 'the St Lucia National Theatre', which in fact had its genesis in the Arts Guild. The Guild scored a victory when the previously banned play *The Banjo Man*, directed by George Odlum with original music by Charles Cadet, was staged as a national production in 1971 and 1972. It finally disbanded in 1974–5.

Browne, Vincent (1922–)
Montserratian playwright and director. A major in the Montserrat Defence Force and warden of university halls in JAMAICA and BARBADOS, Browne is probably the first native playwright from Montserrat (population 15,000) in the Leeward Islands. After writing religious plays for schools, he turned to comedy. His short farce *Big Business*, about the seduction of a mother and daughter by the same suitor, was first produced in 1967 and later in Jamaica, Trinidad (see Trinidad and Tobago),

GUYANA and St Kitts. The satirical comedy *Sunquest*, produced in 1983, also involved a love triangle. Browne's most ambitious effort was probably *And on the Seventh Day*, a historical play on the slave uprising in Montserrat, written to commemorate the 150th anniversary of emancipation. It was directed by the author and presented at the University Centre in Plymouth, the capital, in 1985. In 1984 Browne formed the Montserrat Amateur Dramatic Society for playreadings and annual productions. However, Caribbean dialect plays have seldom been performed, because members are mostly expatriates unfamiliar with the local argot.

Bully, Alwin (1948–)

Dominican playwright, director, actor, designer and arts administrator. Bully gained a BA in English and French at the BARBADOS campus of the UNIVERSITY OF THE WEST INDIES (see Introduction) in 1971, then returned to Dominica to teach at the Dominica Grammar School until 1978. While teaching, he also, in 1971, led the Little Theatre Group. From 1972 to 1988 he was artistic director of the People's Action Theatre which he had founded. This was to become the most active and influential company in Dominica, and Bully wrote and produced his major plays for it: *Streak* (1976), concerned with his country's attitude towards the 'dreadlock rastas'; *The Ruler* (1976), an adaptation of the novel *The Ruler in Hiroona* by G. C. H. Thomas; *The Nite Box* (1977), in which a civil service strike takes place amid a murder mystery; and his folk-musical *Pio-Pio* (1978), about a boy and girl seeking a meaning in life. He also wrote the annually produced *Folk Nativity* (1976); helped translate, and directed, the Creole version of DEREK WALCOTT's (see Eastern Caribbean States) *Ti-Jean and his Brothers* (1981); wrote the radio drama *A Dance in the Dark* (1983), and produced several long-running radio serials and some television documentaries.

In 1978, the year of Dominica's independence (for which he designed the new flag), Bully was appointed Chief Cultural Officer, a position he held for ten years save for a year's secondment to manage the national radio service. Thus he maintained an influence on all aspects of the country's cultural life. He represented Dominica at regional seminars and conferences as well as at international gatherings. He led the Dominica contingents to CARIFESTA (see Introduction) in GUYANA and Barbados, to the Commonwealth Arts Festival in Britain in 1965, to festivals in Guadeloupe in 1977, and to the Martinique theatre festival in 1984 and 1987.

Throughout this period Bully maintained an active interest in theatre as actor, director, playwright, and costume/stage/lighting designer. He conducted workshops and theatre seminars in Caribbean centres, exhibited his art and illustrated two books of poetry. He also composed music and lyrics for some fifty songs and for one full-length cantata. In 1987 he became Subregional Cultural Adviser to UNESCO in JAMAICA. He has won many awards for his work in the arts, the most outstanding being the National Sisserou Award of Honour from the government of the Commonwealth of Dominica.

Edgecombe, David (1952–)

Montserratan playwright, director, radio and television producer, and drama tutor. Edgecombe began writing plays at school and was stage manager, later artistic director, of the Montserrat Secondary Schools Dramatic Association. From 1970, he worked at Radio Montserrat, became editor of the weekly *Reporter*, and formed the Montserrat Theatre Group. In 1971 he left to study communication arts (radio and television) at Concordia University, and remained in Canada for six years, returning to Montserrat in the summers to work at Radio Antilles. In 1973 the Montserrat Theatre Group produced his first mature play, *For Better for Worse*; in 1974 it was staged by the Black Theatre Workshop in Montreal, directed by the author, in a successful run at the Revue Theatre.

Edgecombe's next play, *Sonuvabitch* (1975), was also produced in Montreal, and his third, *Strong Currents* (1977), was commissioned for Canada's entry to FESTAC 77 (see African Theatre, Introduction), the second world Black and African Festival of Arts and Culture, held in NIGERIA. Based on two novels written by the Barbadian Austin Clarke, the play was directed by Jeff Henry, theatre artist from Trinidad (see Trinidad and Tobago) now domiciled in Canada, and ran at the National Theatre in Lagos.

In 1977, on his return to Montserrat, Edgecombe directed *Sonuvabitch* and *Coming Home to Roost* with the Montserrat Theatre Group, of which he was artistic director from 1977 to 1980, resigning because of 'different levels of commitment'. He resumed work with Radio Antilles, concentrating on the arts, and serialized ALWIN BULLY's *Nite Box* and DORBRENE O'MARDE's *Tangled Web*. Meanwhile, his own plays were being produced regularly in neighbouring islands, as well as in the Cayman's, the Bahamas and St Martin. In 1979 *Coming Home to Roost* went on tour to the University of the Virgin Islands in St Thomas for 'Black History Month', and to Cuba for CARIFESTA (see Introduction) 79.

Edgecombe went back to Canada on a Commonwealth Fellowship in 1980 to complete an MA, for which his thesis was the play *Kirnon's Kingdom*, a veiled political statement that was first produced in Montserrat in 1981, taken to BARBADOS for Carifesta 82, and then to Antigua, St Kitts and St Croix. In 1989 the BBC broadcast it worldwide as part of its 'Drama of the Month' series. His play *Heaven* was premiered at the University of the Virgin Islands' Little Theatre in 1991, then toured to other islands. Edgecombe lectures at the College of the Virgin Islands in St Thomas, and is Director of the REICHHOLD CENTER FOR THE ARTS (see Introduction).

Edwards, Gus (1939–)

Antiguan playwright and actor. Edwards was brought up in St Thomas, US Virgin Islands, and in 1959 went to New York City to study for a career in theatre. After playing two minor film roles, in 1977 he became resident playwright with the Negro Ensemble Company. The NEC produced three of his plays in a single season: *The Offering* (1977) and *Black Body Blues* (1978), both directed by Douglas Turner Ward; and *Old Phantoms* (1978), directed by Horacena Taylor. The next year Edwards wrote *Fallen Angels*, on a commission for the North Carolina School of the Arts, where it was first staged.

The NEC also produced his *Weep Not for Me* (1981) at St Marks Playhouse and his *Manhattan Made Me* (1983) at Theatre Four in New York. In 1985 he wrote a television adaptation of James Baldwin's novel *Go Tell It on the Mountain*, which was shown in the 'American Playhouse' series. In 1986 the NEC produced his play *Ramona*.

Edwards has received a Rockefeller Foundation playwright's award, as well as grants from the National Endowment for the Arts and from the Drama League. He has conducted theatre workshops for Lehman College, Bronx, New York, and for the North Carolina School of the Arts. He is a member of the US Dramatists' Guild and the New Dramatists. Since 1983 he has been resident playwright at Arizona State University, Tempe.

O'Marde, Dorbrene (1951–)

Antiguan playwright and director. O'Marde's interest in theatre began at an early age. Then at the UNIVERSITY OF THE WEST INDIES (UWI, see Introduction) Cave Hill campus in BARBADOS he was involved with the Cavite Players, producing plays in the 'Caribbean Plays' series published by the UWI Extramural Department in Trinidad. Returning to Antigua in 1971, he produced his first two plays: *Badplay*, a trickster farce, and *Homecoming*, set during the Black Power period (presented at the Antigua

University Centre, in 1971 and 1972). O'Marde formed the Harambee Open Air Theatre in 1972, but then left to study hospital administration at the University of Toronto, returning to Antigua in 1975. During his absence the Harambee company, led by his brother Andrew and by Colin Simpson, produced Andrew's plays *O Lord, Why Lord* and *Tell It Like It Is*.

In 1976 O'Marde wrote and directed *For Real* and in 1977 *Fly On the Wall*, which toured to Montserrat and Dominica. In 1979 *Tangled Web*, his play about drug-smuggling and gun-running, was staged, featuring in a subplot the current teachers' strike – to which an angry government retaliated by legislating that no civil servant could participate in dramatic activities that criticized it. From 1980 to 1982 O'Marde studied public health at Tulane University, Louisiana. In 1982 he produced a musical comedy, *The Minister's Daughter*, adapted from the novel by the Nigerian Obi Egbuna. In 1983 the Christmas musical *We Nativity*, moving freely between biblical and modern Caribbean eras, was staged. O'Marde next turned his attention to radio and television, in order to reach wider audiences. With ALWIN BULLY he produced the radio drama *Fire Go Bun* for the Family Planning Unit. The Harambee Open-Air Theatre continued to produce contemporary Caribbean plays such as FRANK PILGRIM'S (see Guyana) *Miriamy* and TREVOR RHONE'S (see Jamaica) *Old Story Time*, but by the mid-1980s, having lost its leaders through migration or new responsibilities, the group was forced to disband. O'Marde himself took a position with the Pan-American Health Organization in Barbados.

Peters, Francis (1957–)

Grenadian playwright and drama-group leader. Peters began by writing religious skits for church performance. In 1980–1 he wrote and directed *Discipleship*, a short play on the persecution of Christians by the Romans, and *The Unshakeable Faith*, produced at a secondary school in St George's, capital city of Grenada. His first full-length play, *A Knock at Midnight* (1982), deals with the struggle for sociopolitical freedom on a Caribbean island. He then went to the Jamaica School of Drama (see Jamaica, Cultural Training Centre) on a two-year fellowship. In 1986 he wrote and directed *Struggle*, a play with music set on a Grenada cocoa plantation in the 1950s, which ran for a record eleven performances at the Marryshow Folk Theatre in St George's. Other plays written and produced by Peters include *A New Beginning* (1987), which was taken to Antigua; the religious *My Sword, My Heart, My Life* (1988); *Who is A Servant?* (1990), a political satire. To stage his plays he has formed two production companies: the Christian Dramatic Society (1983) and the Family Theatre (1989). He has also directed other Caribbean plays such as FREDDIE KISSOON'S (see Trinidad and Tobago) *Mamaguy* and TREVOR RHONE'S (see Jamaica) *Old Story Time*.

Philips, Thelma (c.1922–)

Grenadian schoolteacher, drama and dance leader, and schools drama tutor. Philips first performed at the teacher training college that she attended in Trinidad in 1938–9. On her return to Grenada she began work with the university extramural drama group, from which she co-founded, with Alister Bain, the first Grenada folk-dancing company, the Bee Wee Ballet. She led the company on investigations around the island into the indigenous dances as practised by villagers.

From 1950 to 1974 she worked for the government on drama, dance and song productions. Her company represented Grenada at the 1958 Federal Arts Festival in Trinidad; they performed a historical pageant to celebrate Grenada's statehood in 1964, and a dance-drama for Expo 67. These and other productions were scripted by Philips. From 1968 to 1975 she was drama tutor at the Ministry of Education, helping to prepare schools in

Grenada and the sister islands of Carriacou and Petit Martinique for the biennial local drama festivals. She is gratified by the public acceptance of native plays and dances that were formerly held in contempt.

Walcott, Derek (1930–)

The most important Caribbean playwright, and a poet of world rank. Walcott has written thirty-eight plays, half of which have been published. He has also published fifteen volumes of poetry, including the epic *Omeros* (1990). He has received numerous prizes, among them the John D. and Catherine MacArthur Foundation grant in 1981, the 1989 Medal for Poetry awarded by Queen Elizabeth II, and in 1992 the Nobel Prize for Literature.

Errol John and Errol Hill in Walcott's *Henri Christophe*, London, 1952.

Derek Walcott.

Born in St Lucia, Walcott began writing and directing plays while at school. With the support of his twin brother RODDY WALCOTT (also a playwright), he founded the ARTS GUILD OF ST LUCIA, which performed his first published play *Henri Christophe* (1950) about the Haitian revolutionary leader. He attended the UNIVERSITY [College] OF THE WEST INDIES (see Introduction) in JAMAICA (1950–4) and there wrote and staged a number of plays, several of which he later revised and retitled.

After graduating, Walcott taught for two years, then became a feature writer and art and theatre critic for newspapers in Jamaica and later in Trinidad. He wrote an epic drama, *Drums and Colours* (1958), for the Caribbean arts festival held in Trinidad to celebrate the birth of the West Indies Federation. In 1958–9 he studied theatre in the USA with a Rockefeller Foundation fellowship, and on returning to Trinidad he founded and became director of the TRINIDAD THEATRE WORKSHOP, based first at the Little Carib Theatre (see Trinidad and Tobago, BERYL MCBURNIE). For seventeen years he wrote and directed plays with this company, taking productions on tour to other Caribbean territories and to the USA and Canada. Among the most noteworthy of his plays are *The Sea at Dauphin* (1954), *Ti-Jean and His Brothers* (1958), the highly acclaimed *Dream on Monkey Mountain* (1967) which received an Obie in its 1971 production by the Negro Ensemble Company in New York, *The Joker of Seville* (1974), *O Babylon!* (1976) *and Pantomime* (1978).

Walcott's dramas encompass a tension between instinct and intellect – the racial instinct stemming from an African heritage in conflict with an undiminished admiration for European intellectual and artistic achievement. His plays have been produced by theatre organizations in the USA and England, including the Public Theatre in New York, the Arena Stage in Washington, DC, the Goodman Theatre in Chicago and the Mark Taper Forum in Los Angeles. In London the Royal Court Theatre has presented his works, and in 1992 the Royal Shakespeare Company's Other Place theatre in Stratford-on-Avon premiered *The Odyssey*, Walcott's commissioned dramatization of Homer's epic.

In 1981 he was appointed professor of creative writing at Boston University, but returns regularly to the Caribbean to work in theatre, and in 1984 he directed an open-air production of his play *Haitian Earth* in his native St Lucia. In 1991 *Steel*, a musical written with the composer Galt MacDermot and focusing on the steel band as a major force in the Trinidad carnival, was premiered by the American Repertory Theatre in Cambridge, Massachusetts.

Bibliography

C. Cooper, 'A Different Rage: An Analysis of the Works of Derek Walcott, 1974–1976', PhD diss., Univ. of Toronto, 1977; I. Goldstraw, Derek Walcott: An Annotated Bibliography of His Works, New York, 1984; P. Ismond, 'Derek Walcott: The Development of a Rooted Vision', PhD diss., Univ. of Kent, 1974; V. D. Questel, 'Derek Walcott: Contradiction and Resolution', PhD diss., Univ. of the West Indies, Trinidad, 1979; D. Walcott, Henri Christophe, Barbados, 1950; 'Drums and Colours', Caribbean Quarterly, 7, 1 and 2 (Mar./June 1961); Dream on Monkey Mountain and Other Plays, New York, 1970; The Joker of Seville and O Babylon!, New York, 1978; Remembrance and Pantomime, New York, 1980; Three Plays: The Last Carnival, Beef – No Chicken, A Branch of the Blue Nile, New York, 1986.

Walcott, Roddy [Roderick] (1930–)

St Lucian playwright, director, designer and arts administrator. A foundation member of the ARTS GUILD OF ST LUCIA formed in 1950, Roddy Walcott became president when his twin brother, DEREK WALCOTT, left during the Guild's first year to attend university in Jamaica. Roddy ran the Guild for the next eighteen years, and is principally responsible for its achievements. He became its most valued director, organized its tours to other islands and instituted an annual week-long arts festival. He began writing plays in 1956, with three one-acters: *The Harrowing of Benjy, Shrove Tuesday March* and *The One-Eye Is King*. Entered in the Jamaica drama festival of 1957, *The Harrowing of Benjy*, directed by ERROL HILL (see Trinidad and Tobago) for the Federal Theatre Company, won five awards for the most imaginative production, the best West Indian comedy, the best principal actor and the best supporting actor and actress. The play remains one of the most popular in the Caribbean repertoire. Its success prompted Walcott to write two additional plays to form a trilogy: *A Flight of Sparrows*

(1958) and *The Education of Alfie* (1960), neither of which attained the reputation of *Benjy*. His *Malfinis, or The Heart of a Child* (1960), a trial in purgatory of those responsible for the murder of a child, has held for producers a certain gory fascination.

From 1952 to 1967 Walcott was a carnival bandleader-designer and steelband captain in St Lucia. In 1958 his full-length musical, *The Banjo Man*, based on the La Rose festival and selected by a government committee for presentation at the Federal Arts Festival in Trinidad, was banned by the Catholic Church on grounds of profanity. It remained unproduced until 1971, when it was staged as part of St Lucia's Development Day celebrations; in 1972 it represented the island at the CARIFESTA (see Introduction) in GUYANA. Walcott then wrote two more musical comedies: *Chanson Marianne* (1974) on the La Margrit festival, and *Romiel ec Violette* (1974) on the subject of the possible merging of the two competing festivals. He worked closely in his musicals with the St Lucian composer Charles Cadet.

Walcott left St Lucia for Toronto in 1968, and though he continued to write plays his productions dwindled. On a visit home in 1973–4 he gave readings from five unproduced plays and staged *Chanson Marianne*. In 1977 he was appointed the first Director of Culture in St Lucia, a position he held for three years before returning to Canada. In 1989 the St Lucian government invited him back to produce *The Guitar Man's Song*, to mark the tenth anniversary of the island's independence. His *oeuvre* of twenty-six plays includes eight musicals and two screenplays. He has been awarded the OBE for his outstanding theatrical work in St Lucia.

Reggie Carter in Roddy Walcott's *The Harrowing of Benjy*, Jamaica, 1957.

White, Edgar (B.) (1947–)

Montserratan playwright. Though he was taken to New York at the age of five, and has lived mainly in the USA, White retains an African-Caribbean perspective in most of his plays and novels. The first of his twenty plays was *The Mummer's Play*, produced by Joseph Papp at the New York Shakespeare Festival Theatre in 1965. Papp's off-Broadway theatre was to stage six more of his plays. White gained a BA from New York University (1968), then spent 1971–3 at the Yale School of Drama. He has worked with the Cincinnati Playhouse in Ohio and has been artistic director of the Yardbird Theatre Company of Harlem, which has staged his *Lament for Rastafari* (1971) and *The Pygmies and the Pyramid* (1976). In London the Black Theatre Cooperative and the Riverside Studio have performed *Trinity – The Long and Cheerful Road to Slavery* (1982), *The Nine Night* (1983) and *Redemption Song* (1984), among others. Oblique in meaning and ironical in tone, White's plays do not usually attract wide audiences, but *I, Marcus Garvey* (1987), premiered in Barbados, has gone far towards reversing that trend. White lives in New York and London.

GUYANA

Situated on the northeast coast of South America, of which it is the only English-speaking nation, Guyana anchors the eastern chain of Caribbean islands. The Dutch were the first to found a settlement there, pushing the native Amerindians back into the rainforest. Later, both France and Great Britain claimed the area, and it changed hands repeatedly between the warring European powers before the British occupation was confirmed in 1808. In 1831 the three adjacent provinces of Demerara, Berbice and Essequibo, set up by the Dutch, were united into the colony of British Guiana, which in 1966 became the independent nation of Guyana, and in 1970 a republic.

The early settlers had brought in African slaves to work on the sugar plantations. The British outlawed the slave trade in 1807, and when they abolished slavery itself in 1834 the planters sought new sources of labour for this country of mountains and forest, rivers, grasslands and mudflats. It was a search that would produce one of the most racially diverse populations in the Caribbean. Planters came from the tired plantations of islands like BARBADOS, bringing their slaves with them to work the new lands, while liberated Africans captured from slaving vessels were deposited on Guyana's shores. Between 1838 and 1917 some 238,000 East Indians from the Indian subcontinent were introduced into Guyana, as indentured workers. Thirty-two thousand Portuguese came from Madeira under bounty, but abandoned field labour for commerce as soon as their work contracts permitted it. The Chinese came in smaller numbers – some 13,000 by the mid-19th century. The Amerindian word 'Guyana' means 'land of many rivers', but because of its varied populations the country has also come to be known as the land of six peoples – namely, Indian, African, European, Madeiran Portuguese, Chinese and Amerindian.

Records of theatre in Guyana before the late 19th century are incomplete. Providing the first evidence of theatre productions are strolling players from North America, who came in 1800 via Barbados and Grenada, charged $2 a head for each performance, and stayed three months. Where they performed is not known; it was not until 1805 that one M. Campbell constructed in Georgetown a new Union Coffee House, with a second-floor hall to be used for concerts, amateur theatricals, balls and meetings. Reconstructed by a Mr Goepel in 1810, the hall now combined a pit and stage with elegant transparencies on three sides, and bore the grandiose title of Theatre Royal. It was to accommodate both gentlemen amateurs in the tragedy *George Barnwell,* and another professional troupe that played for three months offering comedies and farces, ending its tour with Shakespeare's *Richard III.*

Another company of players visited Guyana in 1817, and in 1826 the Dutch Amateur Dramatic Society were using the theatre. In 1828 this local group built its own theatre by public subscription. However, they soon disbanded, and in 1845 the theatre was sold to the Church of England for use as a chapel. Three other buildings functioned as theatres in the second half of the century: the Anthenaeum, built in 1851; the Assembly Rooms (1857), with the ground floor occupied by the Georgetown Club, and a commodious ballroom and theatre upstairs – the flat auditorium could seat 700, while the gallery held another 100; and the Philharmonic Hall, built by one Charles

Cahuac for staging concerts, but also available for plays and light operas. Without raked seating or an adequately equipped stage, none of these buildings could be considered a proper playhouse. In 1893, when amateur theatre groups were unusually active, a resolution was put to the Georgetown council for the erection of a two-storey building, the upper part to be fitted up as a theatre, at a cost not exceeding $30,000. The council voted against, contending that a theatre would merely increase the burgesses' taxes and that sanitation and water supply were more important priorities.

In 1854 some Portuguese amateur players gave a performance in Georgetown in aid of the girls' orphanage. This was the first dramatic effort by the Portuguese in their adopted country, and its success both on stage and at the box office no doubt inspired subsequent performances by the group at the Philharmonic Hall – even though, since they were given in their native language, the audience must have been limited. In 1897, to mark the anniversary of the restoration of Portuguese independence from Spain, *29, or Honour and Glory*, with a cast of over fifty, was staged in Georgetown, followed the next year by 'a rash of concerts and plays' to mark the fourth centenary of the discovery of the Cape route to India by Vasco da Gama. It was not until the last decade of the century, in a burst of patriotism transcending language, that presentations were made in English.

Apart from Portuguese amateurs, by 1870 the two major drama groups were the whites-only Amateur Dramatic Club and the Histrionic Club for coloureds. Two decades later the same racial distinctions obtained, but the groups were called the Demerara Dramatic Club (for whites) and the Georgetown Dramatic Club (for coloureds). The exclusiveness of the Demerara Club was resisted by some, who in 1898 formed the Demerara Dramatic Company, with membership open to all racial groups on payment of an entrance fee of 48 cents and a small monthly subscription. Women who appeared on stage were exempted from paying fees – an indication of the difficulty of getting respectable middle-class females to perform publicly.

On 1 November 1877 Chinese theatricals of an unspecified kind were recorded for the first and only time in Guyana. And for the next several years the Chinese celebrated their New Year's festival, which no doubt comprised a costumed street parade with music, singing and dancing, including the dragon dance to the beating of the big drum. (Such a parade was seen in Trinidad as late as the 1930s.)

The most important professional companies to visit Guyana in the late 19th century were W. M. Holland's Dramatic Company and E. A. McDowell's English Vaudeville Company. Holland's band of twelve, from New York, opened at the Assembly Rooms in Georgetown on 19 March 1872. It played three times weekly until the leading actor, Wallace Britton, died suddenly of a heart attack and the tour was cancelled. Holland's repertoire had relied on light comedies, and sentimental dramas or melodramas with farcical afterpieces. Schuler's *Fanchon, the Cricket*, based on a tale by George Sand, was his main piece, starring Effie Johns. *Othello* was the only Shakespeare drama to be performed by the company. McDowell's was a more solid outfit. With nineteen members, it performed at the Philharmonic Hall five nights a week for six weeks. Its repertoire included plays by contemporaries such as Boucicault, Bulwer-Lytton, W. S. Gilbert and T. W. Robertson, along with short farces as afterpieces. Performances were of a high order, the actors being led by McDowell's wife, the esteemed Fanny Reeves. The company returned to Guyana in 1886 and again in 1891.

Early this century companies from England began once again to make the long journey to the Caribbean. In 1905 the Frank Benson Shakespeare Company gave performances at the Assembly Rooms that included at least two of Shakespeare's comedies and *Hamlet*. They were followed by the more ambitious Florence Glossop-Harris Company which made its first visit to the Caribbean in 1914, playing mostly Shakespeare. Audiences in Guyana would have been prepared for a season of Shakespeare by the regular lectures on his plays given by J. Veecock, a master at Queen's College, Georgetown, and director-manager of the Georgetown Dramatic Club. This club's halcyon days had been the twenty-odd years up to about 1910 when, with the death of Veecock, it began to fall apart. The Glossop-Harris Company returned for seven more visits between 1920 and 1931, offering lighter dramas and musical comedies.

Curiously, it was the advent of film that generated the first flush of indigenous professional theatre in Guyana. As the crowds flocked to the cinemas, local vaudevillians seized the opportunity to present their dialect playlets before this ready-made audience, using the narrow strip in front of the screen as their stage, a bare minimum of properties and no special lighting or costumes, and relying on audience familiarity with the issues of the moment to sustain interest in the plot. Three leading entertainers appeared at this period: the Portuguese comedian Sidney Martin, who in 1916 published a collection of his sketches and witticisms; the shanty singer Bill Rogers; and SAM CHASE. With remarkable ingenuity, Chase was able to involve his audience in the outcome of his plays. He flourished in the 1940s and 50s.

While the popular entertainers were laying the foundations of a folk-drama, two events conspired to uplift Guyana's two racial majorities, the Africans and the Indians. Beginning in 1931, Cambridge-educated Guyanese schoolmaster NORMAN CAMERON began to write a series of historical plays, to be performed in high schools in Georgetown, that would give the African-Guyanese a sense of their glorious past in Africa and the Middle East, at times using biblical stories to win audience recognition of his principal characters. In the same decade the British Guiana Dramatic Society was formed in the city by a group of young Indians under the guidance of J. B. Singh, a prominent Hindu doctor, and his wife Alice. Active from 1937 to 1948, this group presented ten annual productions of works by Indian playwrights like Tagore and Kalidasa, along with concerts and revues designed to bring to a wider audience images of Indian culture and achievement. In 1945 the group staged *Asra*, probably written by the Guyanese Basil Balgobin. Though set in India, its focus on nationalism and the conflict between traditional and Western values was pertinent to the situation in Guyana.

What was needed was to bring together not only the different races in Guyana but also the urban and rural classes; to create not a melting-pot of cultures but rather an understanding and appreciation of what each group had to offer to the whole. A move in this direction came in 1943 when Harold Stannard, cultural adviser to the British Council in the region, promoted the formation of the Union of Cultural Clubs, which, although presenting at its annual convention mostly British arts, influenced the government to sponsor in 1958 a History and Culture Week with the emphasis on creations of Guyanese origin.

The Sugar Estates Drama Festival, launched in 1956, encouraged plantation workers to combine their skills in the production of one-act plays. Soon drama workshops were being offered to the estate groups. In the same year, Cecile Nobrega broke new ground with her book *Stabroek Fantasy*, from which was devised a musical set in the colourful Stabroek market of Georgetown and among the 'porkknockers' (gold-diggers) of the hinterland. In 1957 the THEATRE GUILD OF GUYANA was established, and two years later secured its own playhouse. It launched its first playwriting competition in 1958 and the first National Drama Festival in 1959. Among those responsible for founding the Guild was BERTIE MARTIN.

The Guild proved to be a driving force in the development of Guyanese theatre. Its modest playhouse was open to all groups and its technical staff were on hand to help in mounting productions. Playwriting workshops and competitions stimulated the writing of local plays, and the Guyana Broadcasting Service added incentive by regularly broadcasting scripts. By 1973 the tally was 175 plays, most of which had been produced on either stage or radio. In one of its most productive decades, beginning in the mid-1960s under the leadership of people like Frank Thomasson and KEN CORSBIE, the playhouse hosted six to eight major productions a year, running some of them for two to three weeks.

The Guild's policy was not to limit itself to Caribbean plays but to include international works of the highest standard, so that indigenous plays could be judged against the best work from anywhere. Among the Guild's established writers are HAROLD BASCOM, BERTRAM CHARLES and FRANCIS FARRIER. Home-produced plays that have been staged overseas include *Miriamy* by FRANK PILGRIM, *The Tramping Man* by Ian McDonald and *Masquerade* by Ian Valz. Among playwrights who have shown promise is PALOMA MOHAMED.

In summer 1972 Guyana held the first CARIFESTA (see Introduction). Twenty-five countries participated, all except Brazil belonging to the Caribbean basin. For its drama contribution the host country presented *Couvade: A Dream of Guyana* by MICHAEL GILKES. In 1976 a new theatre and cultural centre opened. With an auditorium seating 2000 it is considered too large for the average production, yet popular local writers like Bascom succeed in filling it for plays that deal with contemporary issues in a realistic and stageworthy, if predictable, manner. Use of the local argot also enhances the popular appeal. In 1981 RON ROBINSON formed the first registered professional company in Guyana – the Theatre Company. In its first ten years it produced nearly sixty plays, musicals and revues, one-third of which are original Caribbean works. The company has also gone on tours to Caribbean islands and to the USA.

The half-yearly literary magazine *Kyk-over-al* – edited by the late Guyanese poet and essayist Arthur Seymour from 1945 to 1961 and since 1984 revived and co-edited by him and Ian McDonald – has played a significant role in discussing issues of concern to writers and theatre people. It has reviewed local plays, raised questions regarding standards of criticism, published historical articles on Guyanese theatre and reports of festivals and other activities. It was the first serious literary journal, in June 1959, to publish the texts of two prize-winning one-act plays written in the vernacular: *It's Brickdam* by Sheila Van Sertima and *Porkknockers* by SHEIK SADEEK.

Despite Guyana's potential mineral and agricultural wealth, its economy suffered a serious downturn under its late president L. F. S. Burnham, kept in power only because of the threat of a communist regime being installed by his closest rival, the Indian Cheddie Jagan, who was finally elected president in 1992. The depressed state of affairs sent many talented people off to more congenial shores. Among Guyanese theatre people who live and work abroad are playwrights Michael Abbensetts, Jan Carew and Ian Valz; actor-director Ken Corsbie and director-manager HENRY MUTTOO. The highly reputed actor, the late WILBERT HOLDER, worked professionally from Trinidad, and CLAIRMONTE TAITT from Barbados. Writer-director Michael Gilkes and critic Gordon Rohlehr are with the UNIVERSITY OF THE WEST INDIES (see Introduction) in Barbados and Trinidad, respectively.

Bascom, Harold (1951–)

Guyanese playwright and producer. Between 1987 and 1991, his first years writing for the stage, Bascom produced some dozen full-length plays which he staged, generally to full houses, at the 2000-seat National Cultural Centre in Georgetown. His popularity is due partly to the topical issues dealt with in his plays, and partly to his skill in engaging and entertaining the particular audience for whom he writes – the 'market people', as they have been called. Bascom believes their life stories are important and that his comedy-dramas present lessons from which they can learn. Among his most successful are *TV Alley* (1988), *Family Budget* (1989) and *The Visa Wedding* (1989).

Cameron, Norman (1903–83)
Guyanese playwright. Educated at Cambridge University after winning a Guyana Scholarship, Cameron taught at Queen's College, Georgetown, on his return home in 1926, then founded his own high school. He published *The Evolution of the Negro* Book 1 in 1929 and Book 2 in 1934, before embarking on a series of plays aiming to show the glorious past of the African. Among these are *Balthazar* (1931), the story of the third wise man at the birth of Christ; *Adoniya* (1943), about the Ethiopian wife of Moses; *Sabaco* (1947), on the Nubian conquest of Egypt; *Ebedmelech* (1953), on the rescue of Jeremiah by the Ethiopian; *Kayssa* (1959), dealing with conspiracy at the court of the King of Melli in the Sudan; and *The Price of Victory* (1965), a Yoruba legend about Morimi, wife of King Ogun. He also wrote *Jamaica Joe* (1946) and *The Trumpet* (1969). Cameron produced some of these plays in school halls, but they are not often popular on the stage and are usually given readings. Cameron was the first president of the Union of Cultural Clubs, founded in Guyana in 1943.

Charles, Bertram (1937–)
Guyanese playwright, and director of the Related Arts Group. Charles began working in the theatre in Guyana in 1950. In London in 1955, he joined a company called the Related Arts Group, attached to the Park Lane Theatre. In 1957 he enrolled at Goldsmith's College, London University, to study literature, speech and drama. While there he performed in several plays. On his return to Guyana he began writing and producing his own plays, with a company he named The Related Arts Group after the London company. Between 1963 and 1971 he produced some sixteen one-act and full-length plays, among which are *The End of the Affair* (1968), *The Alexin of Our Cure* (1969) and *Within Our Narrow Walls* (1971). Often domestic melodramas, his plays deal with the destruction of family life by infidelity, crime, and guilt for past misdeeds.

Chase, Sam [CHASE, OSWYN ADOLPHUS] (1903–69)
Guyanese comedian. Chase was the premier professional entertainer of his time, playing before urban and rural audiences, in cinemas and in public halls. His career started in the 1920s and lasted for forty-four years. He was a master of timing and could improvise at a moment's notice. His portrayals of women were in no way crude – instead, he relied on ridicule where ridicule was due, always warning his audience that his performance had not the remotest connection to anyone living or dead. He was skilled at involving the audience in deciding the outcomes of his plays, which were based on some contemporary event. At the height of his career he was playwright, musician, producer, promoter and principal actor. Accompanied by a dancing team, he toured the French and Dutch Guianas as well as Trinidad and other Caribbean islands. His plays include *Gentlemen, the King*; *Guardroom Jitters*; and *The Collapsible Bridegroom*.

Corsbie, Ken (1930–)
Guyanese actor, broadcaster and theatre organizer. After serving for a decade as actor and director at the THEATRE GUILD OF GUYANA's playhouse, Corsbie was awarded a three-year British Council scholarship to attend the Rose Bruford School of Drama in Kent and the BBC television and radio training school. On his return home he worked with the Guyana

Broadcasting Service, introducing its radio drama programme. For two years he was a liaison officer for the Caribbean Broadcasting Union and toured the West Indies producing radio documentaries. He returned to the stage in 1973, producing, directing and performing in a series of original shows such as *He-One, Dem-Two* with Marc Matthews, and *All-ah-we* with Matthews and HENRY MUTTOO. These shows toured the islands, putting on over 200 performances. In 1976 Corsbie organized the Conference of Caribbean Dramatists in St Lucia (see Eastern Caribbean States), and launched the THEATRE INFORMATION EXCHANGE (see Introduction), which he coordinated until 1980. He wrote and directed *Barbados Barbados*, a dinner-theatre entertainment, for eight successive winter seasons, and is involved in a thirteen-part series of television documentaries on the cultures of the Caribbean. He has written a school text entitled *Theatre in the Caribbean* (1984).

Farrier, Francis (Quamina) (1938–)
Guyanese playwright for stage and radio, and director-producer. Farrier produced his first play, the one-act *Border Bridge*, in 1963, and in the next three years he staged six more one-acters and the full-length musical comedy *Gaylanda* (1966). He also wrote and produced three half-hour radio plays and, for Radio Demerara, wrote the radio serial *The Tides of Susanberg*, aired in seventy-eight fifteen-minute episodes in 1966. So popular was it that he wrote a sequel, *The Girl From Susanberg*, broadcast in 1968.

In 1969 he won the E. R. Brathwaite Scholarship to study creative writing and drama at the Banff School of Fine Arts in Alberta, Canada. The next year he produced twenty-one half-hour radio plays, nine of them written by him. For production by Station GBS (of the Guyana Broadcasting Service) to mark the first anniversary of the republic of Guyana in 1971, he wrote *Freedom Trail* (on the 1763 Berbice revolution), which was both broadcast and staged in

Georgetown. His play *Journey to Freedom* was produced by the Department of Culture in 1976 and revived in 1978 and 1986. Farrier also wrote the one-act plays *The Slave and the Scroll* (1964) and *The Plight of the Wright* (1966).

Gilkes, Michael (1933–)
Guyanese playwright, director and lecturer in English. Gilkes gained a first-class English degree at London University, then returned to Guyana to teach first at St Stanislaus College then in the Department of English at the University of Guyana. As a member of the THEATRE GUILD OF GUYANA he premiered his first full-length play, *In Transit* (1968), which expressed his wanderlust. In 1970 he returned to England, to the University of Kent, where he obtained a PhD in English and American literature; he spent one more year in Guyana, then moved in 1974 to BARBADOS as lecturer in English at the Cave Hill campus of the UNIVERSITY OF THE WEST INDIES (see Introduction).

In 1978 he founded the Stage One company in Barbados, and was its first artistic director. He has directed a number of important productions including the world première of DEREK WALCOTT's (see Eastern Caribbean States) *Franklin* in Georgetown, Guyana, in 1968; Michael Abbensetts' *Sweet Talk* at the Theatre Guild Playhouse in Georgetown in 1979; DAVID EDGECOMBE's (see Eastern Caribbean States) *Kirnon's Kingdom* for the Caribbean/US theatre conference at St Thomas, US Virgin Islands, in 1980; and ERROL JOHN's (see Trinidad and Tobago) *Moon on a Rainbow Shawl* for Stage One in Barbados. Gilkes's major play is a commissioned drama entitled *Couvade: A dream of Guyana*, first produced at the CARIFESTA (see Introduction) held in Guyana in 1972.

Holder, Wilbert (1935–87)
Actor of stage, radio and television, and writer and director/producer. Born in Guyana, Holder emigrated to TRINIDAD AND TOBAGO in 1962. He was one of the most distinguished actors of the

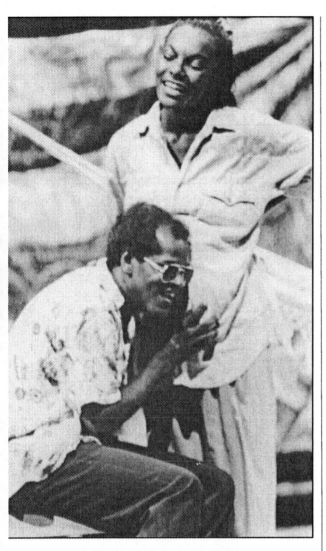

A scene from Michael Gilkes's production of *Couvade*, 1993.

TRINIDAD THEATRE WORKSHOP, a radio broadcaster, and a founder member of the THEATRE GUILD OF GUYANA, playing leading roles in Guild productions such as Archibald MacLeish's *J. B. Julius Caesar*, *Moby Dick*, *A Christmas Carol* and the Guyana musical *Stabroek Fantasy*. In Trinidad he joined the Theatre Workshop and worked closely with DEREK WALCOTT (see Eastern Caribbean States)

for sixteen years, appearing in some ten productions and creating the roles of Jordan and Jackson in Walcott's *Remembrance* (1977) and *Pantomime* (1978), respectively. He toured the Caribbean and the USA, performing in Walcott's *Dream on Monkey Mountain* (1969) at the Eugene O'Neill Theatre in Waterford, Connecticut, and in *Pantomime* at the Hippodrome in Gainesville, Florida.

Holder also worked as a freelance television writer and director, and producer of documentaries and commercials, in Trinidad and other Caribbean countries. For Trinidad and Tobago television he directed thirteen episodes of *Turn of the Tide* (1983), a human-interest drama shot on location in Tobago. He was production manager and associate director of two feature films made in Trinidad – *Bim* and *The Haunting of Avril*. In 1981 he received an award from the Trinidad and Tobago government for his performance in the South African play, *Sizwe Banzi is Dead*. On his death he was awarded the Humming Bird Gold Medal for culture and drama by the Trinidad and Tobago government.

Hopkinson, Slade (1934–93)

One of the best actors in the anglophone Caribbean; director, poet and playwright. Born in Guyana, schooled in BARBADOS; attended university in JAMAICA, taught in Trinidad (see Trinidad and Tobago) – Hopkinson would seem to be the true Caribbean man. He established his skill in performance early, when he played Shakespeare's Julius Caesar at the age of seventeen at his secondary school. At the UNIVERSITY [College] OF THE WEST INDIES (see Introduction) in Jamaica from 1954 to 1957 he undertook a range of roles that included Joxer Daly in *Juno and the Paycock*, Dessalines in Derek Walcott's (see Eastern Caribbean States) *Henri Christophe*, Tiresias in *Oedipus Rex*, Thomas Mendip in *The Lady's Not For Burning*, Tom in *The Glass Menagerie* and King Lear in a production that he directed. Of his performance as Lear, Harry Milner, theatre critic of the *Jamaica Gleaner*, wrote that it was within sighting distance of the great Lears he had seen in London's West End.

Leaving university, Hopkinson formed the West Indian Players in Jamaica, to perpetuate the aims of the defunct Federal Theatre Company. He played Berringer in Derek Walcott's *The Wine of the Country*, the Bolom in his *Ti-Jean and His Brothers*, and the satanic villain in RODDY WALCOTT's (see Eastern Caribbean States) *Malfinis*. For the Players he also directed Derek Walcott's *Malcauchon* and *Ti-Jean*, as well as Roddy Walcott's *Malfinis* and *The Trouble with Albino Joe*.

Moving to Trinidad in 1962, Hopkinson directed DENNIS SCOTT's (see Jamaica) *The Caged*, then attached himself to the TRINIDAD THEATRE WORKSHOP, for which he played the solo role in Beckett's *Krapp's Last Tape* and the professor in Ionesco's *The Lesson*. In 1964 he repeated the title role of *King Lear* in a production directed by ERROL HILL (see Trinidad and Tobago) at the Queen's Hall in Port of Spain. In 1965 he was awarded a two-year fellowship by the Rockefeller Foundation at the Yale School of Drama, where he played Othello.

Hopkinson then spent 1966-8 on the English faculty of the University of Guyana. The THEATRE GUILD OF GUYANA had performed his revolutionary play *Fall of a Chief* in 1962. In 1968 he directed for the Guild his *The Spawning of Eels*, about the dilemma of the scholarship-winner who has to choose between his land and love and the allurements of money and dead scholarship. Returning to Trinidad, he played Lestrade in the 1968 Caribbean touring production of Derek Walcott's *Dream on Monkey Mountain*. In 1970 he formed the Caribbean Theatre Guild from ex-pupils of St George's College in Barataria, Trinidad, whom he had trained and directed in plays such as DOUGLAS ARCHIBALD's (see Trinidad and Tobago) *The Bamboo Clump* and Euripides' *The Trojan Women*. With the Guild he produced Archibald's *The Rose Slip* for touring in country areas, and WOLE SOYINKA's (see Nigeria) *The Lion and the Jewel*. Ill-health then forced him to move back to Jamaica. In 1974 and 1976 Dennis Scott directed Hopkinson's *Sala and Summer Dread*.

In 1977 he moved to Ontario, where he worked at journalism – an old love – and continued to write poetry. Some of his poems appeared in literary journals, and publication of his first book of poems was imminent when he died in February 1993.

Slade Hopkinson.

Martin, Bertie (1905–59)

A Guyanese civil servant who was passionately devoted to the stage. Martin joined the revived Georgetown Dramatic Club in 1945 and became its producer and director two years later. He attended the Bristol Old Vic Theatre School on a British Council scholarship in 1951, and is remembered for his production of a Commonwealth pageant in London to mark the coronation celebrations of Queen Elizabeth II. He was a co-founder of the THEATRE GUILD OF GUYANA in 1957, and worked towards the acquisition of a theatre in Georgetown but was contemptuous of local dialect plays which he considered unworthy of production.

Mohamed, Paloma (1967–)

Guyanese playwright. Mohamed attended Queen's College, Georgetown, and gained a BSc in mass communication at the University of Guyana. She was twenty when her first play, the one-acter *Boo Legge*, was produced by the THEATRE GUILD OF GUYANA in Georgetown. Since then she has written six full-length plays, all premiered by United Performers in Georgetown. *Masquerade in Black* (1989) was considered the best new play of the season; *Reggae Marley* (1989), the best new musical; and *Jezebel* (1990) was produced the following year in Washington, DC. After its presentation in Georgetown, *Mammy* (1990) was selected to represent Guyana at the 1992 CARIFESTA (see Introduction) held in TRINIDAD AND TOBAGO. *Jezebel Two* (1991) and *Benjie Darling* (1992) have also been presented in Georgetown. Mohamed has published short stories for adults and children. She is studying for an MA in international relations and works as an independent television producer.

Muttoo, Henry (1948–)

Guyanese theatre designer, actor and director. Muttoo taught industrial arts in Guyana and in 1973 enrolled at the UNIVERSITY OF THE WEST INDIES (see Introduction) summer school in Trinidad where he studied acting, directing and stage management. He won the Best Actor award in Guyana in 1972 and 1975, and was named best director in the 1975 festival of Caribbean plays. In 1974 he was appointed drama officer at the Guyana National History and Arts Council. From 1976 to 1979 he attend-

ed the Croydon College of Design and Technology, London (gaining a diploma in theatre design), while working as director/ designer in residence at the Keskidee Arts Centre.

From 1980 to 1984 and 1986 to 1988, Muttoo was attached to the Jamaica School of Drama (see Jamaica, CULTURAL TRAINING CENTRE) as production manager and senior tutor in design and technical theatre. In the intervening years he worked as production manager and designer for the Cayman National Theatre Company. From 1989 to 1991 he was administrator of the HARQUAIL THEATRE (see Introduction), Cayman Islands, and then became programme director for the Cayman National Cultural Foundation. He has designed five JAMAICA PANTOMIMES, two grand galas, and scores of commercial stage productions in the Caribbean, North America and Britain. He has won gold and silver awards in Jamaica and the Cayman Islands for his theatrical designs, and has directed nine plays including touring productions of *Whiplash* by Jamaica's Ginger Knight and *Pantomime* by DEREK WALCOTT (see Eastern Caribbean States).

Pilgrim, Frank (1926–89)

Guyanese playwright, journalist and arts administrator. Pilgrim wrote for the London *Observer* and the BBC during 1962-6. He organized and managed the first CARIFESTA (see Introduction) held in Guyana in 1972, and helped organize the Black and African Festival of Arts and Culture (FESTAC, see African Theatre, Introduction) held in Nigeria in 1977. For many years Pilgrim was the cultural officer of the Caribbean Community (Caricom) Secretariat.

In addition to performing for the THEATRE GUILD OF GUYANA in such plays as *Hamlet*, Brazilian Ariano Suassuma's *The Rogues' Trial* (in English translation) and *Barefoot in the Park*, he wrote for the stage and for radio, his major work being the popular comedy *Miriamy*, first staged in Georgetown in 1962, repeatedly revived there and in other Caribbean countries, and produced for Trinidad television in 1987. Pilgrim also wrote the one-acter *Skeleton at the Party*, produced in 1964, and was one of the principal writers for the satiric 'Brink' show, an annual musical revue produced by the Theatre Guild from 1964 to 1969.

Robinson, Ron (1946–)

Guyanese actor, director, theatre manager and broadcaster. Robinson attended Queen's College secondary school, Georgetown, and joined the THEATRE GUILD OF GUYANA, of which he was chairman from 1978 to 1981. In 1981 he formed the Theatre Company, Guyana's first professional company. He has taken leading roles in such plays as *Old Story Time* and *Two Can Play* by TREVOR RHONE (see Jamaica), *Pantomime* and *Beef, No Chicken* by DEREK WALCOTT (see Eastern Caribbean States), *A Streetcar Named Desire* and *Ceremonies in Dark Old Men*. For the Theatre Company he has directed some twenty-five productions including, from the Caribbean, Rhone's *Smile Orange*, Ian Valz's *Masquerade*, ALWIN BULLY's (see Eastern Caribbean States) *Nite Box*, FRANK PILGRIM's *Miriamy*, DAVID EDGECOMBE's (see Eastern Caribbean States) *Sonuvabitch*, and the musical *Raise-up* by Dave Martins. Other works staged for the company include *The Mousetrap, Jesus Christ Superstar, Boeing Boeing, The Odd Couple* and *Long Day's Journey Into Night*. Robinson has also acted in and directed the 'Link' shows – satirical revues with song, dance and drama, patterned on the earlier 'Brink' shows staged by the Theatre Guild. In 1982 and 1985 he organized tours of his company's productions to Caribbean islands, and in 1990 *Raise-up* went to the Cayman Islands, Miami, Mississippi, West Virginia, Washington, DC, New York and Michigan.

Robinson is one of Guyana's leading broadcasters, working both in radio and in television for over twenty-six years. He has trained announcers and operators in Guyana and Antigua (see Eastern Caribbean States). He was the first anchor of GTV news in Georgetown, from 1988 to 1990. In 1990 he was awarded the national Golden Arrow of Achievement for his contribution to theatre and broadcasting in Guyana.

Sadeek, Sheik (1921–)

Guyanese playwright, short story writer, novelist and poet. One of the earliest playwrights of Indian descent in Guyana, Sadeek won the THEATRE OF GUILD OF GUYANA's 1958 playwriting competition with his one-act play *Porkknockers*, about gold-panners in the Guyana hinterland, first produced in 1962. Other prize-winning plays are *Namaste* (1960; produced 1964) and *Fish Koker* (1961; produced 1965). He has also written *Bound Coolie* (1958), *No Greater Day* (1965), *Goodbye Corentyne* (produced 1965) and *Savannah's Edge* (1968). He captures the speech patterns of working-class Indians in Guyana, and publishes his own plays, stories and poems.

Taitt, Clairmonte (1932–)

Guyanese actor. After completing his secondary education in Guyana, Taitt divided his time between broadcasting, the Georgetown Philharmonic Orchestra where he was first violinist and choir conductor, and the THEATRE GUILD OF GUYANA, where he played leading roles in such plays as Lorraine Hansberry's *A Raisin in the Sun* (1965), *The Threepenny Opera* (1966), *The University of Hunger* (1966) by the Guyanese novelist Jan Carew, *Hamlet* (1968), *A Spawning of Eels* (1968) by SLADE HOPKINSON, and *King Lear* (1973). In Guyana he was acclaimed best actor in 1968, 1969, and 1972.

In 1971 Taitt gained a diploma at the British Drama League, London, in play production and drama teaching. He completed courses in radio production at the BBC in 1973, and at Radio Nederland, Holland, in 1982.

In 1976 he emigrated to BARBADOS and there

performed for Theatre 70 and Stage One in a wide variety of Caribbean dramas. An actor of exceptional merit, he has appeared in plays by Michael Abbensetts, RAWLE GIBBONS and ERROL JOHN (see Trinidad and Tobago) ; by MICHAEL GILKES, George Lamming and DENNIS SCOTT (see Jamaica); in two plays each by TREVOR RHONE (see Jamaica) and EDGAR WHITE (see Eastern Caribbean States); and in four by DEREK WALCOTT (see Eastern Caribbean States). His directors have included KEN CORSBIE, Michael Gilkes and EARL WARNER (see Barbados). Taitt was Pa in Lamming's dramatization of his own novel *In the Castle of My Skin* for CARIFESTA 81 (see Introduction) in Barbados, and he created the role of Gavin in the world première of Walcott's *A Branch of the Blue Nile*, staged in Barbados in 1983. He played Peter Quince in the Guyanese localized version of *A Midsummer Night's Dream*, directed by Gilkes in 1986. He has also performed in other Caribbean islands, at the Eugene O'Neill Center in Waterford, Connecticut, and in London, and has worked as an announcer/producer for CBC Radio, Barbados; he is now freelancing in radio broadcasting and drama.

Theatre Guild of Guyana

Founded in 1957 in Georgetown by Lloyd Searwar, Bertie Martin and Arthur Hemstock, the Guild's aims were to sponsor and support productions of Guyanese, West Indian and international plays of the highest standard; to promote the writing of local plays; and to encourage the development of the theatre in all its aspects in (British) Guyana. In 1959 the Guild converted an old police gymnasium into a 200-seat playhouse, later enlarged to hold 300. Over the years the Guild has been an active force in the development of Guyana's theatre, through its training courses in all aspects of theatre and dance, its promotion of local playwrights, its sponsorship of drama festivals and its production of Guyanese and other Caribbean plays, including its annual 'Brink' revues. In its most productive years, the late 1960s and the 70s, it was acclaimed as 'the most vital and active theatre group in the Caribbean'.

Bibliography

K. Corsbie, *Theatre in the Caribbean*, London, 1984; E. Hill, 'The Emergence of a National Drama in the West Indies', *Caribbean Quarterly*, 18, 4, 1972; *Kyk-over-al* (theatre issues), 25 (June 1959), 37 (Dec. 1987), 40 (Dec. 1989); K. Omotoso, *The Theatrical into Theatre: A Study of the Drama and Theatre of the English-speaking Caribbean*, London, 1982.

JAMAICA

Theatre in Jamaica began with the English conquest of the island from Spain in 1655. By 1682 a theatre was in existence, probably situated in the then administrative capital of San Jago de la Vega, or Spanish town, but whether the players were touring professionals from England or resident amateurs is unknown.

In 1733 an English company was successfully performing John Gay's *The Beggar's Opera*, and 'a set of extraordinary good actors' is recorded at the Spanish Town playhouse in 1740–1. In 1776 a new theatre was opened in Spanish Town, at a cost of about £2500; it probably had a level-floor auditorium for dances and assemblies, since from 1792 to 1799 it was taken over by the government to house soldiers.

With the arrival in 1745 of the Irish actor John Moody, the centre of theatrical activity moved to Kingston, the present capital. Supported by local amateurs, Moody mounted a number of Shakespearian productions, then returned to England to recruit a professional company that included David Douglass; once back in Kingston, he set up a theatre in Harbour Street. There he remained until 1749, when he embarked again for England, leaving Douglass in charge of the company. Some years later Douglass abandoned the theatre Moody had set up and established his own in warehouses nearby. In 1755 an English company of comedians led by one Lewis Hallam arrived from America and joined the Douglass troupe. Lewis Hallam junior was a member of the company. When the older Hallam died within the year, Douglass married his widow, became company manager, and after three years took the troupe back to America with, as his principal actor, the eighteen-year-old Lewis. With the outbreak of the American War of Independence imminent, Douglass brought his company, now called the American Comedians, back to Jamaica, where they remained from 1775 to 1785. Eventually Douglass became a printer, leaving Lewis Hallam junior and John Henry as co-managers of the troupe.

The players opened their first season with Romeo and Juliet on 1 July 1775, in a new playhouse situated in the parade ground (now St William Grant Park), which was to remain up to the present day the site of the principal Kingston theatres. Seating 600, this theatre contained a pit at floor level, and a second, stepped, level divided into boxes behind which rose an open gallery. Backless benches were provided throughout the house. In front of the curtain (raised in festoon fashion), the stage floor projected to accommodate entr'acte performances.

This was a slave-holding society, and the theatre catered primarily to the elite. Ticket prices were high, ranging from 6s8d to 13s4d when the average pay for skilled labour was 15s to 20s a week. The players offered a different programme each week, consisting of a major play followed by a farce or burletta, with solo entertainments between scene shifts. Along with Shakespeare, the playwrights most often presented were Cumberland, Mrs Centlivre, Dryden, Garrick, Goldsmith and Sheridan. Bickerstaffe's *The Padlock* was the most popular farce. The company performed occasionally in Spanish Town and on the north side of the island in Montego Bay, where several long rooms had been converted into theatres to accommodate travelling players.

After the American Comedians left the island in 1785, theatrical activity declined. Natural disasters, the successful slave revolt in neighbouring San Domingue and slave uprisings at home preoccupied Jamaica in the ensuing decades. In 1812 a company arrived from Barbados, led by Charles Manning, Jesse Read and Mrs Elizabeth Shaw. They occupied the Kingston Theatre, but did not prosper until joined by William Adamson, also from Barbados. When the Jamaican fever claimed Adamson, his infant son, Read and other players, French-speaking refugees from France and San Domingue took to the stage with comic operettas and vaudevilles. Kingston amateurs also produced *Macbeth*, *Venice Preserv'd* and *She Stoops to Conquer*. It was a period of uncertainty, for the slaves were about to be freed and few could predict the future.

On 1 August 1838 a quarter of a million black slaves were set free: they joined a population of 15,000 whites and 40,000 already free blacks and coloureds. An increase in rowdiness in the theatre – which was to continue until the end of the century – was a problem that had begun before emancipation, when an attempt had been made to segregate the races by building a separate stairway into the theatre for people of colour. Overt segregation was now discontinued, but individuals were disposed to noisily assert their rights as free citizens and, moreover, the theatre continued to address itself to a small section of the population, ignoring the vast majority whose behaviour was patterned on visits to the circus and other popular indigenous entertainments.

The slaves had developed their own modes of performance consisting of music-making, singing, dancing and storytelling; and Christmas masquerades (see African Theatre, Introduction, MASQUERADES IN AFRICA) called jonkonnu, and the Set Girls. Their instruments comprised a variety of home-made drums, rattles, horns, flutes and fiddles; the songs were melancholy and satiric; and the dances often involved role-playing, while the stories suggested survival strategies to ease pain and suffering. Some of these exhibitions were associated with rituals that reached back to an African past. The street masquerades, often sponsored by freemen and women as a holiday pastime, presented elaborately costumed figures including the Actor Boy, who imitated scenes from the theatre. While these various entertainments, carefully controlled, were allowed under the slave system, once the slaves were freed they were expected to abandon such 'barbaric', 'heathen' practices and adopt the behaviour of 'civilized' Christians. But the suppression of Afro-Jamaican expression simply sent it underground, out of sight of the authorities, to emerge years later, in more favourable times, as the native culture.

Meanwhile the theatre on the parade ground, left behind by the American Comedians, had fallen into disrepair. Three more theatres were to be constructed on this site: the first Theatre Royal (1840); the second Theatre Royal (1897), which was destroyed in the great earthquake of 1907; and the Ward Theatre (1912), which is still in use today. All were built for the people of Kingston, and placed under the control of the city council. During the 19th century, members of the Jewish community – owners of the city's major newspaper and of other business interests – played a major role in ensuring the survival of Kingston's public theatre.

The opening of the first Theatre Royal brought a return of professional troupers from overseas, among them the Philadelphian John H. Oxley and his company. Oxley had been a supporting actor to Edwin Forrest, and his Hamlet was viewed as 'the best ever presented to a Kingston audience'. Although his *Macbeth*, containing singing witches and a three-minute sword fight, and a visually spectacular *King Lear*, could fill the theatre, public support was generally disappointing. Nor did Signor Gastaldi's opera company that followed Oxley fare much better. When Oxley later teamed up with Mrs Monier and her daughter Virginia in an attempt to recoup his losses, only his *Othello* in 1842, the first ever production of the play in Jamaica, succeeded in filling the house.

It was time for the Kingston amateurs to take to the boards. Beginning in 1847, no fewer than eight groups competed for honours at the Theatre Royal, the most prestigious being the Kingston Amateur Theatre Association, which offered a major play once a month. There were a French troupe and two black groups, the Ethiopian Amateur Society and the Numidian Amateur Society. Spanish Town also had two amateur groups of its own. This activity terminated abruptly when a cholera epidemic struck the island in October 1850. By one estimate, between 25,000 and 30,000 of the working class perished.

Economic conditions deteriorated in the second half of the century. The planters, now having to pay their labourers, were forced to compete against slave-grown sugar from Cuba and Brazil. In the theatre amateurs held the stage, their most important productions being two original plays in 1853 by the Jamaican Charles Shanahan, a newspaper reporter and president of the amateur Roscian Association. *The Mysteries of Vegetarianism*, a satiric farce on a current dietary practice, and his historical drama *The Spanish Warrior*, based on the career of the New World explorer Balboa, mark the first recorded instance of works written and performed by Jamaicans. The scripts have not survived, nor have any other scripts of local plays produced during this century. Some dramas, farces and skits were published in the press, but no productions of them are recorded.

In 1865 the English actor Charles Kean and his wife, the actress Ellen Tree, visited Jamaica and gave Shakespearian readings and ballad recitations, to great acclaim. Seven years earlier the Jamaican RAPHAEL DE CORDOVA had embarked in the USA on an illustrious career as a humorous reader. Among other Jamaican professionals who worked abroad at this time was the esteemed actor MORTON TAVARES. Also in 1865, the first quartet of black-faced minstrels led by Frank Hussey arrived from New York, followed by other minstrel groups in 1869, 1872 and 1884. They established the tradition of blacking-up to portray comic stereotypes that Jamaican comedians of the populist theatre adopted and maintained into the 1950s and 60s.

October 1865 witnessed the Morant Bay rebellion, started by landless peasants. The uprising was cruelly suppressed by the military, supported by British gunboats under the orders of a sadistic governor. Nineteen of the people's leaders were hanged without trial from the yardarm of one of the gunboats. In an attempt to redress the injury, gunboat officers and crews began a series of seven theatrical productions at the Theatre Royal to raise money for the victims' families. In 1866 Charles Selby's *Robert Macaire* was staged at the temporary barracks in Morant Bay, to which all classes were offered free admission after the first act. Military and naval amateurs continued to perform intermittently until 1869, when a calmer political atmosphere was restored. In that year HENRY G. MURRAY, a black, began to deliver to audiences throughout the country his recitals of humorous stories based on Jamaican manners and customs. His appeal was immediate, and people flocked to hear him. After his death in 1877 his sons Andrew C. Murray and William C. Murray carried on the storytelling profession.

Touring troupers from abroad once again began to visit Jamaica, but few found it profitable, partly because the Kingston playhouse was unkempt and companies were forced to restore it, as well as provide their own scenery, before they could safely perform. Among the most reputable troupes at this time were J. W. Lanergan's, which paid three visits – in 1859, 1860 and 1861–2; E. A. McDowell's company, which played in 1880–1, 1885–6 and 1891; and William F. Burrough's New York Ideal Combination Company, in 1882. There was a distinct trend away from the old-fashioned romantic melodramas and towards contemporary realistic plays by writers such as Tom Robertson and Augustin Daly. These pieces required a more naturalistic approach to acting than hitherto, with greater emphasis on scenic decoration to achieve verisimilitude. Thus companies travelled with their own scene-painter and machinist.

In 1891 Jamaica held a three-month International Exhibition to stimulate trade. A temporary stage was built on the exhibition grounds, and the London Dramatic Company led by Warren F. Hill was installed. Meanwhile, McDowell's company, with the enormously popular Fanny Reeves, occupied the hastily refurbished Theatre Royal. Playing an average of five times a week, these two companies presented some seventy plays – light-hearted comedies, melodramas and historical romances by such authors as W. S. Gilbert, Pinero and Boucicault – in a total of 128 performances.

The challenge of the 20th century was to develop an indigenous drama and theatre that could be identified as belonging to Jamaica and to the Caribbean region. The Murrays had shown that there was a popular audience for local material, and the last decades of the 19th century had witnessed the publication at home and abroad of Jamaican proverbs and Anansi stories. In 1907 Walter Jekyll published for the Folklore Society his collection of Jamaican stories and songs, and in 1913 the Jamaican Astley Clerk published his lecture on the music and musical instruments of Jamaica. The country did not shut out travelling professionals, as G. B. Shaw had urged on his visit in 1911, but gradually the homegrown product began to assert itself as the legitimate theatre of Jamaica. Touring English companies that used the newly built Ward Theatre into the 1930s included the Florence Glossop-Harris Company playing Shakespeare and modern drama, its successor the Empire Players, the W. S. Harkins Dramatic Company and the Klark-Urban Dramatic Company. These continued to provide a model for the schools and for those amateurs for whom theatre was simply an art form devoted to public entertainment of a high

order. The native theatre, on the other hand, drew its energy from two sources: the populist theatre, including the comedians for whom theatre was principally a business catering to the largest audiences; and the art theatre, devoted to the establishment of a national culture.

CHRISTMAS MORNING CONCERTS, most favoured of the variety shows held on public holidays, were seen as opportunities for the seasoned professional as well as for the young and talented tyro to exhibit his speciality before a widely diverse audience. Another instrument for establishing a populist theatre, directed towards the social and political advancement of the Jamaican masses, was the Universal Negro Improvement Association (UNIA), founded in Kingston in 1914 by the Jamaican patriot and world-renowned figure MARCUS GARVEY. From the UNIA stage at Edelweiss Park issued the well known comedians ERNEST CUPIDON and RANNY WILLIAMS. Cupidon is credited with having dramatized two plays and a short story by the popular Jamaican writer H. G. de Lisser, and Garvey himself wrote several plays in 1930–2 aimed at uplifting his working-class audiences; but the most significant playwright of the 1930s was UNA MARSON, whose three plays dealt boldly and realistically with problems faced by the middle class of her time.

Following the workers' riots of 1937–8 that swept the English-speaking Caribbean, Jamaican playwrights supported the nationalist cause with plays such as Frank Hill's *Upheaval* (1939), Roger Mais's *Hurricane* (1943) and W. G. OGILVIE's *One Sojer Man* (1945). The most successful playwright of the period was ARCHIE LINDO, who treated topical issues such as colour prejudice and quasi-historical figures like the infamous White Witch of Rosehall. Two organizations that have had a profound impact on the Jamaican theatre are the LITTLE THEATRE MOVEMENT OF JAMAICA (LTM), formed in 1941, and the Caribbean Thespians (1946). The LTM generates the annual JAMAICA

PANTOMIME, while the Thespians have produced a number of outstanding theatre people including the actors MONA CHIN HAMMOND and CHARLES HYATT, the actor-playwrights EASTON LEE and Mitzi Townshend, and the actor-director RONALD HARRISON.

In 1950, under the aegis of the British Council, Nugent Monck of the Maddermarket Theatre in Norwich, England, visited Jamaica to work with drama students at secondary schools. From this resulted the first island-wide secondary schools drama festival, which has continued to the present day. In 1952 the Dramatic Society of the newly established UNIVERSITY [College] OF THE WEST INDIES (UWI) at Mona, Jamaica, gave its first production. The College, which became a full-fledged university in 1963, is significant because its students have spread the work of the Society throughout the West Indies.

In 1953 ERROL HILL (see Trinidad and Tobago) was appointed drama tutor in the UWI Extramural Department, dealing with the anglophone Caribbean as well as the Dramatic Society on campus. He started a collection of Caribbean plays, and by 1955 had begun to publish them. Also in 1955, a drama festival fostered by WYCLIFFE BENNETT was held as part of the tercentary celebration of British rule. Under the Jamaica Drama League, this festival became an annual event, extending the work done in schools. In 1956 LOUISE BENNETT was named drama officer for the Jamaica Social Welfare Commission. She travelled throughout the island, using the creative group play-making method to help villagers identify their needs and discover ways of satisfying them. In 1958, to herald the opening of the West Indies Federation, the St Lucian playwright DEREK WALCOTT (see Eastern Caribbean States) was commissioned to write an epic drama called *Drums and Colours*, directed by the Jamaican NOEL VAZ, who later became the second drama tutor in the UWI Extramural Department. Important playwrights to emerge in this decade were CICELY WAITE-SMITH (Jamaican by

marriage) whose plays such as *Africa Slingshot* and *Uncle Robert* were greatly admired for their penetrating look at Jamaican society, and BARRY RECKORD, who first offered *Della* to Kingston audiences in 1954, then staged it at the Royal Court Theatre, London, as *Flesh to a Tiger*.

The next phase was the creating of more theatre spaces in Kingston to accommodate the increasing number of drama groups. In 1961, at a cost of £40,000, the LTM built the Little Theatre and rehearsal room. In 1967 playwright TREVOR RHONE and director YVONNE BREWSTER converted a garage into the intimate Barn Theatre. Several small theatres followed suit. Instead of playing for two or three times in the the 1200-seat Ward Theatre, companies could now offer several dozen performances in their much smaller houses, improve their scripts and acting skills and attract bigger audiences over the longer run – all of which helped to professionalize the local theatre. In 1968 the Creative Arts Centre was opened on the university campus, offering yet another theatre space in upper Kingston. The establishment of the Jamaica School of Drama (see CULTURAL TRAINING CENTRE) in 1973 provided two additional performance areas, one an open-air arena.

Several producing companies emerged over the years, to take advantage of the upsurge in live theatre. Few have survived. Among those that have done significant work are the National Theatre Trust formed by LLOYD RECKORD in 1968, and SISTREN, a women's empowerment group of the 1970–80s, led by Honor Ford-Smith. New playwrights whose work merited attention in the 1960s included SAMUEL HILLARY, DENNIS SCOTT and SYLVIA WYNTER. The next two decades witnessed a flow of Caribbean productions to and from Jamaica, inspired in part by the university's Dramatic Society but also by the work of the TRINIDAD THEATRE WORKSHOP, as well as by productions originating in other Caribbean countries. The staging of Caribbean plays in London and in the USA has also opened up new opportunities for professional work to outstanding Jamaican and other Caribbean actors.

By the early 1990s one can distinguish three types of live theatre in Jamaica. The Jamaica pantomime, a traditional form of seasonal entertainment, remains the most all-embracing theatrical experience for the widest audience. Its subject, real or fantasy, always has a contemporary flavour. It combines music and song with dance and speech in vigorous and innovative ways, and can fill the Ward Theatre for several months. Next in popularity is the 'Roots' (Grassroots) Theatre, exemplified by the work of producer Ralph Holness, who offers original plays with an emphasis on sexual behaviour that cater to a mass public. These are the successors to the BIM AND BAM shows of an earlier time, translated to an age of sexual revolution. With small casts and limited scenery, they travel around the country playing in cinemas and public halls. Writer-directors Ginger Knight and BALFOUR ANDERSON also produce shows of this kind, but of a somewhat higher calibre. The third type of theatre consists of original Jamaican and Caribbean plays, plus those from the world repertoire that have a broader appeal than the Roots plays. The leading theatre critic on the island for forty years was the late Irish-born, Yorkshire-raised and Jamaican-wed Harry Milner. His encyclopaedic knowledge of the arts generated reviews that were always informative and often controversial.

There has been a significant development in dance theatre since 1947, when the Jamaican Berto Pasuka formed in London a company called Les Ballets Nègres. His dances, mostly narrative in form, were accompanied by percussive instruments and piano. Pasuka's company toured Europe with great success, demonstrating the wide appeal of dance-drama. In Jamaica the form was adopted by the IVY BAXTER Dance Group, which took four original pieces to the Caribbean Festival in Puerto Rico in 1951. The NATIONAL DANCE THEATRE COMPANY OF JAMAICA, formed in 1962, has continued the tradition, and has won considerable acclaim at home as in tours the world over.

Anderson, Balfour (1953–)

Jamaican playwright, producer, designer, actor and musician. A 1975 graduate of the Mico Teachers' Training College of Jamaica, Anderson taught at primary school for six years, using a role-playing method. He also wrote school plays, participated in the annual schools drama festival, at one point managing three drama groups. He gained a diploma at the National School of Drama in 1984. He then headed the drama programme at the Jamaica Cultural Development Commission, and during 1985–90 travelled the island training rural drama groups. He managed a music group (he sings, plays the guitar and keyboard), and in the early 1980s acquired knowledge of theatre management with the Ed Wallace professional production team.

In 1986 Anderson staged his first major play, *Secret Lovers*, which was produced at the Barn Theatre in Kingston and ran for five months. After two performances in Miami, the play returned to Jamaica for four more months at his 149-seat Green Gables Theatre, before touring the island. In 1987 he scripted the JAMAICA PANTOMIME *King Root*, and during 1988–90 produced six more plays at the Green Gables. He writes comic farces, all with a surprising twist and using three to six characters, on familiar situations.

Baxter, Ivy (1923–93)

Jamaican dancer, choreographer and director of the Ivy Baxter Dance Group, founded in 1950. After attending dance school in Jamaica, Baxter studied dance for eighteen months on a British Council scholarship at the Sigurd Leeder School in London. She returned to Jamaica for the CARIFESTA (see Introduction) hosted by PUERTO RICO in 1952, where her group presented the dances *Manuel Road*, about road workers; *Pocomania*, a folk ritual; *Passing Parade*, a day in the life of a policeman at a busy street corner, and *Village Scene*, based on an Anansi story. The dances were interspersed with Jamaican folk-songs rendered by the Frats Quintet.

Successfully revived at the Ward Theatre in Kingston on the company's return, this programme indicated some of the themes that they would develop in the years ahead: Caribbean folk-dances; interpretations of contemporary life, as in *Rat Passage*, depicting the hardships faced by a stowaway in England; the dance of other countries, as in the *South Sea Suite*; and creative dances to contemporary and classical music. While involved in creating indigenous dance-theatre in Jamaica, they participated in many national and civic occasions and travelled to CUBA, Tinidad (see Trinidad and Tobago) and Washington, DC. After 1962 the Baxter group declined, as the NATIONAL DANCE THEATRE COMPANY OF JAMAICA established itself as the leading dance company on the island.

Bennett, Louise (1919–)

Jamaican folklore artist, dramatist and comedienne. Admired throughout the Caribbean and in America and England for her writing and interpretation of dialect poetry based on Jamaican characters, 'Miss Lou' taught drama at Excelsior School in Kingston, her alma mater. She trained at the Royal Academy of Dramatic Art in London, then became drama officer with Jamaica Welfare, criss-crossing the island on its behalf for six years. She has written dialect plays, written and co-written JAMAICA PANTOMIMES, and was a regular cast member, partnering RANNY WILLIAMS for thirty years. She starred in her last pantomime, *The Witch*, in 1975. Bennett's popular radio programme *Miss Lou's Views* ran in Jamaica for fifteen years. She has been featured in many films, her biggest role being in *Calypso*, made in

Louise Bennett

Haiti and PUERTO RICO. For her work in Jamaican literature and theatre and for promoting Jamaican culture at home and abroad she has received numerous local and international awards, including the Order of Jamaica, the MBE, and the LL D from the UNIVERSITY OF THE WEST INDIES (see Introduction). She is married to Eric Coverley, a retired impresario of CHRISTMAS MORNING CONCERTS and other popular entertainments.

Bennett, Wycliffe (1922–)

Jamaican director, festival organizer, radio and television producer. Bennett began as organizing secretary of the Poetry League of Jamaica (1940–56) and was chairman of the All-island

Speech Festival. In 1958, as a British Council scholar, he gained a diploma in speech and dramatic art from the Royal Academy of Music, London. On a government of Jamaica scholarship he studied in the USA, gaining a BA (Yale, 1966) and an MA in theatre (Columbia, 1972). He studied broadcasting and television in England and the USA, and festival organization in Edinburgh and Wales. He helped to establish the drama festival in Jamaica in 1956, and founded the Jamaica Drama League in 1957. He has been general manager of the Jamaica Broadcasting Corporation and chairman of the Jamaican School of Drama (see CULTURAL TRAINING CENTRE). Among his notable productions are T. S. Eliot's *Murder in the Cathedral*, staged at Scot's Kirk, Kingston, in 1962; Racine's *Phaedra*, in 1963; and Goldoni's *The Servant of Two Masters*, in 1972. He has presented several commemorative spectacles involving thousands of participants at the national stadium in Kingston. Bennett is head of the government Creative Production and Training Centre for media personnel.

Bim and Bam [Lewis, Ed (1914–76) and Wynter, Aston (1913–78)]
Jamaican comedians, perhaps the most popular of all the Jamaican comic duos, whose comedy was based on a long tradition that flourished in the 1920s–60s. In chronological order: Harold and Trim, song and dance team; Cupes (see ERNEST CUPIDON) and Abe, refined comedy; Racca and Sandy, black-face comedy; Slim and Sam, street-corner minstrels; Ike and Mike, refined comedy; Amos 'n Andy, black-face comedy, later Ranny (see RANNY WILLIAMS) and Lee, without black face; and Bim and Bam, originally black-face comedy.

These teams appeared in variety shows such as CHRISTMAS MORNING CONCERTS and at hotels and nightclubs, mostly as stand-up comedians. Racca and Sandy presented the first, and their only, full-length production with *The Burial of A.B.*, which dealt with the death and burial of a notorious policeman and was immensely popular. Bim and Bam followed suit with productions of their own scripted by Bim and requiring a cast of about twelve, including Bim's wife, the entertainer 'Clover'. Their shows include *Healing in the Balmyard*, *The Case of the Baldhead Rooster*, *Laughter in the Court*, *The Black Witch of Trout Hall* and – their most popular of all – *The Case of John Ras I*. Most productions included a court hearing which dissolved into a series of variety acts. Bim and Bam took shows around Jamaica and the Bim, Bam and Clover team toured Bermuda, New York and England. Their spruced-up shows continue to be presented by the producer Oliver Samuels.

Brewster, Yvonne (1938–)
Jamaican actress and producer, and artistic director of the Talawa Theatre Company, London. Brewster left Jamaica in 1956 for England, to study speech, drama and mime at the Rose Bruford College in Kent and at the Royal Academy of Music. She then worked as an actress in London before returning to Jamaica, where she became a radio announcer and television producer.

In 1971 she founded with TREVOR RHONE the Barn Theatre in Kingston, Jamaica, from a converted garage on her family's compound. Later that year in London she directed *Lippo, the New Noah* by Sally Durie, with an African-Caribbean cast at the Institute of Contemporary Arts and, to mark the tenth anniversary of Jamaica's independence, she staged Rhone's *Smile Orange*, which toured to black communities in London. Other productions at this time included DEREK WALCOTT's (see Eastern Caribbean States) *Pantomime* and a musical version of BARRY RECKORD's *Skyvers*. Brewster was also production manager or assistant director on the films *The Harder They Come*, *Smile Orange*, *The Marijuana Affair* and *The Fight against Slavery*.

In 1986 she founded the all-black Talawa Theatre Company, aimed at enriching British theatre and enlarging audiences in the black

Juanita Waterman in Yvonne Brewster's production of *The Importance of Being Ernest*, 1989.

community. She directed seven productions – four by Caribbean authors (*The Black Jacobins* by C. L. R. James, *An Echo in the Bone* by DENNIS SCOTT, *O Babylon* by Derek Walcott, and *The Dragon Can't Dance* by EARL LOVELACE (see Trinidad and Tobago), one Nigerian (*The Gods Are Not to Blame* by OLA ROTIMI), one Irish (Wilde's *The Importance of Being Ernest*, co-pro-duced with the Tyne Theatre Company in Newcastle) and one English (Shakespeare's *Antony and Cleopatra*, co-produced with Merseyside Everyman Theatre in Liverpool) – all staged in venues around London, as well as Newcastle and Liverpool, respectively. In 1988 she directed Rhone's *Two Can Play* at the Bristol Old Vic, and in 1991 Lorca's *Blood Wedding* at the National Theatre in London. In 1992 she took over the renovated Cochrane Theatre in Holborn creating a new home for black theatre in central London. There she directed Soyinka's *The Road* (1992).

Brewster was drama officer of the Arts Council of Great Britain from 1982 to 1984, and has served on the London Arts Board, the British Council's Drama and Dance Advisory Committee, and the Black Theatre Forum. She is a member of the National Theatre Trust and a Fellow of the Royal Society of Arts. In 1993 she was awarded an OBE. She has published two collections of plays: *Black Plays* (1987) and *Black Plays: Two* (1989).

Carter, George (1916–)

Jamaican technical director and lighting designer. For over four decades Carter has worked on every important theatrical production in Jamaica, either as stage manager or as lighting designer. He has tutored stagecraft to extramural classes of the UNIVERSITY OF THE WEST INDIES (see Introduction), is a founding member, technical director and lighting designer of the NATIONAL DANCE THEATRE COMPANY OF JAMAICA, and has served on the advisory board of the Jamaica School of Drama (see CULTURAL TRAINING CENTRE). He has lit intimate productions and large outdoor spectacles and worked on drama festivals in other Caribbean islands, but his most demanding assignment is with the annual JAMAICA PANTOMIME, which leaves its Ward Theatre base in Kingston to play in Montego Bay.

In 1960 Carter received a British Council scholarship to study stage lighting and management in England, followed the next year by an American Council in Education fellowship. He has been awarded the silver Musgrave Medal (1972), the Order of Distinction (1977), the centenary medal of the Institute of Jamaica (1980), and the service award from the Jamaica National Foundation of New York (1992). He is general manager of the LITTLE THEATRE MOVEMENT OF JAMAICA.

Christmas morning concerts

Starting in the 1890s and continuing until the late 1950s, these variety concerts, first introduced on Christmas mornings, became the principal showcases for talented Jamaican entertainers – from singers to gymnasts, from comedians to chalk-talk artists. The shows were held first at the Conversorium and the Coke Memorial Hall in Kingston and later also at the Ward Theatre. Before a mostly working-class audience, popular comedians like Racca and Sandy or BIM AND BAM would present original skits. The impresarios were the well known W. Hylton, Eric Coverley and Vere Johns.

Cultural Training Centre

A complex of four schools – of music, dance, drama, and the visual arts – established in 1975 to prepare young people for professions in the arts. The Centre occupies a ten-acre site in central Kingston and includes an amphitheatre, a studio theatre in the School of Drama, and an auditorium attached to the School of Music. Training programmes at the Centre lead to degrees, diplomas or certificates.

The School of Drama began in 1969 with part-time courses conducted by the non-profit-making LITTLE THEATRE MOVEMENT OF JAMAICA. Its training programme contains an experimental Caribbean laboratory, in which the students investigate traditional folk forms and explore their translation into dramatic theatre.

Cumper, Pat (1954–)

Jamaican playwright. In 1972 Cumper won the Jamaica Scholarship to Girton College, Cambridge University, where she read anthropology and archaeology. Returning to Jamaica, in 1977 she produced her first full-length drama, *The Rapist*, a vernacular piece that received the Best Play award for 1978. Her next play, *Rufus*, directed by DENNIS SCOTT, was not successful, but with her third work, *Coming of Age* (1983), she won the Prime Minister's Award for a play celebrating Jamaica's twenty-one years of independence.

Cumper has co-scripted two JAMAICA PANTOMIMES, and written the plays *Buss Out* (1989), first developed by the SISTREN company, and *Fallen Angel and the Devil Concubine* (1987), first improvised by two actors of the Groundwork Theatre Company in Kingston. The latter has been successfully performed around the Caribbean, and in England, Canada and in the USA. Her other plays include *Jane and Louisa will Soon Come Home* (1990), a dramatization of the novel by Erna Brodber, and *Flameheart*, a docudrama co-written with Maureen Warner Lewis on the life of the Jamaican poet Claude McKay.

Cupidon, Ernest (M.) (1903–40)

Jamaican comedian. A civil servant Cupidon began playing comedy roles c.1928, and appeared on the Edelweiss Park concert stage in shows organized by MARCUS GARVEY. After a short turn at cabaret in England, he returned to Jamaica and staged a number of memorable productions adapted from H. G. de Lisser's stories, including *Susan Proudleigh* (1930), *The Jamaica Bandits* (1931) and *Jane's Career* (1933). Cupidon often played women's roles, and was teamed with Tony Abelton as 'Cupes and Abe', one of Jamaica's earliest and best known comic duos (see BIM AND BAM).

Dawes, Carroll (1932–)

Jamaican director, actress and university lecturer. Dawes took a BA in English at the UNIVERSITY [College] OF THE WEST INDIES (UWI, see Introduction) in 1955, and on a Commonwealth bursary she attended the Rose Bruford College of Speech and Drama in Kent, England. In 1964 she gained a diploma in speech, drama and mime from the Royal Academy of Music and Drama, and a certificate in acting from the Guildhall School of Music and Drama; in 1971 she received a doctorate in fine arts from the Yale School of Drama, Connecticut. From 1968 to 1971 Dawes was lecturer, then assistant pro-

fessor, in the Department of Speech and Communication at Boston College, Massachusetts. Returning to Jamaica, she became acting head of the UWI Creative Arts Centre in 1973, then head of the Jamaica School of Drama (see CULTURAL TRAINING CENTRE) from 1973 to 1976. In 1977 she moved to NIGERIA, where she spent twelve years teaching at the Universities of Calabar, Ife, Ibadan, Ahmadu Bello and Port Harcourt.

Dawes has directed thirty-nine plays, five of them Caribbean and seven African. She has adapted classical plays to the local environment, as with her production of *Macbeth* in Jamaica in 1973; in Nigeria she directed DEREK WALCOTT's (see Eastern Caribbean States) *Dream on Monkey Mountain* in 1979, and Brecht's *The Good Woman of Setzuan* in 1983. Her production of the South African 'workshop' play *Woza Albert!* toured six British universities in 1985. Her stage appearances have included Della, the title role in BARRY RECKORD's play, Margery in *The Country Wife*, Viola in *Twelfth Night*, Lady Macbeth, Oenone in Racine's *Phedre*, Ondine, and Death in *Blood Wedding*.

de Cordova, Raphael (J.) (fl.1858–80)

Jamaican public reader in the USA. De Cordova began to give evening readings from Dickens's Christmas books at Clinton Hall, New York City, in 1858. He was soon writing his own material, composing some forty comic pieces over the next eighteen years, using both rhymed verse and prose. During the American Civil War he gave readings of his patriotic historical poem, accompanied by a projection of campaign views by eminent painters, and music. His most popular presentations, with which he toured many cities, were *Our First Baby*, *Mrs Smith's Surprise Party* and *The Amateur Theatrical Association*.

Forbes, Leonie (1937–)

Leading Jamaican actress. Previously an announcer with the Jamaica Broadcasting

Company, in 1961 Forbes received a two-year scholarship at the Royal Academy of Dramatic Art, London. On graduation she appeared in BBC-TV schools programmes under Robin Midgely and performed in plays produced by black companies.

In 1966 she returned to broadcasting in Jamaica, and at the Garden Theatre, Kingston, played Maria in *Twelfth Night* and Kate in *The Taming of the Shrew*, under the direction of Paul Methuen. While in Australia from 1968 to 1970, she played Portia in *The Merchant of Venice* for the College Players of Queensland in a production that toured schools for three months. Back in Jamaica, she helped to establish the first FM radio station and directed the long-running series *The Fortunes of Flora Lee*. Her stage

Leonie Forbes as Miss Prism in *The Importance of Being Ernest*, Talawa Theatre Company, 1989.

roles at this time included Sister Margaret in James Baldwin's *The Amen Corner*, Mrs Adams in *Moon on a Rainbow Shawl*, and Miss Aggie in TREVOR RHONE's hit play *Old Story Time*, which she played over 400 times in the Caribbean, the USA and Canada. In 1989 she played Miss Prism in the all-black London production of *The Importance of Being Earnest* and Queen Ojuola in OLA ROTIMI's (see Nigeria) *The Gods are Not to Blame*, both plays directed by Jamaican YVONNE BREWSTER. Forbes has appeared in over ten JAMAICA PANTOMIMES, on television and in films.

Garvey, Marcus (Mosiah) (1887–1940)

Jamaican and world-wide black leader, whose rallying cry, 'Race first!', recruited members in their hundreds of thousands into his United Negro Improvement Association located in Brooklyn, New York. After his deportation from the USA in 1927, Garvey set up headquarters at Edelweiss Park in Kingston, Jamaica, where many talented Jamaicans appeared in stage presentations. He wrote and staged four plays, whose scripts have not survived: *The Coronation of an African King*, *Roaming Jamaicans* and *Slavery – from Hut to Mansion* (all in August 1930); and *Wine, Women and War* (January 1932).

Gloudon, Barbara (1935–)

Jamaican playwright, journalist and communications consultant. Gloudon's main contribution to the theatre is in writing the scripts and lyrics for the annual JAMAICA PANTOMIME: from 1969's *Moonshine Anancy*, directed and choreographed by Eddy Thomas, to 1990's *Fifty-fifty*, directed by Brian Heap. One, *The Pirate Princess*, was produced in 1986 by the Temba Theatre Company in London. Gloudon has also authored two plays, *Jack and the Gungo Tree* (1983), for children, and *Appropriate Behaviour* (1985), a comedy directed by Bobby Ghisays for the Citizen Players, Kingston, and by Alby James and Paulette Morrison for the Temba

Theatre Company, London. Gloudon is chairperson of the LITTLE THEATRE MOVEMENT OF JAMAICA and of the Jamaica School of Drama (see CULTURAL TRAINING CENTRE). In 1991 she published a series of short sketches in Jamaican patois under the title *Stella Seh ...* .

Hammond, Mona Chin

Jamaican actress. Having appeared with distinction in a number of productions in Jamaica, Hammond won a scholarship to the Royal Academy of Dramatic Art, London, where she remained to pursue her career. She has played a variety of roles: Lady Macbeth in Peter Coe's *Macbeth* at the Round House; Snow in Genet's *The Blacks*; Mama Benin in MUSTAPHA MATURA's (see Trinidad and Tobago) *Playboy of the West Indies* in 1984, directed by Nicholas Kent; and Rita in the Royal Court production of Michael Abbensetts' *Sweet Talk*. She twice played Tituba in *The Crucible* – at the Young Vic and at the Royal National Theatre, directed by Howard Davies. Her other roles include Mrs Jefferson in Howard Sackler's *The Great White Hope*, Virgie in DEREK WALCOTT's (see Eastern Caribbean States) *O Babylon!*, and Nana in *A Hero's Welcome at the Royal Court*; Lady Bracknell in *The Importance of Being Earnest*, directed by Yvonne Brewster; the mother in *Blood Wedding*; and at the Royal National Theatre, Aase in *Peer Gynt* and the washerwoman in *The Wind in the Willows*. She played Sister 1 and the doctor in the Africa-style production of *Macbeth* conceived and directed by Stephen Rayne, which in 1992 toured colleges in the northeastern USA. For BBC-TV she re-created her role of Mama Benin, and has appeared in Tom Clarke's *Victims of Apartheid*, BARRY RECKORD's *The Beautiful Caribbean*, and the BBC series *Black Silk*.

Harrison, Ronald (1927–)

Jamaican actor, director and designer. A foundation member (1946) and past president of the Caribbean Thespians, Harrison is a strong supporter of the Jamaica Drama League of which he is a past president, and of the annual drama festival. He has played character parts with gusto: Caliban in *The Tempest* (1955); Captain Boyle in *Juno and the Paycock* (1963), for which he received the Best Actor award in the drama festival; and Captain Cotchipee in *Purlie Victorious* (1975). Harrison has directed plays by Caribbean writers, including four by Jamaican W. G. OGILVIE. He has appeared in radio serials and television drama in Jamaica.

Hillary, Samuel (c.1936–)

Jamaican playwright. Hillary won the Ministry of Education playwriting competition in 1957 with his *Geva Charlotte*. In 1960 his *Departure in the Dark* was directed by Orford St John for the Repertory Players in Kingston; and in 1961 *Chippy*, a popular one-acter on a day in the life of a police constable, was produced by the University Dramatic Society in Jamaica and taken on tour in the southern Caribbean. He wrote the script *Banana Boy* for the 1961 JAMAICA PANTOMIME. In 1967 his JONKUNNU play, *Koo-koo, or Actor Boy*, was produced at the Barn Theatre in Kingston, and in 1972 JBC-TV produced a television version of his *Merry Christmas, Mr Murphy, to You and the Missis*. Hillary has written other, unproduced, plays, one of which, *Favours of Lovers*, was awarded the bronze medal in the Jamaica festival literary competition of 1966.

Hyatt, Charles (Eglerton) (1931–)

Jamaican actor. Hyatt established himself as an actor of talent with the Caribbean Thespians and in thirteen productions of the JAMAICA PANTOMIME, before he went to England in 1960 on an Arts Council scholarship. After training at the Theatre Royal, Windsor, he settled in London and for thirteen years worked in television and radio and on the stage. His theatre roles, mostly in the provinces, include:

Zachariah in ATHOL FUGARD's (see South Africa) *The Blood Knot*, directed by Robin Midgley in a Leicester production later presented on BBC-TV with the author playing Morris; and for the Oxford Playhouse, the Governor in Genet's *The Blacks*, which toured Europe. He also appeared in a television drama, *Return to Look Behind* (1963), written for him by Evan Jones. Back in Jamaica in 1974, Hyatt starred in TREVOR RHONE's hit play *Old Story Time* (1979), which ran for four years, followed by Rhone's equally popular two-hander *Two Can Play* (1982). In 1990 he appeared in PAT CUMPER's dramatization of Erna Brodber's novel *Jane and Louisa will Soon come Home*, in an experimental production by EARL WARNER (see Barbados) at the Creative Arts Centre (see Introduction, UNIVERSITY OF THE WEST INDIES) in Jamaica.

Jamaica pantomime

Jamaican version of the traditional English Christmastime revel. It was inaugurated in 1941 with the staging at the Ward Theatre, Kingston, of *Jack and the Beanstalk* by Jack Bruton, specially written for and presented by the LITTLE THEATRE MOVEMENT OF JAMAICA (LTM). In 1943 *Soliday and the Wicked Bird*, written by Vera Bell and designed by the artist Albert Huie, represented the first effort to indigenize the form, but it was not until the 1949 production of *Bluebeard and Brer Anancy*, written by LOUISE BENNETT and NOEL VAZ and directed by Vaz, that the full potential of incorporating the folk-character trickster Anancy, played by RANNY WILLIAMS, was realized. For the next thirty years Williams and Bennett took the leads in every pantomime. From an initial budget of £500 for five performances, the cost of the pantomime in its fiftieth year had grown to over £1,750,000 for a production lasting three months, and playing to audiences totalling 70,000 drawn from every sector of the country. Most consistent of the writers of pantomime scripts and lyrics is BARBARA GLOUDON, now chairperson of the LTM.

Jones, Evan (1927–)

Jamaican writer of plays and of television and film scripts. In 1949 Jones gained a BA from Haverford College, Pennsylvania, where he began to write plays. On graduation he worked at a UN-run Arab refugee camp in Palestine, then spent two years at Oxford University, followed by teaching jobs in the USA. In 1956 he settled in London to become a writer. The first production of one of his plays in his home country was *Inherit this Land*, staged by the LITTLE THEATRE MOVEMENT OF JAMAICA in 1951. In 1962 the Guildford Theatre in Surrey, England, performed *The Spectators*, about tourists in Jamaica; in 1974 GUYANA produced his *In a Backward Country*, about land reform, previously shown on BBC-TV; and in 1970 the Jamaican Theatre Company staged his one-act play, *Go tell it on Table Mountain*. In England Jones is better known for his television and film scripts. *The Widows of Jaffa* (1957), based on his refugee-camp experience, and *The Fight against Slavery* (1976), a drama-documentary series, illustrate his abiding interest in social issues – no doubt acquired from his mother, a Quaker missionary. For director Joseph Losey he wrote four film scripts, of which he considers *King and Country* (1964), on the trial of a war deserter and starring Dirk Bogarde, his best effort. Jones concedes he has become an international writer, but adds: 'Jamaica is my home and ... provides whatever material or inspiration I have ... I've just learned to use that material in an international way.'

jonkonnu

Jamaican Christmas custom, documented since the 18th century, in which costumed characters such as Cow Head, Horse Head, Jack-in-the-Green, Actor Boy, Devil, Policeman and Belly Woman process through the streets accompanied by 'fife and drum music'. The actors, all male, do not remove their masks in public, and, if they speak at all, do so in heavily disguised voices. The custom appears to be a synthesis of European mumming and West African masquerade.

Lee, Easton (1931–)

Jamaican playwright and actor. Lee gave early promise as an actor of merit in productions of the Caribbean Thespians, in the JAMAICA PANTOMIME, and in Kingston's Federal Theatre's 1957 productions of V. S. Naipaul's *B. Wordsworth* and CICELY WAITE-SMITH's *Uncle Robert*. He then wrote *Born for the Sea* (1962), the Easter play *They that Mourn* (1963), and the popular comedy *Tarshan Lace and Velvet* (1969) about courting manners in old Jamaica. He wrote and produced several television plays, such as *Paid in Full* (1965) and *Pretty Medicine* (1966), as well as Christmas plays for children in a Jamaican setting. Lee's major work is *The Rope and the Cross*, written for Easter Day and first presented in Kingston in 1976, then later taken to Trinidad and Canada.

Lee Wah [née Arscott], Mavis (1926–)

Jamaican actress, director and schoolteacher. Arscott had acted in several plays before entering the UNIVERSITY [College] OF THE WEST INDIES (see Introduction) in Jamaica, where during 1951–5 she established herself as the leading undergraduate actress. Among her roles at this time were Knowledge in *Everyman*, Juno in *Juno and the Paycock*, Mrs X in Strindberg's *The Stronger*, Jocasta in *Oedipus Rex* and Amanda in *The Glass Menagerie*. In 1952–4 she was president of the University Dramatic Society.

In Trinidad as Mavis Lee Wah, she appeared for the Drama Guild as Pegeen in *Playboy of the Western World* (1957); in *Bell, Book, and Candle* (1958); in DEREK WALCOTT's (see Eastern Caribbean States) *The Charlatan* (1962), and in the TRINIDAD THEATRE WORKSHOP's (see Trinidad and Tobago) production of this play when it was taken to Jamaica in 1973. For the secondary schools' drama association she played the Nurse in *Romeo and Juliet* (1969) and Lady Macbeth (1974); and she appeared in *A Day in the Death of Joe Egg* (for the alternative National Theatre, 1981); in *Fanlights* by René Marques (1988); again as Amanda in *The Glass Menagerie* (1989); and as the Queen in Shaw's *Dark Lady of the Sonnets* (1990). She is married to JAMES LEE WAH (see Trinidad and Tobago).

Lindo, Archie (1908–89)

Jamaican playwright. As a student at St George's College in Kingston, Lindo acquired a love for elocution and drama; then, as a government officer in the country areas he organized many concerts and recitation contests. A self-educated playwright, he wrote two plays: *Forbidden Fruit* (1942) and *Under the Skin* (1943); and dramatized two novels set in Jamaica: H. G. de Lisser's *The White Witch of Rose Hall* and Mayne Reid's *The Maroon*. His plays were presented at the Ward Theatre and directed by George Bowen. Lindo tried to bridge the gap between the classes by giving dignity to working-class characters. In appealing to audiences from all classes, his plays continued in the pattern set by ERNEST CUPIDON and UNA MARSON.

Little Theatre Movement of Jamaica (LTM)

Started in 1941 by Greta Bourke – remembered for her concept of drama as 'the art where all arts meet' – and Henry Fowler (whom she later married) to raise funds, primarily through theatrical production, for the building of a properly equipped little theatre in Jamaica. Twenty years and forty-five productions later, in 1961 a 615-seat theatre was opened on Tom Redcam Avenue, Kingston. Proceeds from the annual JAMAICA PANTOMIME, developed and produced by the LTM, was a major source of funding for the new theatre. In 1967 the LTM established a school of drama, which was handed over to the government as part of the CULTURAL TRAINING CENTRE in 1975.

Marson, Una (1905–65)

Jamaican black nationalist, feminist, poet and playwright. Having left school early when her parents died, Marson worked at a newspaper office in Kingston, and participated in elocution contests held at Edelweiss Park under MARCUS GARVEY. From 1932 to 1935 she was in England as secretary to the League of Coloured Peoples, for which she wrote, directed and performed in her first play, *At What a Price*, co-authored with Jamaican Horace Vaz. The play, about a country girl who moves to Kingston to seek work and is seduced by her employer, opened in London at the YMCA, then played for three nights at the Scala Theatre. In 1936 Marson returned to Jamaica, founded the Kingston Drama Club, and the following year staged *London Calling*, a comedy of student life in London. In 1938 she presented her most important work, *Pocomania*, revealing the influence of an Afro-religious cult on a young middle-class woman. Returning to England in 1938 she worked on the BBC programme *Calling the West Indies*, which aired the creative work of Caribbean writers.

Murray, Henry G(arland) (fl.1869–76)

Writer and reader of humorous native stories, who probably introduced the tradition into Jamaica. Making frequent use of the Creole language in his enormously popular readings, Murray travelled throughout the island performing to enthusiastic audiences in school halls and other public auditoriums. At his death the tradition was continued by his sons Andrew C. Murray (fl.1879–84) and William Coleman Murray (fl.1887–1900).

National Dance Theatre Company of Jamaica (NDTC)

Formed in 1962 by REX NETTLEFORD from a troupe brought together to mark the attainment of political independence in Jamaica. With dancers initially drawn from the IVY BAXTER Dance Group (1950–63) and others, inspired by the work of BERYL McBURNIE in Trinidad, and with training from Lavinia Williams of Haiti, the NDTC has won acclaim at home and abroad. Narrative forms used by Baxter have influenced its style. With a company of fifty-five, including singers and musicians (all non-stipendiary), and a repertoire of 160 pieces, the group offers two to three seasons of dance a year in Jamaica. It has completed fifty tours overseas, performing in Caribbean countries and in Mexico; at the Kennedy Center in Washington, DC, and the Brooklyn Center in New York; at the O'Keefe Center in Toronto, Canada; at Sadler's Wells Theatre in London; in the USSR, Germany, Australia, China and Japan.

In addition to Nettleford, the company's choreographers include Eddy Thomas, Neville Black, Sheila Barnet, Barbara Requa and Bert Rose. A dance school formed by the company in 1970 was handed over in 1976 to the government to become the Jamaica School of Dance, a part of the CULTURAL TRAINING CENTRE complex.

Nettleford, Rex (1933–)

Jamaican university professor, writer, artistic director, principal choreographer and former lead dancer of the NATIONAL DANCE THEATRE COMPANY OF JAMAICA. Nettleford has choreographed musicals, revues and pantomimes (see JAMAICA PANTOMIME) in Jamaica, and has worked in Britain and on the Broadway musical *Reggae*. A Rhodes Scholar, he teaches at the UNIVERSITY OF THE WEST INDIES (see Introduction), where he is also director of the School of Continuing Studies and of the Trade Union Institute. He has written penetratingly about Caribbean art and culture, and is editor of *Caribbean Quarterly*. He has been a consultant for several international agencies and in Jamaica has been awarded the Order of Merit and the Musgrave Gold Medal.

Ogilvie, W(illiam) G(eorge) (c.1923–92)
Novelist, playwright and teacher. Born in Panama of Jamaican parents, Ogilvie was educated in Jamaica, finishing at the Mico Teachers' Training College. He taught at country schools and at high schools in Kingston. His plays, several of which won awards at drama festivals, include *One Sojer Man* (1945), a comedy directed by Elsie Benjamin; *Legacy* (1959), produced by the Caribbean Thespians; *Jezebel*, winner of the 1955 tercentary award, directed by RONALD HARRISON in 1966; and *The Sudden Guest*, a farce produced as *Star Boarder* (1962) by LLOYD RECKORD. Ogilvie wrote several unproduced plays and two novels, *Cactus Village* and *The Ghost Bank*, both published in Kingston in 1953.

Reckord, Barry (1926–)
Jamaican playwright, director, actor and teacher. Reckord attended Kingston College in Jamaica, from which he won a scholarship in 1950 to Emmanuel College, Cambridge University, where he read English. His first play *Della* (1954), set in the urban underclass area of Trench Town in Kingston, pits the feared Shepherd Aaron against the white doctor for the heroine Della's allegiance. It was first directed in London by his brother LLOYD RECKORD, then staged in Jamaica in 1954 and 1958; under its new title *Flesh to a Tiger* it was presented at the Royal Court Theatre, London, in 1958.

Later plays also deal with issues of class, colour and sex; most have been presented both in Jamaica and in London (where Reckord once taught), and his brother Lloyd has been associated with productions as director and/or actor. The farcical *Miss Unusual* (Kingston, 1956) ridiculed class barriers among Jamaicans, while *You in Your Small Corner* (London, 1960; Jamaica, 1962) treated both colour and class impediments. Reckord's only non-Jamaican play, *Skyvers*, directed by Ann Jellicoe (London,

1963), concerns the problems of teaching in an English comprehensive school.

Of his other plays, *A Liberated Woman* (Jamaica, 1970; London 1971) and *In the Beautiful Caribbean* (BBC-TV and Jamaica, 1972) excited vigorous comment. The first deals with the question of racially mixed marriage and the second depicts a far different Caribbean from that portrayed on tourist brochures. In 1988 the 'adult comedy' *Sugar D* was presented in Kingston under Lloyd Reckord's direction. Barry Reckord's plays have often been dismissed as thesis-driven and melodramatic, but their message is often disquieting.

Reckord, Lloyd (1929–)
Jamaican actor, director and producer. Reckord was involved in amateur theatricals in Jamaica before he left for England in 1951 to study at the Bristol Old Vic Theatre School. After Bristol, he obtained small parts with the Old Vic Theatre Company in London and at the Edinburgh Festival, where he was directed by Tyrone Guthrie. He also appeared in Philip Yordan's *Anna Lucasta* and in the Rodgers and Hammerstein musical *South Pacific*.

In 1954 he directed an early version of his brother BARRY RECKORD's play *Della* in London. This combination would prove fruitful: Lloyd was to direct and/or act in some dozen productions of Barry's plays. In 1954 Reckord was awarded a Smith-Mundt fellowship to study theatre training at the Yale School of Drama, Howard University and the American Theatre Wing. Back in Jamaica in 1956, he started the Actors' Company, for which he directed and acted in foreign and original Caribbean plays, among these Barry Reckord's *Miss Unusual* (1956) and CECILY WAITE-SMITH's *Uncle Robert* (1957). He appeared in his brother's *Flesh to a Tiger* (1958) at the Royal Court Theatre, London, where in 1960 he directed two short plays by DEREK WALCOTT (see Eastern Caribbean States) and Barry Reckord's *You in Your Small Corner*.

Reckord's major contribution to Jamaican

theatre began in 1968 when he established the National Theatre Trust, supported by Kingston merchants, to provide 'a first-class company of actors performing a large and varied repertory of outstanding West Indian plays, the classics, and some of the best of contemporary world drama'. In the first two decades he produced some forty such plays, and established a children's theatre and theatre for schools that toured the island with plays featured in the GCE examinations. His one-man show *Beyond the Blues* – a collection of black writing from Africa, the Caribbean and the USA – travelled to the eastern USA, the Caribbean and Britain, culminating in 1982 with performances at the National Theatre's Cottesloe Theatre in London. He has made two television feature films: *Bodymoves*, and an adaptation of DOUGLAS ARCHIBALD's (see Trinidad and Tobago) glorious comedy *Junction Village*. He has also recently made some video dramas.

Rhone, Trevor (1940–)

Jamaican playwright, screenwriter, director, producer and actor. Rhone acted in the schools drama festival and the JAMAICA PANTOMIME before entering the Rose Bruford College in Kent, England, in 1960 to study theatre. After graduation he returned to Jamaica, taught, and wrote plays and two pantomimes for school production. In 1969 he produced his first major play, *The Gadget.* He founded with YVONNE BREWSTER a production company known as Theatre 77, converting Brewster's garage into a small theatre seating 150. Named the Barn Theatre, this modest playhouse became the model for several others around Kingston.

Rhone's next major play, presented at the Barn Theatre, was *Smile Orange*, a satire on attitudes towards the tourist trade. It ran for 245 performances, thus for the first time establishing indigenous drama as a professional enterprise in Jamaica. He repeated this success with three other plays: *School's Out* (1975), a comedy

Robert McKewley and Eamonn Walker in Trevor Rhone's *Smile Orange*, Talawa Theatre Company, 1992.

of teachers' squabbles in the commonroom; *Old Story Time* (1979), a nostalgic picture of a single mother's struggle for her son's welfare; and *Two Can Play* (1982), on a couple's search for love, compassion and understanding. These plays and others have been staged in other Caribbean islands, and in Miami, Toronto and London.

Rhone co-scripted with Perry Henzell *The Harder They Come* (1972), a full-length feature film on Jamaica. He directed the film of *Smile Orange* in 1976, and *Two Can Play* was produced for television in Kentucky. In 1984 he was awarded the Order of Distinction by the government of Jamaica.

Scott, Dennis (1939–91)

Jamaican poet, playwright, director, actor, dancer and teacher. Scott received a BA in English at the UNIVERSITY OF THE WEST INDIES (see Introduction) in 1970, and a drama-in-education diploma at the University of Newcastle-on-Tyne, England, in 1973. He returned to teach at Jamaica College for four years before becoming director of the Jamaica School of Drama (see CULTURAL TRAINING CENTRE) in 1977, teaching and working in most of the anglophone Caribbean. From 1983 he taught playwriting at the Yale School of Drama, Connecticut, where he was appointed co-chairman of the directing programme. For the Yale Repertory Theatre he directed several plays, including *Othello*, *Miss Julie*, and the US première of the Australian Louis Nowra's play, *The Golden Age*. He did summer work with the National Theatre of the Deaf; with the National Theatre Institute, training young actors and directors; and with the National Playwrights Conference of the Eugene O'Neill Theatre Center in Waterford, Connecticut.

Scott was a member of the NATIONAL DANCE THEATRE COMPANY OF JAMAICA. He wrote some ten plays, and received awards at the Jamaica festival literary competitions in 1966 and 1969. His mature plays are *Echo in the Bone* (1974), which has been produced throughout the Caribbean and represented Jamaica at the Black Arts Festival in Lagos in 1976; and *Dog* (1976), the Jamaican entry at the CARIFESTA (see Introduction) in BARBADOS in 1981. (In the first

Gary McDonald, Leo Wringer, Faith Tingle and Mona Hammond in Dennis Scott's *Echo in the Bone*, Talawa Theatre Company, 1986.

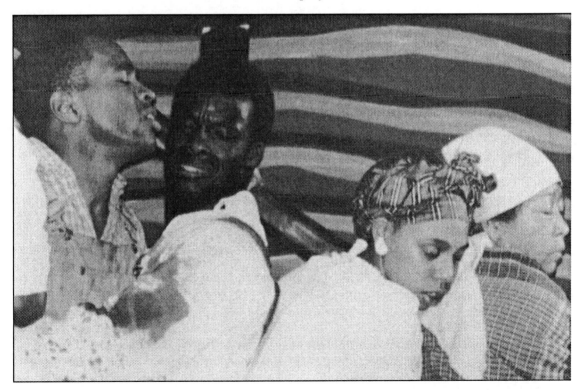

play the murder of a planter by the peasant farmer is explained by a ritualistic return to historical circumstances; in the second, the privileged are humans and the underprivileged are wild dogs.) Scott acted at the Spoleto Festival in Charleston, South Carolina, and at the American Music Theatre Festival in Philadelphia. At the time of his death he was appearing in the highly rated American television series, *The Cosby Show*. His poems have been published in collections in the United States and Britain, and in anthologies in several other countries.

Sistren

Jamaican theatre collective based in Kingston for working-class women. Sistren first performed for the annual Workers' Week celebrations in 1977, choosing its players from employees of a 'make-work' programme for unemployed women. The company soon became professional, and over the years has presented major productions on such issues as women's work, poverty, teenage pregnancy, rape, and the role of women in Caribbean history. Productions derive from public workshops which use drama as a problem-solving device, from research, and from the experience of Sistren members. Plays are built on improvisations that evolve into full-length presentations: *Bellywoman Bangarang* (1978), which won a Jamaica Festival Commission gold medal deals with women's rites of passage; *Nana Yah* (1980) portrays the life of the Maroon warrior Nanny, a national heroine; *'QPH'* (1981) commemorates the women who perished in a fire at the Kingston Alms House; *Domestick* (1982) deals with the abuse of domestic servants; and *Sweet Sugar Rage* (1985) is a documentary film on women's work in the sugar industry.

Sistren has taken its productions to rural Jamaica and to other Caribbean countries. In 1983 it appeared at the London International Festival of Theatre, then performed in the English midlands and in Holland. It is part of a project involving women's organizations worldwide; its principal director is Honor Ford-Smith.

Tavares, Morton [Aaron] (1823–1900)

International Jamaican actor. Tavares performed first on the Kingston stage, then, in a career that spanned half a century, he was to perform in North America, London, Australia, New Zealand and southern Africa. His highest achievement was his appearance at the Theatre Royal, Sadler's Wells, London, in 1869 as Richelieu, Shylock and Iago. His several attempts to establish a viable theatre company in Jamaica were unsuccessful, and he died in poverty near to his beloved Theatre Royal in Kingston.

Vaz, Noel (1920–)

Jamaican director and drama teacher. On the strength of productions he directed for the LITTLE THEATRE MOVEMENT OF JAMAICA (LTM) such as *A Midsummer Night's Dream* (1944), *Arsenic and Old Lace* and A. J. Cronin's *Jupiter Laughs* (1945), as well as two pantomimes (see JAMAICA PANTOMIME), Vaz won a scholarship in 1946 to the Royal Academy of Dramatic Art in London. He chose instead to study at the Old Vic Theatre School under Michel St Denis, in order to observe and assist the director Tyrone Guthrie. He returned to Jamaica and the LTM in 1948, where, with LOUISE BENNETT, he staged the original pantomime *Bluebeard and Brer Anancy* and directed Shaw's *St Joan*. Finding conditions there stifling, he returned to London until 1956, when he joined the UNIVERSITY OF THE WEST INDIES (UWI, see Introduction) as second extramural tutor in drama.

Posted in Trinidad at the time of the imminent West Indies Federation, Vaz directed for the occasion the epic drama *Drums and Colours* by DEREK WALCOTT (see Eastern Caribbean States). In the absence of ERROL HILL (see Trinidad and Tobago), on study leave from

1958 to 1962, he became sole drama tutor for the region, organizing vacation drama schools and supporting the drama society on campus. He began the 'Shakespeare in schools' project, 'to bring to life plays set for examinations', and in the next few years *The Merchant of Venice*, *A Midsummer Night's Dream*, *Macbeth* and *King Lear* were produced and attended by thousands of schoolchildren. With the opening of the Creative Arts Centre on the UWI Jamaican campus in 1968, Vaz taught newly introduced courses in 20th-century theatre techniques. He retired from the university in 1986.

Waite-Smith, Cicely (1910–78)
Playwright. Canadian by birth, Jamaican by marriage, Waite-Smith identified herself with the national movement through her involvement in theatre. She trained in England, and in Paris with Jean-Louis Barrault and Charles Dullin. In Jamaica she devised the improvisational workshop that produced the play *Sleepy Valley* (1952), and wrote plays that contributed to the development of an indigenous theatre. Chief among these were the popular one-acter *Africa Slingshot* (1957), dealing with superstition among village folk, and two middle-class dramas (1958) that were staged at the Ward Theatre in Kingston: *Uncle Robert*, directed by LLOYD RECKORD who also played the title role, and *The Ravishers*, directed by ERROL HILL (see Trinidad and Tobago), also taking the leading role. Waite-Smith was one of the few playwrights of the period to write sensitive dramas of middle-class life. She left Jamaica for England in 1960, and published her autobiography *The Long Run* in 1967.

Williams, Ranny [Randolph] (1912–80)
Jamaican comedian and playwright. Williams first worked at the CHRISTMAS MORNING CONCERTS and then at Edelweiss Park, where he became entertainment manager for MARCUS GARVEY's productions. Here he wrote biblical and musical plays such as *She is a Sheba, Medes and Persians* and *Blacks Gone Wild*. He then toured the island for two years, performing with the 'Chief Little Bear' medicine show. With Lee Gordon as Andy he starred in Amos 'n Andy skits, then discarded 'black face' to become the Ranny and Lee comic duo. Williams was the staple Anancy character in the annual JAMAICA PANTOMIME, in which, teamed mostly with LOUISE BENNETT, he appeared for over thirty-five years. He also partnered her in the long-running radio show *Lou and Ranny*. He featured in several other popular radio shows and wrote two pantomime scripts: *Quashee Lady* (1958) and *Jamaica Way* (1959).

Wynter, Sylvia (1928–)
Playwright, essayist and teacher. Born in Cuba of Jamaican parents, Wynter was taken to Jamaica at age two and educated at St Andrew's High School, from which she won a scholarship to King's College, London University. She gained a BA in Spanish in 1949 and an MA in 1953.

From 1954 to 1958, while in Europe, she became involved in theatre as an actress and dancer. She appeared on the BBC *Caribbean Voices* programme as reader and commentator, and for BBC-TV she did a free translation of Lorca's play *Yerma*, setting it in Jamaica and using Jamaican Creole. In 1958 her full-length play *Under the Sun* was bought by the Royal Court Theatre, London, and a radio version was broadcast in Britain, the USA, Denmark, Canada and Jamaica. The play also gave rise to her novel *The Hills of Hebron* (1962).

In 1962 Wynter returned to Jamaica with her husband, the Guyanese novelist Jan Carew, hoping to start a professional, indigenous, theatre company. In the ensuing years she wrote and produced *Miracle in Lime Lane* (with Jan Carew, 1962) for the Spanish Town Folk Theatre; the musical *Sh-h-h ... It's a Wedding* (1963); *1865 Ballad for a Rebellion* (1965), on the Morant Bay uprising in Jamaica, directed by

LLOYD RECKORD; the pantomime (see JAMAICA PANTOMIME) *Rockstone Anancy* (with Alex Gradussov, 1970)); and *Maskarade* (1973; revised and expanded 1979). Among her important writing are reflections on West Indian writing and criticism and on Afro-Jamaicanism, published in *Jamaica Journal* and *Caribbean Quarterly*.

Bibliography

I. Baxter, *The Arts of an Island*, Metuchen, NJ, 1970; K. Corsbie, *Theatre in the Caribbean*, London, 1984; E. Hill, *The Jamaican Stage, 1655–1900: Profile of a Colonial Theatre*, Amherst, Mass., 1992; R. Nettleford, *Mirror Mirror: Identity, Race and Protest in Jamaica*, Jamaica, 1970, *Caribbean Cultural Identity*, California, 1978, and *Dance Jamaica*, New York, 1985; J. W. Nunley and J. Bettelheim, *Caribbean Festival Arts: Each and Every Bit of Difference*, Seattle, Wash., 1988; K. Omotoso, *The Theatrical into Theatre*, London, 1982; R. Wright, *Revels in Jamaica*, rev. edn, Jamaica, 1986.

PUERTO RICO

Until the 19th century there was only sporadic theatre activity on this eastern island in the Antilles chain. From the time of the Spanish Conquest, the rivalries among the Spanish, French, English and Dutch for possession of the Caribbean islands had resulted in raids and skirmishes that left little time for cultural development or entertainment. Through the 18th century the few existing records show the performance of an occasional Golden Age or religious play, to mark a special event. Although some 130 plays during the 19th century have been documented, only a few are of transcendental value. For the most part, the century remained dominated by foreign imports.

Spanish, Italian, Mexican and Argentine travelling companies staged operas, operettas, zarzuelas (see Dominican Republic, GÉNERO CHICO) and plays from the classic Spanish repertory or the romantic pieces of José Zorrilla, for example. The principal themes of the emerging Puerto Rican theatre ranged from fanciful, escapist works following the romantic model to regionally oriented works with historical or sociopolitical overtones. The acknowledged founder of the Puerto Rican theatre, ALEJANDRO TAPIA Y RIVERA, stepped into the romantic traditions and techniques popular during his time with several historical plays including *Robert D'Evreux* (1856) and *Camoens* (1868). He showed his concern for racial issues and women's roles in *La cuarterona* (*The Quadroon*, 1867) and *La parte del león* (*The Lion's Share*, 1878), respectively. SALVADOR BRAU continued in the traditions of Alejandro Tapia with two romantic plays set in Europe that dealt with concepts of liberty from oppression. His best work is *La vuelta al hogar* (1877), in

which the pirate motif allows him to juggle classic romantic themes. A final play is more realistic and deals with a dominant social problem of the time. Carmen Hernández de Araújo (1821–77) was the island's first woman playwright, and Eugenio Astol (1843–1904) was Puerto Rico's outstanding actor of the romantic period. In the final decade of the century, costumbristic theatre also gained importance through plays such as *El jíbaro* (*The Farmer*, 1878) by Ramón Méndez Quiñones (1847–89).

Before the first theatre houses were built, it was customary for provincial sites to present plays in the model of the Spanish *corral* (an open-air patio). In 1823 the Teatro de Amigos del País (Friends of National Theatre) staged several productions, and in 1834 the first theatre opened in Puerto Rico, not with a play but with opera – an indication of the importance of music in the local culture. (The municipal theatre was remodelled and named the Tapia Theatre in 1950, in honour of Tapia y Rivera, and restored in the 1970s to its colonial grandeur.) Throughout the 19th century the strong hand of the Church, with its active censorship programme, discouraged free expression, but it was not able to suppress the construction of new theatres in San Juan, Ponce, Mayagüez, Arecibo and other towns scattered across the island.

After the War of 1898, Spain ceded control of Puerto Rico to the USA. Until the Commonwealth was created in 1952, Puerto Rico was ruled by a series of American-imposed governors. The changes resulting from this new political status did little to promote theatre on the island, although *El grito de Lares* (*The Cry of Lares*, 1914) by Luis Lloréns Torres (1878–1944) signalled the first of a long series of plays that examined and protested against American intervention. The stimulus for new theatre came in 1938 when EMILIO BELAVAL, as president of the Ateneo Puertorriqueño (Puerto Rican Atheneum), called for the creation of a national dramaturgy. The three plays honoured in the contest sponsored by the Ateneo were by Manuel Méndez Ballester (b.1909), author of *El clamor de los surcos* (*Cry of the Land*); Gonzalo Arocho del Toro (1898–1954), with *El desmonte* (*The Clearing*); and Fernando Sierra Berdecía (1903–62), whose *Esta noche juega el jóker* (*Tonight the Joker Plays*) opened up the painful issue of the Puerto Rican immigrant in New York.

Belaval's theatre group, Areyto, created in 1939, lasted only two seasons, but it succeeded in establishing the basis for other groups and for a new sense of identity in the Puerto Rican theatre. FRANCISCO ARRIVÍ's Tinglado Puertorriqueño (Puerto Rican Stage, 1945) captured the same spirit and was followed by RENÉ MARQUÉS' Teatro Nuestro (Our Theatre, 1950) and the Ateneo's Experimental Theatre (1951), both with the collaboration of José Lacomba (b.1924). The Puerto Rican Cultural Institute, established in 1955, sponsored its first Puerto Rican theatre festival in 1958, an unparalleled opportunity for encouraging new playwrights and fostering theatre in the country. The University of Puerto Rico, unable to present Puerto Rican plays from 1944 until 1956 (from Enrique Laguerre's *La resentida* (*The Sufferer* – about a woman whose family situation in the end-of-century political struggles causes her much anguish and who finally shoots her son) to Arriví's *El murciélago* (*The Bat*) and *Medusa en la bahía* (*Medusa in the Bay*) because of the tense political situation before and immediately after the adoption of commonwealth status, contributed to the training of new directors, actors, designers and technical crew during this period.

Arriví, Belaval, and especially Marqués, set the standards for the new theatre, with plays that ranged from the existentialist/absurdist to social and psychological realist. Their works dealt with life and death, with philosophical and political issues. Arriví's were often lyrical and metaphysical, such as *María Soledad* (*María Solitude*, 1947), but he also dealt with major social issues such as racism, both implicit and explicit in his *Vejigantes* (*Masks*, 1958). Belaval's *La muerte* (*Death*, 1953) played with the nobility of the human spirit in a life-threatening situation, contrasted with its pettiness when the danger passes. Marqués experimented with social commitment, absurdism and biblical motifs, all within vanguard techniques incorporating light and sound. A prolific playwright, he broke new ground with *La carreta* (*The Oxcart*, 1952), which captured the destruction, despair and eventual disintegration of the Puerto Rican family unit brought about by difficult economic conditions. The common denominator running through most of Marqués' plays is his opposition to American encroachment on Hispanic values.

In common with other later writers, MYRNA CASAS picked up both Arriví's lyrical patterns and the historical realism of Belaval with her play *Eugenia Victoria Herrera* (1964), which interprets the national consciousness. Piri Fernández de Lewis (b.1925), working for the Institute of Puerto Rican Culture, wrote and staged plays such as *De tanto caminar* (*So Much Walking*, 1960), depicting with double planes of action the religious doubts of a nun. Her *El grito en el tiempo* (*The Cry across Time*, 1968) celebrated with a 'total theatre' performance the centennial of the famous episode at Lares when Puerto Rico attempted to gain its independence from Spain. In *En el principio la noche era serena* (*In the Beginning the Night was Calm*, 1960) Gerard Paul Marín experimented with a dramatization of suicide in two acts with the same sequence of events but from two different points of view, the subconscious and the social. Of special interest because of his versatility in both narrative and theatre and his mastery of the language is LUIS RAFAEL SÁNCHEZ. Of his nine plays, two deserve particular attention: *La pasión según Antígona Pérez* (*The Passion according to Antígona Pérez*, 1968) for its Brechtian manipulation of classical myth and Latin-American political reality; and *Quíntuples* (*Quintuplets*, 1984), for its illustration of the degenerate condition of Puerto Rican society, using a fine blend of fantasy and reality.

Between 1966 and 1985 collective theatre achieved new levels of popularity and influence, in such groups as El Tajo del Alacrán (the Scorpion's Sting, 1966), headed by Lydia Milagros González (b.1942); Teatro de Guerrilla (Guerrilla Theatre, 1969); Moriviví (1972); Anamú (1973), and many others – all with the function of bringing to the public consciousness a theatre of political protest (not only anti-USA, but also against political conditions on the island). Pedro Santiliz (b.1938) has arranged works especially for street theatre. A host of independent theatre groups were formed in the 1960s and 70s, some of them short-lived, such as El Cemí, Teatro Yukayeke, Teatro la Máscara, Cimarrón, Proscenio and Nuestro Teatro. Travelling groups such as Teatro Rodante and Farándula Universitaria generate across the island interest in the theatre. Ironically, the oldest existing theatre group is still the English-speaking Little Theatre, created in 1931.

Several efforts in the vein of a popularized, experimental theatre have achieved notable success. Teatro del 60 (Sixties Theatre) hit its peak in the 70s and 80s with *Puerto Rico fuá* (*Puerto Rico Poof*) and *La verdadera historia de Pedro Navaja* (*The True Story of Peter the Knife*). The first (by Carlos Ferrari) is a musical review that chronicles the history of Puerto Rico in charmingly satirical tones; the second (by Pablo Cabrera) takes a *Threepenny Opera* approach to a Puerto Rican band of delinquents in 1952, a significant year because of the adoption of commonwealth status. Both established records for the longest runs in Puerto Rican theatre history – twelve and eighteen months respectively. In dance and pantomime theatre Gilda Navarra excels through her directorship of the Taller

de Histriones (Actors' Workshop), which mounted several productions during its existence (1971–85), notably *Ocho mujeres* (*Eight Women*, 1974), which brought a uniquely Puerto Rican flavour to a production that derived from Lorca's *La casa de Bernarda Alba* (*The House of Bernarda Alba*).

Younger writers include José 'Papo' Márquez (b.1950) and Abneil Morales (b.1958), who have struggled against bourgeois influences in the theatre. The best of this generation may be ROBERTO RAMOS-PEREA, whose plays are brutal and closely tied to a contemporary Puerto Rican reality. In addition to creating the National Society of Dramatists and the National Puerto Rican Archive, which publishes the journal *InterMedio de Puerto Rico*, he has written various plays of strong social and political protest, including *Los 200 no* (*The 200 Noes*, 1983) and *Golpes de Rejas* (*Blows on the Bars*, 1988), a vitriolic piece of documentary and collective theatre.

The Puerto Rican theatre in New York is a vital force which owes much of its success to the creative energies of MIRIAM COLÓN. Her Puerto Rican Travelling Theatre has not only supported the Puerto Rican infrastructure but has also played the best of the Spanish-American theatre canon. Jaime Carrero (b.1931) deserves recognition because he is equally adept at writing plays for the island and for a New York public. Among his many successes are *Flag Inside* (1966), an early enactment of Vietnam issues, and *Pipo Subway no sabe reír* (*Pipo Subway Does Not Know How to Laugh*, 1971). Another major writer of this milieu was Miguel Piñero (1958–88), whose *Short Eyes*, a picture of the violence and brutality inside prison, won the New York Drama Critics' Circle Award for best American play of the 1973–4 season. A later play, *The Sun Always Shines for the Cool* (1977), captured all the violence and raw energy of colourful street characters in a New York *barrio*.

Theatre festivals – as many as fifteen a year – have contributed immeasurably to the development of Puetro Rican theatre. In addition to the festival sponsored by the Puerto Rican Cultural Institute, launched in 1958, other events have raised the level of theatre-consciousness: the International Theatre Festival of San Juan has staged the best foreign plays; in the 1970s the Muestras (Showcases), sponsored by the Spanish-born Luis Molina, promoted a consciousness of Third World theatre and provoked a political storm, testing allegiances among theatre groups vying for funding.

The two cultures on the island – Anglo and Hispanic – remain unreconciled. In spite of programmes like Operation Bootstrap, designed to encourage the Puerto Rican economy, over the years New York has lured millions of Puerto Ricans to the mainland. Needless to say, many have returned home disillusioned. Political preferences in Puerto Rico range from independence to statehood (as the fifty-first state of the USA), with the present Commonwealth status in the middle. The spectre of annexation by the USA provides the incentive for groups such as the Comité de Defensa de la Cultura Puertorriqueña (Puerto Rican Cultural Defence League) to use theatre as a weapon in defence of Hispanic identity.

Arriví, Francisco (1915–)

Puerto Rican dramatist, director, critic and essayist; a major figure in Puerto Rican theatre. Arriví studied pedagogy in Puerto Rico, radio and theatre at Columbia University. His early plays *Club de solteros* (*Bachelors' Club*, 1940) and *El diablo se humaniza* (*Humanizing the Devil*, 1941) are fantastic and farcical. *María Soledad* (*María Solitude*, 1947) is a Jasperian search for absolute purity. The trilogy *Máscara puertorriqueña* (*Puerto Rican Mask*, 1956–9) deals with the complex racial and cultural heritage of the Puerto Ricans. Other major plays include *Cóctel de Don Nadie* (*Mr Nobody's Cocktail*, 1964) and the musical *Solteros 72* (*Bachelors 72*). Arriví founded the theatre group Tinglado Puertorriqueño (Puerto Rican Stage) in 1945, and was for many years

director of the theatre wing of the Puerto Rican Cultural Institute, which sponsors the annual theatre festival.

Belaval, Emilio (S.) (1903–72)

Puerto Rican essayist, playwright, director and producer. He studied law at the University of Puerto Rico, and later became president of the Ateno Puertorriqueño (Puerto Rican Atheneum) and a member of the Supreme Court. In 1939 he created Areyto, a popular but short-lived theatre group. Belaval was a major contributor to the development of modern Puerto Rican theatre through his scholarship, his work in promoting theatre, and his plays: *La presa de los vencedores* (*The Victors' Prey*, 1939), *Hay que decir la verdad* (*The Truth Must be Told*, 1940), *La muerte* (*Death*, 1950), *La vida* (*Life*, 1958) and *Cielo caído* (*Fallen Sky*, 1960).

Brau, Sálvador (1842–1912)

Prolific Puerto Rican writer of poetry, novels, essays, stories and dramas. Follower of the romantic models of TAPIA Y RIVERA, Brau dominated in the 1870s and 80s with four principal works. *Héroe y mártir* (1871) presents a sincere but unfocused interpretation of a democratic revolt of the peasants against Charles V in 16th-century Spain; *De los horrores del triunfo* (1874) is another revolutionary play set in 13th-century Sicily. His major work is *La vuelta al hogar* (1877), a tale of pirates in Puerto Rica that resonates with themes from Zorrilla and Espronceda and reflects major romantic themes of disillusion, instinctive choices and redeeming love. His final play, *De la superficie al fondo* (1887), is more realistic, with a focus on the social vice of gambling.

Casas, Myrna (1934–)

Puerto Rican playwright and director. With a doctorate from New York University, Casas is professor of theatre at the University of Puerto

Rico, where she teaches and conducts scholarly research in addition to staging and writing plays. Major works include *Cristal roto en el tiempo* (*Window Broken in Time*, 1960), *Absurdos en soledad* (*Absurds in Solitude*, 1964) and *Eugenia Victoria Herrera* (1964), the latter a strong defence of Puerto Rican territory against foreign intervention or occupation.

Colón, Miriam (1945–)

Director of The Puerto Rican Travelling Theatre (Teatro rodante puertorriqueño), which she founded in 1967. Colón got her start as an actress in Roberto Rodríguez's successful 1954 production of *La carreta* (*The Oxcart*) by RENÉ MARQUÉS, which led the two of them to establish the first Hispanic theatre group in New York, El Círculo Dramático (Drama Circle, 1956). Her company, now firmly established in its own theatre on 8th Avenue, maintains an ambitious bilingual production schedule of Latin American and US Hispanic plays and, during the summer months, takes theatre to marginalized neighbourhoods in the greater New York area. A major objective has been the preparation of theatre professionals and the promotion of new playwrights such as Jaime Carrero and Eduardo Gallardo.

Marqués, René (1919–79)

Puerto Rican director, playwright, short story writer and novelist. Born in Arecibo, he studied agronomy, a career he abandoned after studying literature in Madrid. On his return to Puerto Rico, he founded a little theatre group in Arecibo. A Rockefeller Foundation grant in 1949 allowed him to study at Columbia University and in Piscator's Dramatic Workshop; with a Guggenheim award in 1957, he wrote a novel. In 1951 he helped establish the Teatro Experimental del Ateneo in San Juan, and directed the group for three years. Devoted to maintaining the Hispanic traditions of Puerto Rico, he actively opposed the US

economic and cultural invasion of the island, and favoured independence instead of the Commonwealth status. His plays reflect great experimentation, ranging from the realism/naturalism of *La carreta* (*The Cart*, 1952) to the absurdist vein of *El apartamiento* (*The Apartment/Alienation*, 1964) to a biblical trilogy including *Sacrificio en el Monte Moriah* (*Sacrifice on Mount Moriah*, 1970). His best are *Los soles truncos* (*The Fanlights*, 1958) – still the classic Puerto Rican play because it so effectively combines techniques of poetic staging with the theme of psychological, cultural and political distress – and *Un niño azul para esa sombra* (*A Blue Child for that Shadow*, 1970). Both are complex psychological works on Puerto Rican identity problems.

Ramos-Perea, Roberto (1956–)

Puerto Rican playwright, essayist, short story writer, actor and director. Born in Mayagüez, Ramos-Perea began his career with short plays in the University Theatre of Mayagüez, and later studied theatre in Mexico City. He has directed and acted in several Puerto Rican theatre groups. In addition to *Los 200 no* (*The 200 Noes*, 1983), a violent encounter between a university student and a professor, and *Ese punto de vista* (*That Point of View*, 1984), his work includes a major historical trilogy: *Revolución en el infierno* (*Revolution in Hell*), based on the Ponce massacre of 1937; *Módulo 104, Revolución en el purgatorio* (*Module 104, Revolution in Purgatory*), based on the Puerto Rican penal system during 1980–2; and *Cueva de ladrones, Revolución en el paraíso* (*Thieves' Cave, Revolution in Paradise*), based on the student activist movement.

Sánchez, Luis Rafael (1936–)

Puerto Rican playwright, novelist and university professor. Sánchez' work reveals the influences of Ionesco and of his compatriot RENÉ MARQUÉS. His *Sol 13, Interior* (*Sol 13, Inside*, 1961) consists of a duo – what he calls a *suite de obras* – *La hiel nuestra de cada día* (*Our Daily Gall*) and *Los ángeles se han fatigado* (*The Angels are Tired*), plays thematically linked in contemporary lower-class Puerto Rican settings to classical motifs. *O casi el alma* (*Or Almost the Soul*, 1964) posits Christ and Mary Magdalene in a theological discussion about Puerto Rico. *La pasión según Antígona Pérez* (*The Passion according to Antígona Pérez*, 1968) is an 'American chronicle' of Latin-American revolution using Brechtian techniques and the Antigone dilemma. *Quíntuples* (*Quintuplets*, 1984) consists of six insightful monologues by the Morrison quintuplets and their father, who provide a picturesque and disturbing view of contemporary Puerto Rico, with fantasies of a great circus adventure overlying a Pirandellian play between fantasy and reality.

Tapia y Rivera, Alejandro (1826–82)

Considered the father of the modern Puerto Rican theatre. Tapia left a powerful legacy that is honoured today through the principal theatre of old San Juan that bears his name. Imbued with romanticism, he wrote historical plays with many of the excesses typical of this period. *Robert d'Evreux* (1856), the first of his six plays, was an unnecessarily complex and often unverisimilitudinous interpretation of the English royal family in the early 17th century. *Camoens* (1868) is far superior for its characterization of Portugal's epic poet, author of the *Lusíadas*; *Vasco Núñez de Balboa* (1872) dramatizes an episode in the colonization of America. *La parte del león* (1878) anticipated later concerns about women's role in society. His *La cuarterona* (*The Quadroon*, 1867) was one of the earliest efforts to deal with racial issues concerning land.

Bibliography

F. Arriví, *Areyto Mayor*, San Juan, 1966; J. A. Collins, *Contemporary Theater in Puerto Rico*, San Juan, 1979, and *Contemporary Theater in Puerto Rico: The Decade of the Seventies*, Río Piedras, 1982; A. Garcia de Toro, *Mujer y patria en la dramaturgia puertorriqueña*, Río Piedras, 1987; N. González, *Bibliografía de teatro puertorriqueño (siglos 19 y 20)*, Río Piedras, 1979; A. Morfi, *Historia crítica de un siglo de teatro puertorriqueño*, San Juan, 1980; E. J. Pasarell, *Orígenes y desarrollo de la afición teatral en Puerto Rico*, Santurce, 1969; J. B. Phillips, *Contemporary Puerto Rican Drama*, New York, 1972; E. H. Quiles Ferrer, '1960–1987: La voluntad de existir, in *Escenarios de dos mundos: Inventario teatral de Iberoamérica*, vol 4, Madrid, 1988.

TRINIDAD AND TOBAGO

The sister islands of Trinidad and Tobago were placed by the British under a single administration in 1889. Before that date, their histories were markedly different. Trinidad, most southerly of the Caribbean rim, was seized by Columbus from the Arawak Indians on his third voyage in 1498, and for three hundred years the island remained a Spanish possession. It was largely underdeveloped until 1783, when French planters from the northern islands were given land grants to settle on Trinidad with their slaves. In 1797 British forces took the island, which remained a British colony until 1962.

Tobago changed hands repeatedly between the Dutch, French and English in the 18th-century wars, finally becoming British in 1763. After the abolition of slaves, Trinidad sought to acquire an indentured labour force to replace the Africans who had left the estates. The country brought in Portuguese, Chinese and East Indians; this last group now represents 40 per cent of the population. Tobago remained predominantly African. It was first governed from BARBADOS, then from Trinidad, just eighteen miles away. When the islands were united, Tobago's population was roughly 18,000, while Trinidad, with 200,000 became senior partner of the union. In 1962 they became independent of Great Britain and in 1976 they were declared the Republic of Trinidad and Tobago.

The most important national festival – encompassing original music, singing, masking, street parades, orchestral drumming and various forms of enactment – is the TRINIDAD CARNIVAL, an annual parade that has been in existence for some two hundred years. The Indian community also has a major street festival called 'Hosay', which commemorates the Muslim battle of Karbala and the deaths of the brothers Hasan and Husein. While Tobago participates in this carnival, it has its own equivalent called 'Speech Mas' or 'Speech Band'. These festivals, important as they are, do not overshadow achievements in the regular theatre.

Between 1826 and 1831 Port of Spain, capital city of Trinidad, contained five theatres (or halls converted into theatres), three amateur theatre companies (two English and one French), one professional English touring group and one professional French lyric company. The amateurs played once a month, the professionals twice or three times a week. Most important at this time was the emergence of a resident playwright, E. L. Joseph, a Scotsman who had made Trinidad his home. He wrote and produced a series of local plays that were performed by the Brunswick Amateurs. Among these were *Martial Law in Trinidad* (1832), a musical satire on the militia; *Past and Present*, a farce on social climbers; and several dramatic sketches. Joseph's work is notable for its objective portrayal of both the Creole and the African, and its attempt to capture the different local dialects. He also translated German plays for local production and wrote a *History of Trinidad* (1838).

A period of decline followed, doubtless the result of uncertainty in the years after emancipation. The theatrical drought was relieved periodically by visiting troupers from North America, such as J. W. Lanergan's company in 1858 and E. A. McDowell's in 1886 and 1891. From time to time a locally written play would appear in print or in production. In 1845 *The Count del Santa Cruz* and *The Grand Seignor*, two farces by an unnamed author, were presented by amateurs. In 1847 the *Trinidad Spectator* printed a short play in French, its title taken from the Creole proverb: '*Ca qui pas bon pour z'oies, pas bon pour canards*' ('What's good for the goose is good for the gander'), in which the author defended the reinstatement of the carnival, banned by an outgoing governor. In the 1860s the distinguished Trinidad lawyer M. Maxwell Philip wrote an historical play entitled *Apodoca*, about the Spanish admiral who, defending the island, burned his ships rather than surrender them to a superior British fleet. Neither script nor production record has been traced.

To celebrate the centenary of British rule in the island, long-time resident Lewis Osborne Inniss, a pharmacist born in GUYANA, wrote and produced *Carmelita, the Belle of San José* (1897), followed the next year by *Mura, the Cacique's Daughter*, to mark the anniversary of 'Discovery Day'. These scripts survive – sentimental romances portraying Amerindians who are saved by the British from the cruel Spaniards. However, they completely ignore the existence of Africans, who were then the predominant racial group on the island.

In 1858 the press reported only one functioning theatre in Port of Spain. An attempt to make it into a permanent playhouse failed, and by 1866 there was 'no theatre, major or minor', in the city. To entertain two British princes who were cruising the islands, in 1861 the government had constructed the 'Princes' Building' opposite the Queen's Park Savannah. Though it had no proper auditorium, it was put into service to accommodate visiting theatre companies. When the Trinidad Drama Club was formed in 1897, it pressed immediately for a permanent civic theatre. It was suggested that the Princes' Building be converted into a theatre; but no plan was found acceptable, and the building was put to a multitude of uses until, decrepit, it burned to the ground in 1979.

The 20th century brought an influx of professional companies to the island. Among them were the Frank Benson Shakespeare Company in 1905, and, on repeated visits, the Harkins Dramatic Company, the Florence Glossop-Harris Company and the Empire Players – all English companies of the first order. They performed first at the Princes' Building and later at the Empire Theatre, a large cinema built with a commodious stage and superior acoustics. These visiting groups doubtless inspired the formation of local drama clubs. The Paragon Dramatic Club, launched in 1924 with its own playwright, Cecil Cobham, produced original plays whose titles, in the absence of surviving scripts, suggest the sentimental drama fashionable in an earlier age: among them *False Honeymoon*, *Sold But Not Lost* and *Retribution*. Later writers in this mode were Ethelbert Young of the Thalia Drama Club, Kate Bourne, and Errol Cherrie whose two musical comedies, *Among the Young* and *Chamber in the Moon*, were presented in 1943 and 1944 by the St Cecilia Music Club.

It was left to two schoolteachers, Arthur Roberts and De Wilton Rogers, to bring a sense of realism to the local stage. From 1932 for almost a decade, Roberts produced, with pupils from the Nelson Street Boys' Roman Catholic School, a series of sparkling farces on current affairs in Trinidad: *Divorce* (a controversial subject in Catholic Trinidad); *That Hospital*, about dissatisfaction with the public hospital; *Romance without Sanitation*, on the incidence of tuberculosis; *Obeah*, dealing with belief in the spirit world; *War Gossip*, on the danger of loose talk during the Second World War. Rogers, too, dealt with current topics, but he adopted a more serious approach. In plays such as *Blue Blood and Black* (1936) on the race problem, *Trikidad* (1937) on graft in high places, and *Silk Cotton Grove* (1942) on the uprooting of residents to make way for US military bases, he dramatized issues of grave importance to the ordinary citizen.

Outside the Caribbean, the Trinidadian historian and novelist C. L. R. James had his play *Toussaint l'Ouverture* (1936; later revised and retitled *The Black Jacobins*) presented by the Stage Society in London at the Westminster

The Black Jacobins by C.L.R. James, Talawa Theatre Company, 1986.

Theatre, with Paul Robeson in the leading role. Two Trinidad and Tobago writers who worked for the American stage were Donald Heywood (fl.1920s–30s) and then William Archibald (fl.1940s–60s).

In the 1940s a movement arose towards recognizing folk expression as important to the development of a national culture. The calypso and steel band were defended as vigorous elements of indigenous expression. In 1943 the Trinidadian singer EDRIC CONNOR gave his celebrated lecture to the Music Association on West Indian folk-music, while the Barbados-born Joseph Griffith, bandmaster of the police band, offered his own orchestral compositions at the Princes' Building. In 1948 BERYL McBURNIE, dancer and choreographer, opened her Little Carib Theatre primarily to promote Caribbean dance; a national arts festival was inaugurated with 500 entries; and in 1946 the Whitehall Players was founded by ERROL HILL and ERROL JOHN. This group, merged in 1952 with the New Company into the COMPANY OF PLAYERS, is noted as much for its production record as for the number of outstanding artists it has nurtured.

The 1950s promised much for the theatre, not only of Trinidad and Tobago but of the entire anglophone Caribbean. The publication of Caribbean plays by the Extramural Department of the UNIVERSITY OF THE WEST INDIES (UWI, see Introduction) encouraged writers to write plays and theatre groups to perform them. For the first time audiences in Trinidad and Tobago were exposed to plays by DEREK WALCOTT of St Lucia (see Eastern Caribbean States), when *The Sea at Dauphin* and *Henri Christophe* were staged. Also presented at this time was Errol Hill's *Ping Pong*, the first play about the steel band, which attracted larger audiences than were usually seen then in the live theatre. In 1955 John Ainsworth, a professional actor from England who staged racially integrated productions of *Hamlet* and *Macbeth* (the former playing in Barbados, Trinidad and Guyana), attempted to form a professional theatre company but could not

Freddie Kissoon, Errol Jones and Clinton Browne in Derek Walcott's *The Sea at Dauphin*, Trinidad, 1954.

raise continuing financial support for it.

In 1955 the Drama Guild was founded in San Fernando, Trinidad's second town, where the preponderance of East Indians ensured their participation in the national theatre movement. About 1954 St Clair Wesley Dorant started his Merry Circle group in order to produce his own plays – a total of over thirty. In 1957 FREDDIE KISSOON established the Strolling Players. The major event of the decade was the regional festival of arts held in 1958 to herald the inauguration of the West Indies Federation. The centrepiece was an open-air production of the epic drama *Drums and Colours*, written by Derek Walcott and directed by the Jamaican NOEL VAZ, with actors and production personnel from other Caribbean territories. The festival ignited a rush of theatre activity in Trinidad and Tobago. Of several groups formed in the next few years, Walcott's TRINIDAD THEATRE WORKSHOP (1959) was to prove the most influential.

Once the carnival, the calypso and the steel band were accepted as vital elements of national expression, playwrights were drawn to the challenge. For the mammoth Dimanche Gras carnival show in 1963-5, attempts – generally unsuccessful – were made to structure the presentation around a dramatic story. Of these the most satisfying was the political satire *Whistling Charlie and the Monster* written and directed by Errol Hill in 1964. The next year Hill's calypso verse musical *Man Better Man* represented the country at the Commonwealth Arts Festival in Britain. Of many other carnival-based plays, the best-remembered are: Marina Maxwell's *Play Mas'* (1968), LENNOX BROWN's *Devil Mas'* (1971), RONALD AMOROSO's *The Master of Carnival* (1974), MUSTAPHA MATURA's *Rum and Coca Cola* (1976), EARL LOVELACE's dramatization of his novel *The Dragon Can't Dance* (1984); DEREK WALCOTT's *Steel* (1991), and RAWLE GIBBONS's *I Lawah* (*I Le Roi*, 1986) and his three calypso theatre pieces: *Sing de Chorus* (1991), *Ah Wanna Fall* (1992) and *Ten to One* (1993). In a unique experiment in 1980, the TRINIDAD TENT THEATRE, working with playwright Felix Edinborough, created a number of original musicals in which all stage characters were based on traditional masquerades (see African Theatre, Introduction, MASQUERADES IN AFRICA), identifiable by their costume, movement, speech and behaviour.

To encourage development in the country areas, a Best Village Competition that included the arts was launched by the government in 1967. Although mostly at a rudimentary level, the competition in playwriting and production served to expand interest in the live theatre and, under skilled leadership, village groups could achieve a respectable standard. One such group, the Mausica Folk Performers, appeared in 1984 at the Amateur Theatre Festival in Los Angeles in the musical *Bitter Cassava* written and directed by EFEBO WILKINSON. A secondary schools drama festival, organized in 1965 by JAMES LEE WAH of San Fernando, had by 1972 adjudicated ninety-eight plays, half of them by Caribbean playwrights.

Reinforcing the work of schools and amateur groups, the UWI Extramural Department (now School of Continuing Studies) has since 1964 conducted a summer school in the performing and visual arts. Employing trained and experienced professionals as tutors, the Department has contributed substantially to improving the skills of the younger theatre generation. In 1986 the UWI established a Creative Arts Centre on the Trinidad campus, so that students can now benefit from full-time training and gain academic credit towards their first degree for certain drama courses. In 1985 the National Drama Association of Trinidad and Tobago was established. By allocating productions to different centres during its annual festival, the Association ensures that the best work reaches the widest possible audiences.

With the growth in theatre activity has come a corresponding increase in performance spaces, along with the understanding that a formal proscenium-arch theatre is not neces-sary for staging plays. The auditoriums most often used include the Little Carib, Queen's Hall, the City Hall and Central Bank in Port of Spain, and the Naparima Bowl in San Fernando. Tobago has halls, but no central auditorium for use as a theatre.

Other kinds of theatre exist in Trinidad and Tobago. The Trinidad calypso, in which contemporary events are enacted in song, most often by a single performer, has long been accepted as a unique theatrical form. And speech theatre, a form of storytelling, has been revived in Trinidad and Tobago with notable success. The principal presenter is PAUL KEENS-DOUGLAS, who acknowledges the influence on his work of LOUISE BENNETT of Jamaica. Keens-Douglas is now a roving professional story-teller whose dramatized conversations in dialect prose and verse, published in six book-lets, have inspired storytellers in other Caribbean countries.

The development of Caribbean dance owes much to the pioneering work of Beryl McBurnie, who introduced the themes to which she has devoted her life in the recital *A Trip through the Tropics*, staged in 1940 at the Empire Theatre, Port of Spain. Almost every creative dancer from Trinidad and Tobago has studied under McBurnie, including Percy Borde, Boscoe and Geoffrey Holder, and MOLLY AHYE. The outstanding performer of classical Indian dance is RAJKUMAR KRISHNA PERSAD, who has studied in India and now conducts a school in Trinidad.

Ahye, Molly (1933–)

Dancer, choreographer and folk researcher from Trinidad and Tobago. Ahye joined the Little Carib Theatre (see BERYL MCBURNIE) in 1952 and was a principal performer when she left the Carib in 1965. From 1958 she attended dance classes in the USA and Europe, then in 1968 formed the New Dance Group, later the Oya Kairi Dance Company. With them she toured the Caribbean, Canada, the USA,

London and Glasgow. At the 1975 Festivales d'Espana her company played thirty-two venues over three months. She has introduced sacred dance into churches in Trinidad and Tobago, and participated in stage and television productions as dancer, choreographer and stage director.

Ahye has done extensive ethnographic studies in the Caribbean, Brazil and Nigeria. In 1982 she received an MA in the performing arts (dance) from the American University in Washington, DC, and is studying for a doctorate at New York University. In 1980 she was awarded the Humming Bird Gold Medal for her services to Trinidad and Tobago. She has published *Golden Heritage: the Dance in Trinidad and Tobago* (1978) and *Cradle of Caribbean Dance: Beryl McBurnie and the Little Carib Theatre* (1983).

Alleyne, Eunice (1936–)

Leading Trinidadian actress. Educated in Trinidad and at Boston University, where she took a BSc in communications, Alleyne has been involved in theatre since 1957. She has given star performances in a range of Caribbean plays, from FRANK PILGRIM's (see Guyana) farce *Miriamy* to SAMUEL HILLARY's (see Jamaica) sentimental drama *Departure in the Dark* to DEREK WALCOTT's (see Eastern Caribbean States) tragedy *Ione*. She has also appeared as Solange in Genet's *The Maids* and as Lena in ATHOL FUGARD's (see South Africa) *Boesman and Lena*. As a government officer, Alleyne has worked in broadcasting and public relations, and retired in 1992 as Director of Information.

Amoroso, Ronald [Jim Grant] (1935–)

Playwright and director from Trinidad and Tobago. Amoroso's first play, the one-acter *The Blood Clot*, was staged at the 1970 secondary schools drama festival. Since then he was written sixteen plays including eight folk musicals, mostly for the Best Village Competition. Four

of his works are concerned with the TRINIDAD CARNIVAL, calypso and steel band. His one-acter *The Master of Carnival*, adapted from a story by Euton Jarvis, was judged the most original play at the English-language drama festival in Caracas in 1972.

Archibald, Douglas [Jack] (1919–93)

Playwright from Trinidad and Tobago. An engineer, Archibald had already written several plays when he was discovered by SYDNEY HILL, whose New Company staged his first play *Junction Village* in 1952 to considerable acclaim. Archibald went on to write a dozen or so more, such as *Anne Marie* (1958) and *The Rose Slip* (1962), that have made him one of the most regularly staged playwrights in the Caribbean. His work portrays village life with the same careful observation of manner and speech as he devotes to middle-class characters, and has also been produced in the USA and England. He has written several unproduced plays, including some that explore the early history of Trinidad.

Assoon, Barbara (1929–)

Actress from Trinidad and Tobago. With her performance in *Romeo and Juliet* with ERROL JOHN in 1949 and as Amanda in *The Glass Menagerie* for John's Company of Five the following year, Assoon showed herself to be an actress of sensitivity. In 1952 she was also hailed as the leading female dancer of the Little Carib Theatre (see BERYL MCBURNIE). In 1953 she went to the Bristol Old Vic Theatre School on a British Council scholarship, and played Tituba in the first British production of *The Crucible*. Returning to Trinidad, she played Miriamne to the Mio of ERROL HILL in Maxwell Anderson's *Winterset* in 1955, and was Puck in the Trinidad Dramatic Club's production of *A Midsummer Night's Dream* in 1956. In 1958 she played Rosa in John's prize-winning *Moon on a Rainbow Shawl* at the Royal Court Theatre, London. Thereafter she appeared regularly in the BBC 'Play of the Week' series and in productions at the Royal Court, Stratford East Theatre Royal and the Tricycle Theatre in London. Assoon is senior announcer at Radio Trinidad, but still occasionally performs in London.

Barnes, Belinda (1949–)

Drama instructor and director from Trinidad and Tobago. Barnes trained at the American Academy of Dramatic Arts (1967–70) and in 1976 received a diploma in education at the University of Newcastle-upon-Tyne, England. She taught at the Jamaica School of Drama (see Jamaica, CULTURAL TRAINING CENTRE), and since 1976 has been drama teacher at a secondary school in Trinidad. She has directed JOSÉ TRIANA's (see Cuba) *The Criminals*, which won acting and directing awards at the 1980 national drama festival; Victor Questel's *Two Choices*, winner of the Best Play award at the festival in 1985; Sophocles' *Electra* for the 1987 secondary schools drama festival; DENNIS SCOTT's (see Jamaica) *Dog* in 1988; and ERROL JOHN's *Moon on a Rainbow Shawl* in 1989.

Brown, Lennox (1934–)

Playwright, journalist and poet from Trinidad and Tobago. Brown gained a BA in English from the University of Western Ontario and an MA from the University of Toronto. In Canada he worked as a journalist and as editor-producer for the CBC and the National Network Radio News. He then taught at the University of Hartford, Connecticut, and at Queens College, New York, before returning to Trinidad.

Brown has written some forty plays, many in one act or designed for radio or television. They have been produced in Canada, the USA, the Netherlands and the Caribbean. The Negro Ensemble Company in New York staged *A Ballet behind the Bridge* in 1972 and *The Twilight Dinner* in 1978. The Billie Holiday Theatre in Brooklyn produced *Fog Drifts in the Spring* and *The Trinity of Four* in 1976, and *The Winti Train* in 1977. *Devil*

Crystal Crawford and Jacqueline Allen in Lennox Brown's *Devil Mas'*, Dartmouth College, New Hampshire, 1987.

Mas' was directed by ERROL HILL for Dartmouth College in 1987. The TRINIDAD THEATRE WORKSHOP also presented several radio versions of Brown's plays.

His plays tend to plumb the mystical and mythological consciousness of Caribbeans at home and abroad. He was prize-winner for four consecutive years in the Canadian National One-Act Playwriting Competition and has won other awards.

Company of Players

Theatre group of Trinidad and Tobago. Founded by ERROL HILL and ERROL JOHN in 1946 as the Whitehall Players, with support from the

British Council and headquarters at Whitehall, Port of Spain, the company has had a profound influence on theatre development in the Caribbean. Its first members were trained by professional actors, modern and Shakespearian. Initial productions, staged at the Government Training College for Teachers, Port of Spain, were of English works, until 1949 when Hill and John produced their own. Hill then went to the Royal Academy of Dramatic Art on a British Council scholarship, and John followed to England in 1951.

The Players adopted early on the policy of taking their productions to the people, performing at least twice yearly at hospitals and other institutions, and in the open air in small towns and villages. Until a body of Caribbean works emerged, plays such as Chekhov's farces were adapted to the local idiom. In 1954 the Players combined with SYDNEY HILL's New Company – which in 1952 had brought to light a major Caribbean playwright in DOUGLAS ARCHIBALD – to present a programme of Caribbean plays, followed by DEREK WALCOTT's (see Eastern Caribbean States) *Henri Christophe*. Then the two groups merged into the Company of Players.

The most outstanding company members are Errol John, who became an actor of stage and screen and a world-class prize-winning playwright, and Errol Hill – professor of drama, playwright, and author of drama histories; Percy Borde, a dancer and choreographer in New York; Horace James and Leo Carrera (then Leo Bennett), who worked as actors in Europe (James is now a television producer in Trinidad). Add to these BARBARA ASSOON, an actress and senior announcer on Radio Trinidad; JEAN SUE-WING, who was drama officer for the Trinidad and Tobago government, and Sydney Hill, who was government film officer; FREDDIE KISSOON, who has coached drama in schools and is a playwright and producer for his company, The Strolling Players; and ERROL JONES, who remains one of the leading actors in the West Indies.

Connor, Edric (1915–68)

Singer, actor, film producer and folklorist from Trinidad and Tobago. Within two weeks of his arrival in England in 1944, Connor had made his first broadcast, which launched him on a varied career as singer, actor and stage personality. He made over 300 appearances on BBC-TV and ITV, in addition to countless sound broadcasts.

As one of the early stage actors from Trinidad in England, he played De Lawd in Marc Connelly's *The Green Pastures*, Napoleon in the musical *Calypso* (1948), Joe in Moss Hart and George Kaufman's *You Can't Take It with You*, Joe Major in Joseph Kramm's *The Shrike*, and Gower in *Pericles* at the Shakespeare Memorial Theatre, Stratford-upon-Avon, in 1958; in 1961 he appeared with Rex Harrison at the Royal Court Theatre, London, in *August for the People*. His most persuasive film role was as John Kumalo in *Cry, the Beloved Country* in 1962.

Connor studied film at the Heatherley School of Art, and in 1959 trained as a television producer with the BBC. His films *Caribbean Honeymoon No. 2* and *Carnival Fantastique* were widely acclaimed when shown at the 1960 Edinburgh International Film Festival. His books include *The Edric Connor Collections of West Indian Spirituals and Folk Songs* (1945) and *Songs from Trinidad* (1958). He was married to PEARL CONNOR.

Connor, Pearl (1924–)

Actress and theatre and film agent from Trinidad and Tobago, now resident in Britain. Connor trained under BERYL MCBURNIE at the Little Carib Theatre in Port of Spain, then attended the Rose Bruford School of Speech and Drama in Kent. She worked in the Caribbean service of the BBC and as an actress, last appearing in Lindsay Anderson's *Oh Lucky Man* (1973), shown at the Cannes Film Festival.

With her first husband, the singer, actor and film-maker EDRIC CONNOR, Pearl managed the Edric Connor Agency, later known as the Afro-

Asian Caribbean Management Agency representing Third World artists, writers and filmmakers. Major stage productions cast by the agency include *Suzy Wong, Flower Drum Song, Black McBeth, Hair, Jesus Christ Superstar, Porgy and Bess, Carmen* and *Showboat*. In 1963 Connor established the Negro Theatre Workshop, which provided actors for WOLE SOYINKA's (see Nigeria) *The Road* at the Theatre Royal, Stratford East, London, during the Commonwealth Festival in 1965, and produced a jazz version of the *St Luke Passion* to represent Britain at the first world Black and African Festival of Arts and Culture (see African Theatre, Introduction, FESTAC) in Dakar, SENEGAL, in 1966. The Workshop also collaborated with the Royal Court Theatre in many experimental projects and provided the principal actors for its production of Genet's *The Blacks*.

In 1971 Connor married Joe Mogotsi, leader of the black South African singing group the Manhattan Brothers. Using his expertise, the Agency produced recordings of singers and musicians and organized tours for them throughout the world. In 1972 the Trinidad and Tobago government awarded Connor the Humming Bird Silver Medal for her services to the immigrant community in Britain, and in 1989 she won the Scarlet Ibis award. She is best known as a pioneer and catalyst in the promotion of African-Caribbean and Third World artists in Britain.

Drayton, Kathleen (1930–)

An important manager/organizer of theatrical events. Born in Trinidad, Drayton has contributed to the art and culture of the Caribbean for many years through her involvement with singing, literature and drama. She helped to establish the University Dramatic Society in Jamaica (see Introduction, UNIVERSITY OF THE WEST INDIES) in 1948, and was senior lecturer in the Faculty of Education. She is president of Stage One Theatre Productions, a group of BARBADOS-based dramatists and performers set up to produce Caribbean theatre. The company

has presented leading playwrights such as ERROL JOHN; TREVOR RHONE and DENNIS SCOTT (see Jamaica); and RODDY WALCOTT (see Eastern Caribbean States); and staged the world premières of DEREK WALCOTT's *A Branch of the Blue Nile* (1984) and EDGAR WHITE's (see Eastern Caribbean States) *I, Marcus Garvey* (1987). Stage One has also produced dramatizations of the work of Caribbean writers such as E. K. Brathwaite, Austin Clark, George Lamming and V. S. Naipaul.

Gibbons, Rawle (1950–)

Playwright and director from Trinidad and Tobago, and tutor at the Creative Arts Centre at the Trinidad campus of the UNIVERSITY OF THE WEST INDIES (UWI, see Introduction). Gibbons attended the UWI in Jamaica and Trinidad, gaining an MPhil in 1979 for his thesis, *Traditional Enactments of Trinidad: Towards a Third Theatre*. He has directed plays for the University Players and the Jamaica School of Drama (see Jamaica, CULTURAL TRAINING CENTRE), and in Trinidad for the Yard Theatre, the TRINIDAD THEATRE WORKSHOP and the Creative Arts Centre; such plays include DENNIS SCOTT's (see Jamaica) *An Echo in the Bone* (1976) and *Dog* (1980), C. L. R. James's *The Black Jacobins* (1979), *The Tempest* (1981), DEREK WALCOTT's (see Eastern Caribbean States) *Dream on Monkey Mountain* (1984), and the Nigerian WOLE SOYINKA's *Death and the King's Horseman* (1990). Gibbons wrote and Scott directed *Shepherd* (1981), based on a Spiritual Baptist ritual, for the Jamaica School of Drama's entry to CARIFESTA (see Introduction) held in BARBADOS in 1981. Then in 1984 he wrote *I Lawah*, which toured London and Barbados; in 1991, the experimental *Sing de Chorus*, first in a series of three calypso dramas presented during the carnival season, which encouraged audience participation; and more recently, *Ah wanna fall down* (1992) and *Ten to One* (1993).

Gomez, Joya (1935–)

Actress, voice and speech tutor, and English

teacher from Trinidad and Tobago. Gomez gained a BA from the University of Toronto and a diploma in radio and television arts from Ryerson Polytechnic Institute, Toronto. She has been associated with theatre and the performing arts for many years in Trinidad, Canada and East Africa, serving her apprenticeship in theatre groups such as the Whitehall Players (see COMPANY OF PLAYERS), the TRINIDAD THEATRE WORKSHOP and the TRINIDAD TENT THEATRE. She created the role of Ana in DEREK WALCOTT's (see Eastern Caribbean States) *The Joker of Seville* (1975), played the female role in his *Remembrance* (1978), and Sheila in his *A Branch of the Blue Nile* (1985) directed by EARL WARNER (see Barbados). In 1980 she played the psychiatrist Dr Dysart in Peter Shaffer's *Equus*. For the Tent Theatre she appeared in three carnival plays on its European and Latin-American festival tour in 1982, and created the title role in *Désirée*, a ninety-minute one-woman *tour de force* calling for eight character types – the play opened the National Drama Festival in 1983. She played Mother Courage in 1988 for the Creative Arts Centre (see Introduction, UNIVERSITY OF THE WEST INDIES). Gomez has acted on television in Canada and Trinidad, and in the film *The Rig* (1982) directed by Derek Walcott.

Hill, Errol (1921–)

Actor, director, playwright, author and drama lecturer from Trinidad and Tobago. On the strength of his work with the Whitehall Players (see COMPANY OF PLAYERS) which he founded with ERROL JOHN in 1946, Hill received a British Council scholarship to the Royal Academy of Dramatic Art in London, from which in 1951 he gained a diploma. He was also awarded a diploma in dramatic art from London University. While at the Hans Crescent international student centre in London, he directed Caribbean students in two productions: Sophocles' *Oedipus Rex* (1951) and DEREK WALCOTT's (see EASTERN CARIBBEAN STATES) *Henri Christophe* (1952).

Returning to the Caribbean, in 1953 he was appointed drama tutor at the Extramural Department of the UNIVERSITY [COLLEGE] OF THE WEST INDIES (UWI, see Introduction) in Jamaica. He travelled the Caribbean giving lectures and theatre workshops and arranging summer schools in the performing arts, as well as helping the University Dramatic Society with its campus productions. In 1955 he began to publish Caribbean plays, in order to make them available to theatre groups throughout the region. His first published collection contained his own steel-band play, *The Ping Pong*, plus works by Derek and RODDY WALCOTT (see Eastern Caribbean States), CICELY WAITE-SMITH (see Jamaica) and DOUGLAS ARCHIBALD.

In 1958 Errol Hill received a Rockefeller Foundation fellowship to attend the Yale School of Drama, where in 1962 he gained a BA and an MFA in playwriting. In 1966 he was awarded a DFA in theatre history; his dissertation, *The Trinidad Carnival: Mandate for a National Theatre*, was published in 1972. His calypso verse-play *Man Better Man*, first produced at Yale in 1960, represented Trinidad and Tobago at

Errol Jones and Peter Pitts in Errol Hill's *Man Better Man*, Trinidad and London, 1965.

the Commonwealth Arts Festival in Britain in 1965. It was produced by the Negro Ensemble Company in New York in 1969.

Back in Trinidad in 1962, Hill continued his work as drama tutor for the UWI in the southern Caribbean, while NOEL VAZ (see Jamaica) was appointed drama tutor for the northern region. Hill produced national shows to celebrate the independence of Trinidad and Tobago, and in 1963–4 attempted (with moderate success) to change the Dimanche Gras carnival held at the Queen's Park Savannah into dramatic farces. In 1965 he was seconded to the School of Drama, University of Ibadan, NIGERIA, where he taught theatre history and playwriting and directed. Realizing that the UWI was not yet ready to put drama on its curriculum, in 1967 he moved to the USA to teach first at Richmond College, Staten Island, then at Dartmouth College. He retired from Dartmouth in 1989 as Willard Professor of Drama and Oratory, Emeritus.

Of his plays, *Man Better Man*, *The Ping Pong*, *Strictly Matrimony* and *Dance Bongo* are the most often produced. He has also written and edited books on African-American and Caribbean theatre, including *A Time and a Season: 8 Caribbean Plays*, produced for Jamaica CARIFESTA 76 (see Introduction); *Plays for Today* (1985); and *The Jamaican Stage, 1655–1900: Profile of a Colonial Theatre* (1992).

Hill, Sydney (1923–)

Actor and stage and film director from Trinidad and Tobago. After service in the Royal Air Force (1944–5), Hill gained diplomas in music, speech and drama at Trinity College of Music, London. Back in Trinidad, in 1951 he became Music and Drama Officer with the British Council in Port of Spain. In 1952 he played Horstad in a Whitehall Players' (see COMPANY OF PLAYERS) production of Ibsen's *An Enemy of the People*, and in the same year founded the New Company, for which he directed Patrick Hamilton's *Rope* (1953) – also playing

Granillo – and DOUGLAS ARCHIBALD's *Junction Village* (1954), the first of his plays to be seen on the public stage. For the Company of Players he directed Archibald's *The Bamboo Clump* (1956) and *Anne Marie* (1958), Philip Yordan's *Anna Lucasta* (1956), Tennessee Williams's *Moony's Kid Don't Cry* (1956) and Arthur Schnitzler's 'Dissolution' from *Anatol* (1956), in which he also played Anatol. Other roles at this time include Dessalines in DEREK WALCOTT's (see Eastern Caribbean States) *Henri Christophe* (1954); then in 1955, Attorney Stevens in *The Night of January 16th*, Count Dorante in *The Bourgeois Gentleman*, the Player King and Marcellus in *Hamlet*, and Macduff in *Macbeth*. He played Lysander in *A Midsummer Night's Dream* (1957), De Berrio in Walcott's *Drums and Colours* (1958), staged for the West Indies Festival of Arts, and Tiny Satan in ERROL HILL's *Man Better Man*, presented at the Commonwealth Arts Festival in Britain in 1965.

While he was director-producer of the Trinidad and Tobago government film unit in the mid-50s, Hill received a Canada Council fellowship in film and television. He later joined the School of Public Communication of Boston University, where he gained a BSc in film in 1968 and an MSc in radio and television in 1969. He made numerous documentary films for the Trinidad and Tobago government, such as *The Butler Riots*, *The Life and Times of Captain the Hon. A. A. Cipriani*, *Partnerships in Housing*, *Mama Dis is Mas* (on the parade of carnival bands); and *Eighteen on Steel*, about a steel-band festival.

Hill retired from the civil service in 1983. Since 1990 he has been a lecturer in radio and television broadcasting at the Academy of Media Arts in Port of Spain, and since 1991 a part-time lecturer in voice and speech at the UWI Creative Arts Centre at St Augustine, Trinidad.

John, Errol (1923–88)

Actor and playwright from Trinidad and Tobago. John was a co-founder of the Whitehall

Players (see COMPANY OF PLAYERS) and for a short time ran the Company of Five, until 1950 when he left Trinidad for England as a guest of the British Council. In 1951 he played Haemon in *Oedipus Rex* and in 1952 the title role in DEREK WALCOTT's (see Eastern Caribbean States) *Henri Christophe* in productions directed by ERROL HILL at the Hans Crescent student centre in London. A year later he toured England with the American Negro Theater as Lester in Philip Yordan's *Anna Lucasta*, and appeared in *Cry, the Beloved Country* at St Martin-in-the-Fields, London. Other London stage roles include Paul Prescott in *Local Colour* by Joan Sandler (1954), the Negro in *The Respectable Prostitute* by Jean-Paul Sartre (1954), the Nubian slave in *Salome* by Oscar Wilde (1954); and at the Old Vic the Prince of Morocco in *The Merchant of Venice* (1962), the title role in *Othello* (1962), and Barnardine in *Measure for Measure* (1963). He appeared in starring roles in his own plays for BBC-TV and ATV, and took the lead in a six-part TV series called *Rainbow City*.

In 1957 John won the London *Observer* playwriting competition with his three-act play *Moon on a Rainbow Shawl*, which has been performed in over twenty-five countries including, in translation, Iceland, India and Czechoslovakia. It was first produced in London in 1958, then in New York in a revised version in 1962 with James Earl Jones in the leading role. He also wrote plays for television, of which *Dawn* (1963), *Exiles* (1969) and *The Insider* (1971) were presented by the BBC. Three of his screenplays, *Force Majeure*, *The Disappointed* and *Hasta Leugo*, set in London, the West Indies and Mexico respectively, were published in 1967.

John also played in films such as *The Nun's Story* (1959), *The Sins of Rachel Cade* (1961), *PT109* (1963), *Assault on a Queen* (1966) and *Buck and the Preacher* (1972). He received Guggenheim fellowships to study and write in the USA in 1958 and 1966. By one of his directors he was considered 'a very fastidious actor'; to another he was simply a perfectionist.

Jones, Errol (1923–)

Trinidadian actor. Considered one of the 'heavies' of the Caribbean stage, Jones was an immigration officer for the government of Trinidad and Tobago when he was first attracted to the theatre. He joined the Whitehall Players (see COMPANY OF PLAYERS) and made his stage debut in 1949 in Peter Ustinov's *The Indifferent Shepherd*. For the Players in 1954 he created the part of Afa in DEREK WALCOTT's (see Eastern Caribbean States) *The Sea at Dauphin* and played the title role in the same author's *Henri Christophe*. He starred as Mano in Walcott's epic drama *Drums and Colours*, produced in Trinidad in 1958 to mark the opening of the West Indies Federation.

In 1962 Jones attended the Actors' Studio in New York on a Rockefeller Foundation fellowship. He played Diable Papa in ERROL HILL's musical *Man Better Man*, produced in 1965 for the Commonwealth Arts Festival in Britain, and took the lead role of Makak in Walcott's *Dream on Monkey Mountain* at the Caribana Festival in Toronto in 1967. Other Walcott roles that he created are Catalinion in *The Joker of Seville* (1974), Deacon Doxy in *O Babylon!* (1976), and Otto in *Beef, No Chicken* (1981).

In 1969 and 1974 Jones performed at the Eugene O'Neill Playwrights' Conference in Waterford, Connecticut; he was actor in residence at Grinell College, Iowa, in 1970; and as guest actor with Stage One, BARBADOS, in 1985 he appeared as the senior Garvey in EDGAR WHITE's (see Eastern Caribbean States) *I, Marcus Garvey*. In 1986 he performed at the Caribbean Focus festival in London. He has toured several Caribbean territories, from the Bahamas to GUYANA. His many honours include the National Cultural Council award for acting (1981), the National Drama Association award (1984), the Humming Bird Silver Medal for drama from the government of Trinidad and Tobago (1985), the President's Twenty-fifth Anniversary Award (1987), and the McBurnie Foundation Award (1987). In 1977 he retired from the public service to devote himself fully to acting.

Keens-Douglas, Paul (1942–)

Trinidadian actor, folk poet and dialect writer. Brought up in Grenada, Keens-Douglas gained a degree in sociology from Sir George Williams University, Montreal, then did two years' postgraduate study in sociology at the UNIVERSITY OF THE WEST INDIES (UWI, see Introduction) in Jamaica. In Grenada he performed with a drama group led by THELMA PHILIPS (see Eastern Caribbean States) and with her Bee Wee Ballet group. In Montreal he worked with Jeff Henry, the Trinidadian director and choreographer. In JAMAICA he was associated with the University Dramatic Society and performed in the JAMAICA PANTOMIME *Hail Columbus*, but he was mostly influenced by the folk poetry and performance of LOUISE BENNETT, Jamaica's inimitable oral poet.

Transferring to the Trinidad campus of UWI, Keens-Douglas took a job with Rediffusion and Radio Trinidad. Resettled in the southern Caribbean, with more familiar vernacular and speech cadences, he began to write folk poetry and dialect short stories, which he performed to enthusiastic audiences. His reputation quickly spread throughout the anglophone Caribbean and to Caribbean communities in the USA and Canada. Editions of his poems and short stories include: *When Moon Shine, Tim Tim, Tell Me Again, Is Town Say So, Lal Shop* and *Twice Upon A Time*.

Kissoon, Freddie (1930–)

From Trinidad and Tobago, playwright, actor, teacher; and founder and producer-director of the Strolling Players. In 1962 Kissoon won a British Council scholarship to the Central School of Drama, London, where he gained a certificate in drama and diction as well as the London University diploma in dramatic art.

Having served an apprenticeship with the Whitehall Players and the COMPANY OF PLAYERS from 1951 to 1958 – during which he appeared as Hounakin in DEREK WALCOTT's (see Eastern Caribbean States) *The Sea at Dauphin* and in the title role of his *Ti Jean and His Brothers* – he formed the Strolling Players, a semi-professional group whose first production of three one-acters in 1961 contained two of his own plays, *Zingay* and *Mamaguy* (both published in 1966). The company has since blossomed into one of the most prolific theatrical groups, with a production tally unequalled in the Caribbean. The Players have staged nearly eighty plays, forty-one of them by Kissoon. In 1966 they inaugurated live drama on Trinidad and Tobago television, with the production of *Zingay*. They have given over forty television plays, many of them first seen on the stage, and members have appeared in seven films made in Trinidad. The Strolling Players regularly take their productions around the country on tour. They have also toured other parts of the Caribbean and Toronto.

Kissoon's plays – many of them one-act vernacular farces or melodramas – have been presented in New York, Washington, DC, Montreal, London and NIGERIA on both stage and television. Concerned with contemporary issues, written in a racy style with homespun commentary on manners and morals and a strict observance of propriety, they have won a strong popular following. Kissoon also wrote the seventy-eight episodes of the long-running radio serial *Calabash Alley* (1970–1). In addition, he has written serious full-length works: *King Cobo* (1966) tells the story of a cripple, who out of anger turns to blackmail only to find that his daughter is involved in prostitution; *God and Uriah Butler* (1967), commissioned by the Oilfield Workers' Trade Union, is based on incidents in the life of the labour leader T. Uriah Butler; and *Luisa Calderón* (1992) examines the controversial rule of the first English governor of Trinidad.

Kissoon directs all his plays and has made over 200 stage appearances. In 1987 the government of Trinidad and Tobago awarded him a Humming Bird Medal for his contribution to culture, drama and the theatre. His publications include *100 Exercises in Creative Drama* (1970). Kissoon was a secondary school teacher of English and drama until he retired in 1988.

Lee Wah, James (1931–)

Director, producer and teacher from Trinidad and Tobago. Lee Wah's interest in theatre developed when he was a student at the UNIVERSITY [COLLEGE] OF THE WEST INDIES (see Introduction) at Mona, Jamaica, during 1951–6. Returning to his hometown of San Fernando, Trinidad, he founded the Drama Guild, which he led for twenty years (1956–76). During this period he directed some fifty plays, almost half of them Caribbean, such as RODDY WALCOTT's (see Eastern Caribbean States) *Benjy* (1959), DOUGLAS ARCHIBALD's *Junction Village* (1960) and *The Rose Slip* (1969), SAMUEL HILLARY's (see Jamaica) *Departure in the Dark* (1968), Eric Roach's *New Dancers in the Dooryard* (1970) and ERROL HILL's *Man Better Man* (1975). Non-Caribbean plays that he directed include Synge's *The Shadow of the Glen* (1956) and *The Playboy of the Western World* (1957), Van Druten's *Bell, Book and Candle* (1959), O'Casey's *Bedtime Story* (1961) and *Juno and the Paycock* (1974), WOLE SOYINKA's (see Nigeria) *The Trials of Brother Jero* (1968), Arthur Miller's *A View from the Bridge* (1968), Peter Weiss's *Marat/Sade* (1971) and Joe Orton's *What the Butler Saw* (1972). He also presented *The Merchant of Venice* (1964), *Macbeth* (1973) and *Twelfth Night* (1975).

In 1976 Lee Wah founded the San Fernando Theatre Workshop, of which he is artistic director. There he has continued to combine the productions of Caribbean playwrights like ERROL JOHN, DEREK WALCOTT (see Eastern Caribbean States), Willie Chen and MUSTAPHA MATURA with those of foreign writers such as Tennessee Williams, Samuel Beckett, García Lorca and Eugene Ionesco. In 1964 he started the Secondary Schools Drama Association, which

promotes an annual schools play festival and for which he directed *Romeo and Juliet* in 1969. In 1980 he founded the National Drama Association of Trinidad and Tobago. For the Alternative National Theatre he directed in 1981 *Sweet Talk* by Michael Abbensetts and *A Day in the Death of Joe Egg* by Peter Nichols.

Lee Wah received a one-year fellowship at the Yale Drama School in Connecticut in 1964, and in 1977 he published *Carray! A selection of plays for Caribbean Schools*. He is married to the actress MAVIS LEE WAH.

Lovelace, Earl (1935–)

Novelist and playwright from Trinidad and Tobago. Born in the village of Toco, Trinidad, and brought up in Tobago, Lovelace went to school in Port of Spain, then worked as a proofreader with the Trinidad Publishing Company. He became a government officer first in the Department of Forestry, then in Agriculture. He has been a lecturer in creative writing at the UNIVERSITY OF THE WEST INDIES (UWI, see Introduction) in Trinidad.

Lovelace's rural background is reflected in his plays, some of which he wrote as entries in the annual Best Village Competition. His first play *The New Boss* (1962), written for the independence celebrations and staged out of doors, portrays the newly independent country as an estate turned over to its workers. Three novels followed, and then in 1980 he published *Jestina's Calypso and Other Plays*: the first of this collection, *My Name is Village*, was written for the Matura villagers, who staged it at Queen's Hall, Port of Spain, in 1976; the UWI Players first performed *Jestina's Calypso* at St Augustine in 1978, then *The New Hardware Store* in 1980.

More significant, perhaps, for the promise it holds for Caribbean theatre is Lovelace's attempt to dramatize two of his novels. *The Dragon Can't Dance*, about carnival revellers preparing for their annual festival, was presented at Queen's Hall in 1986. Directed by EARL WARNER (see Barbados), with choreography by Allyson Brown and original music by Andre Tanker, this exercise in dramatization was ambitious if not formidable. In 1988 he dramatized and staged, more successfully, his novel *The Wine of Astonishment* about the Shouter Baptist movement.

Lyndersay, (K. W.) Dexter (1932–)

Technical director, lighting designer, play director and theatre consultant from Trinidad and Tobago. After an apprenticeship with the Little Carib Theatre (see BERYL MCBURNIE) in Trinidad and on tour in JAMAICA, Lyndersay enrolled at the Goodman Theatre School in Chicago, where he gained a BFA, and in 1965 he was awarded an MFA from the Yale School of Drama. He was stage manager and technical director in London and Glasgow for ERROL HILL's *Man Better Man*, the Trinidad and Tobago entry for the 1965 Commonwealth Arts Festival, and in 1966 he was artistic director for Trinidad and Tobago and lighting designer for contingents from the USA and Britain at the first world Black and African Festival of Arts and Culture (see African Theatre, Introduction, FESTAC) in Dakar, SENEGAL.

From 1965 to 1987 Lyndersay was employed in NIGERIA at university theatres in Ibadan, Ahmadu Bello, Calabar and Cross River State. He led performing companies at Ibadan and Calabar, directing the world première of *The Black Jacobins* by C. L. R. James, the African première of Genet's *The Blacks*, the Yoruba *Macbeth*, Samson Omali's *Onugbo Mloko*, and several shorter plays from Egypt, the Caribbean and Nigeria as well as adaptations of Nigerian novels. He was technical director and/or lighting designer for over 250 productions, and consultant for the building of some dozen theatres. In 1970 he gained a certificate in television from the International Institute in Audio-visual Media, Brussels. With his wife Dani Lyndersay he created and directed children's television theatre at Ibadan and Kaduna.

After leaving Nigeria in 1987, Lyndersay was guest lecturer at the International Workshop of the Hogeschool voor de Kunsten at Utrecht, and stage director at the Warrenkam Theatre, Laren, in the Netherlands. The next year he returned to Trinidad to work for the government in the Division of Culture and Creative Arts, as arts director, director of the project Youth Crossroads, director of venues and infrastructure for CARIFESTA (see Introduction) and adviser to the national Best Village programme. He led the Children's Theatre of the Trinidad and Tobago contingent to the first World Children's Theatre Festival in Lingen, Germany, in April 1990. He is the principal academic adviser to the TRINIDAD THEATRE WORKSHOP's School of the Arts, launched in 1991.

Lyndersay's writings include the play *Shaimu Umar* (with Umar Ladan, 1975).

McBurnie, Beryl (c.1915–)

Choreographer, dance teacher and folklorist from Trinidad and Tobago. Having trained at the Mausica Teachers' College in Trinidad, McBurnie became interested in folk-dance during visits to the country with Trinidad's leading folklorist, Andrew Carr. She determined to research Caribbean folk forms and introduce them to the public through dance, music and song.

In 1938 she went to Columbia University, New York, where she was influenced by Martha Graham and Charles Weidman of the Academy of Allied Arts. With Elsa Findlay she studied the eurhythmics of Dalcroze, while teaching the music and dances of the Caribbean at the New Dance Studio and at the Henry Street Settlement Playhouse in New York. Back home in 1940, with a group of young dancers McBurnie presented her first show, *A Trip through the Tropics*, in a sell-out performance at the Empire Theatre, Port of Spain. The show consisted of creative Caribbean and Brazilian dances, along with impressions of New York and modern dances to music by such composers as Wagner, Beethoven and Bach. Returning to New York in 1941, she performed under the name of La Belle Rosette while continuing to teach. In 1942 she replaced Carmen Miranda in the hit show *Sons o' Fun* at the Winter Garden Theatre, New York.

She returned to Trinidad in 1945 to become a dance instructor in the government's Education Department. Her goal was to establish a permanent folk-dance company and a theatre. In 1948, after another research trip to South America, she opened her pre-carnival show *Bele*, in the new Little Carib Theatre, a modest building with an open stage near her home at Woodbrook, Port of Spain. Also in 1948, she presented *Talking Drums*; then in 1949, *Carnival Bele* (in which the Jour Ouvert ballet danced to a steel band), *Sugar Ballet*, *Caribbean Cruise*, and a festival of dance called *Paran'*. For the next several years the Little Carib Dance Company prospered.

In 1950 she became director of dance in the Education Department. She presented *Iere Danses* (*Trinidad Dances*) to raise money for a dancers' scholarship fund, and was sent by the British Council on a dance familiarization tour of England and Europe. During these absences her dance troupe's work continued under leading dancers such as Boscoe Holder, Jeff Henry and Percy Borde. In 1955 the company presented *Danzas* and *Gayap*, in 1957 *Baionga*, and in 1958 – the year of the short-lived West Indies Federation – *Cannes Brûlées*, followed by a history of the West Indies through dance, and *Binaka*. From 1959–65 the Little Carib hosted the initial years of the TRINIDAD THEATRE WORKSHOP directed by DEREK WALCOTT (see Eastern Caribbean States). In 1963 and 1964 the company participated in the Dimanche Gras carnival shows written and produced by ERROL HILL, and in 1965 McBurnie choreographed Hill's *Man Better Man*.

By now the work of the Little Carib Dance Company was recognized overseas. It attended the Caribbean Festival of Arts in Puerto Rico in 1952. In 1953, Pearl Primus took her New York dance company to Trinidad to study the dance forms of the Little Carib. The company performed at the JAMAICA Tercentenary Celebrations in 1955; at the Stratford, Ontario, Festival of Arts in 1958; and at the springtime festival of the Ottawa Philharmonic Orchestra in 1959.

In 1965 the Little Carib building, often under siege for having bypassed the city's building code, closed. By the time it had been rebuilt, three years later, the permanent dance troupe no longer existed, its principal members having left in search of greater professional opportunities. The company had generated the Arawak Dance Company in San Fernando and the Killarney Dance Group in Tobago; early members such as the Holder brothers, Borde, Henry, and Kelvin Rotardier were pursuing successful careers abroad; MOLLY AHYE had founded her Oya Kairi Dance Company in Trinidad. McBurnie herself was now teaching schoolchildren.

In 1959 she was awarded an OBE, and in 1969 the Humming Bird Gold Medal of Trinidad and Tobago. In 1976 the University of the West Indies (see Introduction) conferred on her the honorary degree of Doctor of Laws. She has described some of her dances in a booklet, *Dance Trinidad Dance* (1956).

Maraj, Ralph (1949–)

Playwright, director, actor and teacher from Trinidad and Tobago. A graduate of the UNIVERSITY OF THE WEST INDIES (see Introduction). Maraj has been involved in theatre for over twenty-five years. Starting out as an actor, he won three Best Actor awards in festival competitions. In 1975 he began to write and direct his plays. His political satire *The Missing File* (1982) won him three awards for Best Play, Best Director and Best Actor when it was revived for the National Drama Festival in 1987. Other plays of note include *Under the Sapodilla Tree* (1980), *There Comes a Freedom* (1981) and *The Archbishop and the Prime Minister* (1986).

A scene from Mustapha Matura's *Playboy of the West Indies*.

All – over twenty, to date – are set in Trinidad, and deal with political, social and romantic themes. His dialogue is brisk; the action tends towards the melodramatic.

Maraj has been artistic director of the Drama Guild since 1976 and was president of the National Drama Association for three consecutive terms. He teaches at Naparima College, San Fernando, and was in 1992 appointed Minister of External Affairs by the Trinidad and Tobago government.

Marshall, Stanley (1924–)

Actor and director from Trinidad and Tobago. A retired public service officer, Marshall specializes in character parts. He began his acting career in 1956 with the San Fernando Drama Guild, where he played in Chekhov's *The Marriage Proposal* and in Synge's *The Shadow of the Glen*, as Old Mahon in *The Playboy of the Western World* and as Tiresias in Sophocles'

Antigone; and directed CICELY WAITE-SMITH's (see Jamaica) *The Creatures*.

In 1959 he became a foundation member of the Little Carib Workshop, later the TRINIDAD THEATRE WORKSHOP, under the artistic directorship of DEREK WALCOTT (see Eastern Caribbean States). He created several characters in Walcott's plays, including Moustique in *Dream on Monkey Mountain* (1967), Don Gonzalo in *The Joker of Seville* (1974), Mr Dewes in *O Babylon!* (1976), and Eldridge Franco in *Beef, No Chicken* (1981). He was also cast as the professor in WOLE SOYINKA's (see Nigeria) *The Road* (1966), Uncle Willie in E. M. Roach's *Belle Fanto* (1966) and Old Mack in ERROL JOHN's *Moon on a Rainbow Shawl* (1967), and appeared in plays by other Caribbean authors such as SAM HILLARY and TREVOR RHONE (see Jamaica), EARL LOVELACE, FRANK PILGRIM (see Guyana) and EDGAR WHITE (see Eastern Caribbean States).

Marshall has toured extensively throughout the Caribbean in Theatre Workshop productions, and played in New York and Connecticut. He has appeared on Trinidad, BARBADOS and US television, and has directed Caribbean and foreign plays for the Theatre Workshop (of which he is co-director) and for Malick Folk Performers (of which he is an executive committee member) in Trinidad. In 1989 he received the Trinidad and Tobago national award for drama.

Matura, Mustapha (1939–)

Trinidad-born playwright of East Indian ancestry, who moved to England in 1960 and is considered a major British dramatist. His first full-length play, *As Time Goes By*, produced at the Traverse Theatre in Edinburgh and at the Royal Court in London, won the George Devine and John Whiting awards in 1971. Since then he has written twenty-odd plays and has enjoyed productions in London, Manchester, Edinburgh, Chicago, Washington, DC, and in Trinidad. In 1978 he founded, and is now director of, the Black Theatre Co-operative in London, which has toured Holland, Denmark and Germany.

Matura's plays are set in Trinidad and among Caribbean communities in Britain. They examine the political and psychological effects of colonization on both the colonizer and the colonized. Thus *Play Mas'* (1974) shows how an unpopular government in Trinidad uses carnival to entrap revolutionaries; *Rum and Coca Cola* (1976) reveals the dependency and secret hostility of calypsonians as they await tourists on a beach; and *The Coup* (1991) gives a farcical treatment of an attempted Black Power takeover of government, suggesting the impotence of a newly independent country to cope with world politics. Matura is skilful in his use of dialect, which he often employs to comic effect – especially notable in *Playboy of the West Indies* (1984; published in New York 1988), his adaptation of Synge's *Playboy of the Western World*. By contrast, the transformation of Chekhov's *Three Sisters* into *Trinidad Sisters* (1988) exposes the emptiness at the heart of the colonial's reputed love for the 'mother country'.

Matura has also written extensively for British television, notably for the Channel Four series *No Problem* (1983) and the BBC's *Black Silk* (1985). He has published his plays in pairs or groups: e.g. *As Time Goes By* and *Black Pieces* (1972); *Nice, Rum and Coca Cola* and *Welcome Home, Jacko* (1980); *Play Mas', Independence* and *Meetings* (1982).

Persad, Rajkumar Krishna [Krishna] (1941–)

Dancer from Trinidad and Tobago. Persad began performing Indian dances in the late 1950s, and is perhaps the first such specialist in the country. Having no formal training, he learned the dances by studying them in Indian films, then choreographed them to appropriate music. Dressed in Indian dance costumes, he appeared in local revues and was considered the representative of Indo-Caribbean dance at national events. In 1962 he performed at the Trinidad and Tobago Independence Concert and in 1965 was a member of the group that represented the country at the Commonwealth Arts Festival in Britain. In the same year he received an Indian Government scholarship for dance study in India. He went to Madras, where he learned the Bharat Natyam classical dance as well as regional folk-dances, and received a diploma equivalent to an MA in dance. He has danced at the Lausanne Worldwide Exhibition, on tour in Canada, and at the Carnegie Hall, New York. He founded the Trinidad School of Indian Dance.

Sitahal, Errol (c.1947–)

Actor, director, scene designer and playwright from Trinidad and Tobago. Having gained a BA in English from Bristol University and a diploma in theatre arts from Manchester University, Sitahal taught at the Collège d'Enseignement Général et Professionel, Montreal, from 1970–80. During this time he appeared with the McGill Players' Club, playing the leads in

O'Neill's *The Emperor Jones*, in Pinter's *The Lover*, in *Everyman*, and in LeRoi Jones's *Dutchman*. Other roles have included the Indian in Israel Horowitz's *The Indian Wants the Bronx*, the Emperor in Arrabal's *The Architect and the Emperor of Assyria*, and Pantalone in Hans Sachs' *The Wandering Scholar from Paradise*.

Returning to Trinidad, Sitahal taught English while continuing his theatre work. For the Alternative National Theatre he played roles including Pariag in the dramatized version of EARL LOVELACE's *The Dragon Can't Dance* (1984) and Sookdeo in the stage version of Sam Selvon's *A Brighter Sun* (1985). For Warwick Productions he played Christopher in DEREK WALCOTT's (see Eastern Caribbean States) *A Branch of the Blue Nile* (1985) and Ramsingh in his *Franklin* (1990), produced in BARBADOS. For Hatuey Productions in Trinidad and Tobago he played Ramon in Raoul Pantin's *Sanctuary* (1986) and Don Berrio in Pantin's *Hatuey* (1987).

In Montreal Sitahal directed Jean Genet's *Deathwatch* and the Montreal première of Walcott's *Dream on Monkey Mountain*, for which he created the set. For the Alternative National Theatre in Trinidad he directed and designed Arrabal's *The Architect and the Emperor* (1983), John Whiting's *The Devils* (1984) and ERROL JOHN's *Moon on a Rainbow Shawl*. He also directed his own play *Jahaaji*, which depicts the East Indian experience in Trinidad. He has written three others plays: *Seashango* is a folk-drama set in a Trinidadian village; *A Wreath of Thorns* presents the history of blacks in Canada; and *Monster March* (with Dennis Hall) is a history of the trade union movement in Trinidad (produced in 1987).

Sitahal has won two Canada Council awards for playwriting, and awards from the National Drama Association for his acting and directing.

Springer, Pearl Eintou (1944–)

Actress, storyteller, playwright and poet from Trinidad and Tobago. A librarian, Springer gained an MPhil in information science from the City University of London in 1986. She became an executive member of the Caribbean Theatre Guild in 1970, was director of Black People's Theatre from 1971–4, and from 1980–5 was an executive member of the National Drama Association and of the Writer's Union of Trinidad and Tobago.

In 1977 she adapted for the stage *Minty Alley*, the novel by C. L. R. James, and in 1985 Sam Selvon's novel *A Brighter Sun*. She has written the one-acter *The Trial* (1979), the full-length children's musical *Ti Jean and Mariquite* (1987), and *Anansi, Anansi, Anansi*, a folk-play staged in Birmingham, England, in 1989. She has played the title role in SLADE HOPKINSON's (see Guyana) *Sala*, produced at the Little Carib Theatre (see BERYL MCBURNIE) in 1976. She appeared as Ma Rouse in *Minty Alley* (1978 and 1982), as Lady Macbeth in a 1982 production that toured Trinidad and Tobago, and as Mavis in ERROL JOHN's *Moon on a Rainbow Shawl* in 1985. Her performances as Ma Rouse and Mavis won awards from the National Drama Association.

Springer has appeared as a storyteller in Trinidad and Tobago, England and the USA, and performed poetry at the Edinburgh Festival in 1991. Her published work includes collections of poems, *Out of the Shadows* (1986) and *Focused* (1991); and *Godchild: stories and poems for children* (1988).

Stone, Judy [Judith] (1939–)

Journalist, actress of stage, radio and television, and artistic director of Touchstone Productions. London-born with roots in Trinidad and Tobago, Stone has had a varied career in theatre from the age of six. She trained in speech and drama in London and took the Guildhall and LAMDA certificates. In Trinidad in 1962, she began performing with the Trinidad Dramatic Club and the Phoenix Players until these largely expatriate clubs folded in the late 60s. From 1968–75 she was a member of the TRINIDAD THEATRE WORKSHOP, led by DEREK WALCOTT (see Eastern Caribbean States). During this time she appeared in productions for radio, television and stage, including plays by Walcott and LENNOX BROWN. In 1976 she founded Touchstone Productions, which has staged over twenty plays at numerous venues in Trinidad and Tobago. Four of the plays – Michael Abbensett's *Samba*, MUSTAPHA MATURA's *Independence* and *Rum and Coca Cola*, and FRANK PILGRIM's (see Guyana) *Miriamy* – were by Caribbean authors.

Stone began writing theatre articles for the *Trinidad Guardian* in 1975, and has since produced some 300 weekly 'Theatre Life' columns comprising commentary and interviews on all aspects of theatre, especially current activity in Trinidad and Tobago and the Caribbean generally. She has also written for *Caribbean Contact*, *People Magazine* and *Trinidad and Tobago Review*. She has taught production management at school and adult level, and won the British West Indian Airways award for excellence in journalism in 1988 and 1989, as well as a BBC short story award and other literary awards in fiction and playwriting. In 1992 she won the Cacique award for her contribution to theatre in Trinidad and Tobago. She is working on a study of Caribbean drama.

Sue-Wing, Jean (1927–)

Drama teacher, administrator, actress and director of Trinidad and Tobago. Sue-Wing was a founder member of the Whitehall Players and of the COMPANY OF PLAYERS. She has been a stage manager and production manager, as well as playing the roles of Sheila Birling in J. B. Priestley's *An Inspector Calls* (1949), Juno Boyle in O'Casey's *Juno and the Paycock* (1950), Yette in DEREK WALCOTT's (see Eastern Caribbean States) *Drums and Colours* (1958) and Minee Woopsa in ERROL HILL's *Man Better Man* (1965).

In 1965–6 Sue-Wing studied stagecraft and acting at the British Drama League, London; she gained a BA at the UNIVERSITY OF THE WEST INDIES (UWI, see Introduction) in Trinidad in 1970, and an MA in education from the University of Keele, England, in 1978. As drama

officer in the Ministry for Culture and the Creative Arts for over two decades, Sue-Wing lectured in drama and speech at teachers' colleges in Trinidad and Tobago. In 1971 she devised the first formal schools curriculum in drama. From 1966 to 1987 she taught acting, play production and stage management to UWI extramural students.

Sue-Wing directed, among other plays, the première of DOUGLAS ARCHIBALD's *The Rose Slip* (1962), Henri Gheon's *Journey of the Three Kings* (1963), *Christ in the Concrete City* (1973, with music from Pergolesi's *Stabat Mater*) and RONALD AMOROSO's *The Master of Carnival* (1975). For four decades Sue-Wing has been an adjudicator at speech and drama festivals in Trinidad and Tobago.

Trinidad carnival

In its 200-year history the pre-Lenten Trinidad carnival, essentially an annual parade of original costumes worn by bands of masked revellers, has encompassed many theatrical forms. To the carnival over the years have accreted exhibitions of music, song, dance,

Snake Child by Roland St George, Trinidad Carnival, 1979.

mime and the spoken word that have made it a grand theatrical spectacle and a repository of the nation's performing arts.

Carnival was brought to Spanish-held Trinidad by French colonial planters in the 1780s. Under British rule it continued to be observed by the white elite as a European festival, the free coloureds and black slaves having no part in it. When slavery ended in 1834, the black and coloured masses took over the festival and transformed it into an expression of their new-found freedom. Among the principal 19th-century masquerades (see African Theatre, Introduction, MASQUERADES IN AFRICA) were *canboulay* ('cannes brûlées', or 'burnt canes'), featuring revellers re-enacting scenes from slavery, dread stick-fighters whose music,

Adoration of Hiroshima by Hugh Bernard, Trinidad Carnival, 1985.

dance and pungent argot survive on the contemporary stage, military bands that satirize the armed forces, indigenous creatures of myth and folk-tale, and the ubiquitous calypsonian who emerged as carnival songster and public commentator. During this period repeated attempts by government to suppress the masquerade as a rowdy and indecent exhibition were strenuously resisted, sometimes with rioting and loss of life.

In the 20th century conditions slowly improved, as English replaced French patois in song lyrics and the street parade gained respectability. Costumed bands like the Wild Indians and Burroquites would hold pre-carnival meetings in backyards. Before a growing audience they rehearsed speeches, dances, mimes and playlets, and on carnival eve installed the bands' kings and queens. Calypsonians, now universally recognized professional singers, gave nightly concerts which often ended with a comic sketch that recounted in song a recent topical event. On carnival streets traditional maskers like the Midnight Robber would harangue spectators with threats, in hair-raising encounters, until paid off. The Dragon Band would perform an elaborate street ballet, the Pierrot Grenade would give its version of a spelling-bee. Military bands would exhibit precise drills or make furious assaults on an imaginary enemy.

Carnival music kept pace with developments. When drum-beating was restricted, the skin drums and wooden clappers used to accompany *canboulay* trampers and stick-fighters gave way to the shack-shack (gourd rattle) and bottle-and-spoon ensembles. Then came the bamboo bands and finally the steel orchestras, using discarded petrol drums, which have extended their musical repertoire from calypsos to classics and have spread abroad. Maskers who could afford them hired string bands and later jazz ensembles to accompany their parade, but the bamboo bands and steel orchestras were the creative response of the indigent masquerader whose meagre funds would have been carefully garnered to pay for his costume.

In recent years traditional masquerades have dwindled, as new bands enroll thousands of revellers. Detailed ornamentation in costume and theatrical presentation has been replaced by massed colour effects. Competing carnival kings and queens, whose costumes used to be so extravagantly constructed as to encumber their free movement, have benefited from the designs of Peter Minshall, who employs traditional mask-making techniques in such a way as to free the performer to dance in his costume. In addition, Minshall has presented his masquerade bands as dramatic spectacles that pantomime contemporary concerns such as environmental pollution and nuclear war. In recognition of his skill, the 1992 Olympic Committee in Barcelona invited him to stage the arrival of Columbus' ship in the stadium at the opening ceremony of the games.

Bibliography

B. Brereton, 'The Trinidad Carnival 1870–1900', *Savacou*, Sept. 1975; *Caribbean Quarterly* (Trinidad Carnival issues) 4: 3 and 4, 1956; E. Hill, *The Trinidad Carnival: Mandate for a National Theatre*, Texas, 1972; G. Gohlehr, 'Sparrow and the Language of Calypso', *Savacou*, Sept. 1970, and *Calypso and Society in Pre-Independence Trinidad*, Trinidad, 1990; K. Q. Warner, *Kaiso! The Trinidad Calypso: A Study of the Calypso as Oral Literature*, Washington, DC, 1982.

Trinidad Tent Theatre

Founded by Helen Camps, its artistic director, producer and general manager, the Tent Theatre began with a group of twenty-five trainee performer-technicians and a rented canvas tent measuring 90 feet by 60 in St Clair Gardens, Port of Spain. The theatre was experimental, its principal objective to develop the concept of carnival theatre, preserving the traditional characters and rituals, many of which had been lost from modern street spectacles.

Though formally inaugurated in September 1982, the idea of the Tent Theatre was manifested two years earlier with the production of the musical *Mas in Yuh Mas* (1980), conceived by Camps and written by Felix Edinborough and PAUL KEENS-DOUGLAS. Wayne Berkeley, carnival band leader, designed the costumes; MOLLY AHYE, choreographer and folklorist, ensured that movement and dance were traditionally correct; and Roger Israel arranged the old-time calypsos. Among the carnival characters, using characteristic speech and movement, were the Midnight Robber, Pierrot Grenade, Jab Jab, Jab Molassi, Burroquite, Jammette, Baby Doll, Minstrels, Moko Jumbie, Fireman, Sailor, Bat, Dragon and Dame Lorraine.

In 1981 a new carnival theatre production, *King Jab Jab*, was mounted, which furthered the element of political satire underlying the carnival spirit. In 1982 the Tent Theatre took part in the Latin American Folk Festival in Europe. With a script by Edinborough entitled *J'Ouvert (New Dawn)*, the production implied an end to the threat of nuclear war and the beginning of a new era of peace. Performances were given in London and Rugby (England), Rennes and Bergerac (France); Milan and Rome, West Berlin and Geneva. Its final carnival production was *Go to Hell*, in 1984. The Theatre also produced straight plays such as EDGAR WHITE's (see Eastern Caribbean States) *Like Them that Dream* (1983) and Genet's *The Maids* (1984). An attempt was also made to put together shows called *New Waves* from the old calypsos, but by October 1984 the Trinidad Tent Theatre experiment was over.

Trinidad Theatre Workshop

Founded in Port of Spain in 1959 by DEREK WALCOTT (see Eastern Caribbean States). Following the success of his epic drama *Drums and Colours*, presented in Trinidad in 1958 at the inauguration of the West Indies Federation, St Lucia-born Walcott received a Rockefeller Foundation fellowship to study theatre in New York, at the Circle in the Square under José Quintero and the Phoenix Theatre under Stuart Vaughan. On return to Trinidad, having founded the Theatre Workshop, he assembled a group of talented actors whom he trained for productions of his own plays as well as plays by other Caribbean and foreign writers. Among the outstanding actors who performed for the company are WILBERT HOLDER (see Guyana), Albert La Veau, STANLEY MARSHALL and Claude Reid. For his base Walcott used the Little Carib Theatre established by BERYL McBURNIE, and initially produced under the aegis of the Little Carib Theatre Workshop.

The first production, in December 1959, was a showcase of scenes from Trinidadian and foreign authors. Then in 1962 Walcott's *The Charlatan* was staged, followed in 1964 by the double bill of Ionesco's *The Lesson* and Walcott's one-acter *Malcochon, or The Six in the Rain*, both directed by Walcott. In 1965 the Trinidad Theatre Workshop left the Little Carib Theatre, having been awarded a three-year Rockefeller grant. Between 1966 and 1974, when it returned to the Little Carib Theatre, the company used a variety of venues. In 1966 *The Blacks* by Jean Genet, *Belle Fanto* by E. M. Roach of Tobago, and *The Road* by WOLE SOYINKA of Nigeria were offered at the cramped Basement Theatre of Bretton Hall Hotel, Port of Spain. In 1967 *Moon on a Rainbow Shawl* by ERROL JOHN and in 1968 Walcott's *Dream on Monkey Mountain* were seen at the capacious Queen's Hall. In 1970 Walcott's *Ti-Jean and His Brothers* and *In a Fine Castle* were staged at the City Hall in Port of Spain, and in 1973 his *Franklin, a Tale From the Islands*, at a local high school.

The work of the Theatre Workshop soon began to excite interest beyond Trinidad. In 1967 the company toured BARBADOS, Tobago, GUYANA and Toronto, where it appeared as part of the Caribana festival. In 1968 it visited Antigua and St Lucia (see Eastern Caribbean States), Barbados, St Vincent and Grenada with *Dream on Monkey Mountain* – fast becoming the most celebrated of Walcott's plays in the Workshop's repertoire. In 1969 a performance at the Eugene O'Neill Theatre in Waterford, Connecticut, led to further performances in Los Angeles and New York.

The Workshop staged two more of Walcott's plays – *The Joker of Seville*, its fifteenth-anniversary production in 1974, and *O Babylon!*, in 1976 – before he left the company and began to première his plays with other groups both inside and outside Trinidad. The Theatre Workshop, under the leadership of Albert Laveau, continued to present plays, but less frequently. In 1982 Elliot Bastien's musical *A Nancy Story* and in 1983 EDGAR WHITE's (see Eastern Caribbean States) *Like Them that Dream* were produced at the Little Carib Theatre, but clearly the engine that had driven the company was missing. In 1991 the Workshop obtained a five-year lease on the old Fire Services building in central Port of Spain, to establish a school of the arts (but the government does not plan to renew the lease when it expires).

Wilkinson, Efebo [Lester] (c.1935–)
Playwright and director from Trinidad and Tobago. Wilkinson graduated from the Mausica Teachers' College in Trinidad, and has a BA in theatre arts and an MA in educational theatre from New York University. For the annual Best Village Competitions he has written and produced several plays, and has been artistic director of the Mausica Folk Theatre.

He won first prize in the National Cultural Council competitions for his plays *To Confirm St Peter* (1973) and *Capital Death* (1977); and the Best Play prize for *Bitter Cassava* (1979), *Same Khaki Pants* (1980), *Is Who Kill Cock Robin* (1981) and *De Bocas is Mih Bond* (1982). He has written and produced three children's plays, and for the National Theatre Company he directed RAWLE GIBBONS's *I Lawah* in 1987. Wilkinson is

Director of Culture in the Ministry of Youth, Sports and Culture. He was director of the CARIFESTA (see Introduction) held in Trinidad and Tobago in 1992.

Williams, George (1930–)

Lighting designer and operator from Trinidad and Tobago. Williams's stage experience began at the Little Carib Theatre (see BERYL MCBURNIE). In 1949 he designed lights for the Company of Five's production of *Romeo and Juliet*, then worked for local groups and was lighting specialist at the 1958 West Indian festival of arts.

In 1962 he was awarded a one-year scholarship to the Yale School of Drama for training in technical design and theatrical lighting under Stanley McCandless. From 1963 to 1991 he designed lighting for the Dimanche Gras carnival show at the Queen's Park Savannah, Port of Spain. He has lit productions for CARIFESTA (see introduction) in GUYANA, CUBA, BARBADOS and Trinidad and Tobago; ERROL HILL's *Man Better Man*, at the Commonwealth Arts Festival in Britain in 1965; and presentations at Expo 67 in Canada and Expo 69 in Grenada. He has designed and operated lighting for operas in Trinidad, and since the 1960s has taught stage lighting for extramural classes at the UNIVERSITY OF THE WEST INDIES (UWI, see Introduction). He is tutor in theatrical lighting at the UWI Creative Arts Centre in Trinidad. In 1992 Williams was awarded the Public Service Gold Medal of Merit for his work in art and culture in Trinidad and Tobago.

Bibliography

M. Ahye, *Cradle of Caribbean Dance: Beryl McBurnie and the Little Carib Theatre*, Port of Spain, 1983; K. Corsbie, *Theatre in the Caribbean*, London, 1984; E. Hill, 'The Emergence of a National Drama in the West Indies', *Caribbean Quarterly*, 18, 4, 1972; J. W. Nunley and J. Bettelheim, *Caribbean Festival Arts*, Seattle, Wash., 1988; K. Omotoso, *The Theatrical into Theatre*, London, 1982; G. Rohlehr, *Calypso and Society in Pre-independence Trinidad*, Trinidad, 1990.

INDEX

The index locates names of theatre practitioners and forms of theatre. The latter are identified in *italic*. Substantial references to individuals are indicated in **bold**.

Aaron, Philbert	175
Abah, Oga Steve	7
Abbensetts, Michael	149, 188, 190, 195, 209, 238, 244
Abe Gubegna	33
Abel, Zomo Bel	9, 23
Abelton, Tony	207
aboakyer	38
Acevedo, Carlos	170
Acquaye, Saka	39
Adams, Eliston (Nambulumba)	174
Adams, Robert	148
Addo, Patience	39
Adejobi, Oyin	91
Adejumo, Moses Olaiya	72, **73**, 89, 90, 91
Adelugba, Dapo	77, 78, 87, 88
Adjagnon, Déhumon	15
Afana, Dieudonné	23
Afolayan, Ade	73, 91
Afonso, Sant' Anna	13
Agbeyegbe, Fred	76
Ager Fikir	31, **34**
Ahuma, John	148
Ahye, Molly	**229**, 240, 246
Aidoo, Ama Ata	38, **40**
Ainsworth, John	228
Aiyegbusi, Tunde	88
Akar, John	97
Akman, Anthony	107
Alapini, Julian	15
alarinjo	68, 69, 76, 88, 89
Albuquerque, Orlando de	11
Alfonso, Francisco 'Paco'	160
Alleyne, Eunice	230
Almeida, Júlio de	11
Alphonse, George	175
Amoroso, Ronald	228, **230**, 244
Amouro, Camille	15
anansegoro	39, 41
anansesem	39, 41
Anderson, Balfour	202
Angmor, Charles	39
Angola	11
Antigua	173
Antrade, Costa	12
Apedo-Amah, Morehouse	117
Archibald, Douglas	149, 177, 192, 214, 232, 234, 235, 238, 244
Archibald, William	148, 227
areyto	159, 169
Arriví, Franciso	220, **222**
Arrufat, Antón	161, **165**
Artiles, Freddy	164
Arts Guild of St Lucia	176
Asgarally, Asize	64
Asseng, Protais	9, 23
Assoon, Barbara	**230**, 232
Astelkachew Yihun	34
Astol, Eugenio	219
Attiga-Tsogbe, Kossi	15
Avilés Blonda, Máximo	170, **171**
Awona, Stanislas	23
Axworthy, Geoffrey	87
Ayalneh Mulat	33, **34**
azmari	34
Ba, Thiérno	9, 93
Baba Sala *see* Adejumo	6, 91
Badejo, Peter	80
Badian, Séydou	8, 61
Bain, Alister	180
Baldaque, Fernando	13

Balgobin, Basil — 187
Ballanta-Taylor, N.J.G. — 97
Ballester, Manuel Méndez — 220
Banda, Innocent — 60
Banda, Wilfred — 130
Bandele-Thomas, Biyio — 72
Baralt, Luis A. — 160
Barbados — 153
Barnes, Belinda — 231
Bart-Williams, Gaston — 97
Bascom, Harold — 188
Bastien, Elliot — 247
Baxter, Ivy — 149, **202**
Beier, Ulli — 75
Belaval, Emilio — 220, **222**
Belavin see Bemba,
   Sylvain Bell, Vera — 210
Bemba, Sylvain — 9, **25**
beni — 113
Benin — 15
Bennett, Louise — 149, 201, **203**, 210 216, 217, 229, 237
Bennett, Wycliffe — 201, **203**
Berdécia, Fernando Sierra — 220
Bergés, Añez — 170
Bim and Bam — 202, **204**, 206, 207
Blackwood, Amani — 111
Bondekwe, L.S. — 127
Bongo, Josephine Kama — 24, 37
Borde, Percy — 232, 240
Bori — 65, 70
Botswana — 17
Boudet, Rosa Ileana — 165
Bourke, Greta — 211
Bourne, Kate — 226
Brathwaite, E.K. — 233
Brau, Sálvador — 150, 219, **222**
Brene, José — 162
Brewster, Yvonne — 201, **204**, 208, 209
Breytenbach, P.P.B. — 103
Brown, Lennox — 149, 176, 228, **231**, 244
Browne, Vincent — 176
Bruton, Jack — 210
bufo — 165
Bully, Alwin — 174, **178**, 179, 180, 194
Burkina Faso — 21

Cabrera, Pablo — 221
Cadet, Charles — 177, 183
Cameron, Norman — 147, 187, **189**
Cameroon — 23
Campos, Alexandre Cabral — 13
Campos, Juan Carlos — 171
Cape Verde — 12
Cardoso, Onelio Jorge — 162
Carew, Jan — 188
CARIFESTA — 143
Carrera, Leo (Leo Bennett) — 232
Carrero, Jaime — 221, 223
Carter, George — 206
Casas, Myrna — 220, **222**
Caseley-Hayford, Gladys — 97
Castillo, Efraím — 170
Castillo, María — 170
Caudeiron, Daniel — 174
Cayor, Franz see Tchakouté, Paul
   Cendrecourt, Esme — 147
Central African Republic — 37
Césaire, Aimé — 8, 28, 127, **143**
Céspedes, Francisco Garzón — 164
Chahilu, Ben — 46
Chaka Wacca see Symester, Leon
   Charles, Bertram — 188, **189**
Charles, Pat — 144
Charles, Patricia — 175
Charley, Dele — 98, 99
Charvet, M. — 175
Chase, Sam — 147, 187, **189**
Chenet, Gérard — 93
Chenjerai, Susan — 135
Cherrie, Errol — 226
Chidyamathamba, Basil — 133, 134
Chifunyise, S.J. — 129, 131, 134, **135**
Chigidi, William — 135
Chikwakwa Theatre — 130, **131**
Chikwendere, S. — 136
Chimombo, Steve — 57, 60
Chipunza, N. — 133
Chisiza, Du Jr — 59
Chisulo, Haggai — 130
Christmas morning concerts — 206
Cissé, A.-T. — 43
Clark, Ebun Odutola — 74, 76, 89

Clark-Bekederemo J.P. (J.P. Clark)   69, 73, **74**, 79
Clarke, Austin   179, 233
Clems, Derlene   39
Cobham, Cecil   147, 226
cohaba   169
Collymore, Frank   154, **155**
Colón, Miriam   221, **223**
comedias   169
Company of Players   231
Congo, Republic of   25
Connor, Edric   227, 232
Connor, Pearl   232
Corrieri, Sergio   162, **166**
Corsbie, Ken   145, 188, **189**, 195
Côte d'Ivoire   27
Covarrubias, Francisco   159
Coverley, Eric   203
Cross, Thom   15
Cuba   159
Cultural Training Centre   206
Cumper, Pat   206, 210
Cupidon, Ernest   147, 200, 204, **207**, 210

d'Aby, Amon   27
Dabiré, Pierre   21
Dadié, Bernard   8, 27, **28**
dama   4
Dambará, Kaoberdiano   12
Damirón, Rafael   169
Dandobi, Mahamane   65
Dangarembga, T.   135
Danquah, J.B.   39
Davis, Edgar   174
Dawes, Carroll   207
de Araújo, Carmen Hernández   219
de Cordova, Raphael   199, **207**
de Graft, Joe   38, **40**
de Lewis, Fernández   220
de Lisser, H.G.   147, 200, 207, 211
de Llerena, Cristóbal   169
de Wet, Reza   105
Decker, Thomas   97, 98
Deive, Carlos Esteban   170
del Monte, Don Félix María   169
del Toro, Gonzalo Arocho   220

Dervain, Eugène   9, 27
Dhlomo, Herbert   103, **107**
Dia, Amadou Cissé   93
Diabaté, Massa Makan   61
Diawara, Gaoussou   61
Disla, Reynaldo   170
Do   61
Domínguez, Franklin   170, **171**
Dominica   174
Dominican Republic   169
Dongala, Emmanuel   25
Dorant, St Clair Wesley   228
Dorn, Karl   133
Dorr, Nicolás   162
Dragún, Osvaldo   165
Drayton, Kathleen   233
du Toit, S.J.   103

Easmon, R. Sarif   97
Echavarría (Echevarría), Rubén   170
ECPTO   144
Edgecombe, David   144, 178, 190, 194
Edwards, Gus   179
efe   73
Egbuna, Obi   180
egungun   **4**, 5, 68, 69, 76, 83, 89
ekong   5, 69
Ekossono, R.   23
Elder, Lonne   174
Elébé, Lisembé   127
Elliott, Lorris   149
Ene-Henshaw, James   72
Enekwe, Onuora   72
entremeses   169
Espinosa, Eugenio Hernández   164
Estorino, Abelardo   161, **166**
Etherton, Michael   130, 131
Ethiopia   31
Ewandé, Lydia   8
ewi   89
Eyoh, Hansel Ndumbe   7

Faleti, Adebayo   78
Farrell, Winston   155
Farrier, Francis   188, **190**
Fatunde, Tunde   75

Favory, Henri 64
Felipe, Carlos 160
Ferrari, Carlos 221
Ferreirinha, Felisberto 13
Ferrer, Rolando 160
FESTAC 3
Fiawoo, F. Kawasi 39, 117
Figueiredo, Jaime de 12
Fisseha Beley 34, **35**
Flax, Oliver 173
Fonseca, Carlos Queriós de 13
Forbes, Leonie 207
Ford-Smith, Honor 201
Forget, Yves 64
Fouché, Franck 150
Fowler, Henry 211
Foxá, Francisco Javier 159, 169
francais de moussa 27
Francisco, António 13
Francis, Nigel 175
Franck, A. 37
French, Stanley 176
Fugard, Athol 104, **107**, 133, 134, 210, 230
Fumane, Joao 13

Gabon 37
Gadeau, Koffi 27
Gallardo, Eduardo 223
García Guerra, Iván 170, **171**
Garvey, Marcus 142, 147, 200, 207, **208**, 212, 217
Gathwe, Titus 46
Gbadamosi, Gabriel 72
Gbadamosi, Rashead 72
Gecau, Kimani 134
gelede 4, 15, 68
género chico 171
Getachew Abdi 33
Ghana 38
Gibbons, Rawle 195, 228, **233**, 248
Gibbs, James 55, 56
Gilkes, Michael 157, 188, **190**, 195
Ginebra, Danilo 170
Gloudon, Barbara **208**, 210
Gómez de Avellaneda, Gertrudis 159, **166**
Gomez, Joya 233

González, Lydia Milagros 221
González, Rafael 164
Goyémidé, Etienne 37
Gradussov, Alex 218
griot 8, 9, 27, 93
Guerra, Henrique 12
Guinea 43
Guinea-Bissau 12
Guingané, Jean-Pierre 21
Guridi, Javier Angulo 169
Guyana 185
Gwatiringa, Agnes 135

hadithi 113
Haffner, Charlie 98
Haiti 149
Hammond, Mona Chin 201, **209**
Harawa, Vipya 60
Harper, Peggy 134
Harquail Theatre 144
Harris, Amah 174
Harrison, Ronald 201, **209**, 213
Hemstock, Arthur 195
Henry, Jeff 179, 240
Henzell, Perry 214
Heredia, José María 159
Hernández, Gilda 162, 166
Héssou, Henri 15
Hevi, Jacob 40
Heywood, Donald 227
hiari ya moyo 113
Hill, Errol 143, 149, 176, 177, 182, 183, 192, 201, 216, 217, 227, 228, 230, 231, **234**, 235, 236, 238, 240, 244, 248
Hill, Frank 147, 200
Hill, Sydney 230, 232, **235**
Hillary, Samuel 149, 177, 201, **209** 230, 238, 241
Hinkson, Anthony 155, **156**
Hippolyte, Dominique 150, 176
Hira-Gasy 51
Hoeane, Masitha 19
Holder, Boscoe 240
Holder, Wilbert 188, **190**, 247
Holness, Ralph 202

Hopkinson, Slade	**191**, 194, 243	Kahigi, K.	114
Horn, Andrew	80, 130	*kalankuwa*	70
Hosein, F.E.M.	147	*kalela*	129
Hourantier, Marie-José	24	Kamchedzera, Garton	60
Huidobro, Matías Montes	164	Kamiriithu	46, **48**, 49
Hussein, Ebrahim	6, 114, **115**	Kamlongera, Chris	55
Hyacinth, Steve	175	Kampaoré, Prosper	21
Hyatt, Charles	201, **209**	Kanaventi, Dominic	133, 134
		Kani, John	104
Ijimere, Obutunde (Ulli Beier)	55, 130	Kankan, Jean-Michel	9, 23
Ika, Kalu	72	*kantata*	9, 117, 118
Ikafa, Kwalela	131	Kapumpa, Mumba	130
Imbuga, Francis	46, **48**	Kargbo, Kolosa John	98
Incháustegui Cabral, Héctor	170, **172**	*kasandwon*	39
inganekwane	101	Kasoma, Kabwe	130, **131**
Inniss, L.O.	147, 226	Kateka, Edward	130
intsomi	101	Katiyo, Winston	135
Ipeko-Etomaner, Faustin-Albert	37	Katumba, Jimmy	122, 123, **124**, 125
Iyoel Yohannes	32	Katunde, John W	124
izibongo	101	Kawadwa, Byron	122, 123, **124**, 125
		Kay, Kwesi	40
Jamaica	197	*kayowe*	129
Jamaica pantomime	155, **210**	Keane, Shake	149
James, C.L.R.	148, 205, 226, 233,	Kebede Michael	32
	239, 243	Keens-Douglas, Paul	149, 229, **237**, 246
James, Horace	232	Keita, Fodéba	27, 43
James, Rick	174	Kelepile, Jeppa	18
Jaomanoro, David	51	Kemoli, Arthur	46
Jekyll, Walter	147	Kente, Gibson	104, **110**, 111, 135
John, Errol	148, 149, 175, 190, 195, 227,	Kenya	45
	230, 231, 233, 234, **235**,	Kerr, David	55, 57
	238, 241, 243, 247	Kezilahabi, E.	114
John, Juliana	98	Khaketla, B.M.	18
Johnson, 'Bob'	39	Khaketla, N.M.	19
Jones, Errol	232, **236**	*khoi-san*	101
Jones, Evan	210	Kimotho, Frank	46
jonkonnu	198, 209, **210**	*kinet*	31, 35
Joseph, E.L.	146, 225	King, William	133
Joseph-Hackett, Daphne	154, 155, **156**	Kipanga	45
Junction Avenue Theatre Company	109	Kissoon, Freddie	180, 228, 232, **237**
		Kiyingi-Kagwe, Wycliffe	122, 123, 124, **125**
Ka, Abdou Anta	8, 93, 94	Knight, Ginger	193, 202
Kaba, Alkaly (and Diama)	61	*kodzidan*	39, 41
Kabamba, Hippolyte	127	Koly, Souleymane	9, 27
kachala	129	Konaké, Sory	61
Kaduma, Godwin	116	Konaté, Moussa	61

Konde, Kwame	12
Koné, Amadou	27, 61
Kora	65
kotéba	10, 61
Krio theatre	97, **98**
kuomboka	129
Kuper, Hilda	19
kwagh-hir	5, 70
Kyeyune, Eli	123
La Veau, Albert	247
Labou Tansi, Sony	8, 9, 25, **26**
Lacomba, José	220
Ladan, Umaru	80
Ladipo, Duro	6, 70, 71, 72, 73, **75**, 85
Laedza Batanani	18
lagyah	9
Laguerre, Enrique	220
Lakoju, Tunde	72, 80
Lamming, George	195, 233
Langenhoven, C.J.	103
Lateef, Yusuf	80
Lauten, Flora	162, 164
Lawrence, Raymond	175
Layne-Clark, Jeanette	155
Lee Wah, James	211, 229, **238**
Lee Wah, Mavis	**211**, 238
Lee, Easton	201, **211**
Leloup, Jacqueline	23
Leshoai, B.L.	17
Lesotho	17
Letembet-Ambily	25
Lewis, Maureen Warner	207
Lhongo, Lindo	13
Lhoni, Patrice	25
Lihamba, A(mandina)	114, 116
Lima, Manuel Santos	12
Lindo, Archie	200, **211**
Linstrum, John	55
Little Theatre Movement of Jamaica	211
loas	169
López, Lincoln	171
López, Regino	160
Lovelace, Earl	157, 205, 228, **238** 241, 243
Lovell, Glenville	155, 157
Luaces, Joaquín Lorenzo	160
Lubwa, Cliff p'Chong	125
Lumpa, Gideon	130
Lungu, Craig	130
Lyndersay, Dexter	79, 80, 87, 88, **239**
MacDermot, Galt	182
Macedo, Donald Pereira de	12
Macu, Dujuza ka	105
Madagascar	51
Maddy, Yulisa Amadu	98, **99**, 130
Madzikatire, Safirio	135
Maggiolos, Marcio Veloz	170
mahumbwe	133
Mais, Roger	147, 200
Maité Vera	14
makishi	129
Makonnen Endalkachew	32
Malaku Baggosaw	31
Malamamfumu, Matildah	130
Malawi	53
Mali	61
mammiwata	5
Manaka, Matsemela	105, **110**
Manda, Edwin	129
Mangol, Mwamb'a	127
Maponya, Maishe	105, **110**
Maqina, Mzwandile	105
Maraj, Ralph	240
Margetson, Bobby	173
Marín, Gerard Paul	220
Marques, Alvaro Belo	13, 14
Marqués, René	220, **223**
Márquez, José 'Papo'	221
Marshall, Stanley	**240**, 247
Marson, Una	147, 200, 211, **212**
Martí, José	160
Martin, Bertie	187, **192**, 195
Martins, Dave	194
Martins, Orlando	148
maseve	113
mashawe	129
Mason, Maurice	176
Masquerades	4
Master Yalley	39
Matip, Benjamin	23
Mattewos Bekele	32

Matthews, Marc	190	Morriseau-Leroy, Felix	150
Matura, Mustapha	149, 209, 228, 238, **242**, 244	Moses, Delmance	175
		Mouangassa, Ferdinand	25
Mauritius	63	Moutia, Max	64
Maxwell, Marina	228	Moyo, Aaron	135
Mawugbe, Efo Kodjo	40	Moyo, Stephen	130
Mbarga, M.-C.	23	Mozambique	13
Mbengue, Seyni	93	*mpendoo*	113
Mbewe, Smart Likhaya	58	*Mphihira-Malagasy*	51
Mbogo, Emmanuel	114, **116**	Msora, Bertha	135
Mbowa, Rose	124, **125**	*msunyunho*	113
Mboya, Alakie	47	Mtwa, Percy	105
McBurnie, Beryl	149, 182, 212, 227 229, 230, **239**, 243, 247, 248	Mudaba, Yoka	127
		Mugo, Micere Githae	46, **48**, 49, 134
McDermot, Galt	183	Muhando, P. *see* Mlama, Penina	
McDermot, T.H. *see* Redcam, Tom		Mujajati, G.	135
McDonald, Ian	188	Mukanda, Patterson	130
Mda, Zakes	7, 19, **111**	Mukulu, Alex	123, **125**
Mêlé, Maurice	15	Mulokozi, M.	114
Mendes, Orlando	13	Mulwa, David	46
Mendonça, José	13	Mungoshi, Charles	135
Menga, Guy	9, 25	Muparutsa, Walter	133, 134
Mengistu Lemma	33, **35**	Murray, Henry G. (Andrew & William) 146, 199, **212**	
Mezgebe, Alem	99		
Mg'ombe, James	60	Musengezi, Habbakuk	135
Mieses, Juan Carlos	170	Mutombo-Diba, Valérien	127
Mhlanga, Cont	134, 135	*mutomboko*	129
Mike, Chuck	74	Muttoo, Henry	188, 190, **193**
Milanés, José Jacinto	159	Mvula, Asaf	130
Millán, José Agustín	160	Mvula, Enoch Timpunza	60
Milner, Harry	202	Mvundula	60
Misiye, Andreya	130	Mwansa, Dickson	130
Mittelholzer, Edgar	148	Mwaparra	14
mkwajungoma	113	Mzee Tamaa *see* Suleiman	45
Mlama, Penina	7, 114, **116**		
Mofokeng, Twentyman M.	18	N'Dumbé, Alexandre Kuma	23
Mohamed, Paloma	188, **193**	N'gandu, Mulenga	131
Moktoi, Dave	23	*nachisungu*	129
Moleko, Buti	19	Naipaul, V.S.	211, 233
Molina, Luis	222	Nambulumba *see* Adams, Eliston	
Molina, Tirso de	169	Nasiru, Akanji	71
Mongita, Albert	127	*natak*	64
Montez, Caetano	13	National Cultural Foundation	156
Moody, John	197	National Dance Theatre Co.	
Morales, Abneil	221	of Jamaica	212
Moreira, António Alonso	13	*ncwala*	129

Ndachi-Tagne, D. 23
Ndao, Cheik 8, 93, **94**
Ndébéka, Maxime 8, 9, 25
Ndedi-Penda 23
Nderitu, J. 47
Ndi, Michel 23
Ndo, Daniel 9, 23
Nénékhaly-Camara, Condétto 43
Nettleford, Rex 149, **212**
Ngahyoma, Ngalimecha 114, **116**
Ngandu, Nkashama 127
Ngema, Mbongeni 101, 105, **111**
Ngemera, A. 114
Ngenzhi, Charles 127
Ngombo, Saturnin 127
ngonjera 114
Ngugi wa Mirii 46, 48, 49, 134, 135
Ngugi wa Thiong'o 3, 46, 48, **49**, 122, 134, 135
Ngwenya, Ndema 135
Niane, Djibril Tamsir 43
Niger 65
Nigeria 67
nindo 113
Njoya, Ndam 23, 24
Njugu, Sese 46
Nketia, J.K. 38
Nkosi, Lewis 46
Nobrega, Cecile 187
Nokan, Charles 9, 27
nsombo malimba 129
Ntshona, Winston 104
Ntsime, Joseph M. 17, 18
Nwoko, Demas 88
nyau (kasinja) 4, 129
Nyonda, Paul 37
Nzewi, Meki 72

O'Marde, Andrew 180
O'Marde, Dorbrene 174, **179**
Obafemi, Olu 71, **75**
Obama, Jean-Baptiste 23
ode-lay 5
Odlum, George 177
Ogilvie, W.G. 200, 209, **213**

Ogunde, Hubert 3, 70, 72, 73, **76**, 88, 89, 135
Ogunmola, E.K. 70, 90
Ogunniyi, 'Laolu 72
Ogunshola, Oshola 91
Ogunyemi, Wale 70, **77**, 79, 87, 88
Oliveira, Luna de 13
Omali, Samson 239
Omotoso, Kole 70, **78**, 79
Omtatah, Okoiti 47
Onwueme, Tess 71, 72, **78**
Opperman, Deon 105
Orihuela, Roberto 162, 166
Osanyin, Bode 71, 88
Osofisan, Femi 71, 78, **79**, 88, 90
Osório, Oswaldo 12
Oti, Sonny 70
Owei-Okanza, Jacob 25
Owona, Adalbert 23
Owondo, Laurent 37
Owusu, Martin 40
Oyedepo, Stella 71
Oyekunle, 'Segun 72, 80, 87
Oyono Mbia, Guillaume 8, 9, 23, **24**, 130
Ozidi 69

p'Chong, Cliff Lubwa 123
Pam, Sue 105
Pantin, Raoul 243
Pasuka, Berto 202
Paukwa Theatre Association 114
Paz, Albio 162, 166
Pepetela 12
Pereira, Pedro Paulo 14
Performing Arts Company 80
Persad, Rajkumar Krishna 229, **242**
Peters, Francis 180
Philip, M. Maxwell 226
Philips, Thelma **180**, 237
Phiri, Masautso 129, 130, **131**
Pilgrim, Frank 149, 180, 188, **193**, 194, 230, 241, 244
Piñera, Virgilio 161, **166**
Piñero, Miguel 221
Pita, Santiago 159
Plaatje, Solomon T. 17

Pliya, Jean — 8, 9, 15
Pognon, André — 15
Pomares, Raúl — 163
Porquet, Niangoran — 24, 27
Poupard, Amédée — 64
Prescod, Samuel Jackman — 154
Puerto Rica — 219
pungwe — 133, 134
Purkey, Malcolm — 109

Quiñones, Ramón Méndez — 219
Quintero, Héctor — 162

Rabéarivelo, Jean-Joseph — 51
Rabémanajara, Jacques — 51
Raditladi, Leetile Disang — 17
Rafenomanjato, Charlotte — 51
Rainizablolona, Justin — 51
Rajaonah, Tselatra — 51
Rakotoson, Michèle — 51
Ramana, Rajoo — 64
Ramos, José Antonio — 160
Ramos-Perea, Roberto — 221, **223**
Randrianarivo, Jidy — 51
Reckord, Barry — 149, 201, 204, 207, 209, **213**
Reckord, Lloyd — 201, **213**, 217
Redcam, Tom — 147
Redhead, Wilfred — 177
Reichhold Center — 144
Reid, Claude — 247
Reis, Fernando — 14
Rhone, Trevor — 149, 157, 180, 194, 195, 201, 204, 205, 208, 210, **214**, 233, 241
Ribeiro, Afonso — 13
Ribeiro, Emmanuel — 134
Ritto, Fausto — 13
Roach, Eric — 238, 241, 247
Roberts, Arthur — 148, 226
Robinson, Nellie — 173
Robinson, Ron — 188, **194**
Rodlish, Arthur — 51
Rodríguez, Abraham — 164
Rodríguez, Lázaro — 164
Rogers, De Wilton — 148, 226

Romana Worq Kasahun — 32
Rotardier, Kelvin — 240
Rotimi, Ola — 6, 47, 71, 72, 73, 78, 79, **81**, 130, 205, 208
Rueda, Manuel — 170, **172**
Ruganda, John — 46, 122, 123

Sadeek, Sheik — 149, 188, **194**
Salifou, André — 65
Sall, Ibrahim — 93
Sallah — 70
samariyas — 65
Samuels, Oliver — 205
Sánchez, Herminia — 162, 164
Sánchez, Luis Rafael — 220, **223**
Sánchez, Mario Ernesto — 164
Sangaré, Malian Bakary — 8
Sant'Elmo, Ruy — 13
Santiliz, Pedro — 221
São Tomé e Principe — 14
Scott, Dennis — 157, 192, 195, 201, 205, 206, **215**, 231, 233
Seawar, Lloyd — 195
Seboni, Michael O. — 17
Seck, Douta — 8
sefela — 101
Sekhamane, Afelile — 19
Sekyi, Kobina — 39
selo — 113
Selvon, Samuel — 243
Senegal — 93
Senghor, Leopold — 93, 143
Senghor, Sonar — 93
Sentongo, Nuwa — 123
Serukenya, Wassanyi — 122, 124
Serumaga, Robert — 122, 123, 125, **126**
Setsoafia, B.H. — 117
Severe, Charles — 59
Shanahan, Charles — 146, 199
Shumba, Mupa — 55
Shumba, Simon — 134
Siango, Abbot Benoît-Basile — 37
Sibenke, Ben — 133, 134, **135**
Sierra Leone — 97
Silva, Arnaldo — 13
Silva, Carlos da — 13

Simbotwe, John 130
Simpson, Colin 180
simo 113
Simon, Barney 105
Simon, Lester 174
Singh, J.B. (*also* Alice) 187
Sinxo, G.B. 103
Sistren 201, 207, **216**
Sitahal, Errol 242
Slabolepszy, Paul 105, **112**
Smit, Bartho 112
Sofola, Zulu 72, **82**, 88
Sota, Delta 170
Sousa, Elsa de 11
South Africa 101
Sowande, Bode 71, 73, **83**, 88
Soyinka, Wole 3, 6, 46, 47, 55, 68, 70, 72, 77,
78, 79, **83**, 87, 88, 130,
143, 192, 205, 233, 241, 247
Spencer, Julius 98
Springer, Pearl Eintou 243
St Lucia 175
Stone, Judy 243
Stuart, Joyce 148, 154, 156
Sue-Wing, Jean 232, **244**
Suleiman, Athmani (Mzee Tamaa) 45
Sutherland, Efua 38, 39, 40, **41**
Swaziland 17
Symester, Leon (Chaka Wacca) 174

Taitt, Clairmonte 188, **194**
Takouba 61
Tanzania 113
Tapia y Rivera, Alejandro 219, 222, **224**
Tavares, Morton 199, **216**
Tchakouté, Paul (Franz Cayor) 23
Tekle Desta 33
Tekle Hawariat 31
Tendé 61
Terraza, Manuel 162
Tesfaye Gessesse 33, **35**
teyatur 65
Theatre Guild of Guyana 195
Theatre Information Exchange 144
Thomasson, Frank 188
Tobago (and Trinidad) 225

Togo 117
Tolomoju, Ben 71
Torres, Luis Lloréns 219
Touré, Bachir 8
Townshend, Mitzi 201
Triana, José 161, 164, **167**, 231
Trinidad (and Tobago) 225
Trinidad carnival 244
Trinidad Tent Theatre 246
Trinidad Theatre Workshop 246
Tsegaye Gebre-Medhin 33, **35**
Tsodzo, Thompson 134, 136
Tudor, Joe 154, **156**
Tueche, Jean-Marie 23
Tutuola, Amos 70

U'Tamsi, Felix Tchicaya 8, 9, 25, **26**
Uganda 121
Uhinga, G. 114
Unibadan Masques 87
Ureña, Max Henríques 160
UWI 145

Valz, Ian 188, 194
Van Sertima, J.A. 147
Van Sertina, Sheila 188
Van-Dúmem, Domingos 11
Varela, Victor 164
Vasconcelos, Leite 13
Vaz, Noel 155, 177, 201, 210, 212, **216**,
228, 235
vichekesho 113, 114
Villalona, Rafael 171, **172**
Villoch, Frederico 160

Wachira, Waigwa 46
Waite-Smith, Cicely 149, 201, 211, 213,
217, 234, 241
Walcott, Derek 147, 148, 149 155, 157, 175,
176, 177, **181**, 182,
183, 190, 191, 192, 193, 194,
195, 201, 204, 205, 207, 209,
211, 213, 216, 228, 230, 232,
233, 234, 235, 236, 237, 238,
240, 241, 243, 244, 246

Walcott, Roddy 149, 175, 176, 177, 181, **182**, 191, 193, 234, 238
Wallace, David 130
Warner, Earl 155, **156**, 195, 210, 234
Watene, Kenneth 46, **49**
Weeks, Alan 176, 177
Welsh-Asante, Karium 134
Wenger, Suzanne 775
Werewere-Liking, Nicole 9, 23, **24**, 28
Whaley, Andrew 134, 135
White, Edgar 149, 157, **184**, 195, 233, 236, 241, 246, 247
Wilkinson, Efebo 229, **247**
Williams, George 248
Williams, Lavinia 212
Williams, Ranny 147, 200, 203, 204, 210, **217**
Wilson, Cynthia 157
Wynter, Sylvia 201, **217**
yankama 70

yankamanchi 70
Yero, Kasimu 80
yeye 73
Yirenkyi, Asiedu 38, 39, 40
Yoftahe Negussie 31
Yoruba Travelling Theatre 69, 73, 77, **88**
Young, Ethelbert 226

Zaire 127
Zambia 129
zangbeto 15
Zaourou, Bernard Zadi 8, 9, 24, **28**
Zimbabwe 133
Zinsou, Senouvo 8, 9, **118**
Zirimu, Elvania 122, 123, **126**
Zulu, Y.L. 130

ILLUSTRATION ACKNOWLEDGEMENTS

The Publishers gratefully acknowledge the following for supplying illustrations and granting permission for their use.
While every effort has been made to obtain permission to use photographs, we shall be pleased to make proper acknowledgements in future editions if any errors have been made.

18 Andrew Horn; 56, 59 courtesy of Robert McLaren; 63 courtesy of Dev Virahsawmy; 68, 69, 77, 90, 117, 118 Alain Ricard; 71 courtesy of Martin Banham ; 74, 109 Trevor Faulkner; 82 Ola Rotimi; 83 Maggie Murray/Format; 84, 214 Richard H. Smith; 86 Royal Exchange Theatre, Manchester;
94 courtesy of the Théâtre National Daniel Sorano, Dakar; 102 Ruphin Coudyzer; 106 Joe Louw; 108 Reg Wilson; 115 Frowin Nyoni; 163 Vidal Hernández; 164 Cristóbal López; 181, 183, 203, 208, 215, 227, 228, 231, 234, Errol Hill; 191 Pat Piérro; 192 Wenty Bowen; 205 Raissa Page/Format;
241 Mark Douet/PAL; 244, 245 photos reproduced from Trinidad Carnival, published by Key Caribbean Publications.

Printed in the United Kingdom
by Lightning Source UK Ltd.
102902UKS00002B/125-156